Foreign Independent Tours: Planning, Pricing, and Processing

OTHER BOOKS IN THE
TRAVEL MANAGEMENT LIBRARY
SERIES

LEGAL ASPECTS OF TRAVEL AGENCY OPERATION,
SECOND EDITION

COMPLETE GUIDE TO TRAVEL AGENCY
AUTOMATION, SECOND EDITION

LEGAL FORMS FOR TRAVEL AGENTS

GROUP TRAVEL OPERATIONS MANUAL

GUIDE TO STARTING AND OPERATING A
SUCCESSFUL TRAVEL AGENCY, SECOND EDITION

THE TRAVEL AGENCY PERSONNEL MANUAL

HANDBOOK OF PROFESSIONAL TOUR
MANAGEMENT

FINANCIAL MANAGEMENT FOR TRAVEL AGENCIES

BUDGETING FOR PROFIT AND MANAGING BY
GOALS

GUIDE TO TRAVEL AGENCY SECURITY

THE DICTIONARY OF TOURISM, SECOND EDITION

CAREERS IN TRAVEL AND TOURISM,
SECOND EDITION

A TRAVEL AGENCY POLICY AND
PROCEDURES MANUAL

TRAVEL AGENCY GUIDE TO BUSINESS TRAVEL

Foreign Independent Tours: Planning, Pricing, and Processing

James Poynter

Metropolitan State College
Denver, Colorado

DELMAR PUBLISHERS INC.
MERTON HOUSE TRAVEL AND TOURISM PUBLISHERS

Delmar Staff
Managing Editor: Gerry East
Project Editor: Mary Ormsbee
Production Coordinator: Larry Main
Design Coordinator: Susan C. Mathews

Book Packaged by
Scharff Associates, Ltd.
RD 1 Box 276
New Philadelphia Road
New Ringgold, PA 17960

For information, address Delmar Publishers Inc.
2 Computer Drive West, Box 15-015
Albany, NY 12212

Printed in the United States of America
Published simultaneously in Canada
by Nelson Canada,
a division of International Thomson Limited

10 9 8 7 6 5 4 3 2 1

Library of Congress Cataloging in Publication Data

Poynter, James P., 1939-
    Foreign independent tours.

    (Travel management library)
    Includes index.
    1. Tourist trade. I. Title. II. Series.
G155.A1P68 1989   338.4'791   89-1426
ISBN 0-8273-3120-7 (text). ISBN 0-8273-3121-5 (Instructor's Guide).

CONTENTS

PREFACE

In years gone by, the Foreign Independent Tour, or F.I.T., was considered by many to be the only way to go. That was the era when we had a true difference between first class and economy travel, and those who took first class expected to have their trips tailored for them. After the second world war, this attitude changed drastically with most Americans who traveled internationally, as they chose middle-priced packaged tours or a do-it-yourself travel product. However, recent years have witnessed an increase in the number of individuals who have little time but considerable resources, and the demand for F.I.T.s has returned. In addition, as travel agencies recognize that considerable income can be made in designing F.I.T.s, more and more agencies are adding individual F.I.T. specialists to their staffs, or are creating entire agency specializations in the F.I.T. market.

For the student, this almost-lost art of Foreign Independent Tour development means an opportunity to step into many travel agencies and close a gap. This demand gives the student an edge in getting a first job in a specialization that offers good compensation and an opportunity to take extensive international trips, trips that are often quite luxurious.

This textbook is just an introduction. It is essential for the student to hone his or her skills by developing simple F.I.T.s and then working into increasingly sophisticated F.I.T.s. As the student fine-tunes the ability to satisfy clients with tailored international itineraries, a personal clientele will be built and the assurance of a good income and an interesting career will come with it.

This book is designed for both the student and the practitioner. While the student can find the tools to build basic skills in working with F.I.T.s, many travel agency executives will find the cost sheets and the profit orientation of considerable interest when looking for ways to diversify and to become less dependent on point-to-point domestic air commissions for survival.

Foreign Independent Tours have been revived and today the F.I.T. industry is healthy and growing. Foreign Independent Tours offer the student and the working agent an opportunity to have both an excellent income and an exciting career, but they also offer the agency owner a chance to provide a travel product of the highest quality possible, and a per-sale commission that in many cases is the best possible.

ACKNOWLEDGEMENTS

The author extends thanks to Julie Westhoff of Awanderlust Travel, and to Kate McCarthy of Travel By Dana. Both Julie and Kate contributed information, time, and ideas from the inception of the several-year project that produced this book. Thanks are also extended to David Lundquist of Travel Inc., who is a model of the F.I.T. specialist, and to Lucia (Karakitios) Slater. Lucia brought F.I.T. specialists together to determine what learning elements should be incorporated into a college course in F.I.T. planning. Without her early assistance, this book might never have come about. Finally, thanks to Sorore, Lewis, Robert, and Michael for their patience and understanding during the writing of this book.

DEDICATION

To Patricia Poynter
A dedicated peripatetic F.I.T. traveler

1

WHAT IS A FOREIGN INDEPENDENT TOUR?

INTRODUCTION

Many who hear the acronym "F.I.T." encounter the term for the first time. Whether a student who is new to the industry or an experienced travel agent who has not encountered clients who want tailored international trips, the concept of an F.I.T., or, as it is better known, a foreign independent tour, can be somewhat fearful. Most of us are at least a little apprehensive about those things we encounter for the first time or about which we have little knowledge.

One can enter the world of foreign independent tours with less trepidation if the concentration is placed on the client. In reality, the travel industry as a whole revolves around client needs. The F.I.T. is a product that meets a very specific, well-defined client need. The foreign independent tour meets the needs of those travelers who want something special and individual. As chapter 5 points out, there are several distinctive kinds of foreign independent tour clients, but one should not hastily believe that all F.I.T. clients can be neatly classified or aptly labeled. In reality, any person who wishes to travel internationally makes a choice. That person might travel for business or for pleasure. That person might choose to travel individually or with a group. When the client chooses to travel individually for leisure, the travel industry often labels the trip a foreign independent tour (F.I.T.). The key word here is "choose." The F.I.T. client makes a choice and since the choice lies with the client, then the foundation for the difference between an F.I.T. and any other type of international travel is a client-based foundation.

Some in the industry believe that just because a person travels internationally and does so individually and for leisure purposes, that person by definition is automatically an F.I.T. client. If so, there are many who fall into the F.I.T. category. The 1987 Department of Commerce statistics indicated that seventy-six percent of all United States travelers abroad (outside the U.S.) were F.I.T. travelers. In reporting these statistics, *Travel Agent Magazine* categorized F.I.T. travelers as those international travelers who indicated they were not on prepaid package tours.

1

But those in the industry who work with F.I.T. clients do not consider all people who travel on their own internationally to fall into the F.I.T category. They point out that foreign independent tour clients tend to be upscale clients who are buying many of the same travel products that a person going on a quality packaged tour buys. However, these clients ask that the arrangements be tailored to their specific needs. One can look at the F.I.T client in much the same way as the person who engages an architect to build a house. Some people build homes or have them built from standard *prepackaged* plans, just as some people travel internationally following a set of suggestions taken from published guidebooks. Many others will buy packaged tours without an **escort**, often deciding on the spur of the moment what local sightseeing trips to take, just as some buy homes from a developer or builder who offers a wide range of options (at additional expense) while the house is being built. Others will buy less expensive tract homes, just as there are some who will buy prepackaged, all-inclusive escorted tours. But the individuals who want houses tailored to their exact specifications by an architect are the same type of clients who ask an F.I.T. specialist to tailor-plan foreign independent tours to their specifications.

The person who engages an architect is usually quite particular. The F.I.T. client can also have stringent expectations, and can often see the entire trip unfolding in the imagination well before entering the F.I.T. specialist's office for the first time. F.I.T. clients will spend the money to have the tour designed to their exact specifications. Like the architect's client, F.I.T. clients usually know exactly what they want. The F.I.T. trip can be much more expensive than many other trips, but because it is tailored to meet the dreams of the client, it can be even more memorable. If the F.I.T. specialist considers that what is being designed is a memory that might last for a life time, then, like the architect, the F.I.T. specialist builds a trip that will be remembered fondly by the client. Perhaps more than any other travel specialist, the F.I.T. specialist is in the business of creating and selling dreams.

This chapter will introduce the concept of foreign independent tours. It will identify what the F.I.T. product is and, perhaps more importantly, what the F.I.T. product is not. One way to look at the F.I.T. is to identify the meaning of each of the initials in the acronym. These will be reviewed in depth.

Perhaps the initial that throws off most who consider F.I.T.s is the "I," which stands for "independent." The independent characteristic of an F.I.T. is often thought to pertain to the tour itself. Certainly this is the case. However, it is a more accurate descriptor of the F.I.T. client. Perhaps if any one characteristic describes the F.I.T. client, it is independence. This chapter introduces the very independent nature of F.I.T. clients.

Some people who work in the industry are confused by the term "independent" because they realize that many package tours are in fact undertaken independently. The description of the F.I.T. product identifies what the tour is and what it is not. This chapter distinguishes the concept of a sightseeing trip from the concept of a tour. It then describes why an F.I.T. is quite different from an unescorted package tour purchased by a client and taken independently.

This chapter will also describe an escorted package tour and compare what a client receives from an escorted package tour with what a client receives from a foreign independent tour. Each has advantages and drawbacks. Certainly some packaged escorted tours, like some packaged unescorted tours, have distinct advantages when compared with foreign independent tours. The pros and cons of each type of trip will be measured in detail.

Having examined the optional products for a client on a foreign independent tour, a packaged unescorted tour, or a packaged escorted tour, the chapter will conclude with an analysis of the differences between all three types of tour products.

While chapter one introduces the foreign independent tour and compares it with other types of tour products, chapter two discusses the components of a foreign independent tour. Although many of these components are similar to both the escorted and unescorted package tour, this chapter points out how they can differ considerably when they are tailored to meet the very specific desires of the F.I.T. traveler.

For those who are still unsure of the differences between the various tour products after reading chapter one, a scan of chapter two should clarify the differences.

THE F.I.T. PRODUCT

What is an F.I.T.? The F.I.T. product definition seems simple on the surface: A foreign independent tour. These three words describe an F.I.T., but they do not set absolute boundaries for this type of trip. The initial "F" stands for the word "foreign." There is such a thing as a domestic independent tour, or "D.I.T." But an F.I.T. is differentiated in that the components take place outside of the United States. Therefore, the first word of the F.I.T. acronym, "foreign," presents the first clearcut distinction.

As noted earlier, the second word in the F.I.T. acronym, "independent," engenders some confusion, as the independent aspects of the F.I.T. apply to both the product and the client. While an unescorted package tour is also independent in nature, an F.I.T. is far more than an unescorted package tour. Although an unescorted package tour might be for an individual, a couple, or for a small group (as is an F.I.T.), the F.I.T. connotes the development of a "tailored" tour. In other words, an F.I.T. is a travel program designed to tailor-fit the specific needs and interest of the traveler.

In fact, it is the tailoring aspect of an F.I.T. that makes it unique and sets it apart from every other travel product. In reality, the F.I.T. (and its domestic equivalent) constitutes the only travel product that is individually designed to meet the specifications of the individual traveler.

The F.I.T. is a total package. In many ways it is a package tour very similar to the traditional escorted package tour that is sold in groups. However, this package is one that makes every effort to meet every need of the individual traveler. Typically, the F.I.T. client is an experienced traveler. Often the F.I.T. client will have some very specific ideas as to what he or she wants to do or wants to have included in the tour.

ESCORTED PACKAGE TOUR COMPARISONS

As noted ealier, the F.I.T. can be compared to an escorted package tour. To help understand the differences, consider the following comparisons.

Tour Dates

Dates of the tour provide a starting point for comparison purposes. Escorted package tours depart and return on specific published dates. If these dates are inconvenient for the client, the only choice is to go on the tour anyway (changing other plans that conflict) or not to go on the tour of preference, but to try to find one with more convenient dates. The individual client cannot get the departure or the return dates changed. On an F.I.T., however, the client specifies the exact dates that he or she wishes to leave and to return.

The date arrangements go further, however. On a scheduled package tour each aspect of the tour is planned in advance presumably for the benefit of the largest number of those on the tour. However, on an F.I.T. the client might spend as many or as few days at each destination as she prefers. In this way, the destinations at which the client prefers to spend more time are available. The traveler can complete the tour without being rushed away from a fascinating place or spending too much time at a less interesting place.

Tour Pace

The pace of the tour is also tailored to the individual F.I.T. client. On a scheduled package tour, many tour members might prefer to sleep late some mornings and not go out on another sightseeing trip. Their only option is to miss those events on the tour that are scheduled when they would prefer to sleep. Not so with an F.I.T. The F.I.T. can be tailored to meet the pace of the individual client. If the client prefers to sleep until eleven o'clock in the morning, all sightseeing can be scheduled to start after 11 A.M. On the other hand, if a client prefers to see the sites in the early morning hours, this too can be arranged. In other words, the pace of the tour can be set to the exact specifications of the individual F.I.T. client.

Sightseeing and Activity Choices

Sightseeing destinations and activity choices are another point of comparison between the group tour and an F.I.T. The escorted group member buys the tour with all sightseeing included and with no, or perhaps very few, options available. The options offered tend to be evening activities in a city rather than scheduled daytime sightseeing. If the tour member wanted to go to an art museum, an opera, or some other activity that is not scheduled, he might very well miss the chance. There might not be enough time allocated to include that activity even during scheduled free time. On an F.I.T., however, the schedule is flexible and can usually include all the major sightseeing and other activities that the client wishes to include.

Client Care Comparison

Another major difference between F.I.T.s and package tours is client services en route. On an escorted package tour, an escort handles all details (passport clearance, border crossings, ground and air transfers, hotel check-in and check-out, and often some meal arrangements). The F.I.T. client usually does not have a constant escort. The F.I.T. client might use a "meet and assist" service, which assigns a local guide to meet the client at the airport and arrange transfers to and from the hotel, but seldom do F.I.T. travelers plan more individual assistance than this. On the other hand, local sightseeing firms might provide F.I.T. clients with a wide range of "helping" options. Local sightseeing on a chauffeur-driven basis is often available, but F.I.T. clients can also opt to take a local sightseeing bus. Restaurant meals present another option. Reservations can be made in advance for F.I.T. clients at many of the finer restaurants in the world. A guide can be hired to aid the F.I.T. client in finding the restaurant, translating the menu, and finding the way back to the hotel. The F.I.T. client often suffers a loss of continuity when dealing with local guides, escorts, or chauffeurs, because seldom does one person perform all the above functions. Nevertheless, when such assistance is scheduled, the assistance is individual and the quality of help is usually very good.

Hotel Choice

Still another difference between the escorted package tour and an F.I.T. is the choice of hotels. On an escorted package tour, the tour member has no choice of hotels. The tour bus pulls up to a hotel and the tour members stay

(Courtesy of The Hertz Corporations)

(Courtesy of Railways of Australia)

Fig. 1-1. An F.I.T. lets clients choose the ground transportation that suits them.

there. It might or might not be a hotel preferred by individual tour members. Certainly most travel agents advise their clients that there is a direct relationship between the quality of hotels used on a tour and the cost of the tour. Better quality escorted package tours will include stays in better quality hotels. Less expensive escorted package tours select less deluxe hotels for their tour members. However, even in a quality escorted package tour, individual tour members might prefer a different hotel. The tour member has little choice on an escorted package tour. About the only choice is the opportunity to change rooms if the assigned room is totally to their dislike. Even in this matter, there are times when room-changing is impossible.

On the contrary, an F.I.T. client might choose whatever hotel he or she prefers. As long as there is space available in that hotel at the time reservations are made and the hotel is affordable, whatever hotel the client likes best can be selected and included in the F.I.T. This provides the F.I.T. client with a quality level of preference, the hotel location of preference, and the maximum degree of comfort that budget constraints allow. As in other comparisons between the escorted package tour client and the F.I.T. client, however, the F.I.T. cost is usually greater, since group buying discounts are not available.

Ground Transportation

The escorted package tour client generally travels by motorcoach and all tour members ride on the same bus. Especially in Europe, this bus will take the clients from one destination to another on day trips or from one hotel in one country to another hotel in still another country. These trips can last for several days. Sometimes train transportation is used for group members, and once in a while a group uses a private train car.

The F.I.T. client, on the other hand, can travel either by private car (chauffeur-driven or client-driven), or the client can use public transportation (motorcoach or rail). If the F.I.T. client is going by car, the opportunity to visit sites at his own pace and to visit all the places he wishes to visit is readily available. The F.I.T. expert links sightseeing points together so that the F.I.T. can be done in considerable comfort. On the other hand, if the F.I.T. client uses public transportation, she might have more difficult transfers (even with meet and assist service) than will the escorted motorcoach tour client. Public transportation might use up more of the F.I.T. client's time getting from one sightseeing destination to another, and points of potential interest might be missed for the lack of convenient public transportation.

SUMMARY

The F.I.T. traveler and the escorted motorcoach tour client might both enjoy comfortable, relaxing vacations. But there are trade-offs; neither presents a perfect option for all travelers. The escorted motorcoach tour client knows that someone else will take care of all the mechanics of travel (document processing, transfers, bus and hotel arrangements, etc.). He knows exactly what he will see and where he will stay, and he does not have to worry about baggage transfers, tips, or finding directions. If any problem comes up, he knows the tour guide will be there to take care of it. And perhaps best of all,

Factor	Escorted Tour Packages	Unescorted Tour Packages	F.I.T.
A total "package" tour	Yes	Seldom	Yes
Tailored to the client	No	No	Yes
Flexible departure/ return dates	No	Somewhat Sometimes	Yes
Flexible tour pace	No	Sometimes	Yes
Wide *choice* of sightseeing	Limited	Seldom Included	Yes
Individual client care and attention	Very limited	No	Yes
Choice of hotels	No	Usually, but limited	Yes
Ground transportation			
Tour bus	Yes	Sometimes	Rarely
Sightseeing bus	Yes	Yes	Yes
Rail	Seldom	Rarely	Yes, if desired
Private rent-a-car (client driven)	No	Sometimes	Yes, if desired
Chauffeur-driven car	Rarely	Rarely	Yes, if desired

Fig. 1-2. A summary of the major differences between tour packages and F.I.T.s.

the escorted motorcoach tour client knows he will pay less for his tour package than an F.I.T. client with a similar itinerary will pay. But the escorted motorcoach tour client gives up much freedom of choice and will be regimented into a schedule he might not like. He will miss some sights—and they might be important ones for him. And he might not spend enough time at places that interest him.

The F.I.T. client has chosen a different set of trade-offs. She will see all the sights she most wants to see, and will usually be able to spend as much time seeing them as she wants. Her choice of hotels, restaurants, and ground transportation are as wide as her checkbook can afford. However, the F.I.T. traveler has no constant companion making all travel arrangements, and the quality of service received from local vendors can vary widely. She must keep track of her own baggage transfers, pay tips herself, and often she must find directions totally on her own. And on top of this, the F.I.T. traveler will pay a much higher price for the same services and amenities than would an escorted motorcoach tour member traveling on a similar itinerary. The comparisons are summarized in figure 1-2.

■   ■   ■

❏ *REVIEW QUESTIONS*

1. Name the service that sends a local guide to meet an F.I.T. client at the destination airport and assist in the transfer to the client's hotel?
2. What are the pros and cons of an F.I.T. tour compared to an escorted package group tour?
3. What does the acronym "F.I.T." stand for?
4. If the client likes to sleep late in the morning, is it still possible for him to enjoy an F.I.T.?
5. Does the F.I.T. client have a tour escort traveling with her to handle all the mechanics (border crossings, tipping, hotel check-ins, etc.) for her?

❏ *ROLE PLAY EXERCISE*

Two students may participate in this role play either out of class as a fun way to review the chapter or as an in-class exercise. One plays the role of the travel agency client and the other one plays the role of a travel agent. Please read the script and then pick up the conversation in your own words.

CLIENT: My name is Martha Johnson. My husband and I were on a business trip to Europe last month. It was far too short a time in Europe and we are thinking about returning during the late Spring or early Summer for a real vacation.

TRAVEL AGENT: It's nice to meet you, Mrs. Johnson. My name is (insert your own name). Would you like to take a traditional escorted group tour of Europe or would you prefer that I tailor a tour for you in what we call an F.I.T., a foreign independent tour?

MRS. JOHNSON: Well, I don't know. Would you tell me about the benefits and drawbacks of both options?

Continue on your own.

FOREIGN INDEPENDENT TOUR COMPONENTS

Foreign independent tours are made up of both air and ground arrangements. The travel agent arranges both the air transportation and the details of what happens on the ground (after the client has arrived in the destination countries). Air and ground arrangements must be closely coordinated so that a smooth transition will take place when the F.I.T. traveler journeys from one destination to another. If there is going to be a lengthy time between planes at an airport, a brief city tour (such as those available by ALITALIA for visitors transiting Rome's Fumicino airport and KLM's Amsterdam Schipol airport) or a restful stay in the sponsoring airline's V.I.P. room can often be arranged. Unlike the escorted package tour client, who depends on the tour operator's pre-arrangements or the tour manager's on-the-spot arrangements, the F.I.T. client often expects his travel agent to take care of every detail in advance.

AIR ARRANGEMENTS

Normal ticketing and itinerary processing will need to be undertaken for the F.I.T. client. But often several additional services can be provided to make the F.I.T. client even more comfortable. Many F.I.T. clients travel first-class and thereby can avail themselves of numerous airline-provided amenities—often at no additional cost. Depending upon the air carrier, these amenities can include pre-assigned seating, special meals, sleeperbeds (on a few very long-distance flights), and airport-area ground arrangements. If the client is traveling on an economy or a discounted ticket, the special airline-provided amenities are fewer, but F.I.T. clients can still receive pre-assigned seating and special meals on some flights. If these are areas of importance to clients (and they are for many F.I.T. travelers), the travel agent should be ready to request and confirm them. Providing the F.I.T. client with as much comfort in the air as possible is one of the important factors that marks an agent as a professional.

GROUND ARRANGEMENTS

Ground arrangements can be divided into several categories. These include:

1. Meet and assist service
2. Airport tranfers
3. Accommodations
4. Meal services
5. Entertainment
6. Sightseeing
7. Ground transportation
8. Other ground arrangements

Almost all ground arrangements can be prepared in advance before the client departs on the F.I.T. trip and most ground arrangements can be paid for in advance. Commissions can usually be deducted on almost everything, but the F.I.T. specialist will find that there are some arrangements that the client expects to have, but for which commission is not paid. In spite of this, such details still need to be arranged (a service charge can sometimes be levied to compensate for the agent's time and cost).

Meet and Assist Service

There are two types of "meet and assist" services and both can be of benefit to F.I.T. clients. These two types of service are differentiated by where they are provided and by whom the service is provided. The first meet and assist service takes place at the airport and is provided by airline personnel. This service is normally rendered to V.I.P.'s and to those airline passengers needing special assistance. The person(s) providing the service are referred to by many airlines as P.R.R.s (sometimes called passenger relations representatives or public relations representatives). However, their title may vary from carrier to carrier.

At the origin airport (the airport from which the traveler starts her trip), the V.I.P. F.I.T. client might be met at her car by a passenger relations representative and brought to a V.I.P. room. She is provided with complimentary drinks and sometimes with complimentary snacks, while relaxing in a comfortable lounge chair. Typically there is reading material available (newspapers, magazines, sometimes airline-oriented material) and in some of the larger V.I.P. rooms there is a hostess on duty to serve food and beverages. In other (usually smaller) V.I.P. rooms, the traveler helps herself to food and drinks, which are provided at an open bar. Meanwhile the hostess or the passenger relations representative has taken the traveler's ticket and checked her in (getting a boarding pass for her if she has not already been issued one and making sure she has the seat assignment of choice). When ready to board the airplane, the passenger relations representative escorts the V.I.P. F.I.T. passenger to her seat on the plane, advising the inflight service crew chief of the V.I.P.'s status and any appropriate preferences (what the traveler is drinking, food preferences—if known—and so forth).

At airports where there is a change of planes, a passenger relations representative meets the V.I.P. F.I.T. passenger aboard the plane, or just as she is exiting through the door of the plane and escorts the traveler to a V.I.P. lounge. Similar service is provided as that offered at the originating airport and, of course, the V.I.P. F.I.T. passenger is escorted to her connecting plane at the time it is ready for boarding.

At destination airports V.I.P. F.I.T. passengers are provided with special services as well. Again, a passenger relations representative meets the V.I.P. F.I.T. passenger as she deplanes. She is either escorted through customs and health control or she is escorted to a V.I.P. lounge in the customs area. In the latter case, customs and health officials come to the lounge to conduct customs/health clearance. In many cases the luggage is retrieved for the V.I.P. F.I.T. passenger and brought to the lounge for customs clearance. In most cases, however, luggage is cleared through without being checked. With the most important V.I.P.'s, arrangements are sometimes made for a limousine to meet them on the tarmac (at the foot of the plane) so that after descending the steps of the plane, they go directly to a waiting car to be driven to their hotel. The airline makes arrangements to clear the luggage and have it sent to the hotel.

Most F.I.T. clients, however, are not V.I.P.'s and will not be provided with V.I.P. service by airline-employed passenger relations representatives. Nevertheless, variations of the services described above are often available to the first-class F.I.T. traveler—especially in some of the developing countries where the cost of services is less expensive than in the United States and where the concern about customs and health checks might not be too strong. There are several airports in the world where arrangements can be made for a client to be met by a waiting limousine and whisked to his hotel room with the luggage following. And, although there is a cost involved, this can be arranged for F.I.T. clients, even when they are not considred to be V.I.P.'s. Therefore, if such service is important to the F.I.T. client, check with the airline and the ground operator to see if it is available. But, be sure to check the cost. V.I.P. service extended to F.I.T. clients can be expensive.

The second type of meet and assist service is provided by a "ground operator." Although there are few ground operators who provide only meet and assist services, most are sightseeing firms which offer meet and assist services as one of a menu of services that they provide. They primarily offer sightseeing trips (by private limousine, car, or tour bus). Typically this meet and assist service is only available after the F.I.T. client has gone through passport control, retrieved her luggage, and cleared through inbound customs. As the F.I.T. traveler exits the customs area with her luggage, the meet and assist ground operator will meet her at the customs exit gate. Often the ground operator representative meeting the F.I.T. traveler will hold up a placard with the F.I.T. traveler's name on it. In other cases, the representative might wave a flag with the name of her meet and assist company emblazoned on it. Whatever the technique used for recognition, the F.I.T. traveler should be advised to look for the meet and assist ground operator representative as the traveler exits the customs area since, if they miss each other at this point, they might have great difficulty finding one another at all.

Most meet and assist ground operator representatives speak English and have considerable experience in their job. Their task is to help the F.I.T. client in getting through the airport and transferring the traveler to transportation that will take him to his hotel. The representative usually will assist F.I.T. clients in changing their money at airport banks; filing lost baggage claims, if needed; and/or buying airport souvenirs if the F.I.T. client is so inclined. However, some meet and assist ground operator representatives might have to pick up more than one client and are in an obvious rush. The experienced F.I.T. client will understand when the representative is unable to spend as much time with him at the airport as he might like. The new F.I.T. client on his first independent trip might be disturbed by the cold efficiency with which he is treated by some meet and assist ground operator representatives. An explanation by the travel agent before the client leaves on this trip can sometimes be helpful.

The meet and assist service does not stop at the point of leaving the airport, however. In most cases it includes getting the F.I.T. client to her hotel, resort, or other accommodation. This might be accomplished by privately chauffeured car, van, minibus, or a full-size tour bus. At one extreme, the meet and assist ground operator representative who met the F.I.T. client as she was exiting the customs area will take the client to her (the representative's) own car, she will then drive the client to the hotel, and the representative might bring the luggage into the hotel (or give it to the bellhop). The representative sometimes even assists the F.I.T. client with the check-in procedure prior to leaving the client.

At the opposite extreme, the meet and assist ground operator representative will hail an airport taxi, give directions to the taxi driver, and leave it up to the F.I.T. client and the driver to get to the hotel. Often in such circumstances, the client does not feel well taken care of and, in fact, in some such circumstances, the taxi driver charges the F.I.T. client for the trip (sometimes even charging too much) in spite of the fact that the travel agent arranged and paid for the F.I.T. client to be met at the airport *and* transferred to the hotel.

In most cases, however, transfer to the hotel is accomplished in a van or a tour bus. Sometimes the van or bus will stop to let off each of the F.I.T. clients at their respective hotels. In many cases, an escort or guide will be on board the bus. If so, this person will talk about the sights that are passed while driving from the airport to the hotels, explain the hotel check-in processes, and tell clients where they should meet for local sightseeing trips, which they might or might not have already booked and paid for. It, therefore, behooves the travel agent to book his F.I.T. clients on sightseeing trips offered by the same company he has worked with to provide meet and assist services. This is not a hard, fast rule. But by having the same company provide meet and assist services, transfers, and sightseeing trips is often a convenience for the F.I.T. clients.

Airport Transfers

The provision of airport transfers for clients is another service often requested by F.I.T. clients. Obviously, if they have asked for a full meet and assist service that includes a transfer from the airport to their hotel, then arranging for airport transfers would be a duplication of effort. However, there are many—especially experienced—F.I.T. clients who do not want to pay for an airport meet and assist service. They feel that they only need to arrange for a transfer from the airport to their hotel (and back when their stay in the city is over).

Airport transfers can be booked on a round trip or on a one-way basis. One quite logical option for an F.I.T. client is to have full meet and assist (including transfer) service upon arrival at a destination and to have only transfer service (from the hotel back to the airport) when she is ready to return home or to proceed to her next destination.

Accommodations

Accommodations can be quite luxurious or Spartan. The late Bert Hemphill, founder of Hemphill Tours (now Hemphill-Harris Tours) and one of the world's best F.I.T. experts, once said, "I can put a wealthy executive in Africa for two days on a safari, but I had better get him into a Hilton on the third day." Many F.I.T. clients want to experience life like a native and in some parts of the world there is no choice but to do so. However, a larger number of F.I.T. clients will want the comforts of home after a very short time of "going native." Many American F.I.T. clients enjoy unique accommodations like castles, houseboats, floating barges, country estates, an Israeli kibbutz, etc. Finding the unique out-of-the-way quality inn is an accomplishment on which many F.I.T. specialists build their reputation.

Booking accommodations normally consists of four steps:

1. Finding accommodations of a type and at a price that is desirable to the F.I.T. client
2. Requesting a reservation for the accommodation selected

3. Paying for, or putting a deposit down on the accommodation selected—thereby confirming the reservation request
4. Preparing and giving accommodation documentation to the F.I.T. client

The client should be able to leave on her trip carrying with her full accommodation documentation and having full confidence that all details have been taken care of. At the very least this should include:

1. Directions to the place where she will be spending the night(s)
2. A payment voucher or receipt, indicating that full or partial payment has been made and accepted
3. A confirmation from the receiving property, indicating that they have received the room request and have confirmed acceptance of the client for the room requested

Joseph and Mary were not the last to be turned away at the inn. It continues to happen every evening. It is the travel agent's responsibility to do everything possible to make sure the persons who are turned away do not include the F.I.T. clients.

Meal Services

Treating the palate is one of the major experiences many F.I.T. clients look forward to when traveling. Indeed the unique cuisines of many countries are an experience to look forward to. There are restaurants throughout the world that are justly famous and many clients feel that it would be a crime to be near some of these restaurants and not eat there. In spite of this many travelers go to Vienna and miss the Sacher Hotel's dining room and its famous "Sacher Torte"; many visit England and never partake of a truly British "High Tea," and there are even a few who go to Germany in the Fall and miss the chance to spend an evening at a Munich beer hall during Octoberfest.

All travelers must eat and drink. They might do so in a way that will give them pleasant memories, no memories, or bad memories for the rest of their lives. Part of the job of an F.I.T. specialist is to make sure the trip is a pleasant memory. Hotels and resorts might include meals in some of the hotel package plans and this is something F.I.T. clients sometimes want. Some of the best local foods can be eaten in pensions, hotels, resorts, and other places that provide both accommodations and meal services. But much hotel and resort food is neither unique nor memorable. Many F.I.T. clients will expect you to include a luau in Hawaii or couscous in Morocco. It is the responsibility of the F.I.T. specialist to learn where the best restaurants and other dining facilities are, to suggest them, and, where possible, to include them in the itinerary and pre-pay them. The Medieval Feasts in

British, Irish, Swiss, and a host of other countries' castles are examples of memorable food-and-drink evenings that can be reserved in advance, scheduled on the F.I.T. client's itinerary, and paid for in advance.

The travel agent's responsibility in relation to meal services is similar to what the travel agent is expected to do in relation to accommodations. He should:

1. Find special dining facilities of a type and at a price that is of interest to the F.I.T. client
2. Request a reservation for the dining facility (sitting—if a dinner show or if two or more sittings are offered), table or section (if appropriate)
3. Pay for or make a deposit for the meal (if this is needed and it often is
4. Obtain a dining confirmation (in writing)
5. Prepare and give the F.I.T. client appropriate documentation (directions to the dining facility, receipts for payment, meal vouchers, etc.).

Entertainment

Entertainment opportunities are extremely varied throughout the world, and for the F.I.T. client the variety of entertainment options is even greater than it is for many other travelers. Adding to the travel agent's difficulty in pre-booking entertainment are the wide differences in taste. Some F.I.T. clients want only cultural entertainment. The whole purpose of many trips is to see plays, operas, ballets, or concerts. Others prefer night clubs. Others want Las Vegas extravaganzas. And still others want quiet, intimate entertainment (like dancing to the music of a small after-dinner band or a romantic gondola serenade along the canals of Venice).

The travel agent booking entertainment for an F.I.T. client must start with a knowledge of the range of entertainment in the destination city or area. She must then get to know the client's entertainment preferences. If it is a client the agent knows well and for whom many previous F.I.T. trips have been booked, the agent will probably already have a "feel" for what the client's preferences are. Some clients are shy about discussing their preferences in entertainment and it might take several conversations before the agent gets to know the type of entertainment that is appropriate and desired. But of paramount importance is knowing client entertainment preferences. Most of us have known people who walk out at the hint of an off-color joke or who are so bored they sleep through a live play or an opera. To include such entertainment for those for whom it is inappropriate is not only a waste of money, it is also a waste of time and often leads to the client selecting another agent for his next trip. Therefore, getting to know the client, the client's entertainment tastes, what is available within these entertainment taste guidelines, and booking entertainment the client will find pleasantly memorable is a challenge each agent faces with each F.I.T.

client. As with accommodations and meal service, the travel agent needs to reserve the entertainment, make a deposit or full payment for it, obtain a reservation and a payment confirmation, and prepare and give the client full documentation relating to the entertainment that has been booked.

Sightseeing

Sightseeing opportunities constitute one of the main reasons for a traveler to take an F.I.T. trip instead of an escorted package tour. For most package tour clients the sightseeing that is included is either too much or too little, too rushed or too slow, too inclusive, or not inclusive enough, too early in the day or too late in the day, too crowded, too noisy, and often not really what the client wanted. The F.I.T. client has the unique opportunity of having sightseeing tailored to her needs. She can go where she wants to go when she wants to go and can spend as much or as little time seeing the sights as she wishes (within the limitations of the sight itself, of course). Obviously, one cannot see the sun rising over the Acropolis, except during sunrise and one cannot tour the cavernous insides of the pyramids after they close to tourists in the early evenings. Generally, however, the F.I.T. client has more of an oppportunity to visit the sights that she wants to visit than a traveler taking any other type of organized trip.

Again, knowledge is important. The F.I.T. specialist is expected to know everything that is worthwhile visiting at the F.I.T. client's vacation destination(s). To do this the agent should consult sightseeing guides and escorted tour package brochures *before* making recommendations unless the specialist is very experienced with the destination. Again, it will be important to know the interest areas of the client. Armed with this knowledge, the F.I.T. specialist can make some verbal recommendations and can draft out a possible itinerary (first rough draft itinerary) based upon what the client wants to see/do, the financial costs, the client's time constraints, and the times the sights are open to tourists.

After reaching agreement with the client, the agent reserves sightseeing trips in a manner similar to the way in which he books a tour. He calls the sightseeing company's toll-free number, verbally requests reservations, and compares his verbal request with the sightseeing company's written confirmations once he gets the confirmation and bills. After pre-paying for the sightseeing, the agent prepares or coordinates sightseeing documentation (vouchers, etc.) and gives these to the client right before the F.I.T. client leaves on the trip.

Ground Transportation

Sometimes ground transportation is needed for F.I.T. clients and other times it is not. A busy business executive, for example, with only two weeks of vacation time and taking a ten-day European trip might elect to fly to

Rome on an APEX fared ticket, taking stopovers in London and Paris en route, and will fly back from Rome. While in each of these three cities a meet and assist airport transfer service company has been booked. Sightseeing trips are scheduled with hotels booked that are near the sightseeing bus pick-up point or hotels are used which are themselves pick-up points for sightseeing buses. Entertainment can be reached by taxi, or in many cases, on foot. Ground transportation, therefore, is not needed and having a rental car, for example, might be more of a hindrance than a help.

For many F.I.T. clients, however, ground transportation is important. The greatest flexibility will be provided by a rental car or chauffeur-driven car/limousine.

Rental car arrangements are made in the same way that they are made for rental cars in the United States. The car rental company's toll-free number is called, the type of car desired is selected, the dates of pickup and return are advised, and a voucher request is processed. However, there are some distinct differences. By and large the rental cars in Europe are European makes of car, many of which are new to Americans. Also, the configuration on the cars can often be different. For example, many cars rented in England, where driving is on the opposite side of the street as compared to American driving, have the drive mechanism on the right-hand side of the automobile. This can take some getting accustomed to. Therefore, when asking for a car, it will be necessary to determine what particular configuration clients prefer and to match what car rental companies have available.

In addition, many of the car rentals will carry charges with which we are not familiar in the United States, such as value added tax. These need to be clarified in advance.

Rental cars for F.I.T. clients have both advantages and disadvantages. Obviously, the flexibility is considerable in that the client has the opportunity to visit a site at her convenience. However, the driver might have much less opportunity to view the scenery than if she were traveling on a sightseeing bus or some other vehicle since she will be occupied with driving. This reduces her ability to sit back, relax, and be a tourist. In addition, finding locations can sometimes be difficult and time consuming, resulting in much less time being spent at the destination. One answer to both of these problems is chauffeur-driven cars and for those who can afford this approach, it provides a number of benefits. The client, who otherwise would be driving the car, is able to sit back and relax and take in the scenery. The chauffeur, an experienced driver, knows exactly where the destinations are, therefore, no time is wasted in trying to find the points of interest. In addition, the chauffeur is normally trained as a guide. He can point out and discuss points of interest along the way and he can provide historical and other commentary while visiting the major sightseeing destinations.

The bus system in Europe is good and provides yet another alternative means of transportation for the F.I.T. client. Many Europeans utilize buses for sightseeing purposes on a regular basis. Although many American are not aware of it, an agent can request reservations and tickets in advance. However, with the exception of the Europabus system, agents usually suggest that their F.I.T. clients make arrangements on the spot. Since bus service is frequent and reliable in Europe, advance reservations are usually not needed. In addition, there is no commission paid to the agent and getting up-to-date factual schedules can be very difficult, it not impossible.

Other Ground Arrangements

Other ground arrangements can be quite varied, arrangements can include home stays, meetings with counterparts and/or dignitaries, attending fashion shows, and special sporting event attendance or participation (balloon rides or races, for example). Many reference publications will be needed to dig out what is available and how to book it and pay for it in advance. The "Specialty Travel Index," State and/or National Tourist Bureau, and The European or Pacific Travel Planner are examples of some of the most often used references that help the F.I.T. specialist to book other ground arrangements of specific interest and/or value to the F.I.T. clients.

SUMMARY

Tour components are made up of both air and ground arrangements. It is the responsibility of the travel agent to find out what will best fit the client's interest, budget, and convenience, reserve arrangements that have been selected, confirm the arrangements, pay for the arrangements when pre-payment is allowed or expected, and prepare documentation for the client so that she will have all the needed information, confirmations, and receipts while traveling.

The travel agent F.I.T. specialist interfaces between service vendors and the F.I.T. client. The most important service provided by the agency F.I.T. specialist is to find out what is available and to select from the range of available options that best fit the F.I.T. client. This is true in every area from pre-flight at the origin airport, in flight, at transfer airports, at the destination airport(s) and on the ground at every destination.

The F.I.T. specialist interfaces with airline reservationists and airline passenger service representatives to make certain that airport and airplane services are provided. He interfaces with sightseeing firms to arrange meet and assist services so that the client is met at the airport and helped to waiting transportation. He works out transfer arrangements—usually with the same sightseeing firms—so the client receives smooth, quality transportation from the arrival airport to the hotel or other accommodation and back after the stay at the destination is over. The F.I.T. specialist interfaces with hotel, resort, and other reservationists to make certain accommodations are reserved, confirmed, booked, and documents issued.

Special meal arrangements and entertainment is researched. Meal and entertainment options are provided to the F.I.T. client and by reviewing the pros and cons of each option, special meal functions and entertainment activities are selected, requested, confirmed, paid for, and documents (usually vouchers) are issued.

Sightseeing options are researched also and the selection process with the client is entered into. Again, sightseeing is requested, confirmed, paid for, and the documents are issued.

Car rental, train, bus and other ground transportation options are reviewed for each destination area. Once selected, they are paid for, confirmed, and documented.

The travel agent ties all arrangements together by listing the components in a detailed itinerary and a documentation package that flows sequentially from the hour of departure to the hour of return home.

■   ■   ■

❏ *REVIEW QUESTIONS*

1. There are two groups of foreign independent tour components discussed in this chapter. One is air arrangements. The other is:
2. What is the title of the person at the airport who normally handles the meet and assist duties?
3. What type of services are usually provided by the meet and assist ground operator representative?
4. What did Bert Hemphill say about F.I.T. client accommodations?
5. What are five areas of responsibility that a travel agent has in relationship to handling an F.I.T. client's meal service?

❏ *ROLE PLAY EXERCISE*

Two students can participate in this role play either out of class as a fun way to review entertainment booking points made in the chapter or as an in-class exercise. One student plays the role of the travel agency's F.I.T. client and the other plays the role of the travel agent F.I.T. specialist. Please read the script and then pick up the conversation in your own words.

TRAVEL AGENT: Thank you for coming in Mrs. Johnson. I am getting ready to set up ground arrangements for your trip to Europe in June and would like to discuss entertainment options with you. Would you give me an idea of the kinds of entertainment you most enjoy and the kind of entertainment you are looking forward to while visiting Europe?

CLIENT: Well, my interests are a little different than my husband's. And, of course, we will be traveling together. We will need to do things together, too. What are some of the options and how do most people handle this kind of problem?

Continue on your own.

3

THE F.I.T. CLIENT/AGENT BOOKING PROCESS

Several meetings with clients are typically scheduled by travel agent F.I.T. specialists. These meetings have several purposes. The first contact will generally be a meeting during which the highlights of the trip are discussed. Major budget considerations are determined and the agent gets a rough idea of what the client wants. The next meeting identifies broad options and gives the client a general idea of what is practical. At the same meeting, or at subsequent meetings, trip details and a final itinerary are worked out. At the final meeting documents are turned over to the client.

A large number of meetings can be held. However, professional F.I.T. specialists realize that while they must provide a quality travel product to their client, they must also make a profit for the agency. The more time they spend in talking with the client, the less profit the travel agency will make. Since travel agents are paid on a salary (normally), the old adage of "Time is money" definitely applies. Therefore agents will often attempt to reduce the number of meetings to no more than two or three. In reality this can be done often if the agent touches base with the client by phone when there are key points that need to be resolved.

THE INITIAL CONTACT

The initial contact with the travel agency can come from the client calling and requesting information, or from the client walking into the agency, sitting at the desk of a counselor, and asking for trip information. In either case, the initial contact is often very brief. The client advises the agent of the destination(s) and the approximate duration of the trip, the number of people going on the trip, and usually the client provides some rough indication of budget constraints. However, none of these details might be firm at this stage. Some clients come in with an exact knowledge of every detail, including departure and arrival dates for each destination, the names of each person traveling, hotel names at each destination, sites to be visited and how long at each site, ground transportation preferences, and an exact budget. Clients can range from not being sure about anything to being absolutely certain about all the details. Most agents at this point will suggest to a client that the agent will research her needs and get back to the client with some specific options. Many agents will suggest that there might be tour brochures showing itineraries covered by tours for the same destination areas even though the F.I.T. client will not be taking an escorted tour. By looking at the tour brochures, the client can get an understanding of the major sites that might be practical to visit during a specific block of time.

After the F.I.T. specialist advises the client that he will research the trip, it is important to do so as rapidly as possible. The research at this stage might require little work on the part of the agent. He will need to consult the various guides to determine what can be done within the time and budget constraints that the client has identified. In almost every case, there will be a number of options and the agent might want to rough out two or possibly even three scenarios.

The second meeting will often be much longer than the initial meeting. At this meeting concentration should focus on the amount of time to be spent in each major city and the major sights to be seen. It is not at all unusual for a client to tell the agent that she wants to spend a certain amount of time in each of a number of different countries and for the agent to sketch out the itinerary the client has identified, only to find out the client has forgotten to point out some other most important aspect of the trip, thus changing the entire itinerary. It is, therefore, suggested at a very early stage the client be asked to prioritize destinations and sights in terms of "most important" down to "least important." In many cases it will be a sight that is more important than a specific destination.

At this meeting, or at a subsequent meeting, the client will be asked questions relating to specific interests regarding hotels, the need for meet and assist services, airport transfers, accommodations, meal services, entertainment, sightseeing, ground transportation, and other arrangements. It is suggested that each of these be covered as a specific category as they relate to each destination city. If the agent will make notes during this discussion, the agent should be able to take this series of notes and put together a total draft package. Prior to the next meeting with the client, this draft package should be mailed to the client for the client and any travel companions to review in detail. It is suggested that wide margins be left so that the client or the travel companions can make notes. They should record on the draft itinerary package anything they prefer to have changed.

Most F.I.T. specialists will try to make this meeting the key—if possible the last meeting for gathering preference information and getting initial deposits. Ideally no more face-to-face meetings will be held until the client picks up the final documents. Everything else can be done by phone or mail. It is at this time that the client and the agent settle on firm, in a few areas still rather broad, constraints regarding the trip. Such things as the exact countries to be visited (sometimes even the exact cities), a total dollar figure per person to be spent (sometimes calculated on a per diem basis), and the most important sites to be visited are discussed.

It is also at this second meeting that the agency specialist needs to undertake a client analysis investigation. Before the agent can start making arrangements for the specific details of the trip, a good understanding of what the client's preferences are as it relates to the type of hotel (or other accommodations), types of meals, entertainment, and even the type of railcar preferred needs to be developed. A tremendous amount of time can be spent by the agent in changing and rebooking services if the client analysis does not occur at this stage.

Before the next meeting the agency specialist should have prepared a complete itinerary in typed form of what the client might want to do and see. This is mailed to the client in advance, so that there can be an opportunity to study it, go over it with the spouse or other travel companions, and make changes. There is considerable advantage to giving the client this itinerary in advance and then suggesting that the client have it for at least a weekend for review prior to the next meeting.

If there are numerous changes to be made, another meeting with the agent can be scheduled, where these changes can be discussed in detail. However, if the agent has done a good job analyzing his clients and has done a good job of researching, putting together and presenting the F.I.T., no further meetings are necessary until the client is ready to pick up the documents. If there are only a few changes to be made, this can be done by telephone or by mailing the draft package back to the agent. In either case when the agent gets the changes back, the agent needs to work up a final package, keeping in mind the exact desires of the client. In this final package, first, second, and third options should be identified as it needs to be pointed out to the client that not all of the first choices are available when the booking process starts.

Once the final package is identified, the agent will want to contact suppliers and confirm each detail of the trip. Whenever there is a hangup, and there might very well be, the client should be advised what the options are. This should be done by phone in most cases. After all details have been confirmed in accordance with the preferences identified by the client, a final meeting will be held during which final payment will be made and all documents are turned over to the client.

■   ■   ■

❏ *REVIEW QUESTIONS*

1. What are some of the reasons why a client might be asked to prioritize destinations and sights in terms of "most important" down to "least important"?

2. What things happen during the final client/agent meeting?
3. In most cases is the first client/agent meeting longer or is it the second meeting that is longer? Why?
4. Why might an agency F.I.T. specialist give an F.I.T. client tour brochures?
5. How does the adage "Time is money." apply to the F.I.T. client/agent booking process?

❏ *ROLE PLAY EXERCISES*

Two students can participate in this role play either out of class as a fun way to review the treatment of a client's list of priority (most important down to least important) destinations and sights or as an in-class exercise. One student plays the role of the travel agency's F.I.T. client and the other plays the role of the travel agent F.I.T. specialist. Please read the script and then pick up the conversation in your own words.

TRAVEL AGENT: You have a long list of destinations and sights you want to see and do in Europe, Mrs. Johnson. Thank you for taking the time to prioritize the destinations and sights. I know it must have been difficult, but I am sure you have realized that this is one of the best ways to determine what should be eliminated, since the trip is so short and there are only so many destinations that can be visited and sights seen on any trip. Let's . . .

CLIENT: (interrupting)   Oh, but you don't understand. I want to see all these places and I want to do everything on the list I gave you. It was awfully hard to rank them. I concluded we will have to get it all in during the trip. I'm sure you can do that, can't you?

Continue on your own.

INITIAL ITINERARY PLANNING

At an early stage in the development of an F.I.T., the F.I.T. specialist prepares an initial draft of the client's itinerary. There is disagreement as to what parts should be developed first or the order in which the F.I.T. development steps should be taken. F.I.T. specialists initiate F.I.T.s in different ways. However, there is a tendency among F.I.T. specialists to require some data before the initial itinerary is prepared. Essential information to gather in advance includes:

1. Total duration of trip (normally number of days, from departure to date of return home)
2. Countries and cities to be visited with approximate number of days to be spent in each
3. What the client considers to be the highlights she wants to include in the F.I.T.

Of course, the more specific the information available, the more complete one can expect to prepare the initial itinerary draft, and in many cases, the fewer drafts of the itinerary that will be needed.

THE LOGICAL F.I.T. SEQUENCING APPROACH

Armed with the above rough data, the F.I.T. specialist undertakes the task of putting the itinerary together. There is a logical approach that is often used. This logical approach is to start with the first day of the itinerary and to plan each activity day by day. Going along with this approach, the F.I.T. specialist often will prepare a geographically sequenced trip, for example, from the west and working east, on an itinerary that provides as little backtracking as possible. This geographical approach is not only logical, but it also fits in with air fares, which might include such things as stopover privileges at an additional, but relatively small cost.

THE TRIP FOCUS APPROACH

In spite of the fact that starting with a logical time sequencing from day one until the last day of the trip and a logical geographical sequencing, planning the trip from one direction to the opposite without backtracking is the most apparently logical way to start, many F.I.T. specialists find from experience that such an approach does not provide them or their clients with the kind of itinerary that is ultimately accepted or preferred. Many agents, therefore, will attempt to identify what is expected to be for the client the single most important event or destination. Once this has been identified, the specialist will work from that point in the trip both forward and backward to tie in the balance of the trip. Many agree that by identifying the major focus (or perhaps two major points) and building the trip around it, a more pleasurable trip results and fewer itinerary changes are requested by the client.

INITIAL ITINERARY SPECIAL EVENTS

Often F.I.T.s are centered around special events. These events might be a golf tournament in Scotland, a Christmas performance of the Vienna Boy's Choir, oiled wrestling matches in Turkey, or any one of thousands of other unique events. When special events are included in the itinerary, and especially when such events are the major focus point of the itinerary, they often require structuring the balance of the itinerary around the special event. The major reason is that many of these special events will be held once a year (or less often) on specific dates. In addition, many special event tickets are difficult to obtain and frequently when there is a special event that is popular worldwide; hotel accommodations and ground transportation arrangements are sold out for a long time in advance. This necessitates very early reservations and strong penalties are often levied in case changes are made. Obviously, when such special events are included, they must be considered prior to those activities which can be scheduled at any time and/or which are offered on either a daily or weekly basis.

COUNTRY/CITY ITINERARY STARTING POINT

Normally the original itinerary starts with just a listing of the city and/or country to be visited for each date on the itinerary. These listings are then modified by adding flight schedules for the air trips to and from each country/city and ground transportation (normally either rail or car). Special circumstances can occur that result in the itinerary being modified from the initial city/country listing. For example, the itinerary might need to be modified to some extent when slower transportation is utilized (such as canal barge transportation—popular in several European countries) or a cruise is scheduled (for instance, a Rhine cruise from Rotterdam to Basle).

ACCOMMODATIONS AND THE INITIAL ITINERARY

After developing the country/city and transportation details, the F.I.T. specialist will turn to either the accommodation arrangements or to sight-seeing arrangements. Most often, it is the accommodation arrangements that are planned next. Many clients prefer downtown city hotels. When they do, the options to select from are normally rather large. With downtown hotels usually few changes to other details of the itinerary need to be made. However, if a client indicates that he prefers to stay in castles, mansions, pensions, at a farm, or any of a number of other alternatives, the accommodation details might affect the amount of time that can be spent in a specific country/city and the details might need to be altered accordingly. In such cases, the F.I.T. specialist will normally work out accommodation recommendations and alternatives relating to any changes in country/city arrangements that need to be made to adjust to the accommodation arrangements.

In developing original itinerary accommodation recommendations, the F.I.T. specialist will identify those accommodations that, after usually brief research, appear to be best suited for the client. If the client has advised that she prefers to stay in unusual accommodations (such as those noted previously), this type of accommodation is selected. However, rarely does the F.I.T. specialist make reservations for accommodations at this stage. Usually a recommendation is discussed with the client prior to making firm reservations. Often the F.I.T. specialist will need to research such books as the *STARS List of Elegant Properties,* the *Official Hotel and Resort Guide (OHRG),* specialized books on accommodations such as *Castles in Europe,* and so forth. The research undertaken at this time is not done to finalize arrangements. It is simply to provide recommendations and alternatives for the client to consider. Many F.I.T. specialists provide the client with two or three alternative accommodation suggestions for each night. In other words, the F.I.T. specialist usually provides the traveler with several options for the evening's stay (pointing out the pros and cons of each accommodation option).

INITIAL ITINERARY SIGHTSEEING

Sightseeing is important to many clients and most F.I.T. travelers will stress the importance of seeing certain specific sites in their initial conversation. Arrangements for these sightseeing trips are usually included in the initial itinerary. As with hotel recommendations, the initial itinerary sightseeing suggestions are not finalized with confirmed reservations at this stage. The sightseeing options are simply sketched in. Some F.I.T. specialists will review the appropriate pages of the *Gray Line Sightseeing Book* or the *American Sightseeing International Book* with their F.I.T. clients. They advise the client that the full range of sightseeing trips detailed are available options. They go on to advise that if the client would prefer to have one or more of the sightseeing trips listed in the reference books, those trips can be substituted for any already listed as itinerary suggestions or the itinerary can possibly be changed to provide additional time to include the sightseeing trips selected from the reference material. In this way the client is able to select from a wide range of options rather than only evaluate the specific recommendation made in each time block by the F.I.T. specialist.

INITIAL ITINERARY MEAL RECOMMENDATIONS

Although many F.I.T. specialists do not include meal recommendations in the initial itinerary, special meal functions are often included. These may be such events as medieval banquets, casino dinner shows, and night club dinner shows. A few of these might be included at this stage, but unless there is some special restaurant or other entertainment/food service facility that is special, the meal functions are normally left until the development of a later itinerary. Many clients will want to make local arrangements for meals with a list of suggestions from the F.I.T. specialist. Other clients will prefer to have most meals arranged in advance. The details of normal day-to-day arrangements, if they are to be included in the F.I.T., are normally found in the later itinerary drafts. As with sightseeing options, some F.I.T. specialists will provide the client with a range of restaurant, dinner show, and other meal suggestions at every destination so that the client can select those of preference.

INITIAL ITINERARY SPECIAL EVENTS

Special events, as noted earlier, often constitute the real reason for an F.I.T. Since it is around many of these special events that F.I.T.s are often prepared, they must be included in the initial itinerary draft. It is suggested that even though it is only the initial itinerary, considerable detail should be provided to the F.I.T. client relating to the events that are of special significance. This is often presented in the form of one or more paragraphs describing the arrangements that are suggested for the client. Such things as the location of seating at the Rose Bowl game, the acoustics one can expect to enjoy in one's private box at La Scala or the carriage arrangements made to transfer the clients from their hotel to the Grand Ballroom for the Viennese New Year's Ball, are all discussed in some detail even in the initial itinerary.

It must be remembered that this is what makes the F.I.T. special to the client. To a great extent, it is the glamour associated with special events that the client is buying. Reading the itinerary over and over and savoring the upcoming events are just as important before leaving on the F.I.T. as treasuring the special F.I.T. memories after the trip is over. It is here that one must remember the adage "Sell the sizzle as well as the steak."

SUMMARY

While the initial itinerary is not intended to be a final itinerary complete in all details, it does include specific recommendations based on the major points of the trip. By working from the high point of the trip focus and planning in both directions and then sequencing the trip on a day-by-day basis, moving geographically from one direction to the opposite, the F.I.T. specialist is able to provide a country/city framework on which to build the balance of the F.I.T. Since special events often constitute the trip focus, these events need to be planned first and they need to be discussed in the itinerary in considerable detail. After identifying the special events in a country/city and geographically scheduling the balance of the itinerary, the F.I.T. specialist adds accommodation arrangement recommendations. The next step is to include sightseeing suggestions and alternatives on the initial itinerary. Finally, special meal functions are included. Before leaving the initial itinerary, it is important to go back to the special events section making certain that all details of the events are discussed in a manner that will make the trip seem as glamorous, romantic, and/or exciting as the client envisions it to be.

By preparing an initial itinerary with specific recommendations and a number of optional choices, the client is given a framework from which to work. Details that will make the trip very special can be selected. Special touches that make it a tailored trip can be added. If all is done right, the F.I.T. should be a memorable experience fondly remembered for many years.

■　　　　　■　　　　　■

❏ REVIEW QUESTIONS

1. What are the logical sequencing approaches often used by F.I.T. specialists in preparing an initial itinerary?
2. What is the trip focus approach in preparing an F.I.T. initial itinerary?
3. Should meal functions be planned in the initial itinerary? Why? Why not?

4. Give an example of an accommodation arrangement that might change the itinerary date and/or country/city schedule.
5. What three sightseeing guides are often utilized in preparing F.I.T. sightseeing recommendations for clients?

❏ ROLE PLAY EXERCISE

Two students can participate in this role play either out of class as a fun way to review initial itinerary planning or as an in-class exercise. One student plays the role of the travel agency's F.I.T. client and the other plays the role of the travel agent F.I.T. specialist. Please read the script and then pick up the conversation in your own words.

TRAVEL AGENT: I am very pleased to provide you with this initial itinerary, Mr. and Mrs. Johnson. We have attempted to include all the points that you stressed are special to you. As you will see, I am making some very specific recommendations on special meal functions. Would you review the entire itinerary very briefly and let me know what you like about it and what you would prefer to have changed?

CLIENT: (After having rapidly reviewed the initial itinerary) This certainly is interesting. It does give us most of the things that we want. However, I have a question. In this section (pointing to a page in the itinerary), you give the details for a picnic for us. How crowded will it be in this meadow in southern France? Will we be bothered by mosquitoes? Will we need to bring some type of repellent with us? Do we get to choose what food we will have or will they just give us a basket with our having to take whatever is in it?

Continue on your own.

INITIAL ITINERARY PLANNING

ITINERARY SAMPLE NUMBER ONE

EUROPE ITINERARY
FOR
MR. AND MRS. CARL JOHNSON

JUNE 29, 1982	TUESDAY	Depart Memphis on AA #248 at 11:55 A.M. Arrive New York LaGuardia Airport at 3:55 P.M. Depart New York on SAS #912 at 7:00 PM
JUNE 30, 1982	WEDNESDAY	Arrive Copenhagen at 8:30 A.M. HOTEL SCANDINAVIA AMAGER BLVD. 70 COPENHAGEN Remainder of day at leisure to relax and recover from "jet lag."
JULY 1, 1982 JULY 2, 1982 JULY 3, 1982	THURSDAY FRIDAY SATURDAY	Sightseeing in Copenhagen should include a view of the "Little Mermaid" statue; perhaps a boat tour along the picturesque canals; walk down the pedestrian street called the Stroejet and visit some of the many fine shops, such as Illums Bolighus (my favorite), visit Rosenborg Castle and see the Crown Jewels, visit Christiansborg Palace; spend time at the wonderful Tivoli Gardens; walk around the Nyhavn, the harbor area that retains the air of a seaport town from another century; see the Changing of the Guard at Amalienborg Palace Square. You might also enjoy seeing the Latin Quarter, the university section of the city where outdoor cafés abound.

JULY 4, 1982	SUNDAY	Depart on M.S. Polaris at 6:00 P.M.
JULY 5, 1982	MONDAY	At sea, cruising through Kattegat and Skagerrak to the Norwegian fjord country.
JULY 6, 1982	TUESDAY	Today you will pass through Norway's narrow, mountain-rimmed bays heading for Lysefjord underneath the cliff of Prekestolen (Pulpit Rock). You will climb to the top of the cliff, then stop briefly at Stavanger, Norway's "oil city."
JULY 7, 1982	WEDNESDAY	Today you will visit Bergen, where you will see Composer Edvard Grieg's house, visit the Fanroft Stave Church built by the Vikings, see the waterfront with its 14th and 15th century buildings.
JULY 8, 1982	THURSDAY	This morning the ship enters the 125 mile long Sognefjord, the longest and deepest of all the fjords. At Flaam you will board the Flaamsbanen for a 45-minute ride to Myrdal. You then connect to the train to Voss, the ski resort where Knute Rockne was born, and then reboard the Polaris at Gudvangen.
JULY 9, 1982	FRIDAY	During the night the Polaris sails into the gentle Nordfjord to anchor at the village of Loen. You will see the breathtaking blue-white Briksdal glacier overhanging the valley walls, traveling either on foot or by horse and buggy. You will sail in the afternoon.
JULY 10, 1982	SATURDAY	Today you will sail the Storfjord through a landscape of dazzling beauty where giant waterfalls plunge down the mountainside.

JULY 10, 1982 (Continued)	SATURDAY	Geiranger lies at the innermost part of the fjord. You will travel over the Romsdal Valley and Trollstigen, which comes down the cliff in eleven serpentine turns. Rejoin the ship in late afternoon.
JULY 11, 1982	SUNDAY	Today you will sail to Trondheim, where you will see the landmarks of the Nidaros Cathedral and the nearby village of Hell—a favorite postmark for visitors. BRITTANIA HOTEL DRONNINGENSGT 5, TRONDHEIM
JULY 12, 1982	MONDAY	Depart Trondheim on SAS #549 at 9:35 A.M. Arrive Oslo at 10:25 A.M. GRAND HOTEL KARL JOHANSGT 31, OSLO Afternoon at leisure to explore some of the city or to relax.
JULY 13, 1982	TUESDAY	Sightseeing of Oslo should include the old and new sections of the city, the university, the Royal Castle, the cathedral, town hall, and Vigeland Sculpture Park.
JULY 14, 1982	WEDNESDAY	Depart Oslo on SAS #482 at 11:35 A.M. Arrive Stockholm at 12:30 P.M. GRAND HOTEL S. BLASEHOLMSHAMMEN 8, STOCKHOLM
JULY 15, 1982 JULY 16, 1982	THURSDAY FRIDAY	Sightseeing of Stockholm should include Old Town, the town hall, and the Riddarholm Church, the Royal Palace, the Millesgarden Sculpture Park, and go to the western suburbs to the royal residences at Drottningholm, where

JULY 15, 1982	THURSDAY	you can visit the palace and the
JULY 16, 1982	FRIDAY	famous Royal Court Theatre.
(Continued)		

JULY 17, 1982   SATURDAY   Depart Stockholm on SAS # 901 at
11:30 A.M.
Arrive New York, JFK Airport, at
3:30 P.M.
Clear customs, then take taxi to
hotel near Laguardia.
MARRIOTT HOTEL,
LAGUARDIA AIRPORT
102-05 DITMARS BLVD.

July 18, 1982   SUNDAY   Depart LaGuardia Airport on
US AIR #229 at 7:10 A.M.
Arrive Pittsburgh at 8:25 A.M.
Depart Pittsburgh on US AIR 405
at 10:15 A.M.
Arrive Memphis at 10:57 A.M.

This will end what I hope will be a perfect trip.

(Itinerary developed by Julie Westhoff, Awanderlust Travel, Denver, Colorado.)

INITIAL ITINERARY PLANNING

ITINERARY SAMPLE NUMBER TWO

EUROPE ITINERARY
FOR
THE CARL JOHNSON FAMILY

October 10—Wednesday

TWA # 840 ($881)			**TWA #742** ($792)	
Leave LAX	8:30 A.M.		Leave Denver	10:15 A.M.
Arrive Kennedy	4:30 P.M.		Arrive Kennedy	3:55 P.M.

TWA # 740			**TWA # 740**	
Leave Kennedy	6:20 P.M.		Leave Kennedy	6:20 P.M.
Arrive Munich	9:50 A.M.		Arrive Munich	9:50 A.M.
	10/11			10/11

Pick up car (9 passenger VW Mini Bus). Interrent (800) 421-6878
$367.00 + 14% (976.50 DM) tax per week. Unlimited mileage.

October 11—Thursday

Arrive in Munich. Pick up car and visit sites in Munich. Drive to
Innsbruck to spend the night, going through Fuessen (Bavarian Alps),
stopping at King Ludwig's fantastic Newschwanstein Castle and
Hohenschwangau Castle, Alpsie.

October 12—Friday

Visit sites in Innsbruck and drive to Liechtenstein and see sites, possibly
spend the night. (See Hotel Meierhof.)

October 13—Saturday

On to Interlocken—see sites and spend the night.

October 14 & 15—Sunday and Monday

Leave for Locarno, stopping at Zermott to spend morning and part of
afternoon.

Side trips: Boat trip to Lago Maggori
             Como
             Stresa

October 16 & 17—Tuesday and Wednesday

On to Venice, stopping for lunch in Desenzano. Spend the night in Venice and sightsee the next day or two.

October 18 & 19—Thursday and Friday

Drive to Florence and spend day and night. Visit the Duomo, Pitti Palace, David, Vecchie, Mercato Centrale, etc.

October 20—Saturday

On to Seravalle and Assisi, possibly through San Gimignano (walk through towers recalling days when rival families strived to build higher than their neighbor) and possibly on to Rome and spend night. If possible, take night ride to Tivoli Fountains.

October 21—Sunday

See Rome and spend night (Hotel Venezia—see book.)

October 22—Monday

Drive to Sorrento and take boat to Capri. Tour Capri, Blue Grotto (if open), etc. Then it's back to Sorrento for dinner and walk around the town. Spend the night at Hotel Loreli.

October 23—Tuesday

Leave Sorrento and head up coast to San Vincenzo and spend night.

October 24 through 29—Wednesday through Sunday

Aosta—visiting: Biela, Chialamberto, Carvena, Matterhorn (Italian Side), Castles, Courmayeur, etc., as well as Aosta Valley itself (the little Rome of the Alps).

October 29—Monday

Leave Aosta and head for Chaumonix, France, Granoble, and surrounding Savoy area—spend night.

October 30 & 31—Tuesday and Wednesday

On to Morten and Bern, Switzerland and spend two days—visit sites.

November 1—Thursday

Start up Rhine River to Strasburg and spend night, seeing sites along the way.

November 2—Friday

Go to Heidelberg and surrounding areas and spend night.

November 5—Monday

Going home!

TWA # 743

| Leave Frankfurt | 1:55 P.M. |
| Arrive Kennedy | 4:05 P.M. |

TWA # 849

| Leave Kennedy | 6:10 P.M. |
| Arrive LAX | 8:58 P.M. |

TWA # 743

| Leave Frankfurt | 1:55 P.M. |
| Arrive Kennedy | 4:05 P.M. |

(Go through customs and get back on plane)

| Leave Kennedy | 6:25 P.M. |
| Arrive Denver | 8:40 P.M. |

(Itinerary developed by Julie Westhoff, Awanderlust Travel, Denver, Colorado.)

INITIAL ITINERARY PLANNING

ITINERARY FORM SAMPLES

ITINERARY FOR _____

TRIP _____

Lv
_____
Ar
_____

Lv
_____
Ar
_____

Lv
_____
Ar
_____

Lv
_____
Ar
_____

Lv
_____
Ar
_____

Lv
_____
Ar
_____

Lv
_____
Ar
_____

Because schedules are sometimes subject to change without notice, or delayed, we should like to suggest in the interest of good service, that you check the above departure times before leaving for the airport or station.

(Courtesy of Julie Westhoff, Awanderlust Travel, Denver, Colorado.)

ITINERARY DRAFT WORKSHEET FOR:

	SUN	
	MON	
	TUES	
	WED	
	THUR	
	FRI	
	SAT	
	SUN	
	MON	
	TUES	
	WED	
	THUR	
	FRI	
	SAT	
	SUN	
	MON	
	TUES	
	WED	
	THUR	
	FRI	
	SAT	
	SUN	
	MON	
	TUES	
	WED	
	THUR	
	FRI	
	SAT	
	SUN	
	MON	
	TUES	
	WED	
	THUR	
	FRI	
	SAT	

Form IW 5 © WILLOW PRESS Inc., Hauppauge. NY 11788

(Courtesy of Willow Press. Reprinted with permission.)

Date	Recd	Paid	Explanation
TOTAL			
Ticket No.			

Name Phone R: / B: ____

Address ____

Name Phone R: / B: ____

Address ____

DATE	CITY	FLIGHT	TIME	CONFIRMED	CLASS	
	Lv					
	Ar					
	Lv					
	Ar					
	Lv					
	Ar					
	Lv					
	Ar					
	Lv					
	Ar					
	Lv					
	Ar					
	Lv					
	Ar					

(Courtesy of Julie Westhoff, Awanderlust Travel, Denver, Colorado.)

INITIAL ITINERARY PLANNING

SCANDINAVIAN ITINERARY DEVELOPMENT EXERCISE NUMBER ONE

SITUATION: Our good friend, Mrs. Johnson, and her close friend, Mrs. Taymore, want to visit Scandinavia. Since Mrs. Taymore lives in Memphis and Mrs. Johnson wishes to visit with her friend before and after the trip, the departure and arrival city for the trip will be Memphis. They wish to leave the last Tuesday in June and fly to Copenhagen, where Mrs. Taymore grew up. After spending several days with relatives in Copenhagen, they wish to fly on the second Sunday morning in July to Trondheim where they want to overnight. Take them on a morning flight the next day (Monday) to Oslo. On Wednesday they wish to fly to Stockholm during the late morning. After spending Wednesday night, Thursday, Friday, and Saturday in Stockholm, they want to fly back to Memphis on Sunday. Using the flight schedule simulations on the next pages, plan flights on the itinerary short form following the simulated flight schedules.

INITIAL ITINERARY PLANNING

SCANDINAVIAN ITINERARY DEVELOPMENT EXERCISE NUMBER ONE

JUNE

S	M	T	W	T	F	S
28	29	30				

JULY

S	M	T	W	T	F	S
			1	2	3	4
5	6	7	8	9	10	11
12	13	14	15	16	17	18
19	20	21	22	23	24	25
26	27	28	29	30	31	

Fig. 4-1. Scandinavian itinerary development exercise planning calendar.

ITINERARY SHORT FORM

DATE	AIRLINE/ FLIGHT	DEPARTURE AIRPORT	TIME DEPART	ARRIVE	ARRIVAL AIRPORT

HOTELS _____   RENTAL CARS _____

Fig. 4-2. A standard itinerary short form.

To NEW YORK NY/NEWARK, NJ   EDT NYC
E-EWR (NEWARK INTERNATIONAL)
J-JFK (KENNEDY)   L-LGA (LA GUARDIA)
P-HPN (WESTCHESTER COUNTY)
S-JRE (EAST 60TH STREET HELIPORT)
T-TSS (EAST 34TH STREET HELIPORT)
W-JRA (WEST 30TH STREET HELIPORT)
ALSO SEE LONG ISLAND MACARTHUR, N.Y.,
AND LONG ISLAND REPUBLIC, N.Y.

Freq.	Leave	Arrive	Flight	Class	Eq	MI	S

▲MEMPHIS, TENNESSEE   CDT MEM

Freq.	Leave	Arrive	Flight	Class	Eq	MI	S
	9:00a	12:31P L	NW 790	FYBMQ	DC9	B	0
X7	9:05a	12:32P L	NW 630	FYBMQ	72S	B	0
7	9:05a	12:32P L	NW 630	FYMBnQn	72S	B	0
	12:20P	3:52P E	NW 792	FYBMQ	DC9	S	0
	12:25P	7:15P L	NW 472	FYBMQ	72S	S	0
	12:30P	3:59P L	NW 632	FYBMQ	D9S	L	0
	3:55P	7:30P L	NW 636	FYBMQ	D9S	S	0
X6	4:15P	10:53P L	NW 538	FYBMQ	D9S	S	2
	7:55P	11:23P E	NW 796	FYBMQ	DC9		0
	8:05P	11:27P L	NW 988	FYBMQ	727		0

CONNECTIONS

Freq.	Leave	Arrive	Flight	Class	Eq	MI	S
	7:10a	9:15a ATL	DL 540	FYBMQ	D9S	B/S	0
	10:21a ATL	12:25P E	DL 194	FYBMQ	72S	S	0
	7:25a	9:45a CVG	DL 864	FYBMQ	72S	B/S	0
	10:37a CVG	12:20P L	DL 352	FYBMQ	72S		0
	8:40a	11:25a DTW	NW 290	FYBMQ	757	B/S	0
	12:05P DTW	1:35P P	NW 1146	FYBMQ	D9S	S	0
	8:49a	9:53a STL	TW 580	FYBMQ	DC9	S/	0
	10:58a STL	2:12P L	TW 140	FYMBQ	72S	L	0
X67	8:49a	9:53a STL	TW 580	FYBMQ	DC9	S/	0
	11:10a STL	2:31P E	TW 402	FCYMB	L10	L	0
67	8:49a	9:53a STL	TW 580	FYBMQ	DC9	S/	0
	11:10a STL	2:31P E	TW 402	FYBMQ	727	L	0
	8:49a	9:53a STL	TW 580	FYBMQ	DC9	S/	0
	10:52a STL	3:07P J	TW 298	FYBMQ	72S	L	1
	8:50a	11:01a ATL	DL 646	FYBMQ	D9S	S	0
	11:50a ATL	1:45P	DL 478	FYBMQ	72S	S	0
	9:00a	10:36a ORD	UA 522	FYBMQ	73S	S	0
	11:30a ORD	2:27P E	UA 968	FYBMQ	D8S	S	0
	9:00a	10:36a ORD	UA 522	FYBMQ	73S	L	0
	12:00n ORD	2:53P L	UA 72	FYBMQ	767	L	0
	10:30a	1:43P CLT	PI 1270	FYBHQ	73S	S/	1
	3:35P CLT	5:15P J	PI 1452	FYBHQ	73S	S/	0
	10:40a	12:45P ATL	DL 1238	FYBMQ	72S	L	0
	1:24P ATL	3:23P L	DL 482	FYBMQ	72S	L	0
	10:40a	12:45P ATL	DL 1238	FYBMQ	D9S	S	0
	1:23P ATL	3:25P E	DL 740	FYBMQ	757	L	0
	11:27a	12:27P STL	TW 638	FYMBQ	DC9		0
	1:20P STL	4:54P J	TW 344	FCYMB	L10	L	0
	11:27a	12:27P STL	TW 638	FYMBQ	DC9		0
	1:35P STL	4:58P L	TW 114	FCYMB	767	S	0
	11:27a	12:27P STL	TW 638	FYMBQ	DC9		0
	1:55P STL	5:21P E	TW 136	FYBMQ	72S	S	0
	12:25P	2:35P ATL	DL 508	FYBMQ	D9S	S	0
	3:56P ATL	5:59P L	DL 918	FYBMQ	72S	S	0
	2:00P	4:08P ATL	DL 718	FYBMQ	757	D	0
	5:02P ATL	7:15P L	DL 860	FYBMQ	763	D	0
	2:00P	4:08P ATL	DL 718	FYBMQ	757	D	0
	5:05P ATL	7:20P E	DL 422	FYBMQ	72S	D	0
X6	2:31P	4:01P ORD	UA 567	FYBMQ	73S	S/	0
D-21OCT	4:30P ORD	7:30P E	UA 308	FYBMQ	D10	D	0
X6	2:31P	4:01P ORD	UA 567	FYBMQ	73S	D	0
E-24OCT	4:30P ORD	7:30P E	UA 308	FYBMQ	D10	D	0
	2:31P	4:01P ORD	UA 567	FYBMQ	73S	S/	0
	5:00P ORD	8:04P L	UA 82	FYBMQ	72S	D	0
X6	2:31P	4:01P ORD	UA 567	FYBMQ	73S	S/	0
	5:30P ORD	8:40P E	UA 144	FYBMQ	D10	D	0
X7	3:52P	6:03P ATL	DL 305	FYBMQ	D9S	S	0
	6:59P ATL	9:10P E	DL 432	FYBMQ	767	D	0
X67	3:52P	6:03P ATL	DL 305	FYBMQ	D9S	S	0
	7:02P ATL	9:10P L	DL 178	FYBMQ	767	D	0
6	3:52P	6:03P ATL	DL 305	FYBMQ	D9S	S	0
	7:02P ATL	9:10P L	DL 178	FYBMQ	757	D	0
X6	4:25P	6:55P CMH	NW 1164	FYBMQ	72S	D	0
	7:35P CMH	9:05P E	CO 476	FYBMQ	737		0
	5:25P	7:42P CVG	DL 302	FYBMQ	72S	S	0
	8:29P CVG	10:15P L	DL 720	FYBMQ	72S		0

To NEW YORK NY/NEWARK, NJ   EDT NYC

Freq.	Leave	Arrive	Flight	Class	Eq	MI	S
X6	5:30P	7:13P ORD	UA 342	FYBMQ	73S	D	S 0
	8:00P ORD	11:03P L	UA 88	FYBMQ	72S	S	0
X6	5:30P	7:13P ORD	UA 342	FYBMQ	73S	D	S 0
	8:30P ORD	11:29P E	UA 596	FYBMQ	D10	S	0
X67	5:40P	7:48P ATL	DL 524	FYBMQ	M80	S	0
	8:44P ATL	10:50P E	DL 748	FYBMQ	D8S	S	0
6	5:40P	7:48P ATL	DL 524	FYBMQ	D9S	S	0
	8:44P ATL	10:50P E	DL 326	FYBMQ	767		0
7	5:40P	7:48P ATL	DL 524	FYBMQ	M80	S	0
	8:44P ATL	10:50P E	DL 748	FYBMQ	767		0
	6:23P	7:25P STL	TW 596	FYMBQ	DC9		0
	8:25P STL	11:45P L	TW 444	FCYMB	L10	S	0
	6:23P	7:25P STL	TW 596	FYMBQ	DC9		0
	8:30P STL	11:56P E	TW 70	FYMBQ	M80		0
	8:40P	10:51P ATL	DL 1031	FYBMQ	D9S		0
	11:52P ATL	1:45a E	DL 186	FnYnBnMQ	763		0

To MEMPHIS, TENNESSEE   CDT MEM

▲NEW YORK NY/NEWARK, NJ   EDT NYC
P-HPN J-JFK L-LGA T-TSS E-EWR S-JRE W-JRA

Freq.	Leave	Arrive	Flight	Class	Eq	MI	S
X7	6:30a L	8:05a	NW 631	FYnMBnQn	D9S	B	0
X7	8:50a L	12:57P	PI 1629	FYBHQ	73S	*	2
		PI1629 * MEALS SL/SL					
	9:45a L	11:23a	NW 633	FYBMQ	72S	B/S	0
	9:50a E	11:15a	NW 791	FYBMQ	DC9	S	0
	1:15P L	2:54P	NW 635	FYBMQ	M80	L/S	0
	1:20P E	2:50P	NW 793	FYBMQ	DC9	S	0
	5:20P E	7:02P	NW 637	FYBMQ	72S	D	0
X6	5:35P E	7:05P	NW 795	FYBMQ	DC9	S	0
6	5:35P E	7:05P	NW 795	FYnMBnQn	DC9	S	0

CONNECTIONS

Freq.	Leave	Arrive	Flight	Class	Eq	MI	S
X17	5:30a L	7:31a ATL	DL 929	FnYnBnMQ	D8S	B	0
	8:29a ATL	8:35a E	DL 409	FYBMQ	D9S	B/S	0
17	5:30a E	7:31a ATL	DL 929	FnYnBnMQ	767	B	0
	8:29a ATL	8:35a E	DL 409	FYBMQ	D9S	B/S	0
	6:30a L	8:24a CVG	DL 425	FYBMQ	73S	S	0
	9:04a CVG	9:20a	DL 733	FYBMQ	73S		0
	6:30a L	8:37a CVG	DL 745	FYBMQ	72S	B	0
	9:04a CVG	9:20a	DL 733	FYBMQ	73S		0
	6:55a L	8:34a STL	TW 223	FYMBQ	M80	B	0
	9:38a STL	10:52a	TW 512	FYMBQ	DC9		0
	7:05a L	8:36a STL	TW 111	FYMBQ	M80	B	0
	9:38a STL	10:52a	TW 512	FYMBQ	DC9		0
	7:30a E	8:40a ORD	UA 123	FYBMQ	D10	B	0
	9:50a ORD	11:27a	UA 597	FYBMQ	73S	S/	0
	8:00a L	9:21a ORD	UA 63	FYBMQ	73S	S/	0
	9:50a ORD	11:27a	UA 597	FYBMQ	73S	S/	0
	8:30a L	10:51a ATL	DL 803	FYBMQ	763	B	0
	11:56a ATL	12:05P	DL 946	FYBMQ	D9S	S	0
	8:30a E	10:38a ATL	DL 799	FYBMQ	757	S	0
	11:56a ATL	12:05P	DL 946	FYBMQ	D9S	S	0
	10:00a L	12:12P ATL	DL 107	FYBMQ	L10	S	0
	1:25P ATL	1:35P	DL 1661	FYBMQ	73S	S	0
X6	10:30a E	11:39a ORD	UA 231	FYBMQ	D10	S	0
	12:45P ORD	2:17P	DL 893	FYBMQ	73S	L/S	0
X6	11:00a L	12:12P ORD	UA 69	FYBMQ	72S	L	0
	12:45P ORD	2:17P	UA 893	FYBMQ	73S	L/S	0
X7	12:10P L	2:24P ATL	DL 477	FYBMQ	D9S		0
	3:12P ATL	3:22P	DL 305	FYBMQ	D9S		0
X67	12:10P E	2:13P ATL	DL 403	FYBMQ	D8S	L	0
	3:12P ATL	3:22P	DL 305	FYBMQ	767	L	0
6	12:10P E	2:13P ATL	DL 403	FYBMQ	D9S		0
	3:12P ATL	3:22P	DL 305	FYBMQ	D9S		0
	12:10P L	2:24P ATL	DL 477	FYBMQ	763	L	0
	4:45P ATL	4:55P	DL 933	FYBMQ	M80	S	0
X6	12:10P E	2:13P ATL	DL 403	FYBMQ	D8S	L	0
	4:45P ATL	4:55P	DL 933	FYBMQ	M80	S	0
	12:50P L	2:23P STL	TW 403	FYBMQ	L10	L	0
	3:29P STL	4:36P	TW 511	FYMBQ	DC9		0
	1:00P L	2:14P ORD	UA 73	FYBMQ	72S	L	0
	3:30P ORD	5:02P	UA 1277	FYBMQ	73S	S/	0
	1:02P E	2:27P STL	TW 75	FYBMQ	72S	L	0
	3:29P STL	4:36P	TW 511	FYMBQ	DC9		0
6	1:30P L	2:42P ORD	UA 129	FYBMQ	D10	S	0
	3:30P ORD	5:02P	UA 1277	FYBMQ	73S	S/	0
	3:00P	4:45P CLT	PI 1167	FYBHQ	72S	S/	0
	5:28P CLT	6:08P	PI 1258	FYBHQ	733	D	0
	3:56P J	6:18P STL	TW 573	FYBMQ	72S	S	1
	7:11P STL	8:26P	TW 602	FYBMQ	DC9		0
X6	4:00P E	5:17P ORD	UA 79	FYBMQ	767	D	0
	6:44P ORD	8:23P	UA 937	FYBMQ	73S	D/S	0
	4:10P E	6:14P CVG	DL 565	FYBMQ	72S	S	0
	6:39P CVG	6:57P	DL 1047	FYBMQ	D9S	S	0
	4:16P E	6:10P CVG	DL 1187	FYBMQ	757	S	0
	6:39P CVG	6:57P	DL 1047	FYBMQ	D9S	S	0
X67	4:15P L	5:42P STL	TW 235	FCYMB	L10	D	0
	7:11P STL	8:26P	TW 602	FYBMQ	DC9		0
67	4:15P L	5:44P STL	TW 235	FCYMB	727	D	0
	7:11P STL	8:26P	TW 602	FYBMQ	DC9		0
	4:20P J	5:35P BWI	PA★ 895	YBMQ	DH7	S	0
	6:15P BWI	7:15P	NW 985	FYBMQ	D9S	D	0
1	4:30P J	5:39P BWI	NW 917	FCYMB	767		0
	6:15P BWI	7:15P	NW 985	FYBMQ	D9S	D	0
X6	4:30P E	5:49P ORD	UA 145	FYBMQ	D8S	D/S	0
	6:44P ORD	8:23P	UA 937	FYBMQ	73S	D/S	0
	4:30P L	6:13P STL	TW 251	FYBMQ	72S	D	0
	7:11P STL	8:26P	TW 602	FYBMQ	DC9		0
X6	6:00P L	8:00P CLT	PI 1492	FYBHQ	733	D	0
	8:47P CLT	10:15P	PI 1545	FYBHQ	73S	S	1
	6:05P J	7:43P PIT	US 559	YBHQM	D9S	S	0
	8:15P PIT	9:04P	US 523	YBHQM	D9S		0
	6:20P E	8:32P ATL	DL 765	FYBMQ	757	D	0
	10:11P ATL	10:20P	DL 665	FnYnBnMQ	M80		0
	6:55P	9:10P ATL	DL 729	FYBMQ	763	D	0
	10:11P ATL	10:20P	DL 665	FnYnBnMQ	M80		0

Fig. 4-3. *Official Airline Guide* flight schedules for Scandinavian itinerary development exercise.

To COPENHAGEN, DENMARK   CPH

NEW YORK NY/NEWARK, NJ, USA 4426/3849   **NYC**

USD	FF	C	732.00	1464.00	Y	732.00	1464.00
	NW	F	1799.00	3598.00	C	907.00	1814.00
					Y	899.00	1798.00
	SK	F	1907.00	3814.00	C	961.00	1922.00
	TW	F	1799.00	3598.00	C	907.00	1814.00
					Y	899.00	1798.00
	FF	EX/4403	YH	630.00	YL	515.00	YO 599.00
		EX/4999	YH	995.00	YL	799.00	
	NW	EX/1026	YL	815.00			
		EX/1320	YH	846.00	YL	646.00	
		EX/1047	ML	548.00	MO	778.00	
		EX/1900	ML	361.00			
		EX/4154	YJ	595.00	YK	695.00	YL 495.00
		EX/4402	YO	791.00			
	SK	EX/1198	K	361.00			
		EX/1224	QJ	595.00	QK	695.00	QL 495.00
		EX/4400	YH	1105.00	YL	857.00	
		EX/4402	YH	909.00	YL	646.00	
		EX/4413	YL	1012.00	YL	816.00	
		EX/4999	QK	791.00	YH	965.00	YK 791.00
	TW	EX/1179	KO	778.00			
		EX/4402	QH	846.00	QL	646.00	QO 791.00
		EX/4504	BH	1011.00	BL	815.00	

E-26MAR D- 1APR	4	1650	JFK	0910 +1	CPH	SK	902	FCMK	D10 1
E-26MAR D- 1APR	SPEC 1730 OP 25 MAR	JFK	0700 +1	CPH	SK	912	FCMK	D10 0
	1730	JFK	0800 +1	CPH	SK	912	FCMK	D10 0
E- 1MAY D-21SEP	X56	1735	JFK	0910 +1	CPH	SK	902	FCMK	763 1
E- 6NOV	3	1745	LGA	0945 +1 NW 36	CPH 72S-BOS-D10	NW	36	CYBMQ	• 1
E- 1NOV D- 5NOV	3	1745	JFK	1125 +1 NW 36	CPH 72S-BOS-D10	NW	36	CYBMQ	• 2
E- 2APR D-27APR	4	1750	JFK	0910 +1	CPH	SK	902	FCMK	D10 1
E- 6NOV	15	1755	LGA	0945 +1 NW 36	CPH 72S-BOS-D10	NW	36	CYBMQ	• 1
E- 1NOV D- 5NOV	5	1755	JFK	1125 +1 NW 36	CPH 72S-BOS-D10	NW	36	CYBMQ	• 2
	34	1830	JFK	0745 +1	CPH	FF	32	CY	747 0
D-19MAR		1830	JFK	0800 +1	CPH	SK	912	FCMK	D10 0
D-20MAR D-25MAR	X67	1830	JFK	0800 +1	CPH	SK	912	FCMK	D10 0
E- 2APR D-23SEP		1830	JFK	0800 +1	CPH	SK	912	FCMK	D10 0
	X47	1830	JFK	1020 +1	CPH	TW	816	FCYMB	L10 1
E-24SEP		1930	JFK	0800 +1	CPH	SK	912	FCMK	D10 0

CONNECTIONS

	7	1750	JFK	0650	AMS	KL	642	FCMB	747 0
		0830	AMS	0950 +1	CPH	KL	173	CMB	310 0
D-30DEC	X7	1750	JFK	0650	AMS	KL	642	FCMB	747 0
		0830	AMS	0950 +1	CPH	KL	173	CMB	310 0
	X6	1815	JFK	0545	MAN	BA	172	FJMSB	747 0
		0745	MAN	1030 +1	CPH	BA 5106	CMSBL	B11 0
		1830	JFK	0755	FRA	LH	401	FCM	D10 0
		0900	FRA	1025 +1	CPH	SK	630	CMB	D9S 0
	X26	1830	JFK	0710	MAD	IB	954	PCYM	D10 0
		1055	MAD	1400 +1	CPH	IB	502	CMK	72S 0
	26	1830	JFK	0710	MAD	IB	954	PCYM	D10 0
		1055	MAD	1525 +1	CPH	IB	504	CMK	D9S 0
		1900	JFK	0640	LHR	BA	174	FJMSB	747 0
		0935	LHR	1220 +1	CPH	BA	750	CMSB	757 0

EX 25 DEC

		1900	JFK	0640	LHR	PA	2	PJYBM	747 0
		0935	LHR	1220 +1	CPH	BA	750	CMSB	757 0
	357	1930	JFK	1215	HEL	AY	112	FCBM	D10 1
		1310	HEL	1360 +1	CPH	SK	713	CMB	DC9 0

EX 23 DEC, 25 DEC, 28 DEC, 30 DEC

	37	1930	JFK	1215	HEL	AY	112	FCBM	D10 1
		1630	HEL	1760 +1	CPH	AY	815	CM	D9S 1
	357	1930	JFK	1215	HEL	AY	112	FCBM	D10 1
		1755	HEL	1835 +1	CPH	AY	863	CM	D9S 0
D- 9DEC	5	2000	JFK	0620	KEF	FI	614	CMBKQ	D8S 0
		0730	KEF	1130 +1	CPH	FI	202	CMBKQ	72S 0
E-16DEC	35	2000	JFK	0620	KEF	FI	614	CMBKQ	D8S 0
D-21DEC		0730	KEF	1130 +1	CPH	FI	202	CMBKQ	72S 0
E-23DEC	34	2000	JFK	0620	KEF	FI	614	CMBKQ	D8S 0
		0730	KEF	1130 +1	CPH	FI	202	CMBKQ	72S 0

OP 22 DEC

E- 1NOV	27	2000	JFK	0620	KEF	FI	614	CMBKQ	D8S 0
D-13DEC		0720	KEF	1245 +1	CPH	FI	232	CMBKQ	72S 1
E-15DEC	247	2000	JFK	0620	KEF	FI	614	CMBKQ	D8S 0
		0720	KEF	1245 +1	CPH	FI	232	CMBKQ	72S 1
	6	2000	JFK	0620	KEF	FI	614	CMBKQ	D8S 0
		0745	KEF	1250 +1	CPH	FI	220	CMBKQ	72S 1

EX 24 DEC, 31 DEC

	46	2100	JFK	1205	HEL	AY	106	FCBM	D10 0

	1240	HEL	1320 +1	CPH	AY	803	CM	M80 0
	2100	JFK	0840	LHR	BA	176	FJMSB	747 0
	1130	LHR	1415 +1	CPH	SK	502	CMB	M80 0

EX 24 DEC

X25	2120	JFK	1050	FRA	LH	403	FCM	D10 0
	1235	FRA	1400 +1	CPH	SK	632	CMB	D9S 0
	2120	EWR	0900	LGW	VS	002	JYB	747 0
	1130	LHR	1415 +1	CPH	SK	502	CMB	M80 0
D-29NOV	23	2120	EWR	0900	LGW	VS	002	JYB	747 0
	1510	LGW	1755 +1	CPH	BA	758	CMSBL	B11 0
E-30NOV	X6	2120	EWR	0900	LGW	VS	002	JYB	747 0
	1510	LGW	1755 +1	CPH	BA	758	CMSBL	73S 0
D-28NOV	1457	2120	EWR	0900	LGW	VS	002	JYB	747 0
	1510	LGW	1755 +1	CPH	BA	758	CMSBL	73S 0
	X1	2135	JFK	1035	AMS	KL	644	FCMB	74M 0
	1210	AMS	1325 +1	CPH	SK	552	CMBK	D9S 0
	1	2135	JFK	1035	AMS	KL	644	FCMB	74M 0
	1210	AMS	1325 +1	CPH	SK	552	CMBK	D9S 0

To TRONDHEIM, NORWAY   TRD
ARPT VAERNES 20.0MI/32.0KM 65MIN

COPENHAGEN, DENMARK   **CPH**

DKK	F	2625		5250 Y			2085		4170
D-14DEC	1247	2210	CPH	2350		SK	842	CMBK	DC9 0
E-15DEC	X6	2210	CPH	2350		SK	842	CMB	DC9 0
D-15JAN									

EX 23 DEC, 25 DEC, 26 DEC, 27 DEC, 28 DEC, 29 DEC, 30 DEC

E-16JAN	1247	2210	CPH	2350		SK	842	CMBK	DC9 0
D-14DEC	35	2210	CPH	2350		SK	842	CMB	DC9 0
E-16JAN	35	2210	CPH	2350		SK	842	CMB	DC9 0

To OSLO, NORWAY   OSL
From TRONDHEIM, NORWAY 0/246   **TRD**

NOK	Y		825		1650				
E-31OCT	X67	0700		0750	FBU	BU	131	CMB	73S 0
E-31OCT	X7	0800		0850	FBU	BU	141	CMB	73S 0
	X7	0830		0920	FBU	SK	361	Y	D9S 0
		0830		0940	FBU	SK	133	CMB	73S 0
	X67	0910		1000	FBU	BU	149	CMB	73S 0
	X7	0930		1020	FBU	SK	341	Y	D9S 0
	X67	1045		1135	FBU	BU	137	CMB	F27 1
	7	1140		1230	FBU	SK	365	Y	D9S 0
	X7	1150		1240	FBU	BU	159	CMB	73S 0
E-31OCT	X67	1240		1330	FBU	BU	285	CMB	73S 0
		1425		1515	FBU	BU	136	CMB	73S 0
	X6	1525		1615	FBU	BU	151	CMB	73S 0
	X6	1600		1650	FBU	SK 1345	Y	D9S 0
	X6	1625		1715	FBU	BU	143	CMB	73S 0
		1725		1815	FBU	BU	161	CMB	73S 0
	X36	1800		1850	FBU	SK	349	Y	D9S 0
	X6	1825		1915	FBU	BU	145	CMB	73S 0
	X6	1925		2015	FBU	BU	157	CMB	73S 0
	X6	2025		2115	FBU	BU	147	CMB	73S 0
	3	2100		2150	FBU	SK	355	Y	D9S 0
	X56	2135		2225	FBU	SK 1355	Y	D9S 0
E- 4NOV	5	2210		2300	FBU	BU 1165	CMB	73S 0

To STOCKHOLM, SWEDEN   STO
OSLO, NORWAY 308/257

NOK	F	1810		3620 Y			1260		2520
E-31OCT	2345	0705	FBU	0800	ARN	SK	482	CMBK	D9S 0
D-18NOV									
E-19NOV	2345	0705	FBU	0800	ARN	SK	482	CMBK	M80 0
D-14DEC									
E-31OCT	1	0705	FBU	0800	ARN	SK	482	CMB	D9S 0
D-18NOV									
E-19NOV	1	0705	FBU	0800	ARN	SK	482	CMB	M80 0
D-14DEC									
E-15DEC		0705	FBU	0800	ARN	SK	482	CMBK	M80 0
D-15JAN									

EX 22 DEC, 23 DEC, 24 DEC, 27 DEC, 28 DEC, 29 DEC, 30 DEC, 2 JAN, 3 JAN, 4 JAN, 5 JAN, 6 JAN

E-16JAN	2345	0705	FBU	0800	ARN	SK	482	CMBK	M80 0
E-16JAN	1	0705	FBU	0800	ARN	SK	482	CMB	M80 0
E-27SEP	34	0800	FBU	0855	ARN	SK	902	FCMK	763 0
	1234	0805	FBU	0900	ARN	SK	484	CMB	DC9 0
D-14DEC	X67	0905	FBU	1000	ARN	SK	486	CMB	D9S 0
E-15DEC	X7	0905	FBU	1000	ARN	SK	486	CMBK	D9S 0
D-15JAN									

EX 22 DEC, 23 DEC, 24 DEC, 26 DEC, 27 DEC, 28 DEC, 29 DEC, 30 DEC, 31 DEC, 2 JAN, 3 JAN, 4 JAN, 5 JAN, 6 JAN, 7 JAN

E-16JAN	X67	0905	FBU	1000	ARN	SK	486	CMB	D9S 0
D-14DEC	6	0905	FBU	1000	ARN	SK	486	CMBK	D9S 0

Fig. 4-3. Continued

```
D- 7JAN        1105 FBU 1200   ARN   SK  490   CMBK    D9S 0
E- 8JAN  X7    1105 FBU 1200   ARN   SK  490   CMBK    D9S 0
E- 8JAN  7     1105 FBU 1200   ARN   SK  490   CMBK    M80 0
E- 1NOV  246   1120 FBU 1215   ARN   FI  302   CMBKQ   72S 0
D-14DEC  2     1415 FBU 1510   ARN   SK 1496   CMBK    D9S 0
E-15DEC  57    1415 FBU 1510   ARN   SK 1496   CMBK    D9S 0
D-15JAN
E-16JAN  7     1415 FBU 1510   ARN   SK 1496   CMBK    D9S 0
E- 4NOV  5     1415 FBU 1510   ARN   SK 1496   CMB     D9S 0
D-14DEC
E-16JAN  5     1415 FBU 1510   ARN   SK 1496   CMB     D9S 0
E-18NOV  X7    1505 FBU 1600   ARN   SK  498   CMB     D9S 0
E-19NOV  X67   1505 FBU 1600   ARN   SK  498   CMB     M80 0
         EX  22 DEC, 23 DEC, 26 DEC, 27 DEC,
             28 DEC, 29 DEC, 30 DEC,  2 JAN,
              3 JAN,  4 JAN,  5 JAN,  6 JAN
E-19NOV  6     1505 FBU 1600   ARN   SK  498   CMB     D9S 0
E- 4NOV  5     1605 FBU 1700   ARN   SK 1480   CMB     D9S 0
         X6    1625 FBU 1725   ARN   SU  636   Y       TU3 0
         X6    1705 FBU 1800   ARN   SK  708   CMB     D9S 0
         X6    1805 FBU 1900   ARN   SK 1484   CMB     D9S 0
         X6    2005 FBU 2100   ARN   SK 1488   CMB     D9S 0
         EX  22 DEC, 23 DEC, 26 DEC, 27 DEC,
             28 DEC, 29 DEC, 30 DEC,  2 JAN,
              3 JAN,  4 JAN,  5 JAN,  6 JAN
```

Eff./Dis.	Freq.	Leave	Arrive		Flight	Class	Eq	S

To NEW YORK NY/NEWARK, NJ, USA   NYC
ALSO SEE LONG ISLAND MACARTHUR, N.Y., USA
AND WHITE PLAINS, N.Y., USA

STOCKHOLM, SWEDEN 4700/3917   STO

```
SEK FF  C    5305      10610   YH          4795    9590
                               YL          3780    7560
    NW  F    13185     26370   C           6445   12890
                               Y           6720   13440
    PA  P    13185     26370   J           7125   14250
    SK  F    13980     27960   Y           7125   14250
    TW  F    13185     26370   C           6445   12890
                               Y           5340   10680

    FF  EX/1116   YL          3750
        EX/4403   YH          5095   YL     4080
        EX/4999   YH          6555   YL     5165
    NW  EX/1188   BL          3495   BO     3995   BZ     4195
        EX/1320   YH          5605
        EX/1900   BL          3390
        EX/4402   YL          4265
    PA  EX/4400   YH          7825   YL     6410
        EX/4999   BH          6710   BL     5430   MH     5605
        EX/4999   ML          4265
    SK  EX/4400   YH          7825   YL     6410
        EX/4402   YH          5995   YL     4665
        EX/4942   MH          5605   ML     4265
        EX/4981   K           5390
        EX/4999   YH          6440
    TW  EX/1251   QJ          4195   QL     3495   QO     4000
        EX/1320   ML          5430
        EX/3527   MH          6710
        EX/4402   BH          5605   BL     4265
        EX/4999   QH          4515   QL     3980

E-31OCT 267  0905 ARN 1415   JFK   TW  817   FCYMB   L10 1
E- 1NOV 246  1015 ARN 1705   LGA   NW   37   CYBMQ    •  2
D- 5NOV      NW   37   D10-BOS-72S
         5   1110 ARN 1340   JFK   FF   35   CY      747 0
D-25MAR X35  1140 ARN 1410   JFK   SK  903   FCMK    D10 0
E-26MAR X3   1140 ARN 1310   JFK   SK  903   FCMK    D10 0
D- 1APR
E- 2APR X3   1140 ARN 1410   JFK   SK  903   FCMK    D10 0
D-30APR
E- 1MAY      1140 ARN 1410   JFK   SK  903   FCMK    D10 0
D-23SEP
E-24SEP X3   1140 ARN 1510   JFK   SK  903   FCMK    D10 0
D-25MAR X3   1140 ARN 1525   JFK   SK  901   FCMK    D10 1
E-26MAR 3    1140 ARN 1425   JFK   SK  901   FCMK    D10 1
D- 1APR
E- 2APR 3    1140 ARN 1525   JFK   SK  901   FCMK    D10 1
D-26APR
```

```
E-27SEP 3    1140 ARN 1635   JFK   SK  901   FCMK    763 1
E-31OCT 15   1145 ARN 1415   JFK   TW  827   FCYMB   L10 0
D-25MAR      1235 ARN 1540   JFK   PA   45   PJYBM   310 0
E- 2APR      1315 ARN 1540   JFK   PA   45   PJYBM   310 0
E-26MAR      1335 ARN 1540   JFK   PA   45   PJYBM   310 0
D- 1APR
```

```
                 CONNECTIONS
         0800 ARN 1120   BRU   SK  593   CMB     D9S 1
         1345 BRU 1545   JFK   SN  541   FCYBH   74D 0
    235  0815 ARN 1015   AMS   SK  555   CMB     D9S 0
         1315 AMS 1525   JFK   KL  641   FCMB    747 0
    146  0815 ARN 1015   AMS   SK  555   CMB     D9S 0
         1315 AMS 1525   JFK   KL  641   FCMB    747 0
         0825 ARN 1055   ZRH   SR  413   FCYML   310 0
         1230 ZRH 1515   JFK   SR  100   FCYML   D10 0
         0830 ARN 1005   LHR   BA  777   CMSBL   73S 0
         1400 LHR 1645   JFK   BA  177   FJMSB   747 0
         EX  20 DEC, 23 DEC, 24 DEC, 25 DEC,
             26 DEC, 27 DEC,
         0920 ARN 1125   FRA   SK  635   CMB     D9S 1
         1330 FRA 1600   JFK   LH  404   FCM     D10 0
```

```
         1010 ARN 1210   AMS   KL  192   CMB     737 0
         1315 AMS 1525   JFK   KL  641   FCMB    747 0
         EX  25 DEC
         1030 ARN 1140   CPH   SK  409   CMB     D9S 0
         1230 CPH 2120   JFK   SK  911   FCYMB   D10 0
    45   1125 ARN 1315   HEL   AY  792   CM      D9S 0
         1405 HEL 1715   JFK   AY  105   FCBM    D10 0
    367  1125 ARN 1315   HEL   AY  792   CM      D9S 0
         1405 HEL 1715   JFK   AY  111   FCBM    D10 1
         1700 JFK 1745   JRE   PA  829   F       LMO 0
D-23NOV X67  1235 ARN 1405   LHR   BA  779   CMSBL   73S 0
         1900 LHR 1750   JFK   BA    3   R       SSC 0
E-28NOV X67  1235 ARN 1405   LHR   BA  779   CMSBL   73S 0
D-16DEC  1900 LHR 1750   JFK   BA    3   R       SSC 0
         1235 ARN 1540   JFK   PA   45   PJYBM   310 0
         1700 JFK 1815   EWR   PA  979   F       LMO 0
    X67  1235 ARN 1405   LHR   BA  779   CMSBL   73S 0
         1830 LHR 2115   JFK   BA  179   FJMSB   747 0
E- 1NOV 267  1305 ARN 1615   KEF   FI  303   CMBKQ   72S 1
         1655 KEF 1800   JFK   FI  615   CMBKQ   D8S 0
         EX  18 DEC, 25 DEC
    4    1330 ARN 1535   KEF   FI  307   CMBKQ   D8S 1
         1655 KEF 1800   JFK   FI  615   CMBKQ   D8S 0
         EX  29 DEC
D-14DEC 3    1330 ARN 1440   CPH   IB  415   CMB     D9S 0
         1630 CPH 2120   MAD   IB  953   PCYM    D10 0
D-11DEC 7    1325 MAD 1520+1 JFK   SK  903   CMBK    D9S 1
         1330 ARN 1440   CPH   SK  415   CMK     D9S 1
E-18DEC 37   1330 ARN 1440   CPH   IB  415   CMBK    D9S 0
         1630 CPH 2120   MAD   IB  953   PCYM    D10 0
         1325 MAD 1520+1 JFK   SK  903   CMBK    D9S 0
D-20NOV 67   1335 ARN 1505   LHR   BA  779   CMSBL   73S 0
         1900 LHR 1750   JFK   BA    3   R       SSC 0
E-27NOV 67   1335 ARN 1505   LHR   BA  779   CMSBL   73S 0
D-11DEC  1900 LHR 1750   JFK   BA    3   R       SSC 0
    67   1335 ARN 1505   LHR   BA  779   CMSBL   73S 0
         1830 LHR 2115   JFK   BA  179   FJMSB   747 0
         EX  24 DEC, 25 DEC
    37   1430 ARN 1540   CPH   SK  417   CMBK    D9S 0
         1630 CPH 2120   MAD   IB  505   CMK     D9S 1
         1325 MAD 1520+1 JFK   IB  953   PCYM    D10 0
         EX  28 DEC
D-23NOV  1500 ARN 1635   LHR   SK  527   CMB     D9S 0
         1900 LHR 1750   JFK   BA    3   R       SSC 0
E-27NOV  1500 ARN 1635   LHR   SK  527   CMB     D9S 0
D-16DEC  1900 LHR 1750   JFK   BA    3   R       SSC 0
         1500 ARN 1635   LHR   SK  527   CMB     D9S 0
         1830 LHR 2115   JFK   BA  179   FJMSB   747 0
         EX  24 DEC, 25 DEC
```

Fig. 4-3. Continued

```
To MEMPHIS, TENNESSEE        CDT   MEM          6   12:10P E   2:13P ATL   DL   403   FYBMQ   767 L   0
▲NEW YORK NY/NEWARK, NJ           EDT   NYC             3:12P ATL  3:22P     DL   305   FYBMQ   D9S      0
P-HPN  J-JFK  L-LGA  T-ISS  E-EWR  S-JRE  W-JRA        12:10P L   2:24P ATL   DL   477   FYBMQ   763 L   0
X7   6:30a L    8:05a      NW   631  FYnMBnQn D9S  B  0        4:45P ATL  4:55P     DL   933   FYBMQ   M80 S   0
X7   8:50a L   12:57P      PI  1629  FYBHQ   73S  *  2   X6   12:10P E   2:13P ATL   DL   403   FYBMQ   D8S L   0
                          PI1629 * MEALS BL/SL                 4:45P ATL  4:55P     DL   933   FYBMQ   M80 S   0
     9:45a L   11:23a      NW   633  FYBMQ   72S  B/S 0        12:50P L   2:23P STL   TW   403   FCYMB   L10 L   0
     9:50a E   11:15a      NW   791  FYBMQ   DC9  S   0        3:29P STL  4:36P     TW   511   FYMBQ   DC9      0
     1:15P L    2:54P      NW   635  FYBMQ   M80  L/S 0   6   1:00P L   2:14P ORD   UA    73   FYMBQ   72S L   0
     1:20P E    2:50P      NW   793  FYBMQ   DC9  S   0        3:30P ORD  5:02P     UA  1277   FYMBQ   73S S   0
     5:20P L    7:02P      NW   637  FYBMQ   72S  S   0        1:02P E   2:27P STL   TW    75   FYMBQ   72S L   0
X6   5:35P E    7:05P      NW   795  FYEMQ   DC9  S   0        3:29P STL  4:36P     TW   511   FYMBQ   DC9      0
6    5:35P E    7:05P      NW   795  FYnMBnQn DC9  S  0   6   1:30P E   2:42P ORD   UA   129   FYBHQ   D10 S   0
           CONNECTIONS                                        3:30P ORD  5:02P     UA  1277   FYMBQ   73S S/0
X17  5:30a E    7:31a ATL   DL   929  FnYnBnMQ D8S  B   0        3:00P L   4:45P CLT   PI  1167   FYBHQ   72S S/0
     8:29a ATL  8:35a     DL   409  D9S  B/S 0        5:28P CLT  6:08P     PI  1258   FYBMQ   733 D   0
17   5:30a E    7:31a ATL   DL   929  FnYnBnMQ 767  B   0        3:56P J   6:18P STL   TW   573   FYMBQ   72S S   1
     8:29a ATL  8:35a     DL   409  D9S  B/S 0        7:11P STL  8:26P     TW   602   FYBMQ   DC9      0
     6:30a E    8:24a CVG   DL   425  FYBMQ   767  B   0   X6   4:00P L   5:17P ORD   UA    79   FYBMQ   767 D   0
     9:04a CVG  9:20a     DL   733  73S            6:44P ORD  8:23P     UA   937   FYBMQ   73S D/S0
     6:30a L    8:37a CVG   DL   745  FYBMQ   72S  B   0        4:10P L   6:14P CVG   DL   585   FYBMQ   D9S S   0
     9:04a CVG  9:20a     DL   733  73S            6:39P CVG  6:57P     DL  1047   FYBMQ   D9S S   0
     6:55a L    8:34a STL   TW   223  FYMBQ   M80  B   0        4:15P L   6:10P CVG   DL  1187   FYBMQ   757 S   0
     9:38a STL 10:52a     TW   512  FYMBQ   DC9      0        6:39P CVG  6:57P     DL  1047   FYBMQ   D9S S   0
     7:05a E    8:36a STL   TW   111  FYMBQ   M80  B   0   X67  4:15P L   5:42P STL   TW   235   FCYMB   L10 D   0
     9:38a STL 10:52a     TW   512  FYMBQ   DC9      0        7:11P STL  8:26P     TW   602   FYMBQ   DC9      0
     7:30a E    8:40a ORD   UA   123  FYBMQ   D10  S   0   67   4:15P L   5:44P STL   TW   235   FCYMB   72S D   0
     9:50a ORD 11:27a     UA   597  73S  S/0        7:11P STL  8:26P     TW   602   FYMBQ   DC9      0
     8:00a L    9:21a ORD   UA    63  FYBMQ   72S  B   0        4:20P J   5:35P BWI   PA★  895   YBMQ    D47 S   0
     9:50a ORD 11:27a     UA   597  73S  S/0        6:15P BWI  7:15P     NW   985   FYBMQ   D9S D   0
     8:30a L   10:51a ATL   DL   803  FYBMQ   763  B   0   1   4:30P J   5:39P BWI   TW   917   FCYMB   767      0
     11:56a ATL 12:05P     DL   946  D9S  S   0        6:15P BWI  7:15P     NW   985   FYBMQ   D9S D   0
     8:30a E   10:38a ATL   DL   799  FYBMQ   757  B   0   X6   4:30P L   5:49P ORD   UA   145   FYBMQ   D8S S   0
     11:56a ATL 12:05P     DL   946  D9S  S   0        6:44P ORD  8:23P     UA   937   FYBMQ   73S D/S0
     10:00a L  12:12P ATL   DL   107  FYBMQ   L10  B   0        4:30P L   6:13P STL   TW   251   FYMSQ   72S D   0
     1:25P ATL  1:35P     DL  1661  FYBMQ   73S  S   0        7:11P STL  8:26P     TW   602   FYMBQ   DC9      0
X6   10:30a E  11:39a ORD   UA   231  FYBMQ   D10  S   0   X6   6:00P L   8:00P CLT   PI  1492   FYBHQ   733 D   0
     12:45P ORD  2:17P     UA   893  73S  L/S 0        8:47P CLT 10:15P     PI  1545   FYBHQ   73S      1
X6   11:00a L  12:12P ORD   UA    69  FYBMQ   72S  L   0        6:05P J   7:43P PIT   US   559   YBHQM   D9S S   0
     12:45P ORD  2:17P     UA   893  73S  L/S 0        8:15P PIT  9:04P     US   523   YBHQM   D9S S   0
X7   12:10P L   2:24P ATL   DL   477  FYBMQ   763  L   0        6:20P E   8:32P ATL   DL   765   FYBMQ   757 D   0
     3:12P ATL  3:22P     DL   305  D9S            10:11P ATL 10:20P     DL   665  FnYnBnMQ M80      0
X67  12:10P E   2:13P ATL   DL   403  FYBMQ   D8S  L   0        6:55P L   9:10P ATL   DL   729   FYBMQ   763 D   0
     3:12P ATL  3:22P     DL   305  D9S            10:11P ATL 10:20P     DL   665  FnYnBnMQ M80      0
```

(Reprinted by special permission from the October 1988 edition of the *Official Airline Guide*, North American edition. Copyright © 1988, Official Airline Guide. All rights reserved.)

Fig. 4-3. Continued

5

F.I.T. CLIENT PROFILES

Little study has been directed toward the types of people who become F.I.T. clients. However, some F.I.T. specialists agree that we can break these clients generally into two large groups, with many others still who belong to neither group. The first group is often called "empty nesters," and comprises the young-at-heart seniors with a yen for travel. The second group is called the "adventurous," and spans all ages, occupations, and interests: these men and women share only the desire for adventure. Naturally, these groups are not mutually exclusive.

EMPTY NESTERS

In October 1988, *Travel Agent Magazine* described the "silver opportunities" provided by a distinctive group of travelers, the empty nesters. The article described these clients as men and women in their fifties or sixties whose family responsibilities have decreased while their disposable income increased. Their children have grown and moved on and their mortgages are paid. Many are at the peak of their earning power or have retired. According to *Travel Agent Magazine,* this group has more discretionary income than any other group in the United States population. With the time and money to spend, travel often becomes a way of life for the empty nesters.

Many of these seniors started their travels as package tour clients, seeing some part of the world from a tour bus. After a number of these tours, they discover places they want to return to and experience more thoroughly. These travelers share experiences with friends and find they have missed some interesting spots on the tours; romantic, beautiful places that the tours did not include, and little-known places of interest, or calm, unique attractions. And they find that the tours do not satisfy their special interests. They do not have the time on a tour to look up their geneaology in the libraries of their ancestors' country. They do not have the time on a tour to walk the shores or fields where our wars were fought and to contemplate what the battles were like. At most a tour might give them a few minutes.

So empty nesters find their special interests often require a tour tailored to their own needs. They know what they want. They have the time, money, interest, knowledge, and desire to travel. The empty nesters want and often insist on working with a travel counselor who understands them, their idiosyncracies, interests, and destinations. Above all, these gentlemen and gentlewomen insist on having an experienced travel agent who is an expert in the F.I.T. travel product.

THE ADVENTURESOME

Some have labeled the adventuresome F.I.T. clients "yuppies," perhaps because many of them are young. These adverturesome clients do represent a new breed of F.I.T. client, but do not be mislead—they are not all young. In fact, a growing number of the empty nesters want adventure, too. Some say that adventure travel is the fastest-growing segment of the travel product range and that adventure-seekers account for much of the F.I.T. portion of travel.

Many adventure-oriented clients also began on packaged group travel programs. Perhaps they took high school bicycling trips of Europe, spent college summers mountain-trekking in the Himalayas or on jeep excursions into the Australian Outback. But sooner than most who started traveling later in life, they tired of organized expeditions. Instead, they wanted to do it on their own.

Who are the adventuresome F.I.T. clients? Generally they are young people with a large disposable income. These are the professionals who graduated from college into high-paying fields. Before age thirty, some have earned salaries that exceed their parents' incomes by multiples. They are single and have long vacations. They are also young couples with no children and two high incomes. They can take several short trips each year or, by saving vacation time, a two- or three-week annual vacation. A few inherited their money. A few others got their money from the divorce courts. And a growing number work hard for a year or for a few years, quit their jobs, and travel while they feel they are still young enough to enjoy it.

Like the empty nesters, many of these young people know exactly what they want in adventure travel. They expect the travel agent to package the trip expertly and handle the mundane details, leaving them time to enjoy the excitement of living the adventure.

Others do not know what they want. They will come to the F.I.T. specialist with a rough idea of what they want to do or the challenge they want to experience. It is then the agent's challenge to assemble a trip that satisfies the client's appetite for adventure without exceeding it.

A few examples will help identify the F.I.T. specialist's challenge. A twenty-year-old college drop-out worked at manual labor jobs for more than a year and ran every morning before going to work. When he had saved what he thought was enough money, he went to a travel agency and asked the agent to arrange for him to run the Pamplona bulls. This is an annual event in which the young men of Pamplona, Spain, run with the bulls brought for the bull-fight ring. It is a dangerous sport in which a number of young Spaniards are gored each year and since the young American had never left the United States, fought bulls, or spoken any language other than American English, it is understandable that the travel agent had some concerns about setting up an F.I.T. for this particular outdoorsman.

Another example is Elsie, a young woman who plans to climb a Nepalese mountain. She has saved, held fund raising events, and friends even sold tee shirts picturing her climbing the mountain. When the funds were raised, her travel agent arranged for her and her equipment to travel on a most unusual F.I.T. to Nepal. The F.I.T. specialist worked with Elsie to schedule air travel to Katmandu, Nepal (change of planes in England and India). He contracted with a ground agent to have a landrover in Katmandu. He arranged a local preclimb shopping excursion to buy the necessary additional climbing gear in and around Katmandu. He also arranged in advance a hotel stay in Katmandu, transfer to the village at the foot of the mountain Elsie planned to climb, sherpas to go with her to the base camp (and beyond), emergency medical stand-by arrangements, and other minute details that are not a part of the standard agency sale.

THE FAMILY REUNION

Although empty nesters and the adventuresome are the two largest client groups, some other F.I.T. client groups are significant in size. One of these is the family reunion. Seldom is the family reunion F.I.T. the size that most of us think about when we consider a family reunion, however. Usually it's two, three, or at most, five people traveling together. A balloon tour operator has pointed out that families reuniting constitute his largest client base. Grandma and Grandpa might not be able to lure the family to home for the annual Thanksgiving dinner anymore. So they invite their grown children to balloon through the Pyrenees with them and watch how rapidly son and daughter get time off from work, friends and other commitments to join their parents for a week of ballooning and other adventures in Europe. The parents and grandparents who long to be with the younger family members are finding F.I.T.s ready-made enticements to add spice to their lives and give their children memories that last a lifetime.

THE SPECIALLY INTERESTED

Those with special interests constitute another large segment of F.I.T. clients. Of course, the empty nesters and the adventuresome also often have special interests that motivate their travel. However, there are many who have very specific interests and who do not fall into the categories of empty nesters or the adventuresome. An F.I.T. associate recently remembered a client with a keen interest in snakes. He studies them, breeds them, and seems to enjoy catching them. The F.I.T. specialist works with him to arrange trips to countries where specific snakes breed. The F.I.T. client travels throughout the world. He captures snakes and brings them back for his collection.

Another F.I.T. specialist has a client who collects coins. She travels throughout the world exploring the shops and meeting with local collectors to increase her coin collection.

Still another F.I.T. specialist works with a client who buys and renovates antique cars. He has brought cars and parts of cars back from nearly one hundred countries. After restoring the automobiles, he often sells them for a considerable profit. He has more than financed his trips from the sale of renovated automobiles. Collectors present the F.I.T. specialist with the challenge of bringing back items they collect. This might present little difficulty for the coin collector F.I.T. client, but for the snake collector and the automobile collector, bringing back the snakes and cars can sometimes present the F.I.T. specialist with a distinct challenge.

Clients with special interests are not only collectors. Other large categories of special interest F.I.T. clients include spectators and athletes. The two do not necessarily go together. Spectators might be clients who go to other countries to view sporting events. There are, for example, F.I.T. clients who travel from country to country to watch soccer games, golf matches, polo matches, and just about any sport there is. Sometimes these trips are booked as package tours, but most of the time the trip is arranged as an F.I.T..

Other spectators go to museums—often to a series of museums in several countries featuring a specific artist or group of artists. Some go for musical events. Again, this might be a series of similar events (for example, the better operas of Europe in a specific season) or it might be for a series of musical events in a single city. Theater and ballet goers also fall into this spectator F.I.T. client category.

SPORTS ENTHUSIASTS

Sports enthusiasts constitute still another group of F.I.T. clients. Many an F.I.T. specialist has arranged game fishing trips for clients who want to catch the big fish. An associate had a cowboy for a client. Although he lives in a city, he travels almost weekly from one rodeo to another throughout the United States, Canada, and other countries. An internationally-known bodybuilder travels to contests all over the world. And, notes the F.I.T. specialist, he insists on hotel rooms that are quiet, where fans will not bother him or other noise will not disturb his rest before contests, and on hotels with dining rooms that can provide the stringent diet he maintains.

BUSINESS PROFESSIONALS

Business professionals are not often thought of as F.I.T. clients, but a growing number of them are leaving their commercial travel agents and finding F.I.T. specialists who will tailor their overseas trips. While the average commercial agent will get flights at the best possible price and hotel rooms at better-than-commercial, agency-negotiated special rates, chief financial officers and others with vital, sensitive, and financially-critical business to attend to in other countries are beginning to value the quality of the travel and the trip above the cost savings related to the trip. They find out that F.I.T. specialists can and do provide the tailored quality so very important to financially sensitive business dealing.

SUMMARY

Although this chapter has not covered all categories of F.I.T. clients, it provides a breakdown of many of the larger ones. Clearly the largest group is the empty nesters. A second large group is the adventuresome. Still other client groups include family reunions and special-interest travelers. Sports lovers and business professionals are others for whom an F.I.T. specialist is an important and a logical travel choice.

■   ■   ■

❏ REVIEW QUESTIONS

1. What is the largest group of F.I.T. clients and what kind of trips does this client group take?
2. The adventuresome are sometimes called "yuppies." What adjectives best describe this client type?
3. How might the F.I.T. family reunion differ from the kind of family reunion most of us think about right away when we hear the term, "family reunion"?
4. Why might collectors prefer to take an F.I.T. instead of an escorted package tour?
5. What kinds of expectations do sports enthusiasts bring to the travel agent when booking an F.I.T.? Give some examples.

6. Why are some CEOs and CFOs turning away from commercial travel agents and turning to F.I.T. specialists to plan their trips to other countries?
7. Can you name any other F.I.T. client types not discussed in the chapter? If so, what are they? How do they differ with the clients described in this chapter?

❑ ROLE PLAY EXERCISE

Two students may participate in this role play either out of class as a fun way to review the chapter or as an in-class exercise. One student plays the role of a travel agent who specializes in selling cruises while the other is an F.I.T. specialist. Please read the script and then pick up the conversation in your own words.

CRUISE SPECIALIST: I have heard of travel agents specializing in the sale of F.I.T.s, but I have never met anyone who sells F.I.T.s more than other travel products. It must be hard developing an F.I.T. client base.

F.I.T. SPECIALIST: Most of it is done by word of mouth. Perhaps more than any other travel product, the F.I.T. must be of top quality. Once you provide the best possible quality time after time and get a reputation for doing an excellent job, the word spreads.

CRUISE SPECIALIST: But what kinds of people take F.I.T.s? Isn't it just a few rich people? Isn't your client base dying out?

F.I.T. SPECIALIST: Whoa! Let's take one question at a time. The client base is steadily growing and, while most F.I.T. clients have more money than the average client, there are lots of them that I would not categorize as being "rich." Now let me tell you what types of clients F.I.T. travelers are . . .

Continue on your own.

6

The F.I.T. CLIENT ANALYSIS

One of the most important facets of developing an F.I.T. is to understand what is appropriate for the specific F.I.T. client(s) for which the F.I.T. is developed. The unique quality of an F.I.T. is that it is designed to be a tailored trip, meeting the exact specifications of the F.I.T. client(s). Unless the F.I.T. specialist understands what the preferences are, unless there is a good "feel" for the likes and dislikes of the client(s), unless the F.I.T. specialist senses that she can screen a multitude of options and select those which the F.I.T. client(s) most desire, having a truly tailored travel product will not be possible. Keeping in mind the constraints of time and the ability to draw from the clients the true understanding of their preferences, this task is crucial. It is not at all unusual for the traveler to spend thousands of dollars on a trip and return home disappointed. If this is the case, it is likely that the very important step of analyzing the F.I.T. client has not been accomplished satisfactorily.

SETTING

The setting for the client analysis ideally is one that is condusive to conversation and to listening. In too many cases the F.I.T. specialist attempts to determine preferences while at the same time juggling the papers of other clients and answering the phone. There might be constant interruptions and the F.I.T. specialist's ability to listen and to hear the nuances of what the client is saying is considerably lessened. Ideally the setting will be one in which the F.I.T. specialist and the clients are in a separate room (perhaps a conference room) and there will be no interruptions. The agent should have access to a number of resource publications and documents without having to leave the room and the agent should be able to give undivided attention to the clients. Some agents prefer to have no files, no brochures, no other possible distractions in the room. They prefer only a pad, a pen, and conversation. Some agents tape record this session to listen to later in order to pull out specific details. These are all workable options when the analysis is conducted in a meeting room-type setting. But unfortunately, the setting where most agents work is at a desk near other counselors, with other clients coming and going, with the phones ringing and interrupting, and with a stack of additional work close enough for distraction. The more one can structure the setting so that listening and open communications are possible, the more one can expect to determine exact preference details.

LISTENING

The key to true client analysis is listening. In many cases agents will dominate the conversation by giving the client far too many detail options regarding the trip. In conducting a true client analysis the agent asks questions and then listens. All of us have our own preferences. We might feel that the little inn in the Bavarian Alps would be perfect for everyone. But our preferences can get in the way of what will really be perfect for the individual client currently being worked with. No place is perfect for everyone. Only by listening can we decide what the client's preferences are. Agent contributions are beneficial in the conversation, but we should strive for a ratio of listening (for example, having the client talk) far more than contributing (talking ourselves).

QUESTIONING

If one is to understand the F.I.T. client's preferences, it will often be necessary to ask insightful questions. In many cases the F.I.T. client might not be sure of what is most important to see or to do on the trip. It is not at all unusual for an F.I.T. specialist to converse with a client who believes that one set of preferences is what he wants for the trip, only to find that through questions it is possible to discover there is some site or some activity which is in the back of the mind of the client, but has never been brought out, and which really is the key (the most important) factor relating to the trip. This usually is not something purposely hidden by the client. There is seldom a game of "You try to find out what's important to me" being played. After all, it is the client's money. However, in many cases the client is really not sure of what is important to see and to do on the trip and what is not. F.I.T. specialists are continually surprised at what clients ultimately decide to do when one compares the ultimate decisions with what the client indicated as preferences at the beginning of the F.I.T. development process, and it is not at all unusual to find a considerably different set of priorities.

As pointed out, discovering the truth in preferences means asking many questions. Here are a few important ones: "Where do you want to go"?;

"What do you want to do"?; "Are you a day or a night person"?; "Do you want to be on the go all the time, or do you prefer a leisurely pace"?; "What kinds of things are important to you"?; "What are your priorities?"; "If you have to choose between X an Y, which would you prefer"?

As the conversation develops, attempt to get into greater detail. Try to find out whether or not there is an underlying reason for the trip that is not really apparent. Sometimes there are several reasons given for taking the trip. Try to determine the true strengths of these reasons and how they will interact or relate to the client's set of priorities. Before the conversation is finished, ask about specific preferences. Make certain that you understand clearly how independent the client wants to be. Will the client feel comfortable going through international airports without assistance? Or does the client really want and need meet and assist services? Determine whether or not the client is the adventuresome type who would prefer to find her own way not just through the airport, but also in the rural areas of the country(ies) being visited.

Ask questions designed to determine the level of sophistication of the traveler. Many who travel internationally for the first time have apprehensions that they hesitate to express. They might have read about an American tourist who was arrested in another country, but hesitate to express concern along these lines. Many F.I.T. specialists make certain to point out the potential legal problems and, especially for single clients, they recommend registering with the American embassy upon arrival in a new country. The right questions can help an F.I.T. specialist determine apprehensions such as legal problems, health concerns, and so forth. By initiating questions designed to overcome these concerns, the F.I.T. specialist might be able to open the door to a willingness to express concern about these same problems.

Ask questions to determine what type of accomodations the client will be most comfortable with. Research points out that the typical F.I.T. client is seldom really happy in accommodations that are less comfortable than those found in his home environment.

Ask questions relating to food and beverages. Some clients will not want anything special in relation to food and drinks. Meal functions are of little importance to them. They tend to be people for whom having a hot meal each day is not particularly important. They tend to be people who will not talk about food and beverages. On the other hand, the client who talks about good meals on previous trips, who knows and discusses fine cuisine, will probably find special meal services of great importance. In this case, ask questions relating to what types of meals are important. Ask where the client usually dines while on domestic trips or on previous international trips. By asking questions about past trip meals and preferences, the agent will get a good feel for what the client prefers.

However, sometimes the client has saved for many years to take this trip and she wants it to be very special; she wants to experience things she has not experienced before. One F.I.T. client recently advised that she had always wanted to attend a performance of La Scala and had never attended an opera before. She might very well find out that the opera is not what she had expected, but a highlight of the trip in the planning of the trip and the main reasons for it, is the La Scala performance. This must be included in the F.I.T.

In terms of sightseeing, ask questions related to trips where the client has done sightseeing before and how she felt about these previous excursions. Was she happy with them? There are persons who say that if you've seen one castle, you've seen them all. Obviously, for this type of person seeing historic homes and castles is not the type of sightseeing preferred. On the other hand, there are those who prefer to see countryside (tulips in bloom in Holland, the fall foliage, etc.) to seeing art museums. It is important, therefore, to determine what kind of sightseeing the F.I.T. client prefers and to ask questions relating to what is wanted.

When it comes to ground transportation, again, ask questions. Does the client want to drive a car himself? Some want the convenience of a car, but are concerned about missing the sights if they are driving. For these people chauffeured cars or limousines would be a good option. Still others would prefer to go by train. It is important to determine the client's preferences and this can best be done by asking questions.

Fig. 6-1. Know the level of comfort your clients expect when they travel abroad. (Courtesy of BritRail Travel International, Inc.)

Probe deeply with your questions to determine what other types of ground transportation are wanted. Clients need to know that transportation problems can occur in other countries. Flights between medium-sized countries in Africa, Asia, and Latin America might involve roundabout itineraries since, in many countries, cities might be connected by direct flights only once or twice per week. Frequently, only propeller aircraft is available. The aircraft might be crowded and dirty, and clients should be prepared to encounter live animals on board (usually chickens or other small farm animals). Fellow passengers might never have flown before and exhibit considerable fear of flying. Landing might be on makeshift landing strips. Ground transportation might require fording streams, riding in open-air jeeps, hiking some distance where roads are blocked, riding donkeys, camels, or other animals, or riding in crowded trains that hire professional "pushers" to push people into the train so that the car doors can be closed. Although these transportation experiences can be uncomfortable, they can also be memory highlights. Certainly one can ask questions that will reveal the readiness of an F.I.T. client to withstand these transportation arrangements. If the client is unwilling to face these challenges, the F.I.T. specialist must consider scheduling travel on major air carriers and between the most metropolitan cities, rather than plan itineraries that take the client into more rural communities.

Finally, ask questions, that might elicit a hidden reason for taking an F.I.T. The president of a large travel agency in Denver cites a case of F.I.T. clients for whom an entire Pacific itinerary was scheduled. After having planned all the aspects of the itinerary, reservations made at appropriate hotels and for sightseeing trips, the clients suddenly came to the realization that the major reason they wanted to make the trip was to visit a World War II battlefield on which the man had fought. By including the battlefield visit, the entire itinerary had to be changed. However, it was so important to the clients that the trip was changed to accommodate the battlefield visit. Sometimes probing questions can discover these, not completely thought through, but still very important aspects of an F.I.T. tour. By discovering them in an early meeting with clients, considerable time and expense will be saved by not having to make changes later. In addition, of course, it can be expected that the clients will return from their trip happier than they would otherwise.

FINANCIAL ANALYSIS

Understanding exactly what the client can afford on the F.I.T. is very important. Financial matters are sensitive matters to most clients. Therefore, the financial aspects need to be treated with diplomacy and tact. Two examples will point out why. In a well-known agency in Pittsburgh a client requested reservations in a very expensive hotel in Europe. The new agent did not book that hotel. She reserved a room in a less expensive one. When asked the reason why a cheaper hotel was booked, the agent replied: "The other hotel was so expensive." It is important that F.I.T. specialists understand what is affordable for their clients and what their clients prefer and book that, even though it might not be in the price range of the F.I.T. specialist.

Another example from the same source, points out that one day a cleaning woman, who worked in the building in which her agency is located, entered and booked a very expensive trip. Knowing that it was the cleaning woman, the agents did not take her as seriously as they should have. The woman had saved for many years for her "dream trip." By analyzing correctly that this was a trip of a lifetime for which the expenses had been saved, the agent could have handled the financial details of the trip better and with greater tact.

It's not possible to judge the financial position of all clients by the way they carry themselves or the way they dress. Even if we were able to make such judgments, we would still not know what the financial priorities of a client are. It is therefore important to ask questions in a manner that will save face for the client, but that still will give the client what is desired. Sometimes it is from fear of insulting the client, or having the client say "no," that agents offer other options that are less expensive and less desirable than a client really wants or really can afford. By using either/or options, it is possible to narrow down exactly what the client prefers. For example, a recent F.I.T. client was asked about hotel choices in Seoul, Korea. The agent asked if he would prefer a western hotel, although it might be quite a bit more expensive, or if he would prefer a local hotel at a lesser cost. Determining that the client preferred a western hotel, the F.I.T. specialist also determined that the expense factor was not as important. Next the F.I.T. client was able to quote the price ranges of three western hotels. Again, by giving an option, the client was able to say which price range he preferred. Finally, the F.I.T. specialist working within the stipulated price range, asked if the client preferred an executive floor room at the higher end of the price range, or if something on a lower level and a more modest room would be satisfactory. By providing such either/or options, the F.I.T. specialist can rapidly come to a conclusion relating to price range, without insulting or underestimating the financial condition or financial preferences of the client.

SUMMARY

In determining an F.I.T. client's range of preferences, it is important to undertake the client analysis discussion in a setting that lends itself to few distractions. Conference facilities are usually better than the agent's desk, but just getting away from the noise and potential interruptions of the general agency work area is usually better than having the client sit at the agent's desk. Both client and agent will then be able to better concentrate on the task of determining preferences. As the F.I.T. specialist undertakes the analysis section, the specialist should strive to ask open-ended questions and listen in order to catch all the nuances that reflect client preferences. The ratio of listening more than talking should be strived for by F.I.T. specialists. Questioning, in fact, is a very important key to successful client analysis. Insightful questions, open-ended questions, and either/or option questions all lend themselves to gathering the data needed to put together a good F.I.T. Remembering that clients are usually happier when their travel lifestyle is equal to or better than the lifestyle they lead at home, one can ask questions about travel preferences on domestic trips and lifestyle preferences at home to begin to determine the kinds of things that might be important to the client when making a trip abroad. The same concept applies to determining food and beverage preferences (find out what these preferences are when the client eats in local restaurants or while on domestic trips for instance), hotel preferences, ground transportation preferences, and activity levels (amount of sightseeing, duration of trips, times of starting and stopping sightseeing activities, etc.). Perhaps the greatest area of sensitivity relates to money and the possibility of selling an under or over priced product. Asking a number of questions and starting with an area of the trip that lends itself to specific price levels (such as hotel costs), one can begin to determine price range preferences in many areas of the F.I.T. plan and the F.I.T. specialist can generally apply the same standards to other aspects of the trip.

The F.I.T. specialist/client analysis meetings can be time consuming and sometimes be frustrating for the F.I.T. specialist. However, if the specialist will keep in mind that a good job of client analysis will usually result in very little or no backtracking in terms of making changes. The agent will soon learn to value the client analysis process and regard the time and effort spent as time and effort well spent.

■   ■   ■

❏ *REVIEW QUESTIONS*

1. Why is conducting an F.I.T. client analysis an important part of developing a successful F.I.T.?
2. What type of setting is the best for conducting F.I.T. client analyses?
3. During the analysis the F.I.T. specialist both talks and listens. What type of talking-listening ratio should the F.I.T. specialist strive for?

4.   What three types of questions are beneficial to include during a client analysis?

5.   What is one way to avoid embarrassing the client talking about the financial aspects of an F.I.T. while at the same time not underselling the F.I.T. product developed for the client?

❏ *ROLE PLAY EXERCISE*

Two students may participate in the role play either out of class as a fun way to review F.I.T. client analysis or as an in-class exercise. One student plays the role of the travel agency's F.I.T. client and the other plays the role of the travel agent F.I.T. specialist. Please read the script and then pick up the conversation in your own words.

TRAVEL AGENT: Thank you for taking this time out to meet with me, Mr. and Mrs. Johnson. It is important that I get a very good idea of what your preferences will be in regards to your trip in June. Please feel free to tell me all the things that are important to you to see and do, but I would also like you to tell me the kinds of things that you might not be interested in. What activities do you expect to look back at after the trip and say that these were the highlights?

CLIENT: Gambling in Monte Carlo is something we have always wanted to do.

TRAVEL AGENT: Would you clarify that for me a little more? What type of gambling is important to you? How extensive do you want your gambling experience to be?

Continue on your own.

7

AIR VENDOR SELECTION

AIR CARRIER SELECTION

When selecting air carriers for F.I.T. clients, several factors need to be considered. Should it be a carrier based in the United States or should it be the airline of a different country? Should the same carrier be used throughout the itinerary (when possible) or should there be different carriers on each of several segments of the routing? Should the least expensive carrier be used? How important is service, food, seat size, aircraft size, or in-flight amenities? These are all factors that need to be considered. Before making a determination of a carrier, review the following important pros and cons to be determined and weighed.

THE DEGREE OF SELECTION

In some cases there will be little or no choice in the selection decision. When reviewing the possible flights between points on the itinerary, the F.I.T. specialist will find there might be few flights to choose from at the time the client wishes to travel. All flights may be on one carrier, or in some cases, only two carriers fly between the destination points. This is particularly true in the middle part of Africa, and in some parts of Asia and in the Pacific; as well as between some cities in Latin America. In such cases the decision will be made by the availability factor alone (if there is only one carrier). However, when there are two or more carriers operating flights at about the same time, other selection features can be considered.

CONVENIENCE

Convenience is usually one of the major factors in the selction of an air carrier for a particular flight. Scheduling, departure/arrival, airport location convenience, ease of airport transiting, on-going flight reconfirmation convenience and flight change convenience should be considered.

SCHEDULE CONVENIENCE

Nonstop flights are generally preferred by most F.I.T. clients. Not only do they arrive before flights with one or more stops, but for people who get air sick, there is less landing and take-off up and down stress. There is certainly less interruption of the client on longer flights than on those where one or more stops are involved. For example, figure 7–1 shows a direct flight from London to Rome (BA 552) that takes only a total elapsed time of 140 minutes (subtract 1 hour for going through one time zone change). On the other hand, the same trip can be scheduled between the two cities with one stop (ET 711) and take a total elapsed time of 4 hours (240 minutes) again taking into consideration that there is a 1 hour time difference due to traveling through one time zone change. Therefore, unless clients have indicated otherwise, nonstop flights should normally be scheduled.

However, there are times when a client prefers to take a carrier with one or more stops to make plane changes rather than to take nonstop flights. One of the more common situations is when a client requests a flight that will stop at an airport with a particularly good duty-free shop in order to take advantage of bargains that might be available at that shop.

By working with the list of duty-free shops in the *Official Airline Guide,* a client can often be scheduled on flights that will stop at airports with duty-free shopping opportunities at either no additional cost or at very little additional cost and with little additional time expenditure. The following list of flights from Brussels, Belgium, and back to New York City provides the traveler with an opportunity to fly with Sabena (the flag carrier of Belgium) on a nonstop flight or the option to stop in London for an hour of shopping in Paris' Charles de Gaulle airport duty-free shop by returning via Trans World Airlines (TW803) instead. To find out where a flight stops, turn to the "FLIGHT ITINERARIES" section of the *Official Airline Guide* (usually just a few pages after the yellow advertising pages at the beginning of the *OAG*) and look up the airline carrier and flight number. As can be seen in figure 7-2, TW 803 originates in Brussels (BRU). It makes a stop at Paris' Charles de Gaulle airport (CDG) and New York City's John F. Kennedy airport (JFK) and then completes its itinerary in San Francisco (SFO).

There are also clients who collect countries and wish to make every possible stop that will allow them to get a new stamp in their passports showing that they have been to another country. You might want to make these clients aware of the Travelers Century Club, an organization to which a growing number of F.I.T. clients belong. This is an organization made up of individuals who have traveled to one hundred or more countries or areas in the world. For those who are interested in obtaining additional informa-

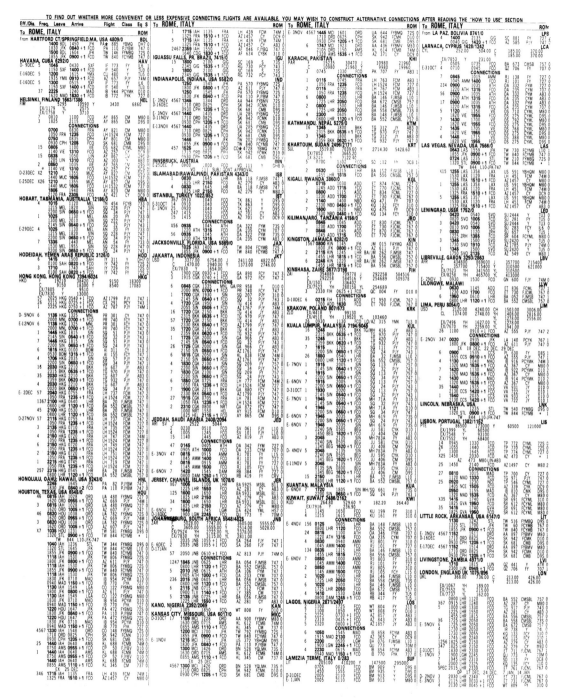

Fig. 7-1. Sample page from the *OAG*. (Reprinted by special permission from the *Official Airline Guide* Worldwide edition, October 1988. Copyright © 1988, Official Airline Guide. All rights reserved.)

To NEW YORK NY/NEWARK, NJ, USA   **NYC**
ALSO SEE LONG ISLAND MACARTHUR, N.Y., USA
AND WHITE PLAINS, N.Y., USA

BRUSSELS, BELGIUM 4211/3662   **BRU**

```
BFR        P  70640  141280  J   39560      79120
    SN     F  70640  141280  C   39560      79120
    TW     F  70640  141280  C   39560      79120
    PA  EX/1024  YL  19990
        EX/1159  YH  37100  YL  33560
        EX/4400  YH  30910  YL  23520  YO  25810
        EX/4504  YH  38900  YL  34930  YO  34930
    SN  EX/1988  YH  37100  YL  33560
        EX/4354  YK  33560
        EX/4400  YH  30910  YK  25810  YL  23520
        EX/4452  YZ  19990
        EX/4486  YZ  16990
        EX/4960  YH  38900  YL  34930
        EX/4999  YK  34930
    TW  EX/1095  YH  37100  YL  33560
        EX/1179  Q   19990  QH  27810  QL  19990
        EX/1179  QO  23990
        EX/4400  BH  30910  BL  23520  BO  25810
        EX/4502  MH  38900  ML  34930
        EX/4999  MO  34930
```

```
             1      0950       1415   JFK  TW 803 FCYMB  L10 1
D-25MAR              1130       1510   JFK  PA 131 PJYBM   *  1
                PA   131 310-LHR-747
E- 2APR              1145       1530   JFK  PA 131 PJYBM   *  1
                PA   131 310-LHR-747
E-26MAR              1230       1510   JFK  PA 131 PJYBM   *  1
D- 1APR         PA   131 310-LHR-747
E-24SEP  357  1245       1535   JFK  SN 541 FCYBH  74D 0
E-25SEP 1246  1245       1535   JFK  SN 541 FCYBH  747 0
E-26MAR       1345       1435   JFK  SN 541 FCYBH  74D 0
D- 1APR
E- 2APR       1345       1535   JFK  SN 541 FCYBH  74D 0
D-26APR
E-27APR  4    1345       1535   JFK  SN 541 FCYBH  74M 0
D-25MAY
E-28APR  X4   1345       1535   JFK  SN 541 FCYBH  74D 0
D-31MAY
E- 1JUN 1246  1345       1535   JFK  SN 541 FCYBH  747 0
D-23SEP
E- 1JUN  357  1345       1535   JFK  SN 541 FCYBH  74D 0
D-22SEP
D-25MAR
              1345       1545   JFK  SN 541 FCYBH  74D 0
         567  1400       1600   JFK  TW 769 FCYMB  L10 0
         234  1400       1620   JFK  TW 769 FCYMB  767 0
         57   1455       1710   JFK  TK 581        Y    310 0
                     CONNECTIONS
       X25  0715   0815      FRA  LH 1715 FCM  727 0
            1000 FRA 1235    JFK  LH  400 FCM  D10 0
       X67  0740   0745      LGW  AE  029 CYBQM 733 0
            1130 LGW 1555    JFK  BA  173 FJMSB 747 1
            0755   0845      CDG  SN/AF 641 CYB  733 0
            1100 CDG 0845    JFK  AF  001   R   SSC 0
```

A

```
       X23  0755   0845      CDG  SN/AF 641 CYB  733 0
D-23DEC          1100 ORY 1300    EWR  CO   57 PJYBM D10 0
D-23DEC     CF05   0805      LHR  SN  601 CYBK  733 0
            1030 LHR 0920    JFK  BA    1   R   SSC 0
D-23DEC  X7 0810   0810      LHR  BA  387 CMSB  73S 0
            1030 LHR 0920    JFK  BA    1   R   SSC 0
E-27DEC X17 0810   0810      LHR  BA  387 CMSB  73S 0
            1030 LHR 0920    JFK  BA    1   R   SSC 0
         X7 0810   0810      LHR  BA  387 CMSB  73S 0
            1100 LHR 1345    JFK  BA  175 FJMSB 747 0
            0815   0945      CPH  SN  761 CYB   73S 0
            1230 CPH 1455    JFK  SK  911 FCMK  D10 0
         7  0945   0945      LHR  BA  389 CMSBL 73S 0
            1100 LHR 1345    JFK  BA  175 FJMSB 747 0
         6  0945   1125      YMX  NX  300  YB   D8S 0
            1720 YMX 1845    JFK  LA  161 PCY   767 0
                    EX  31 DEC
            1050   1150      FRA  LH 1717 FCM   727 0
            1330 FRA 1600    JFK  LH  404 FCM   D10 0
```

To NEW YORK NY/NEWARK, NJ, USA   **NYC**
ALSO SEE LONG ISLAND MACARTHUR, N.Y., USA
AND WHITE PLAINS, N.Y., USA

```
         X7 1100        1100      LGW  AE  031 CYBQM 733 0
            1300 LGW 1540    EWR  VS  001  JYB  747 0
            1120        1200      AMS  KL  384  CM   F28 0
            1315 AMS 1525    JFK  KL  641 FCMB  747 0
            1245        1245      LHR  BA  393 CMSBL 757 0
            1400 LHR 1645    JFK  BA  177 FJMSB 747 0
                   EX  20 DEC,  23 DEC, 24 DEC, 25 DEC,
                       26 DEC, 27 DEC
D-23NOV     1245        1245      LHR  BA  393 CMSBL 757 0
            1900 LHR 1750    JFK  BA    3   R   SSC 0
E-27NOV     1245        1245      LHR  BA  393 CMSBL 757 0
D-16DEC     1900 LHR 1750    JFK  BA    3   R   SSC 0
         2  1355        1435      AMS  OK  738       757 0
            1730 AMS 1940    JFK  KL  643 FCMB  74M 0
         1  1420        1600      YMX  NX  300  YB   D8S 0
            1720 YMX 1845    JFK  LA  161 PCYK  767 0
            1505        1550      AMS  KL  386  CM   F27 0
            1730 AMS 1940    JFK  KL  643 FCMB  74M 0
                   EX  25 DEC, 26 DEC, 31 DEC
         X6 1545        1545      LHR  SN  607 CYBK  73S 0
            1830 LHR 2115    JFK  BA  179 FJMSB 747 0
                   EX  25 DEC
D-23NOV  X7 1615        1615      LHR  BA  395 CMSBL 73S 0
D-16DEC     1900 LHR 1750    JFK  BA    3   R   SSC 0
E-28NOV  X7 1615        1615      LHR  BA  395 CMSBL 73S 0
D-16DEC     1900 LHR 1750    JFK  BA    3   R   SSC 0
         X7 1615        1615      LHR  BA  395 CMSBL 73S 0
            1830 LHR 2115    JFK  BA  179 FJMSB 747 0
                   EX  24 DEC
D-23NOV     1745        1745      LHR  SN  609 CYBK  73S 0
            1900 LHR 1750    JFK  BA    3   R   SSC 0
E-27NOV     1745        1745      LHR  SN  609 CYBK  73S 0
D-16DEC     1900 LHR 1750    JFK  BA    3   R   SSC 0
```

FLIGHT

```
TW-TRANS WORLD AIRLINES,          JFK DCA  3              803 BRU CDG JFK SFO
  INC. AND TRANS WORLD       783 AUH BAH FRA LHR               1
        EXPRESS                   JFK DCA  2              803 CDG JFK SFO  67
    753 LHR BOS STL SEA      783 MCT DOH CDG LHR         804 JAX ATL JFK CDG
    754 SFO BOS LHR               JFK DCA  7              807 FCO CDG BOS STL
    758 PDX SEA JFK FRA      784 MCT JFK LHR DOH              X257
        TXL                       MCT  7                 807 CAI CDG BOS STL
    760 SFO LAX LHR               DIS AFT OCT30               257
    761 LHR LAX SFO          784 DCA JFK LHR BAH         810 SEA STL BOS CDG
    763 LHR JFK SAN ONT           MCT  6                     FCO X357
    764 LAX BOS LHR               EFF OCT31              810 SEA STL BOS CDG
    768 DCA JFK BRU MUC      784 DCA JFK LHR BAH             CAI  357
        56                        AUH  5                 812 BOS CDG TLV
    768 DCA JFK BRU  7        784 DCA JFK LHR DOH         814 JFK AMS HAM TXL
    769 BRU JFK DTW MKE           AUH MCT  4             815 TXL HAM AMS JFK
        5                         EFF OCT31                  LAX
    769 MUC BRU JFK DTW       784 DCA JFK LHR BAH         816 JFK GEN CPH  23
        MKE  234                  MCT  3                 816 JFK ARN CPH  156
    774 STL BOS LHR               EFF OCT31              817 GEN CPH JFK MSP
    780 BOS JFK LHR          784 DCA JFK LHR BAH             SLC  7
    781 LHR JFK MCO               AUH MCT  3                 DIS AFT OCT30
    782 MCO JFK LHR               EFF OCT31              817 ARN CPH JFK MSP
    783 MCT BAH FRA LHR       784 DCA JFK LHR BAH             SLC  267
        JFK DCA  6                SHJ MCT  2                  EFF OCT31
    783 AUH BAH LHR JFK           EFF OCT31              819 CDG JFK STL
        DCA  5               796 ORD STL LGW FRA         820 JFK ZRH BUD
    783 MCT AUH DOH LHR       800 JFK CDG BRU  4          821 BUD ZRH JFK LAX
        JFK DCA  4           800 JFK CDG TLV X456        825 TLV CDG BOS SFO
    783 AUH BAH CDG LHR       801 CDG JFK IAH AUS             X167
                             803 TLV CDG JFK SFO
                                 X167
```

B

Fig. 7-2. (A) Sample OAG Brussels to New York City flight schedule. (Reprinted by special permission from the October 1988 issue of the *Official Airline Guide*, Worldwide edition. Copyright © 1988, Official Airline Guide. All rights reserved.) (B) TW803 flight itinerary. (Reprinted by special permission from the October 1988 edition of the *Official Airline Guide* Worldwide edition. Copyright © 1988, Official Airline Guide. All rights reserved.)

tion on the club, contact the organization at the following address and phone number: Travelers Century Club, 16000 Ventura Blvd., Suite 200, Encino, CA, 91436, 800-252-2103. F.I.T. specialists might wish to keep data on file on the club so that F.I.T. clients who collect countries can have information on membership without writing for it.

You can assist clients who collect countries by breaking up their flights and adding collectable stopover countries. On very long flights, for example, from the west coast of the United States to Asian countries, clients might prefer a flight that lands at some point in between in order to get off the plane, stretch their legs, and add another stamp to their passport. Sometimes this can be provided at no additional cost whatsoever. Traditionally Korean Air flight 001 (KE 001), for example, stops in both Honolulu (where passengers can get off, walk around and rest, but cannot get another passport stamp, since Hawaii is a part of the United States) and Tokyo (where the same rest opportunities are available, but an additional passport stamp can be obtained as well) en route to Seoul, Korea. Although some clients will definitely prefer to get to Seoul as rapidly as possible and will not want to take advantage of these stopover opportunities, there certainly will be others who will welcome the chance to land in Hawaii and Tokyo, get off the plane, stretch their legs for awhile, and add another country's stamp to their passports. One should be careful to advise such clients that while most air carriers will allow clients to deplane at stops such as this one so that they can get off, stretch, and walk around the customs cleared sections of the terminal building, there are some carriers that have a policy of not allowing passengers to deplane and there are flights where restrictions in airports because of weather or other conditions inhibit offering the standard practice of allowing passengers to deplane and this opportunity might not be extended to passengers. Check with the air carrier to find out if the deplaning experience is normally offered on the flight the client is considering. Because of weather and security variations throughout the world, clients should never be promised that they will have an opportunity to deplane at en route stops to a final destination.

On some very lengthy itineraries experienced travelers will often ask for a change of planes or for a one or two day stopover in order to break-up the monotony of a very long flight. Less experienced travelers should be advised of the jet lag and boredom that can result in lengthy flights and given the option to take flights with stops, especially when there will be no difference in fares.

The major factor relating to schedule convenience for most F.I.T. clients is the time of departure and the time of arrival. Many experienced travelers prefer to plan nothing but a flight on a day when they will be flying between cities that are some distance apart. They prefer to fly at a time that will provide them with the greatest amount of convenience and time for sleeping well, both the night before the flight and the night after the flight. They often request and want a flight that gives them time for a leisurely breakfast (or other meal) and transfer to the airport. One of the best departure times for such flights is 10:00 A.M. or 11:00 A.M. If the F.I.T. client is making a flight that is between 1 and 6 hours in length (and most flights that are not crossing an ocean are at least this short), the client can sleep fairly late, have breakfast, check out of the hotel after the rush of early morning departures (and the lines often associated with these rushes), make a leisurely transfer to the airport, catch the plane without a long airport wait, make a leisurely transfer through the destination airport and to the destination hotel, get settled into the new hotel room, have a leisurely hotel dining room dinner, and still get to bed in time for them to have a full night of rest before tackling the next morning's sightseeing activities. Lunch aboard the plane is usually provided. This is exactly what many experienced F.I.T. travelers want when they are making a change of locations that involves a flight and a hotel change. It is interesting to note that the Hemphill-Harris World Air Cruise, one of the most expensive of all travel products and a tour marketed to the same type of clientele as are luxury F.I.T.s, makes an effort to schedule as many of their flight departures as possible at 10:00 A.M.

But it is not just the time of departure that is important in schedule convenience. The time of flight arrival is perhaps even more important. If at all possible, the client should have a flight that allows an arrival at the destination hotel by 6:00 P.M. This means that if the hotel is located close to the airport, a 5:00 P.M. arrival will often be sufficient. However, keeping in mind the time it takes to clear customs (if it is an international flight), claim bags, obtain ground transfer service, and taking into consideration the distance between the airport and the hotel, the flight arrival time might have to be as early as 4:00 P.M. or sometimes even earlier in order to get to the destination hotel by 6:00 P.M.

One of the best ways to determine the amount of time needed in order to get a client to a destination hotel by 6:00 P.M. is an *Official Airline Guide Travel Planner*. These publications are produced by the same company that issues the *Official Airline Guides,* which show flight schedules. The travel planner comes in three editions. There is one for European countries, one for Pacific countries, and one for North America. Travel planners do not exist for Latin America or Africa. For flights going into those areas, it is better to consult with the air carrier and request information relating to ground transportation time.

If one is working with a destination in the geographical area covered by one of the three editions of the travel planner, the publishers make it easy to look up the exact information needed on ground transportation time. Review figure 7–3 with the listing for Budapest, Hungary. One turns in the alphabetical listing to the country of Hungary and then under the city alphabetical listing one finds that Budapest, being the capital and the largest city in the country, is highlighted in especially large letters. In addition, city maps are provided for all major cities and there is one for Budapest. The city map is always on a grid and each of the major hotels is listed by a number and a grid reference. This makes it easy to identify where

HUNGARY

THE BASICS

TIME
Hungary is 6 hours ahead of U.S. Eastern Time.
Banking Hours: 8:30 AM-3:00 PM (Mon-Fri)
Business Hours: 8:30 AM-5:00 PM
Shopping Hours: Food Stores:7:00 AM-6:00/8:00 PM. Shops: 10:00 AM-6:00 PM
                   (Mon-Fri); 10:00 AM-2:00 PM (Sat)

TOBACCO/LIQUOR
Import Allowances
Tobacco: 1 carton of cigarettes for travelers 18 years of age or older.
Liquor: 1 quart of liquor for travelers 16 years of age or older.

PUBLIC HOLIDAYS & CALENDAR OF EVENTS

MARCH
17-26   Spring Festival, **Budapest**
18-23   "Travel" Exhibit, **Budapest**
23   Festival Orchestra, **Budapest**

TOURIST BOARD OFFICES
Ibusz Hungarian Travel Bureau:
Budapest, Felszabadulas Ter 5, 1053 Budapest. Tel. 181-120.
North America
New York, NY 10111, 630 Fifth Ave., Ste. 2455. Tel. 212/582-7412.
Europe
Belgrade, Yugoslavia 11000, Strahinjica Bana 47. Tel. 623-826.
Berlin, German Dem. Rep. 102, Karl Liebknecht St. 9. Tel. 212-35-59.
Brussels, Belgium 1040, 6 Rue de Luxembourg. Tel. 511-4-85.

Frankfurt, German Fed. Rep. 6000 Baseler St. 46-48. Tel. 252-018.
London, England W1R 9TG, Conduit St. Tel. 493-02-63.
Madrid, Spain 8, Juan Alvarez Mendizabel No. 1 111, Piso 6. Tel. 241-25-44.
Moscow, U.S.S.R., ul. Gorkogo 26/1. Tel. 299-8010.
Paris, France 75002, Rue de Quatre Septembre 27. Tel. 742-5025.
Prague, Czechoslovakia 11000, Praha, ul. Kaprova 5. Tel. 22-40-08.
Rome, Italy 00185, Via V.E. Orlando 75. Tel. 485-871.
Sofia, Bulgaria 6, ul. G. Dimitrov 44. Tel. 89-21-36.
Stockholm, Sweden 10326, Beridarebanan 1. Tel. 20-40-40.
Vienna, Austria A-1010, Krugerstrasse 4. Tel. 529-260.
Warsaw, Poland 00517, ul. Marszalkowska 80. Tel. 25-99-15.
Pacific Asia
Tokyo, Japan 106, Togensha Bldg., 3rd Fl., 12-10 Roppongi 4-chome, Minato-Ku. Tel. 404-80-89.

DESTINATIONS AND ACCOMMODATIONS
Hotel Listings: The Hungarian Government has established ratings for hotels. These rating classifications appear in parenthesis within the individual hotel listings. A decode of the classifications follows:

★★★★★ = Luxury
★★★★ = Upper First Class
★★★ = First Class
★★ = Tourist
★ = Economy

All room rates presented are for guideline purposes only and should be confirmed directly with the hotels or their Sales Representatives. In some instances, service charges and/or taxes may be included in the room rate range.

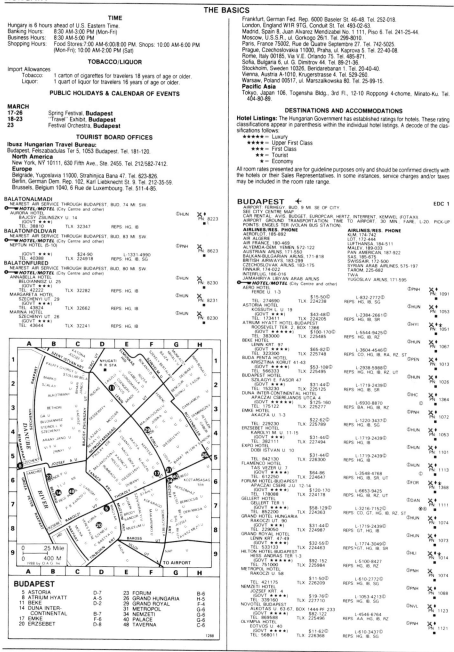

Fig. 7-3. Sample page from the *OAG Travel Planner and Hotel/Motel Guide.* (Reprinted by special permission from the January-March 1989 edition of the *Official Airline Guide Travel Planner and Hotel/Motel Guide* European edition. Copyright © 1989, Official Airline Guide. All rights reserved.)

BUDAPEST (CONT.) EDC 1

HOTEL/MOTEL (City Centre and other)

PALACE HOTEL ⓈPNH ✕♦
RAKOCZI U 43 PN 1083
(GOVT ★★★) $13-62Ⓒ L-721-3437Ⓒ ■
TEL 136000 TLX 224217 REPS HG, IB, SG

PARK HOTEL ⓈPNH ✕♦
BAROSS TER 10 PN 1087
(GOVT ★★) $13-48Ⓒ L-721-2661Ⓒ ■
TEL 131420 TLX 226274 REPS HG, IB, SG

RAMADA GRAND HOTEL ⓈDAN ✕
MARGITSZIGET PN 1138
(GOVT ★★★★) $52.92 L-2883-5100 ■
TEL 111000 TLX 226682 REPS HG, IB

STADION HOTEL ⓈHUN ✕♦
IFJUSAG UTJA 1-3 PN 1143
(GOVT ★★★) $31-44Ⓒ L-1719-2439Ⓒ ■
TEL 631830 TLX 225685 REPS HG, IB, PE, SR

TAVERNA HOTEL ✕
VACISTR 20 PN 1056
(GOVT ★★★) $32-50Ⓒ L-1774-2772Ⓒ ■
TEL 384999 TLX 227707 REPS HG, IB

THERMAL HOTEL MARGITSZIGET ⓈDAN ✕♦✱
MARGITSZIGET PN 1138
(GOVT ★★★★★) $76-124Ⓒ L-4213-6875Ⓒ ⓂⒶ ■
TEL 111000 TLX 225463 REPS HG, IB, RZ, UT

VOLGA HOTEL ⓈPNH ✕♦
DOZSA GY U 65-67 PN 1134
(GOVT ★★★) $17-62Ⓒ L-942-3437Ⓒ ■
TEL 408314 TLX 225120 REPS HG, IB, SG

VOROS CSILLAG HOTEL ⓈHUN ✕
REGE U 21 PN 1121 ■
TEL 750522 TLX 225125 REPS HG, IB

WIEN HOTEL ⓈPNH ✕
BUDAORSI U 88-90 PN 1118
$15-50Ⓒ L-832-2772Ⓒ ■
TEL 665400 TLX 224469 REPS HG, IB, SG

BUK
NEAREST AIR SERVICE THROUGH BUDAPEST, BUD, 135 MI SW

DEBRECEN EDC 52
NEAREST AIR SERVICE THROUGH BUDAPEST, BUD, 125 MI NE RAIL HUNGARIAN STATE

DOBOGOKO
NEAREST AIR SERVICE THROUGH BUDAPEST, BUD, 27 MI NW

HOTEL/MOTEL (City Centre and other)

NIMROD HOTEL ⓈPNH ✕♦
PN 2099
$25-42Ⓒ L-1386-2328Ⓒ ■
TEL 2627644 TLX 225085 REPS HG, IB, SG

DUNAUJVAROS
NEAREST AIR SERVICE THROUGH BUDAPEST, BUD, 40 MI SW

HOTEL/MOTEL (City Centre and other)

ARANY CSILLAG HOTEL ⓈHUN ✕
VASMU UT 39 PN 2400
$27-29Ⓒ L-1497-1608Ⓒ ■
TEL 18045 TLX 29321 REPS HG, IB

EGER
NEAREST AIR SERVICE THROUGH BUDAPEST, BUD, 78 MI NE

HOTEL/MOTEL (City Centre and other)

EGER HOTEL ⓈHUN ✕♦
SZALLODA U 1-3 PN 3300
(GOVT ★★★) $19-29Ⓒ L-1053-1608Ⓒ ■
TEL 13233 TLX 633²⁵ REPS HG, IB, SR

PARK HOTEL ⓈHUN ✕
KLAPKA U 8 PN 3300
$33-35Ⓒ L-1830-1940Ⓒ ■
TEL 13233 TLX 63355 REPS HG, IB

SENATOR HOTEL ⓈHUN
DOBO TER 11 PN 3300
$21-29 L-1164-1608 ■
TEL 20466 TLX 63355

GYOR EDC 96
NEAREST AIR SERVICE THROUGH BUDAPEST, BUD, 84 MI NW

HOTEL/MOTEL (City Centre and other)

RABA HOTEL ⓈHUN ✕
ARPAD U 34 PN 9021
(GOVT ★★) $32-34Ⓒ L-1774-1885Ⓒ ■
TEL 15533 TLX 24365 REPS HG, IB

HEVIZ
NEAREST AIR SERVICE THROUGH BUDAPEST, BUD, 125 MI SW

HOTEL/MOTEL (City Centre and other)

THERMAL HOTEL AQUA ⓈDAN ✕✱
KOSSUTH L U 13-15 PN 8380
$41-69Ⓒ L-2273-3825Ⓒ ⓂⒶ ■
TEL 11090 TLX 35247 REPS CO, HG, IB, ST

THERMAL HOTEL HEVIZ ⓈDAN ✕♦
KOSSUTH L U 9 PN 8380
$41-69Ⓒ L-2273-3825Ⓒ ⓂⒶ ■
TEL 11190 TLX 35286 REPS HG, IB, UT

KAPOSVAR EDC 82
NEAREST AIR SERVICE THROUGH BUDAPEST, BUD, 134 MI SW

HOTEL/MOTEL (City Centre and other)

DOROTTYA HOTEL ⓈPNH ✕♦
ENGELS U 2 PN 7400
$11-38Ⓒ L-610-2107Ⓒ ■
TEL 14110 TLX 13243 REPS HG, IB, SG

KECSKEMET
NEAREST AIR SERVICE THROUGH BUDAPEST, BUD, 50 MI SE RAIL HUNGARIAN STATE

HOTEL/MOTEL (City Centre and other)

ARANYHOMOK HOTEL ⓈHUN ✕♦
SZECHENYI TER 3 PN 6000
(GOVT ★★) $27-34Ⓒ L-1497-1885Ⓒ ■
TEL 20011 TLX 26327 REPS HG, IB

KESZTHELY
NEAREST AIR SERVICE THROUGH BUDAPEST, BUD, 119 MI SW RAIL HUNGARIAN STATE

HOTEL/MOTEL (City Centre and other)

HELIKON HOTEL ⓈDAN ✕♦
BALATON-PART PN 8360
(GOVT ★★★) $19-58Ⓒ L-1053-3216Ⓒ ⓂⒶ ■
TEL 11330 TLX 35276 REPS HG, IB

MARGITIZIGET IS.
NEAREST AIR SERVICE THROUGH BUDAPEST, BUD, 10 MI NW

MATRAFURED
NEAREST AIR SERVICE THROUGH BUDAPEST, BUD, 58 MI NE

MISKOLC EDC 46
NEAREST AIR SERVICE THROUGH BUDAPEST, BUD, 100 MI NE

HOTEL/MOTEL (City Centre and other)

PANNONIA HOTEL ⓈHUN
KOSSUTH LAJOS U 2 PN 3525
$19-31Ⓒ L-1053-1719Ⓒ ■
TEL 88022 TLX 62778 REPS HG, IB

MISKOLC-TAPOLCA
NEAREST AIR SERVICE THROUGH BUDAPEST, BUD, 110 MI NE RAIL HUNGARIAN STATE

HOTEL/MOTEL (City Centre and other)

JUNO HOTEL ⓈHUN ✕♦
CSABAI U 2-4 PN 3519
(GOVT ★★★) $35-37Ⓒ L-1940-2051Ⓒ ■
TEL 64133 TLX 62332 REPS HG, IB

PECS EDC 72
NEAREST AIR SERVICE THROUGH BUDAPEST, BUD, 122 MI SW

HOTEL/MOTEL (City Centre and other)

NADOR HOTEL ⓈHUN ✕
SZECHENYI TER 15 PN 7621 ■
TEL 11477 TLX 12200 REPS HG, IB

PALATINUS HOTEL ⓈHUN
KOSSUTH L U 5 PN 7621
$36-37 L-1996-2051
TEL 33022 TLX 12652

PANNONIA HOTEL ⓈHUN ✕
RAKOCZI UT 3 PN 7621
(GOVT ★★★) $36-37Ⓒ L-1996-2051Ⓒ ■
TEL 13322 TLX 12469 REPS HG, IB

SIOFOK
NEAREST AIR SERVICE THROUGH BUDAPEST, BUD, 75 MI SW RAIL HUNGARIAN STATE

HOTEL/MOTEL (City Centre and other)

BALATON HOTEL (5-10) ⓈPNH ✕
PETOFI SETANY 9 PN 8600
(GOVT ★★) $24-72 L-1331-3992 ■
TEL 10655 TLX 224108 REPS HG, IB, SG

EUROPA HOTEL (5-10) ⓈPNH ✕
PETOFI SETANY 15 PN 8600
(GOVT ★★★) $26-96 L-1441-5322 ■
TEL 13411 TLX 224108 REPS HG, IB, SG

HUNGARIA HOTEL (5-10) ⓈPNH ✕
PETOFI SETANY 13 PN 8600
(GOVT ★★) $24-90 L-1331-4990 ■
TEL 10677 TLX 224108 REPS HG, IB, SG

LIDO HOTEL (5-10) ⓈPNH ✕
PETOFI SETANY 11 PN 8600
(GOVT ★★) $24-72 L-1331-3992 ■
TEL 10633 TLX 224108 REPS HG, IB, SG

SOPRON EDC 99
NEAREST AIR SERVICE THROUGH BUDAPEST, BUD, 136 MI NW

HOTEL/MOTEL (City Centre and other)

LOVER HOTEL ⓈHUN ✕♦
VARISI U 4 PN 9400
(GOVT ★★★) $27-37Ⓒ L-1497-2051Ⓒ ■
TEL 11061 TLX 249123 REPS HG, IB

PALATINUS HOTEL ⓈHUN ✕
UJ U 23 PN 9400
$17-26Ⓒ L-942-1441Ⓒ ■
TEL 11395 TLX 249146 REPS HG, IB

PANNONIA HOTEL ⓈHUN ✕
LENIN KRT 75 PN 9400
$21-23Ⓒ L-1164-1275Ⓒ ■
TEL 12180 TLX 249116 REPS HG, IB

SZEGED EDC 62
NEAREST AIR SERVICE THROUGH BUDAPEST, BUD, 105 MI SE

HOTEL/MOTEL (City Centre and other)

HUNGARIA HOTEL ⓈHUN ✕
KOMOCSIN TER 2 PN 6720
(GOVT ★★★) $36-37Ⓒ L-1996-2051Ⓒ ■
TEL 21211 TLX 82408 REPS HG, IB

ROYAL HOTEL ⓈHUN ✕
KOLCSEY U 1 PN 6720
$36-37Ⓒ L-1996-2051Ⓒ ■
TEL 12911 TLX 82403 REPS HG, IB

TISZA HOTEL ⓈHUN ✕♦
WESSELENYI U 1 PN 6701
$19-32Ⓒ L-1053-1774Ⓒ ■
TEL 12466 TLX 82358 REPS HG, IB

SZEKESFEHERVAR EDC 22
NEAREST AIR SERVICE THROUGH BUDAPEST, BUD, 47 MI SW RAIL HUNGARIAN STATE

HOTEL/MOTEL (City Centre and other)

ALBA REGIA HOTEL ⓈHUN ✕♦
RAKOCZI U 1 PN 8000
(GOVT ★★★) $33-35Ⓒ L-1830-1940Ⓒ ■
TEL 13484 TLX 21295 REPS HG, IB

SZEKSZARD
NEAREST AIR SERVICE THROUGH BUDAPEST, BUD, 86 MI SW

HOTEL/MOTEL (City Centre and other)

GEMENC HOTEL ⓈPNH ✕♦
MESZAROS LAZAR U 2 PN 7100
$16-42Ⓒ L-887-2328Ⓒ ■
TEL 11722 TLX 14240 REPS HG, IB

SZOMBATHELY EDC 94
NEAREST AIR SERVICE THROUGH BUDAPEST, BUD, 150 MI SW RAIL HUNGARIAN STATE

HOTEL/MOTEL (City Centre and other)

CLAUDIUS HOTEL ⓈHUN ✕♦
BARTOK B KRT 39 PN 9700
(GOVT ★★) $32-33Ⓒ L-1774-1830Ⓒ ■
TEL 13760 TLX 37262 REPS HG, IB

ISIS HOTEL ⓈHUN ✕
RAKOCZI FERENC U 1 PN 9700
$17-28Ⓒ L-942-1552Ⓒ ■
TEL 14990 TLX 37385 REPS HG, IB

SAVARIA HOTEL ⓈHUN ✕
MARTIROK TERE 4, BOX 507 PN 9700
$32-34Ⓒ L-1774-1885Ⓒ ■
TEL 11440 TLX 37200 REPS HG, IB

TATA
NEAREST AIR SERVICE THROUGH BUDAPEST, BUD, 54 MI NW

HOTEL/MOTEL (City Centre and other)

DIANA HOTEL ⓈPNH ✕♦
REMETESEGPUSZTA PN 2890
$14-34Ⓒ L-776-1885Ⓒ ■
TEL 80388 TLX 27237 REPS HG, IB

TIHANY
NEAREST AIR SERVICE THROUGH BUDAPEST, BUD, 88 MI SW

HOTEL/MOTEL (City Centre and other)

CLUB TIHANY HOTEL ⓈHUN ✕✱
REV U 3 PN 8237
(GOVT ★★★★) ■
TEL 48088 TLX 32272 REPS HG, IB

VISEGRAD
NEAREST AIR SERVICE THROUGH BUDAPEST, BUD, 30 MI NW

HOTEL/MOTEL (City Centre and other)

SILVANUS HOTEL ⓈPNH ✕♦
PN 2025
$25-42Ⓒ L-1386-2328Ⓒ ■
TEL 2628311 TLX 225720 REPS HG, IB, SG

Hotel Information/Facilities
- AH&MA Member
- ♦ — Conference Rooms
- ✕ — Restaurant on premises
- ■ — 8% or more commission
- Ⓟ — Free Airport Pick-up
- Ⓢ — Hotel System affiliation
- ✱ — Rooms for Handicapped
- Reps — Hotel Representatives
- NP — New Property
- RP — Renovated Property

Hotel Rate Plans
- Ⓐ — American Plan
- Ⓒ — Continental Plan
- Ⓜ — Modified American Plan

General Information
- ✈ — Scheduled Airline Service
- EDC — European Dialing Code
- L — Local currency

Note: Government hotel ratings, (in parens), are explained in detail at the beginning of this section. Hotel/Motel room rate ranges are for guideline purposes only. Always CONFIRM rates when booking reservations. Mileage and direction indicated under the off-line destination is **from** the airport **to** the off-line point.

Fig. 7-3. Continued

a hotel is located in the city. A mileage chart on each of the maps shows the approximate mileage. By utilizing this, one can tell fairly rapidly how far a specific location in a city is from the city center or from any other major location. This makes it particularly nice if a client is planning sightseeing trips or visits to specific places within walking distance. Although some city maps do not include the airport on the map, most will show where the airport is located. On the map of Budapest, the bottom right-hand corner shows a reference saying, "To Airport" with an appropriate arrow.

To provide even more information relating to the timing to get from the airport to the hotel, the listing on Budapest (as is customary with all major city listings) shows that the airport is located nine miles southeast of the city. Three lines further down the listing there is a note that states, "Airport Ground Transportation: Time to Airport 30 Min.; . . ." This provides the reader with an understanding of the minimum amount of time a client will need if traveling between the airport and the city center. It is normally wise to add a minimum of thirty minutes to deplane and go through customs and, if one is picking up a rental car or waiting for an airport bus, an additional thirty minutes of time at the airport before being able to depart for the hotel is usually wise to schedule. In addition, it should be kept in mind that the time from airport to city center is normally the minimum amount of time and usually refers to the time it would take to drive that distance at a light-traffic driving time. If the client will be traveling from the airport to the city center at a high traffic time (for example, five in the afternoon for many cities), additional driving time needs to be allowed. Also if there is road construction (you can find out if there is major road repair work being done by asking the air carrier flying your client into the city) or if the hotel is not located in the center of the city, but is located on the other side of the city from the airport, additional time will be needed.

Some might question why an early evening (by 6:00 P.M.) arrival at the destination hotel is important. There are several reasons why many experienced F.I.T. clients prefer a 6:00 P.M. (or even a little bit earlier, if possible, hotel arrival on the day of a flight. A major one, of course, is the practice of hotel overbooking. Almost all major hotels overbook. If an F.I.T. client arrives by 6:00 P.M., the hotel is not usually full. Therefore the clients will be accommodated if they have a reservation, one that is confirmed. An arrival at 8:00 P.M. might mean that they will be turned away even with confirmed reservations. Since most major hotels guarantee reservations for arrival after 6:00 P.M. only with advance payment or a credit card guarantee, it is at or around 6:00 P.M. that hotels start reviewing their room status and determining which categories (often, including those who do hold guaranteed reservations) of those with reservations will be turned away. Obviously, if F.I.T. clients can make it to the hotel and get checked in before this review, their chances are much better—and their chances of getting a good room are better (the lesser quality rooms are usually assigned to guests last).

Perhaps the most important reason for experienced F.I.T. clients to prefer a 6:00 P.M. hotel arrival, however, is the ability to get settled into their room, have a leisurely dinner, and get a good night's sleep so they will be totally rested the next day and be able to take maximum advantage of the activities scheduled the next day. A 6:00 P.M. arrival allows the client the time needed to make a change in hotel room, if needed; to reivew the activities scheduled for the next day; or perhaps the time to take a leisurely evening stroll in the neighborhood of the hotel. For those who want evening activities (night clubs, dinner dancing, etc.), there is often enough time to include some of these activities after getting settled into the hotel.

AIRPORT LOCATION CONVENIENCE

The location of departure and arrival airports is also a factor to be considered in air carrier selection. Often international flights depart from several airports serving a large city and there are three or more airports where a flight can land near the destination city. These airports can be a long way from each other and a long distance from the city. International flights leaving from Washington, D.C., for example, might depart from close in National airport (just across the Potomac from downtown Washington), from the Baltimore/Washington airport (between the two cities, but closer to Baltimore), or from Washington's Dulles airport (twenty-six miles through the Virginia countryside from Washington, D.C.). If the client is departing from downtown Washington, it will make little difference whether the flight takes off from Baltimore/Washington or from Dulles. (There will be some differences since the frequency of transfers and the city to airport distance is different.) However, if the client lives in the Washington, D.C., area, and is leaving from home, the Dulles airport will be much more convenient if the client lives in Virgina and Baltimore/Washington will be more convenient if the client lives in Maryland. The location of the F.I.T. client's home vis a vis the airport could make a two-hour transfer time difference and this should be considered by selecting a carrier that leaves from the closest airport.

The same consideration is given to the client's hotel location vis a vis the airport location in cities outside the United States. If one were leaving from London, for example, one has a choice of four airports. However, two of them have all of the international flights and both (Heathrow and Gatwick) are some distance from downtown London. Again, the travel planner (European edition) will help in identifying the airport that can be of greatest convenience for the client. The following travel planner exerpt, figure 7–4, from London, under the very first listing for the city indicates that Heathrow airport is fifteen miles west of London. The next line indicates that

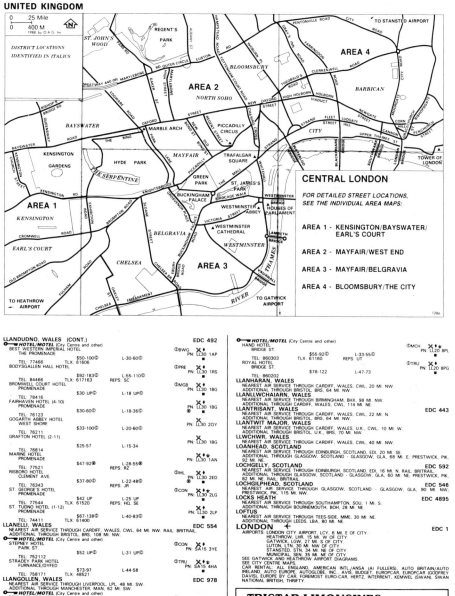

UNITED KINGDOM

CENTRAL LONDON

FOR DETAILED STREET LOCATIONS, SEE THE INDIVIDUAL AREA MAPS:

AREA 1 - KENSINGTON/BAYSWATER/ EARL'S COURT

AREA 2 - MAYFAIR/WEST END

AREA 3 - MAYFAIR/BELGRAVIA

AREA 4 - BLOOMSBURY/THE CITY

LLANDUDNO, WALES (CONT.)   EDC 492
⊙━ *HOTEL/MOTEL* (City Centre and other)
BEST WESTERN IMPERIAL HOTEL   ①BWG ✕♦
THE PROMENADE   PN: LL30 1AP
$50-100ⓒ   L-30-60ⓒ
TEL: 77466   TLX: 61606
BODYSGALLEN HALL HOTEL   ①PRE ✕♦
PN: LL30 1RS
$92-183ⓒ   L-55-110ⓒ
TEL: 84466   TLX: 617163   REPS: SC
BROMWELL COURT HOTEL   ①MGB ✕♦
PROMENADE   PN: LL30 1BG
$30 UPⓒ   L-18 UPⓒ
TEL: 78416
FAIRHAVEN HOTEL (4-10)   ✕♦
PN: LL30 1BG
$30-60ⓒ   L-18-36ⓒ   ⊛
TEL: 76123
GOGARTH ABBEY HOTEL   ✕♦
WEST SHORE   PN: LL30 2QY
$33-100ⓒ   L-20-60ⓒ
TEL: 76211
GRAFTON HOTEL (2-11)   ✕♦
PN: LL30 1BG
$25-57   L-15-34
TEL: 76814
MARINE HOTEL   ✕♦⁂
PROMENADE   PN: LL30 1AN
$47-92⊛   L-28-55⊛
TEL: 77521   REPS: RZ
RISBORO HOTEL   ①IHL ✕♦
CLEMENT AVE.   PN: LL30 2ED
$37-80ⓒ   L-22-48ⓒ   ■
TEL: 76343   REPS: JR
ST. GEORGE'S HOTEL   ①CON ✕♦
PROMENADE   PN: LL30 2LG
$42 UP   L-25 UP
TEL: 77544   TLX: 61520   REPS: HQ, SE
ST. TUDNO HOTEL (1-12)   ✕♦
PROMENADE   PN: LL30 2LP
$67-138ⓒ   L-40-83ⓒ
TEL: 74411   TLX: 61400
LLANELLI, WALES   EDC 554
NEAREST AIR SERVICE THROUGH CARDIFF, WALES, CWL, 64 MI. NW. RAIL: BRITRAIL.
ADDITIONAL THROUGH BRISTOL, BRS, 108 MI. NW.
⊙━ *HOTEL/MOTEL* (City Centre and other)
STEPNEY HOTEL   ①CON ✕♦
PARK ST.   PN: SA15 3YE
$52 UPⓒ   L-31 UPⓒ
TEL: 752112
STRADEY PARK HOTEL   ①TRU ✕♦
FURNANCE/DYFED   PN: SA15 4HA
$73-97   L-44-58
TEL: 758171   TLX: 48521
LLANGOLLEN, WALES   EDC 978
NEAREST AIR SERVICE THROUGH LIVERPOOL, LPL, 48 MI. SW.
ADDITIONAL THROUGH MANCHESTER, MAN, 62 MI. SW.
⊙━ *HOTEL/MOTEL* (City Centre and other)
BRYN DERWEN HOTEL   ①MGB ✕♦
ABBEY RD.   PN: LL20 8EF
$33 UPⓒ   L-20 UPⓒ
TEL: 860583
BRYN HOWEL HOTEL   ✕♦
PN: LL20 7UW
REQUEST RATES
TEL: 860331
CHAIN BRIDGE HOTEL   ①CON ✕♦
BERWYN   PN: LL20 8BS
$45 UPⓒ   L-27 UPⓒ
TEL: 860215

⊙━ *HOTEL/MOTEL* (City Centre and other)
HAND HOTEL   ⑤MCH ✕♦⁂
BRIDGE ST.   PN: LL20 8PL
$55-92ⓒ   L-33-55ⓒ   ■
ROYAL HOTEL   REPS: UT   ①TRU ✕♦
BRIDGE ST.   PN: LL20 8PG
$78-122   L-47-73
TEL: 860202
LLANHARAN, WALES
NEAREST AIR SERVICE THROUGH CARDIFF, WALES, CWL, 20 MI. NW.
ADDITIONAL THROUGH BRISTOL, BRS, 64 MI. NW.
LLANLLWCHAIARN, WALES
NEAREST AIR SERVICE THROUGH BIRMINGHAM, BHX, 98 MI. NW.
ADDITIONAL THROUGH CARDIFF, WALES, CWL, 114 MI. NE.
LLANTRISANT, WALES   EDC 443
NEAREST AIR SERVICE THROUGH CARDIFF, WALES, CWL, 22 MI. N.
ADDITIONAL THROUGH BRISTOL, BRS, 64 MI. NW.
LLANTWIT MAJOR, WALES
NEAREST AIR SERVICE THROUGH CARDIFF, WALES, U.K., CWL, 10 MI. W.
ADDITIONAL THROUGH BRISTOL, U.K., BRS, 70 MI. NW.
LLWCHWR, WALES
NEAREST AIR SERVICE THROUGH CARDIFF, WALES, CWL, 40 MI. NW.
LOANHEAD, SCOTLAND
NEAREST AIR SERVICE THROUGH EDINBURGH, SCOTLAND, EDI, 20 MI. SE.
ADDITIONAL THROUGH GLASGOW, SCOTLAND - GLASGOW, GLA, 68 MI. E, PRESTWICK, PIK,
92 MI. NE.
LOCHGELLY, SCOTLAND   EDC 592
NEAREST AIR SERVICE THROUGH EDINBURGH, SCOTLAND, EDI, 16 MI. N. RAIL: BRITRAIL.
ADDITIONAL THROUGH GLASGOW, SCOTLAND - GLASGOW, GLA, 60 MI. NE, PRESTWICK, PIK,
82 MI. NE. RAIL: BRITRAIL.
LOCHGILPHEAD, SCOTLAND   EDC 546
NEAREST AIR SERVICE THROUGH GLASGOW, SCOTLAND - GLASGOW, GLA, 90 MI. NW;
PRESTWICK, PIK, 115 MI. NW.
LOCKS HEATH
NEAREST AIR SERVICE THROUGH SOUTHAMPTON, SOU, 1 MI. S.
ADDITIONAL THROUGH BOURNEMOUTH, BOH, 28 MI. NE.
LOFTUS   EDC 4895
NEAREST AIR SERVICE THROUGH TEES-SIDE, MME, 30 MI. NE.
ADDITIONAL THROUGH LEEDS, LBA, 80 MI. NE.
LONDON ✈   EDC 1
AIRPORTS: LONDON CITY AIRPORT, LCY, 6 MI. E OF CITY.
HEATHROW, LHR, 15 MI. W OF CITY.
GATWICK, LGW, 27 MI. S OF CITY.
LUTON, LTN, 30 MI. NW OF CITY.
STANSTED, STN, 34 MI. NE OF CITY.
MUNICIPAL, SEN, 35 MI. NE OF CITY.
SEE GATWICK AND HEATHROW AIRPORT DIAGRAMS.
SEE CITY CENTRE MAPS.
CAR RENTAL: ALL ENGLAND, AMERICAN INTL/ANSA (AI FULLERS), AUTO BRITAIN/AUTO
IRELAND, AUTO EUROPE, AUTOGLOBE, INC., AVIS, BUDGET, EUROPCAR, EUROPCAR (GODFREY
DAVIS), EUROPE BY CAR, FOREMOST EURO-CAR, HERTZ, INTERRENT, KEMWEL (SWAN), SWAN
NATIONAL BRITISH, THRIFTY.

TRISTAR LIMOUSINES

London, Heathrow & Gatwick Airports
Chauffeured Volvo & Daimler Limos
Small group transfers, luxury buses

RES: 1-800-321-6622   In VA: 1-804-758-2365
IN ENGLAND: 0-800-282-611 or 01-759-9819

━━━━ *INFORMATIONAL LISTING* ━━━━

Fig. 7-4. (Reprinted by special permission from the January-March 1989 edition of the *Official Airline Guide Travel Planner and Hotel and Motel Guide* European edition. Copyright © 1989 Official Airline Guide. All rights reserved.)

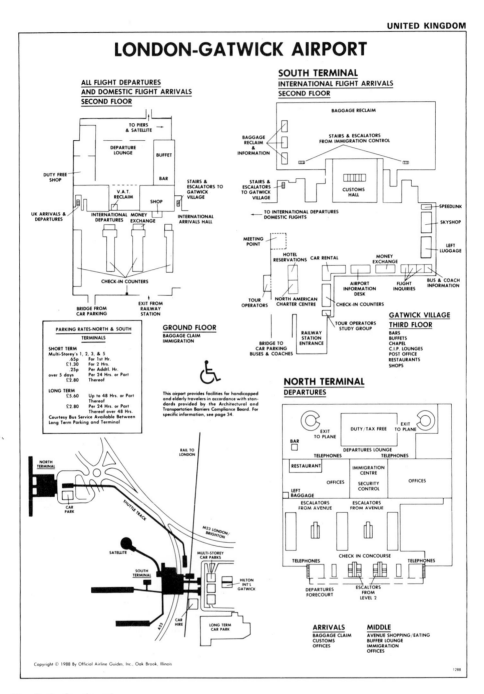

Fig. 7-4. Continued

UNITED KINGDOM

LONDON - HEATHROW AIRPORT

TERMINAL 1 — Domestic Airlines, British Airways, Domestic & European Flights (except Paris & Amsterdam), Aer Lingus, Cyprus Airways, El Al, Icelandair, Sabena and South African Airways

FIRST FLOOR - DEPARTURES

DOMESTIC
DEPARTURE LOUNGE

INTERNATIONAL
DEPARTURE LOUNGE

DOMESTIC
ARRIVALS

BUFFET

IMMIGRATION

GROUND FLOOR

ARRIVALS
AIRBUS TO TOWN; HOTEL
   COURTESY COACHES
AIRPORT INFORMATION DESK
BANK
CUSTOMS
DOMESTIC BAGGAGE CLAIM
GROUND TRANSPORTATION
HOTEL/RAIL INFORMATION
IMMIGRATION
INTL. BAGGAGE CLAIM
RAIL/AIR COACH LINK
TRANSFER BUS TO TERMINALS 2, 3
   & 4

DOMESTIC
DEPARTURES

SKYSHOP

ELEVATORS

SHOPPING
CONCOURSE

TO BALCONY
BARS AND
RESTAURANTS

BANK

INTERNATIONAL
DEPARTURES

SKYSHOP

AIRLINE CHECK-IN COUNTERS

LIFTS TO ARRIVALS
FORECOURT

ELEVATORS

AIRLINE TICKET &
INFORMATION DESKS

WALKWAY TO QUEEN'S
BUILDING & TERMINAL 2

TERMINAL 2 — European Airlines (except Aer Lingus, Air Malta, Cyprus Airways, Icelandair, KLM, NLM, Sabena)

FIRST FLOOR

POST
OFFICE

ARRIVALS

TO DEPARTURES

STAIRS
TO 2ND
FLOOR

DEPARTURE LOUNGE

GROUND FLOOR
CHECK-IN AREA
ELEVATORS

BALCONY
BAR
BUFFET
COFFEE SHOP
RESTAURANT

BAGGAGE
CLAIM

CUSTOMS

IMMIGRATION

BANK

AIRLINE DESKS

SKYSHOP

BANK

FIRST FLOOR
ADDITIONAL FACILITIES:
BAGGAGE CLAIM
BAR
BUSINESS CENTER
CAFETERIA
CAR RENTAL
DUTY FREE SHOP
RAIL & HOTEL INFORMATION

AIRPORT
INFORMATION DESK

TRAVEL DESKS

SHOPS

PASSENGER RAMP
FROM GROUND FLOOR
AND TO CAR PARK 2

WALKWAY TO QUEEN'S BUILDING & TERMINAL 1

PASSENGER RAMP TO
GROUND FLOOR SUBWAYS
AND UNDERGROUND

TUNNEL TO & FROM CENTRAL TERMINAL

DOMESTIC DEPARTURE
LOUNGE

SHORT TERM
PARKING

TERMINAL 1

TERMINAL 3 ARRIVALS

SHORT TERM
PARKING

UNDERGROUND STATION & PASSENGER SUBWAYS

TERMINAL 3 DEPARTURES

QUEEN'S BUILDING

SHORT TERM
PARKING

EMERGENCY MEDICAL CENTER
OBSERVATION DECK

HEATHROW TERMINALS 1, 2, 3 STATION
(PICCADILLY LINE)

BUS STATION

TERMINAL 2

BUSINESS
CENTER

TERMINAL 4

SHORT TERM
PARKING

A30

HEATHROW TERMINAL 4 STATION
(PICCADILLY LINE)

Fig. 7-4. Continued

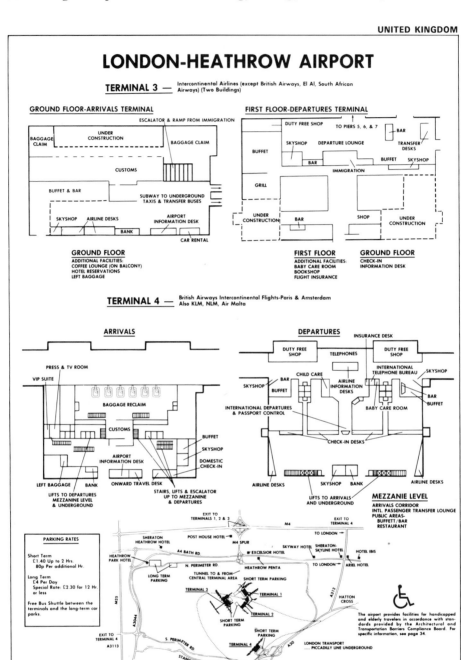

Fig. 7-4. Continued

UNITED KINGDOM

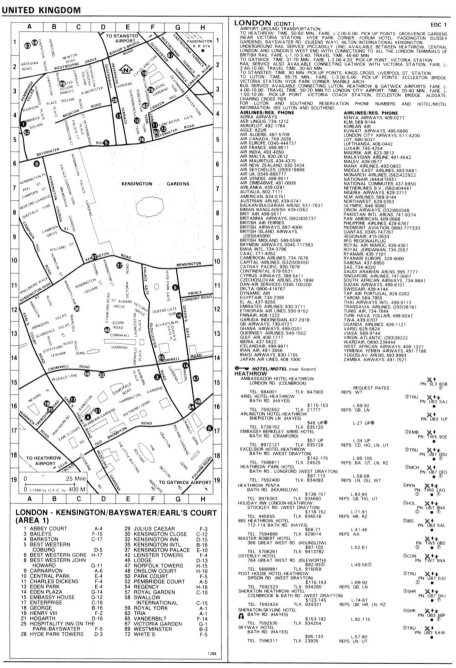

LONDON (CONT.) EDC 1

AIRPORT GROUND TRANSPORTATION:
TO HEATHROW: TIME, 50-60 MIN.; FARE, L-2.00-6.00. PICK-UP POINTS: GROSVENOR GARDENS (NEAR VICTORIA STATION), HYDE PARK CORNER, FORUM HOTEL, PADDINGTON (SUSSEX GARDENS), BAYSWATER RD. (QUEENS WAY). HILTON INTERNATIONAL KENSINGTON. UNDERGROUND RAIL SERVICE (PICCADILLY LINE) AVAILABLE BETWEEN HEATHROW, CENTRAL LONDON AND LONDON'S WEST END WITH CONNECTIONS TO ALL THE LONDON TERMINALS OF BRITISH RAIL. FARE, L-1.10-3.40; TRAVEL TIME, 45-60 MIN.
TO GATWICK: TIME, 31-70 MIN.; FARE, L-2.00-4.20. PICK-UP POINT VICTORIA STATION. RAIL SERVICE ALSO AVAILABLE CONNECTING GATWICK WITH VICTORIA STATION. FARE, L-3.40-10.00; TRAVEL TIME, 30-40 MIN.
TO STANSTED: TIME, 50 MIN. PICK-UP POINTS: KINGS CROSS, LIVERPOOL ST. STATION.
TO LUTON: TIME, 65-75 MIN.; FARE, L-3.00-5.00. PICK-UP POINTS: ECCLESTON BRIDGE, VICTORIA STATION, HYDE PARK CORNER, MARBLE ARCH.
BUS SERVICE AVAILABLE CONNECTING LUTON, HEATHROW & GATWICK AIRPORTS. FARE, L-4.00-10.00. TRAVEL TIME, 50-70 MIN.TO LONDON CITY AIRPORT: TIME, 20-40 MIN.; FARE, L-1.50-10.00. PICK-UP POINT: VICTORIA COACH STATION, ECCLESTON BRIDGE, ALDGATE, CHARING CROSS PIER.
FOR LUTON AND SOUTHEND RESERVATION PHONE NUMBERS AND HOTEL/MOTEL INFORMATION, SEE LUTON AND SOUTHEND.

AIRLINES/RES. PHONE	AIRLINES/RES. PHONE
ADRIA AIRWAYS	KENYA AIRWAYS, 409-0277
AER LINGUS, 734-1212	KLM, 568-9144
AEROFLOT, 492-1764	KOREAN AIR
AIGLE AZUR	KUWAIT AIRWAYS, 486-6666
AIR ALGERIE, 487-5709	LONDON CITY AIRWAYS, 511-4200
AIR CANADA, 759-2636	LOT, 580-5037
AIR EUROPE, 0345-444737	LUFTHANSA, 408-0442
AIR FRANCE, 499-9511	LUXAIR, 745-4254
AIR INDIA, 493-4050	MAERSK AIR, 623-3813
AIR MALTA, 930-2612	MALAYSIAN AIRLINE, 491-4542
AIR MAURITIUS, 434-4375	MALEV, 439-0577
AIR NEW ZEALAND, 930-3434	MANX AIRLINES, 493-0803
AIR SEYCHELLES, (293)518888	MIDDLE EAST AIRLINES, 493-5681
AIR UK, 0345-666777	MONARCH AIRLINES, (582)422922
AIR VENDEE, 499-9511	NATIONAL (444)415551
AIR ZIMBABWE, 491-0009	NATIONAL COMMUTER, 437-6950
AIRLANKA, 439-0291	NETHERLINES B.V., (582)404441
ALITALIA, 602-7111	NIGERIA AIRWAYS, 629-3717
AMERICAN, 834-5151	NLM AIRLINES, 568-9144
AUSTRIAN ARLNS, 439-0741	NORTHWEST, 629-5353
BALKAN-BULGARIAN ARLNS, 637-7637	OLYMPIC, 846-9080
BIMAN BANGLADESH, 439-0362	ORION AIRWAYS, (332)850348
BRIT AIR, 499-9511	PAKISTAN INTL. ARLNS, 741-9374
BRITANNIA AIRWAYS, (582)405737	PAN AMERICAN, 409-0688
BRITISH AIR FERRIES	PHILIPPINE AIRLINES, 629-6767
BRITISH AIRWAYS, 897-4000	PIEDMONT AVIATION, 0800-777333
BRITISH ISLAND AIRWAYS,	QANTAS, 0345-747767
(293)545900	REGIONAIR, 415-0633
BRITISH MIDLAND, 589-5599	RFG REGIONALFLUG
BRYMON AIRWAYS, 0345-717383	ROYAL AIR MAROC, 439-4361
BWIA INTL, 734-3796	ROYAL JORDANIAN, 734-2557
CAAC, 771-4052	RYANAIR, 435-7101
CAMEROON AIRLINES, 734-7676	RYANAIR EUROPE, 328-4000
CAPITAL AIRLINES, (532)505550	SABENA, 437-6950
CATHAY PACIFIC, 930-7878	SAS, 734-4020
CONTINENTAL, 679-5531	SAUDI ARABIAN ARLNS, 995-7777
CYPRUS AIRWAYS, 388-5411	SINGAPORE AIRLINES, 747-0007
CZECHOSLOVAK AIRLN, 255-1898	SOUTH AFRICAN AIRWAYS, 734-9841
DAN-AIR SERVICES, 0345-100200	SUDAN AIRWAYS, 499-8101
DELTA, 0800-414767	SWISSAIR, 439-4144
DYNAMIC AIR	TAP AIR PORTUGAL, 828-0262
EGYPTAIR, 734-2395	TAROM, 584-7955
EL AL, 437-9255	THAI AIRWAYS INTL, 499-9113
EMIRATES AIRLINES, 930-3711	TRANSAVIA AIRLINES, (293)38181
ETHIOPIAN AIR LINES, 930-9152	TUNIS AIR, 734-7644
FINNAIR, 408-1222	TURK HAVA YOLLARI, 499-9247
GARUDA INDONESIAN, 437-2918	TWA, 439-0707
GB AIRWAYS, 730-0721	UGANDA AIRLINES, 409-1121
GHANA AIRWAYS, 499-0201	VARIG, 629-5824
GUERNSEY AIRLINES, 549-1502	VIASA, 568-9144
GULF AIR, 408-1717	VIRGIN ATLANTIC, (293)38222
IBERIA, 437-5622	WARDAIR, 0800-234444
ICELANDAIR, 499-9971	WEST AFRICAN AIRWAYS, 409-1327
IRAN AIR, 491-3656	YEMENIA, YEMEN AIRWAYS, 491-7186
IRAQI AIRWAYS, 930-1155	YUGOSLAV ARLNS, 493-9993
JAPAN AIR LINES, 408-1000	ZAMBIA AIRWAYS, 491-7521

HOTEL/MOTEL (near Airport)
HEATHROW

AMBASSADOR HOTEL-HEATHROW		
LONDON RD. (COLNBROOK)		PN: SL3 8QB
	REQUEST RATES	
TEL: 684001 TLX: 847903	REPS: WT	
ARIEL HOTEL-HEATHROW		①TRU
BATH RD. (HAYES)		PN: UB3 5AJ
$115-153	L-69-92	
TEL: 7592552 TLX: 21777	REPS: GB, LN	
ARLINGTON HOTEL-HEATHROW		①TRU
SHEPISTON LN. (HAYES)		PN: UB3 1LP
$45 UP⑨	L-27 UP⑨	
TEL: 5736162 TLX: 935120		
EMBASSY-BERKELEY ARMS HOTEL		⑥EMB
BATH RD. (CRANFORD)		PN: TW5 9QE
$57 UP	L-34 UP	
TEL: 8972121 TLX: 935728	REPS: GD, HQ, LN, UT	
EXCELSIOR HOTEL-HEATHROW		①TRU
BATH RD. (WEST DRAYTON)		PN: UB7 0DU
$142-175	L-85-105	
TEL: 7596611 TLX: 24525	REPS: BA, GT, LN, RZ	
HEATHROW PARK HOTEL		⑥MCH
BATH RD., LONGFORD (WEST DRAYTON)		PN: UB7 0EQ
$97-113	L-58-68	
TEL: 7592400 TLX: 934093	REPS: LN, QU, WT	
HEATHROW PENTA		⑨PEN
BATH RD. (HOUNSLOW)		PN: TW6 2AQ
$138-157	L-83-94	
TEL: 8976363 TLX: 934660	REPS: GB, HQ, UT	
HOLIDAY INN LONDON-HEATHROW		①HOL
STOCKLEY RD. (WEST DRAYTON)		PN: UB7 9NA
$118-152	L-71-91	
TEL: 445555 TLX: 934518	REPS: HR, RZ	
IBIS HEATHROW HOTEL		①IBS
112-114 BATH RD. (HAYES)		PN: UB3 5AL
$68-77	L-41-46	
TEL: 7594888 TLX: 929014	REPS: AA	
MASTER ROBERT HOTEL		①CON
366 GREAT WEST RD. (HOUNSLOW)		PN: TW5 0BD
$87-102	L-52-61	
TEL: 5706261 TLX: 9413782		
OSTERLEY HOTEL		①TRU
764 GREAT WEST RD. (ISLEWORTH)		PN: TW7 5NA
$82-93⑨	L-49-56⑨	
TEL: 5689981 TLX: 915059		
POST HOUSE HOTEL-HEATHROW		①TRU
SIPSON RD. (WEST DRAYTON)		PN: UB7 0JU
$115-153	L-69-92	
TEL: 7592323 TLX: 934280	REPS: GB, LN	
SHERATON HEATHROW HOTEL		①SHR
COLNBROOK & BATH RD. (WEST DRAYTON)		PN: UB7 0HJ
$123-145	L-74-87	
TEL: 7592424 TLX: 934331	REPS: GB, HR, LN, RZ	
SHERATON-SKYLINE HOTEL		①SHR
BATH RD. (HAYES)		PN: UB3 5BP
$153-192	L-92-115	
TEL: 7592536 TLX: 934254		
SKYWAY HOTEL		①TRU
BATH RD. (HAYES)		PN: UB3 5AW
$95-133	L-57-80	
TEL: 7596311 TLX: 23935	REPS: LN, UT	

LONDON - KENSINGTON/BAYSWATER/EARL'S COURT (AREA 1)

1	ABBEY COURT	A-4
3	BAILEYS	F-15
4	BARKSTON	C-17
5	BEST WESTERN COBURG	D-5
6	BEST WESTERN GORE	H-17
8	BEST WESTERN JOHN HOWARD	G-11
9	CARNARVON	A-6
10	CENTRAL PARK	E-4
11	CHARLES DICKENS	F-4
13	EDEN PARK	E-4
14	EDEN PLAZA	G-14
15	EMBASSY HOUSE	G-12
17	ENTERPRISE	C-16
18	GEORGE	B-16
19	HENRY VIII	F-2
21	HOGARTH	D-16
25	HOSPITALITY INN ON THE PARK-BAYSWATER	F-5
28	HYDE PARK TOWERS	D-3
29	JULIUS CAESAR	F-3
30	KENSINGTON CLOSE	C-12
32	KENSINGTON INN	D-15
35	KENSINGTON INTL.	B-16
37	KENSINGTON PALACE	E-10
42	LEINSTER TOWERS	F-4
46	LODGE	D-13
47	NORFOLK TOWERS	H-15
48	ONSLOW COURT	H-16
50	PARK COURT	F-5
52	PEMBRIDGE COURT	A-5
54	REGENCY	H-16
57	ROYAL GARDEN	C-10
58	SWALLOW INTERNATIONAL	C-15
59	ROYAL YORK	A-1
63	TRIA	A-1
65	VANDERBILT	F-14
67	VICTORIA GARDEN	G-1
69	WESTMINSTER	B-3
72	WHITE'S	F-5

1288

Fig. 7-4. Continued

Gatwick airport is twenty-seven miles south of the city. Listings show airport codes (LHR for Heathrow and LGW for Gatwick). In looking up flight departures, one can rapidly determine the airport from which each flight departs. In many cases, Heathrow would be preferable for F.I.T. clients since it is much closer to London, almost half the distance from London as Gatwick.

An additional convenience for clients provided by the travel planner is a map of major airports. In the case of Gatwick and Heathrow, the concourses and terminal maps for both are provided. By taking a few minutes to study the maps, one can rapidly get a good feel for the amount of time that might be required for the client to get through the airport and to the waiting plane, for example, from arrival at the airport to the actual departure gate. In some cases this might be a very short period of time while in other cases it might be a much longer time. It should be noted also that where there are several terminals at an airport, the travel planner lists the carriers that depart from or arrive at each of the terminals. This also assists in scheduling and advising clients so that they will know the terminal from which they are leaving and therefore will be able to transit from arrival at the airport to their departure gate as rapidly as possible. Some F.I.T. specialists even include departure and arrival airport and terminal maps with client itineraries for the client to carry during the F.I.T., thereby making airport transit especially easy.

Still another convenience provided by the travel planner is a listing of the airport ground transportation time. The listing for Heathrow indicates, "TO HEATHROW: TIME, 50 – 60 MIN.; Fare, L–2.00–6.00." This information provides the F.I.T. specialist with an understanding of the minimum amount of time that one should consider taking between downtown and the departure airport (for London this is fifty to sixty minutes for Heathrow and seventy minutes for Gatwick). It also provides information relating to the local ground transportation cost (for England it is quoted in United Kingdom pounds, the currency of England), and the pick-up points for ground transportation (and for London, a note that rail service is available to both airports from downtown London). For London, if one travels by rail, the fare, the departure points in London (Victoria Station, for example), and the travel time required are all indicated.

COST

Cost is a factor that is usually thought of first in the selection of an air carrier for an F.I.T. Certainly cost is important, although it is not always the single most important F.I.T. carrier selection factor. Clients might stress the importance of being on a budget, but a client who can afford an F.I.T. also wants and expects comfort. If there is only a small cost difference between solid comfort and real discomfort in flying conditions, almost all F.I.T. clients will opt to pay the cost difference and will select comfort. Therefore, it is important to determine what carrier provides the best price, but it is equally important to check out other carriers and what they have to offer for a price close to the best price. If a carrier offering much more comfortable flight conditions is available at only a small percentage of greater cost, give the client the option and let the client make the decision. Even if the decision is to opt for the less expensive choice, the client will usually appreciate your extending the option.

A second factor relating to cost is the agency commission. Obviously, selecting a carrier that provides the comfort desired at the best price is an important criterion in carrier selection. However, there might be several carriers all offering essentially the same degree of service and quality at the same price. Selecting a carrier that will pay a better-than-average commission makes the final choice an easy one in many cases. Getting the best possible commission and earning the highest possible overrides keep the travel agency profitable and keeps the earnings of the F.I.T. specialist at a most satisfactory level as well.

IN-FLIGHT CONSIDERATIONS

Comfort and the receipt of amenities during the flights are important considerations as well. These might include such things as give-aways, in-flight movies, in-flight stereo, the food that is served during the flight, the courtesy of in-flight service personnel, seat comfort (leg room, ease of getting in and out, size, degree of recline), and how big the aircraft is. Although most F.I.T. specialists know the importance of each of these factors, it is easy to overlook one or more aspects of in-flight comfort, leaving the F.I.T. client less than happy. Prepare a checklist and put a blank copy in each F.I.T. client's file. Check off each comfort consideration for each flight before turning the documents over to the client. Experienced F.I.T. specialists know that some carriers are known for having flights people would rather not have been on, and some carriers concentrate on making their in-flight services extra special. In addition where special requests from F.I.T. passengers are a consideration, there are some carriers that are definitely easier to work with in getting these requests met than other carriers.

Give-Aways

While is it improbable that any carrier is selected for its give-aways (Japan Air with its free Japanese business cards might be the exception), some in-flight give-aways are definitely more memorable than others. Sleeping masks, toiletry kits, and slippers are common give-aways. The quality of these might vary considerably. Some airlines still provide free playing cards, free headsets, and free drinks—even in the economy section of the plane. Generally speaking, the more free give-aways that are geared toward in-flight comfort, the more comfortable one can expect the F.I.T. client to be while flying to the next destination.

In-Flight Movies

When they were first introduced, in-flight movies were very important to clients. The airlines knew it and many a client was swayed to fly with one carrier over another because a popular recently released film was being shown en route. Today many carriers have included commercials with their films. Some carriers show inexpensive, out-of-date films, reservationists sometimes do not know what film will be shown on a flight and passengers often would not prefer to see the film. Certainly when the screen is directly in front of a passenger and it is necessary to lean very far back in one's seat to see the full screen, viewing the in-flight movie is not a pleasant experience. In addition, since many carriers turn out all the lights and close the window shades during the film showing, those clients who would prefer to play cards, read, or look out the window at the scenery being flown over, may feel that they have been inconvenienced. The answer is to find out what your client prefers. If the client wants to see the movie, make sure a comfortable viewing seat is selected. If other activities are preferred, request a seat in a section of the plane, if there is one, where the movie will not be shown.

In-Flight Stereo

One of the most pleasant aspects of a long flight for many clients is the ability to listen to good music. Having the availability of in-flight stereo music is especially important to clients. Although in-flight stereo is common and expected on flights across the Atlantic or Pacific oceans, other flights might or might not offer this amenity. If in-flight stereo is on your checklist to check out while comparing possible carriers for a flight segment, this can be one additional aspect that can help make a difference in carrier selection.

In-Flight Food and Beverages

Many a carrier has been turned down or selected because of its food and beverages. It is not uncommon for F.I.T. clients to ask to fly on a carrier of a country in order to get a chance to eat the food specialties native to that country. This sometimes happens on air segments between two countries for which the air carrier is not a native carrier. However, F.I.T. specialists should know that the native carriers of some Islamic countries do not allow alcohol on their flights and do not serve alcoholic beverages. This factor alone has discouraged many F.I.T. clients from flying with such carriers. Generally these carriers try to make up for not serving alcohol by providing better quality meals and more give-aways than their competitors. For an F.I.T. client who wants to drink, the meal differences seldom make up for having drinks. For those who do not drink, such flights are sometimes considered a nice change. In either case, if a flight on which alcoholic drinks are not served is to be considered, definitely check first with the client.

The cuisines of the world offer a major reason people want to travel. As much as our finer restaurants in the United States might try to duplicate the atmosphere of eating a special native meal in the country of origin, it is simply not the same. Many carriers search throughout their country to find the best chefs to prepare the food served on their flights. And there are carriers that have won some of the world's highest culinary awards for their in-flight meals. This is especially true in first class, the class preferred by many F.I.T. clients. If special meals are important to the F.I.T. client (this should be determined in the client analysis session), make sure that carriers who are noted for their meal service are chosen when you make your selection. Many carriers produce fine menus for their first-class service, those who are especially proud of their cuisine will usually provide copies of their menus to the F.I.T. specialist on a gratis basis upon request.

In-Flight Personnel

There are those who say luck is the only way to get top-quality in-flight staffing and certainly luck seems to be the only factor in many cases. Nevertheless, those who have flown extensively agree that some crews and crew members are excellent while others are far from good. Good in-flight people can often make the difference between a comfortable, pleasantly memorable flight and one the F.I.T. client will be happy to leave. But depending totally on luck to get good service is risking the happiness of the client.

Many of the in-flight staffing problems United States-based carriers face are not encountered by carriers based in other countries; while carriers outside the United States face some problems United States-based carriers do not face. Understanding these differences helps to identify those carriers most likely to provide the best service. United States carriers face a combination of unions (in some cases) and are in intense competition (in all cases). This combination keeps in-flight personnel from being able to provide all the services they might otherwise be willing to provide (because of union rules) and keeps pressure on to pay low in-flight salaries. As a result, one seldom encounters in-flight personnel in the United States who have fifteen to twenty years of experience or people who can look to substantially higher salaries in the future if they do an exceptional job in serving the clients on a daily basis. However, the work ethic in the United States is much stronger than in some other countries, resulting in a quality of service that is often superior to that rendered in other countries where there is a much lower work ethic. In addition, United States-based in-flight service crews know they can get fired if they do not perform to an acceptable quality standard. In some other countries and with some other carriers jobs are guaranteed no matter how the passenger is treated.

There are, however, airlines that pride themselves on their service. Crew members consider themselves to be professionals and in the standards of their countries being a flight crew member is an important status factor. Some of these airlines train their crew members on a continuous basis and the quality of service on the plane is definitely superior to average crew member service.

Identifying the carriers with such exceptional service is sometimes a challenge. Discussing carrier selection with experienced F.I.T. experts can sometimes give one some good choices. Even better is questioning F.I.T. clients after they have completed each trip. If a question relating to crew satisfaction is included in the post-trip discussion, a list of better and less-than-desireable carriers from the stand point of crew services can be put together in a very short time. However, because service quality standards can and do change, it is necesary to constantly update one's data and not depend upon information gleaned five or even ten years ago.

Seat Comfort

Seat comfort is to a considerable degree, a matter of statistics. Each airline provides seating charts and factual data on how wide the seat is, what the amount of leg room is and what the greatest angle of recline is in each category of seating (first class, business class, economy and discount class) on each of the planes that they fly. The F.I.T. specialist should study this data for those carriers that F.I.T. clients use. There are definite differences between carriers and between aircraft flown. Generally speaking, the larger the aircraft flown, the larger the seat; the more expensive the class of service, the larger the seat. Therefore, as a general rule, first-class passengers flying in 747's and 1011 aircraft will have the largest seats. Some carriers on longer flights provide what they call "beds" for first-class passengers flying across the Pacific Ocean on a Boeing 747 aircraft. By booking passengers on a larger aircraft, the F.I.T. specialist might be able to provide them with more seat comfort than by booking a flight on a smaller plane. Economy or discounted seats on a 747 often are actually larger than some smaller aircraft seats in first class.

The size of seats, however, is not the only factor relating to seat comfort. Leg room and the degree of chair recline are also important factors. Many carriers put as many chairs into an aircraft as possible—especially if the flight is a popular one. Even on long international flights, it is not at all unusual for a traveler seated in the economy/discounted section to find his knees pushing the tray table up when the seat in front is reclined.

One F.I.T. specialist commented, "There are no seats on the plane other than on the nonsmoking aisle." She meant that this type of seat is the only one she books (unless the client requests another type of seat). Aisle seats often do provide a little more leg room. Even more leg room is provided in the seats in the emergency exit row and in the front row of a section of seats. Because of the curvature of the aircraft, there are sometimes two seats toward the back of a section that have considerable leg room. This can be ideal for a couple traveling together.

The degree of recline is a factor many travel agents forget to consider. In some first-class sections, seats recline to a complete horizontal position, making for a very comfortable snoozing position. However, the degree of recline tends to become smaller as one progresses back from first class to business class to economy/discount class. Even in the first-class section, those seats at the very back row with the partition separating cabins immediately behind them will often not recline at all.

A new factor in airline seat competition has recently been introduced by Northwest Airlines. This is a built-in television at the back of each airplane seat slightly above the fold-out tray table. This feature offers the passenger the option of selecting one of several closed-circuit television programs and provides the traveler with a far wider range of entertainment options than has previously been available. Although Northwest is the first carrier to introduce this feature and it is already installed on its flights to the Far East, other airlines are seriously considering the introduction of back-of-the-seat built-in television consoles as well.

A final factor to consider in seating is the material from which seats are made. A carrier recently publicized that its aircraft seats were upholstered in pure leather. Those traveling on the carrier reported the seats to be less comfortable than the traditional fabric covering. Some fabrics, to be more durable, are rough and feel coarse to the touch. They may last longer, but they can be much more uncomfortable.

To get the best possible seats for your F.I.T. clients, make seating reservations in advance wherever possible. Many F.I.T. specialists will note the first day seating reservations are taken on flights for an itinerary being worked on in advance. They will place these dates in their computer reservation queues and access this queue each day as soon as they arrive at the agency. By being one of the first to reserve a seat, they can select the very best possible seats for their F.I.T. clients.

Size of Aircraft

The size of the aircraft is important for reasons other than just the size of the seats (although this is a very big factor). Larger aircraft often provide more amenities. Some have lounge sections in all classes of service. Some have separate sections for viewing films and sections where films are not shown. The largest planes provide much more room to get up and walk during a long flight. And, because of walk-in freezers and ovens, the food and beverage options are far greater in the larger aircraft. Finally, those who tend to have a fear of flying tend to fear it a lot less when they are on a very large aircraft rather than when flying in a small plane. By seating such clients in the middle of the plane, they can often avoid looking out windows at all and especially on a night flight, it is sometimes not too hard for them to imagine that they are not flying at all.

To determine the size of an aircraft, go back to the *Official Airline Guide* listing and look at the equipment code in the flight listing. This will be the second column from the right in the flight listing. Earlier in this chapter a reference was made to the *Official Airline Guide* listing of British Air flight number 552 (BA 552) from London to Rome. In reviewing that listing, one can see that the equipment flown on that flight is a "757." The equipment statistics are listed in the Worldwide edition of the *Official Airline Guide* under the title: "Airline Performance Statistics." By looking at the excerpt from a recent Worldwide edition of the *Official Airline Guide* (figure 7–5), one finds that the "757" code refers to a Boeing 757 (All Series). Going across the entry line on the listing for this code, one finds some keys to aircraft size relative to other aircraft. For example, the Boeing 757 can carry a passenger capacity of either 178 or 224 persons. This is much smaller than some other aircraft. For example, the Boeing 747, listed immediately before the Boeing 757, carries 430 passengers. Obviously, therefore, the Boeing 747 is a much larger aircraft than the Boeing 757. Other factors that indicate size are span and length. In reviewing the listing for the Boeing 757, one finds that the span is 124′ 6″ while the length is 155′ 3″. Again, this is considerably smaller than other aircraft, such as the 747 listed immediately before it. By reviewing these statistics in the Worldwide edition of the *OAG,* one can rapidly determine the relative size of the aircraft on which a client is being scheduled to fly.

GROUND CONSIDERATIONS

As important as in-flight considerations are in the selection of an air carrier, they should not be the only factors considered in selecting a carrier. Help while the F.I.T. client is on the ground is also important—especially in a country or area that is less developed or very different than the United States in its customs and culture. A number of countries give very definite preference in providing ground services to those flying in and out on the native carrier. This was so prevalent in Russia that Pan Am World Airways discontinued flights into Moscow for several years. Pan Am flyers were

AIRCRAFT PERFORMANCE STATISTICS

Code	Aircraft Type	No. of Engines	Aircraft Categories	Wide Body	DIMENSIONS: Span		Length		Gross Weight lbs.	Passenger Capacity#	TYPICAL PERFORMANCE: Pay load lbs.	Cruising Speed m.p.h.	Range miles	Pressurized
					ft.	in.	ft.	in.						
ATR	AEROSPATIALE/AERITALIA ATR 42 (ALL SERIES)	2	T		80	7	73	10	32,446	42/49	10,603	277		YES
SSC	AEROSPATIALE-BRITISH AEROSPACE (BAC) CONCORDE	4	J		83	10	203	9	400,000	108/128	25,000	1,400	3,800	YES
CRV	AEROSPATIALE CARAVELLE (ALL SERIES)	2	J		112	6	118	10	127,870	128/140	29,100	512	2,150	YES
NDH	AEROSPATIALE DAUPHIN HELICOPTER (ALL SERIES)	1	H				43	6	6,615	14		196	423	NO
AGH	AGUSTA A109 HELICOPTER	2	H		36	1	35	1 3/4	5,402	6		165	351	NO
AB3	AIRBUS INDUSTRIE (ALL SERIES)	2	J	YES	147	1	175	11	313,060	201/345	68,000	576	2,100	YES
AN2	ANTONOV AN22	4	T		211	3 1/2	189	7 1/2	551,156	28	99,208	375	3,107	
AN4	ANTONOV AN24	2	T		95	10	77	3	42,997	50	8,150	295	807	NO
AN6	ANTONOV AN26	2	T		95	9 1/2	77	2 1/2	49,297	50		280	342	
BEC	BEECHCRAFT (ALL SERIES)	2	T or P											NO
BEB	BEECHCRAFT BARON	2	P		37	10	28	0	5,120	4/6	1,965	225	1,085	NO
BEQ	BEECHCRAFT QUEEN AIR	2	P		50	3	35	6	8,800	7/11	3,578	214	1,185	NO
BEO	BEECHCRAFT TWIN BONANZA	2	P		45	11 1/2	31	6	6,300	5	2,230	201	1,110	NO
BE8	BEECHCRAFT 18	2	P		49	8	35	3	9,900	11/15	4,055	256	1,515	NO
BE9	BEECHCRAFT C99	2	T		45	8	44	6	10,900	15	5,123	280	1,150	NO
BH2	BELL HELICOPTER (ALL SERIES)	1	H		33	3	39	1	3,200	4	860	140	341	NO
70M	BOEING 707 (MIXED PASSENGER/FREIGHTER)	4	J		145	9	152	11	336,000	145	83,447	615	5,750	YES
707	BOEING 707 PASSENGER (ALL SERIES)	4	J		130	10	145	1	258,000	100/181	52,000	615	6,325	YES
727	BOEING 727 PASSENGER (ALL SERIES)	3	J		108	0	133	2	170,000	70/131	35,900	622	3,000	YES
72M	BOEING 727-100 (MIXED PASSENGER/FREIGHTER)	3	J		108		133	2	160,000	96	30,500	600		YES
72S	BOEING 727-200	3	J		108	0	153	2	191,000	145	40,670	622	2,400	YES
737	BOEING 737 PASSENGER (ALL SERIES)	2	J		93	0	94	0	111,000	115/138	29,093	577	1,300	YES
73M	BOEING 737-200 (MIXED PASSENGER/FREIGHTER)	2	J		93	0	100	2	125,000	115/130	33,561	573	1,800	YES
73S	BOEING 737-200/200C PASSENGER	2	J		93	0	100	2	120,000	115/130	34,050	577	2,300	YES
733	BOEING 737-300	2	J		94	9	105	7	135,000	138	35,500	550	2,500	YES
74M	BOEING 747 (MIXED PASSENGER/FREIGHTER)	4	J	YES	195	8	231	10	785,000	238	165,710	600	5,500	YES
747	BOEING 747 PASSENGER (ALL SERIES EXCEPT SP)	4	J	YES	195	8	231	10	833,000	452	134,000	557	6,500	YES
74L	BOEING 747 SP	4	J	YES	195	8	184	9	700,000	430	98,000	564	6,730	YES
757	BOEING 757 (ALL SERIES)	2	J		124	6	155	3	220,000	178/224	38,940	560	2,440	YES
767	BOEING 767 (ALL SERIES)	2	J	YES	156	1	159	2	312,000	211/290	69,000	550	4,500	YES
B11	BRITISH AEROSPACE (BAC) ONE-ELEVEN (ALL SERIES)	2	J		88	6	93	6	78,500	74/79	17,600	550	1,430	YES
VGP	BRITISH AEROSPACE (BAC-VICKERS) VANGUARD PASSENGER	4	T		118	0	122	10 1/2	146,500	97/139	21,500	405	2,910	YES
VCV	BRITISH AEROSPACE (BAC-VICKERS) VISCOUNT (ALL SERIES)	4	T		93	8 1/2	85	8	72,500	75	14,500	352	1,725	YES
HS7	BRITISH AEROSPACE (HAWKER SIDDELEY) 748 (ALL SERIES)	2	T		98	6	67	0	46,500	40/56	11,363	275	850	YES
TRD	BRITISH AEROSPACE (HAWKER SIDDELEY) TRIDENT (ALL SERIES)	3	J		95	0	114	9	135,500	103	24,500	606	2,700	YES
J31	BRITISH AEROSPACE JETSTREAM 31	2	T		52	0	47	1 1/2	12,566	18		282	1,380	YES
141	BRITISH AEROSPACE 146-100	4	J		86	5	85	10	74,600	88	17,277	460	1,450	YES
142	BRITISH AEROSPACE 146-200	4	J		86	5	93	8	89,500	100	21,000	460	1,450	YES
BNI	BRITTEN-NORMAN ISLANDER	2	P		49	0	35	8	6,300	10	2,000	260	425	NO
BNT	BRITTEN-NORMAN TRISLANDER	3	P		53	0	43	9	9,350	18	4,000	180		NO
CS2	CASA (CONSTRUCCIONES AERONAUTICAS, S.A.) NURT. C212 AVIOCAR	2	T		62	6	45	10	16,427	22/28	6,077	230	1,400	NO
CNA	CESSNA (ALL SERIES)	1 or 2	T or P											NO
CN2	CESSNA STATIONAIR 206	1	P		35	10	28	0	3,600	4/7	1,792	169	702	NO
CNT	CESSNA STATIONAIR 207	1	P		35	10	31	9	3,800	4/7	1,729	185	581	NO
CN4	CESSNA 402 TWIN TURBO	2	P		39	11	36	1	6,300	4/8	2,436	239	562	NO
CVR	CONVAIR (ALL SERIES)	2	T or P		105	4	79	2	54,600	56	11,200	350	1,100	YES
CV8	CONVAIR 880	4	J		120	0	129	4	193,000	90/104	25,650	615	2,994	YES
CWC	CURTISS-WRIGHT C46 COMMANDO	2	P		108	1	76	4	40,000	40/60	12,000	220	1,600	NO
DAM	DASSAULT-BREGUET MERCURE	2	J		100	3	114	3	120,150		32,850	574	1,094	YES
DHT	DEHAVILLAND OF CANADA DHC6 TWIN OTTER	2	T		65	0	51	9	12,500	20	4,420	209	745	NO
DH7	DEHAVILLAND OF CANADA DHC7 DASH-7	4	T		93	0	80	7	43,000	50	15,000	275	850	YES
DH8	DEHAVILLAND OF CANADA DHC8 DASH-8	2	T		84	0	75	6		32		300	691	
DHP	DEHAVILLAND OF CANADA BEAVER	1	P		48		30	3	5,100	10	1,800	143	733	
DHO	DEHAVILLAND OF CANADA OTTER	1	P		58	0	41	10	8,000	10	2,100	132	960	NO
DHB	DEHAVILLAND OF CANADA TURBO BEAVER	1	T		48	0	35	3	5,370	10	1,800	157	750	NO
DHH	DEHAVILLAND HERON	4	P		71	6	48	6	13,500	14/17	2,100	195		NO
DOS	DORNIER DO28 SKYSERVANT	2	P		51	1/4	37	1/4	8,852	15	3,000	160	708	
DO8	DORNIER 228 (ALL SERIES)	2	T		55	7	49	3	12,570	19	6,000	231	1,065	NO
EMB	EMBRAER EMB 110 BANDEIRANTE	2	T		50	2	49	5	12,500	19	5,000	262	900	NO
EM2	EMBRAER EMB 120 BRASILIA	2	T		64	10 3/4	64	8 1/2	12,295	30		288	628	YES
FK7	FAIRCHILD-HILLER FH227	2	T		95	2	83	1	43,500	44/52	11,500	294	1,520	YES
SWM	FAIRCHILD SWEARINGEN METRO	2	T		46	3	59	4	12,500	19	3,950	294	2,139	YES
F27	FOKKER F27 FRIENDSHIP/FAIRCHILD (ALL SERIES)	2	T		95	2	82	2	45,000	40/56	13,500	265	1,450	YES
F28	FOKKER F28 FELLOWSHIP (ALL SERIES)	2	J		82	3	96	2	73,000	85	19,623	523	1,055	YES
CD2	GOVERNMENT AIRCRAFT FACTORIES N22/N24 NOMAD	2	T		54	0	43	0	8,500	12/16	3,000	165	850	NO
GRA	GULFSTREAM AEROSPACE CORP. (GRUMMAN) ALBATROSS G-111	2	A		96	8	61	3	31,000	28	7,965	160	1,500	NO
GRG	GULFSTREAM AEROSPACE CORP. (GRUMMAN) GOOSE	2	A		49	0	38	4	8,000	10	2,000	160	825	NO
GRS	GULFSTREAM AEROSPACE CORP. (GRUMMAN) GULFSTREAM (SERIES II, III)	2	T		78	4	63	9	36,000	18/37	4,300	345	2,300	YES
GRM	GULFSTREAM AEROSPACE CORP. (GRUMMAN) MALLARD	2	A		66	8	48	4	12,750	10	1,950	180	1,245	NO
HPH	HANDLEY PAGE HERALD	2	T		113	0	96	10	82,000	60/74	12,000	266	3,150	YES
HPJ	HANDLEY PAGE JETSTREAM	2	T		52	0	47	1	12,550	14/18	4,100	250	1,440	YES
IL4	ILYUSHIN IL14	2	P		104	0	69	11	36,380	18/24	4,800	224	1,250	NO
IL8	ILYUSHIN IL18	4	T		122	8 1/2	117	9 1/2	119,000	75/125	30,860	403	1,860	YES
IL6	ILYUSHIN IL62	4	J		141	3 1/2	174	2	347,224	186	50,706	528	5,716	YES
ILW	ILYUSHIN IL86	4	J	YES	157	8 1/4	197	6 1/2	454,152	350		575		YES
LOE	LOCKHEED ELECTRA L188	4	T		99	0	104	6 1/2	116,000	66/104	22,000	405	2,750	YES
LOM	LOCKHEED ELECTRA L188 MIXED CONFIGURATION	4	T		99		104	6	116,000			390	2,200	
L10	LOCKHEED L1011 (ALL SERIES)	3	J	YES	155	3	177	7	430,000	250/400	95,500	615	3,450	YES
L15	LOCKHEED L1011-500	3	J	YES	155	4	164	2 1/2	496,000	246/330	115,000	580	5,998	YES
MR4	MARTIN 404	2	P		93	3	74	7	44,900	44	9,500	255	900	YES
DC3	MCDONNELL DOUGLAS DC3/DAKOTA C47	2	P		95	0	64	6	25,200	21/30	7,380	207	1,330	NO
DC4	MCDONNELL DOUGLAS DC4/SKYMASTER C54	4	P		117	6	93	11	73,800	44/80	11,440	230	2,750	NO
DC6	MCDONNELL DOUGLAS DC6 (ALL SERIES)	4	P		117	6	101	6	93,200	52/80	12,310	309	3,070	YES
DC8	MCDONNELL DOUGLAS DC8 (ALL SERIES)	4	J		142	3	150	5	315,000	116/176	34,000	544	7,010	YES
D8S	MCDONNELL DOUGLAS DC8 (ALL 60/70 SERIES)	4	J		142	3	187	4	325,000	259	66,665	580	7,150	YES
D8M	MCDONNELL DOUGLAS DC8 (MIXED PASSENGER/FREIGHTER)	4	J		142	4	187	5	325,000	180/259	66,665	600	3,700	YES
DC9	MCDONNELL DOUGLAS DC9-10 AND 20 SERIES	2	J		93	3	104	4	98,000	90	20,850	593	2,200	YES
D9S	MCDONNELL DOUGLAS DC9-30, 40, 50 AND 80 SERIES	2	J		93	3	125	6	121,000	125	27,925	593	2,700	YES
D95	MCDONNELL DOUGLAS DC9-50	2	J		93	3	133	5	122,200	139	32,615	593	2,550	YES
M80	MCDONNELL DOUGLAS DC9 SUPER 80	2	J		107	10	147	10	140,000	137/172		576	3,060	YES
D10	MCDONNELL DOUGLAS DC10 (ALL SERIES)	3	J	YES	155	3	182	3	455,000	250/380	98,490	608	6,350	YES
MIH	MIKHAIL MIL HELICOPTER	2	H		50	2 1/2	108	10 1/4	26,455	28		140	311	
MU2	MITSUBISHI MU2	2	T		39	2	39	5	11,575	8		347	1,606	
YS1	NIHON (NAMCO) YS11	2	T		105	0	86	3	51,800	52/60	12,550	292	1,980	YES
ND2	NORD AVIATION 262/MOHAWK 298	2	T		71	10	63	3	23,370	27	5,810	240	500	YES
PN6	PARTENAVIA P68	2	P		39	4 1/2	31	4	4,387	7		185	1,312	
PL6	PILATUS TURBO PORTER	1	T		49	8	35	9	4,850			151	644	
PAZ	PIPER AZTEC	2	P		37	4	31	2	5,200	6	2,151	206	1,519	NO
PA6	PIPER AERO STAR 601	2	T		34	2	54	9	5,500	6	240	250	1,400	YES
PAC	PIPER CHEROKEE	1	P		32	10	27	8	3,400	6/7	1,544	167	856	NO
PAH	PIPER NAVAJO/MOHAVE/CHIEFTAIN	2	P		40	6	34	6	7,000	8		254	1,019	NO
PAS	PIPER SENECA	2	P		38	11	28	6	4,570	6/7	1,747	219	1,036	NO
PA1	PIPER T-1040	2	T		41	1	36	8	9,000	9	3,800	250	900	NO
ACD	ROCKWELL COMMANDER (ALL SERIES)	2	P		49	6	35	1	6,750	5/7	2,750	205	1,220	YES
SF3	SAAB-FAIRCHILD 340	2	T		70	4	63	9	25,020	34		300	920	YES
SA2	SAUNDERS ST-27-ST2	2	T		71	6	59	0	13,500	23		230		NO
SHP	SHORT BROS. SKYLINER	2	T		64	11	40	0	12,500	19	4,600	188	694	YES
SHS	SHORT BROS. SKYVAN	2	T		64	11	40	1	12,500	19		188	694	
SH3	SHORT BROS. 330	2	T		74	8	58	0	22,000	30	7,500	218	1,137	NO
SH6	SHORT BROS. 360	2	T		74	10	70	10	26,000	36	7,500	244	1,151	NO
S58	SIKORSKY S-58ET HELICOPTER	1 or 2	H		56	0	47	3	13,000	7/16		127	278	NO
S61	SIKORSKY S61 HELICOPTER	1 or 2	H		62	0	72	0	19,000	26/28	6,000	139	282	NO
TU3	TUPOLEV TU134	2	J		95	2	112	9	98,100	64/72	14,330	546	1,490	YES
TU5	TUPOLEV TU154	3	J		123	2 1/2	157	1 3/4	198,410	164	44,090	605	3,280	YES
WLH	WESTLAND W30 HELICOPTER	2	H		43	8	52	2	12,350	17/21			100	
YK2	YAKOVLEV YAK 42	3	J		112	2 1/2	119	4 1/4	114,640	100/120	20,000	510	621	YES
YK4	YAKOVLEV YAK40	3	J		82	1	66	9	35,270	34/40	5,070	342	1,240	YES

Fig. 7-5. The size of an aircraft can be located in the performance statistics printed in the *OAG*. (Reprinted by special permission from the October 1988 edition of the *Official Airline Guide* Worldwide edition. Copyright © 1988, Official Airline Guide. All rights reserved.)

always treated far worse than those flying on Aeroflot, the Russian national carrier. When they arrived, they had to wait to clear customs, immigration, and health checks until all Aeroflot flights had been cleared. Fewer inspectors were assigned to clear Pan Am passengers, resulting in longer lines, and baggage checks were more frequent. Clients were told by the Russian airport staff people that they would be treated better if they flew with Aeroflot and they were encouraged to change their outbound flights from Pan Am to Aeroflot. Pan Am was allowed to have only one office in Moscow, while Aeroflot maintained offices in many locations. This made changes in schedules and reconfirmations much easier with Aeroflot.

The same type of prejudice is prevalent in many countries. Usually it is toned down considerably from the extreme Pan Am/Aeroflot example given previously, but the preferential service given to those flying with the national carrier is provided by government officials in many countries of the world. Therefore, F.I.T. specialists should always consider the native carrier when selecting an air carrier for their clients. It might mean the difference between a comfortable transit through the arrival and departure airports and a transit that is very uncomfortable. It might also mean the difference between spending hours to reconfirm flight changes and the ability to reconfirm or change on-going or return flights in a very short time.

SUMMARY

The cost, the comfort, and the convenience of the F.I.T. client all need to be considered in selecting an air carrier vendor. Sometimes there is only one choice available, but most of the time a wide range of choices of carriers exists. Scheduling convenience is usually the first criterion used in selecting a carrier. Most travelers do not want to wait several hours to take a flight on a carrier. On the other hand, convenience is sometimes sacrificed when there will be a major difference in the comfort level. Other convenience factors that are to be considered include airport location, transit time, transit convenience, on-going flight connections, and the availability of nonstop flights. Cost is important. Usually a client will take a less expensive flight if the class of service is reasonably good and the timing is good. Cost, therefore, is often the deciding factor in the selection of an air carrier. In-flight amenities such as stereo, in-flight films, and larger seats can all be important to F.I.T. clients. A part of these amenities include give-aways, such as free Japanese business cards provided to clients on Japan Air. Food and beverage is sometimes important. Many Western clients prefer to fly on a carrier that serves alcoholic beverages when traveling to a country in the Middle East where alcoholic beverages are not allowed. Native carriers, which do not serve alcoholic beverages, are sometimes preferred by those who do not drink and those who want to get a chance to taste the native food prior to arrival. In-flight personnel can make a big difference. Experienced flight attendants can make a world of difference in the comfort level of passengers on long as well as short international flights. Size of aircraft and seating comfort tend to go together and both make a difference in the comfort of passengers. The larger carriers have larger seats (the economy section seats on many 747's are as large as the first class seats on the 707's). In addition, there are lounges on some of the larger aircraft, allowing passengers to have some ability to move around the aircraft. Ground considerations are also important. Native carriers are sometimes given preferential treatment when clearing passengers through customs, immigration, baggage, and health checks upon arrival in the destination country.

All in all, there are a number of factors that go into considering an air carrier for an F.I.T. client. If one is not sure which of these factors will be of importance to the particular client, it behooves the F.I.T. specialist to ask. An economical, comfortable flight can go a long way toward earning a repeat client. An uncomfortable, expensive flight can sometimes mean losing a client.

■   ■   ■

❏ *REVIEW QUESTIONS*

1. What are the major criteria for selecting an air carrier for an F.I.T. client?
2. What makes the degree of selection sometimes quite limited?
3. What aspects of convenience should be considered in selecting an air carrier?
4. Why might an F.I.T. client prefer to fly with a carrier that has one or more stops en route as compared with nonstop flights?
5. What is the major factor relating to schedule convenience for most F.I.T. clients?
6. What is considered one of the best flight departure times for F.I.T. clients? Why?
7. At what time are most of the departures of the Hemphill-Harris World Air Cruise scheduled?
8. By what time do F.I.T. clients prefer to arrive at destination hotels? Why?
9. If there is a choice of international departure airports in a city, what factors should be considered in selecting a departure airport for the F.I.T. client?
10. Under what circumstances should the F.I.T. specialist select an air carrier that pays a higher than normal commission?
11. Which in-flight considerations can be important to F.I.T. clients? Why?

12. What are some of the give-aways provided by international air carriers?
13. Why should a flight without in-flight movies be selected for F.I.T. clients who prefer not to watch a movie?
14. Why would an F.I.T. specialist not select a native carrier for a client flying to the Middle East? Why might the F.I.T. specialist select the middle eastern country's native carrier?
15. How does the F.I.T. specialist find out which carriers are known for their international cuisines?
16. What factors might an F.I.T. specialist use to determine the expected quality of service from in-flight personnel?
17. What type of equipment generally provides the largest seats with the best amount of leg room?
18. Why might an F.I.T. client be more comfortable on a 747 than on a 707 aircraft?

❏ ROLE PLAY EXERCISE

Two students may participate in this role play either out of class as a fun way to review the chapter or as in in-class exercise. One plays the role of the client and the other plays the role of the travel agency's F.I.T. specialist. Please read the script and then pick up the conversation in your own words.

F.I.T. SPECIALIST: You will be staying in Paris for two days and then flying on to Leningrad. When it comes to selecting air carriers for these flights, do you have any preferences?

F.I.T. CLIENT: I would prefer a larger aircraft, but I guess there are a large number of airlines that fly to London, aren't there? Do many fly from London to Leningrad?

F.I.T. SPECIALIST: Yes and no. There are ten to twelve airlines that fly to London when one takes into consideration both international airports that serve London. But there is only one airline that flies directly from London to Leningrad, Aeroflot, the Russian national carrier. Even with a change of planes in Amsterdam or Paris, you will be flying into Leningrad with Aeroflot.

F.I.T. CLIENT: I guess I am stuck with Aeroflot. What are the advantages and disadvantages of flying with them? In other words, what should I expect? And of the ten or twelve that fly to London, are there any differences that I should consider, other than price of course?

F.I.T. SPECIALIST: Let's start with the good and bad aspects of flying with Aeroflot. The major benefit you will find in flying with them is . . .

Continue on your own.

AIR VENDOR SELECTION

AIR CARRIER SELECTION EXERCISE

ASSIGNMENT: You are the travel agency's F.I.T. specialist. Mrs. Johnson is at your desk discussing the upcoming trip of Mr. and Mrs. Johnson to Acapulco. You have discussed alternative air carrier choices. You have found that there are no direct flights from Denver to Acapulco, but the following options are available.

7:15a	10:25a	IAH		CO	440	FYQMV	727	B	0
	11:05a	IAH	12:35p	CO	233	FYQMV	72S	L	0
7:40a	10:23a	DFW		FL	130	FYQKV	73S	F	0
	11:25a	DFW	12:43p	AA	369	FYBQM	72S	L	0
9:00a	2:35p	MEX		MX	945	Y	72S	LS	2
	3:25p	MEX	4:10p	MX	311	Y	D95	L	0
9:00a	3:00p	MEX		MX	919	Y	72S	LS	2
	7:00p	MEX	7:45p	MX	729	Y	72S	S	0
3:35p	8:10p	MEX		MX	917	Y	72S	DS	1
	9:45p	MEX	10:35p	MX	317	Y	M80	S	0

Taking into consideration the points raised in this chapter, select flights for Mr. and Mrs. Johnson and show them on the itinerary on the next page. Explain your reasons for the selections you made below.

REASONS: _____

_____

_____

_____

AIR VENDOR SELECTION

AIR CARRIER SELECTION EXERCISE

ITINERARY FOR _____

TRIP _____

_____ Lv _____

_____ Ar _____

_____

_____ Lv _____

_____ Ar _____

_____

_____ Lv _____

_____ Ar _____

_____

_____ Lv _____

_____ Ar _____

_____

_____ Lv _____

_____ Ar _____

_____

_____ Lv _____

_____ Ar _____

_____

_____ Lv _____

_____ Ar _____

_____

Because schedules are sometimes subject to change without notice, or delayed, we should like to suggest in the interest of good service, that you check the above departure time before leaving for the airport or station.

HOTEL VENDOR
SELECTION FACTORS

MAJOR SELECTION FACTORS

There are four major factors to be considered when selecting a hotel for a client. These are: (1) the cleint, (2) the hotel as it relates to F.I.T. travel, (3) the location, and (4) the cost. These factors have not been listed in their order of importance. All four major selection factors are important and a hotel should meet the minimal levels of expectancy in all four areas if it is to be considered. It should not be presumed that the four major selection factors are comprehensive. If several hotels seem to equally meet the four major criteria, additional criteria can be determined in order to make a final selection. In addition, the client may have special criteria that must be met. For example, if the client is in a wheelchair, handicap ramps and elevators will be essential and will become one of the first determinants to be considered. In studying the major selection factors, each will be considered on its own.

The Client

As discussed in the chapter on client analysis, it is essential that the travel agent know the client, the client's interests, requirements, and preferences. Knowing the specific client's needs might take time to develop, but if the client is to be happy with the hotels selected, taking the time to identify specifics relating to the client's needs will be well worth it. Since these factors seldom change radically, once the preferences are determined, they can be drawn upon for future F.I.T.s. Some of the kinds of questions that might be considered are:

1. Does a client prefer a close-in, downtown, street-front hotel in the shopping, theater, or financial district or does the client prefer a hotel with grounds, gardens and/or a scenic view?

2. Is a small, business-like, rapid in-and-out lobby preferred or does the client expect a large well-appointed lobby?
3. Would the client prefer an intimate small hotel where most or all staff members know his/her name or is a vast spread-out hotel with many choices of dining rooms, in-hotel entertainment, and facilities/services more desirable?
4. Would the client prefer a room facing the street with some street noise, but with a sweeping view or would a quieter inside or back-of-the-hotel room with less or no view be preferable?
5. How important is twenty-four-hour room service?
6. Must the room be expensive and very well appointed or is a comfortable but more modestly appointed room acceptable?
7. How large a bathroom does the client expect to have and are there any specific bathroom facilities (such as a phone in the bathroom) required by the client?
8. Does the client insist on a venerable hotel with an excellent reputation or is a sleek, modern, recently built hotel preferred?
9. Does the client insist upon a large amount of personal service and if so, what range of staff-to-client ratio should the travel agent be looking for?
10. How esential is it that local sightseeing companies have a desk in the hotel and/or use the hotel as a pick-up and drop-off point?
11. Are hotel health clubs, golf courses, tennis courts, swimming pools, and other sporting facilities important?
12. If at a beach location, does the client insist on being right on the beach, or would across the street be okay? How essential is it to have a beach front room as compared to one with a beach view or a room not providing a view of the beach?
13. How important is the concierge to the client? Is this a client who can be expected to rely heavily on the hotel's concierge or is the client so worldly that very little or no concierge reliance can be expected?
14. What type of housekeeping service is expected? Does the client expect triple sheeting, down comforters and pillows, maid service two or three times a day, turn-down service, etc.?
15. If the client will be driving, is valet parking preferred or would the client prefer the convenience of self-parking?
16. Does the client expect to be on an executive suite floor with appropriate executive services, limited elevator access, and a serve-yourself buffet dining facility on the floor?
17. How important is having an English-language newspaper slipped under the door each morning?
18. Is in-room coffee and/or an in-room stocked bar important?

These are a few of the kinds of questions the F.I.T. specialist needs to ask of the client in order to determine the hotel that will best meet the client's needs. In most cases the ideal hotel will not be found. A compromise might need to be made. If so, the F.I.T. specialist will need to know exactly what facilities and/or services the client might prefer to have, but will not be able to have in the available choice of hotels. And, the F.I.T. specialist will need to point out the pros and cons of hotel alternatives when compromises must be made or when there are two hotels that seem to closely meet the needs of clients. A good example is the Grande Bretagne and the King George hotels in Athens. They are similar in deluxe facilities and in an excellent location. Nevertheless, there are F.I.T. clients who have very definite preferences for each of them. Both cater to royalty and both are considered top F.I.T. client hotels. However, there are definite differences between the two hotels and it would be beneficial for the F.I.T. specialist to describe the differences for an F.I.T. client who has never been to Athens before.

The Hotel as It Relates to F.I.T. Travel

Some hotels cater to and are excellent for F.I.T. clients. Others cater to budget travelers, conventions and groups, or overnight business professionals. Others cater to a mixed clientele group, including F.I.T. clients. It would be nice if the hotel guides would add a section to the individual property descriptions pointing out the target audience(s) of each property. If they did, a large number of hotels would be eliminated immediately for consideration for F.I.T. clients. Perhaps it is for that reason that no guide publishes target audience data. Nevertheless, it is part of the job of the F.I.T. specialist to identify those properties that want F.I.T. clients and that make a real effort to attract F.I.T. clients. If the F.I.T. specialist has not been to the hotel or to the destination city, reading guide descriptions and talking to booking representatives of the hotels should help. For example, Scott Feinerman, North American marketing and sales manager for the Carlton Hotel, Singapore, and the Sahid group of hotels, Indonesia (213-662-4772), advises that he is always delighted to get a call from F.I.T. specialists having clients who are traveling to the Far East. Many of his hotels are in the more exotic cities of the world and he is especially pleased to advise about locations, sites, and to discuss the pros and cons of the hotels and make specific recommendations appropriate to individual clients. Matching the hotel and its amenities to the preferences of the F.I.T. client results in repeat clients and strong word-of-mouth referrals. Many hotel representation executives feel the same as Scott and take the time to provide exact recommendations and the reasons for them.

Some who are new to developing F.I.T.s express concern about finding hotel representation firms. Indeed, locating lists of representative firms can sometimes be a challenge. The following resources provide lists of thousands of international hotels and their representative companies. Almost all hotel representative companies have toll-free "800" numbers in the United States and can be called at no expense to the travel agency. Perhaps the most comprehensive hotel and hotel representative listings are in the *Official Hotel and Resort Guide* (O.H.R.G.). This guide comes in three editions and is available from the following source: Official Hotel and Resort Guide, 1845 West Carroll, Chicago, Illinois, 60612.

The first edition of the *O.H.R.G.* is devoted to hotels and resorts in the United States and except for booking overnight stays in gateway cities, it is of little value to F.I.T. specialists who, by definition, work on international client trips. The second edition covers Europe (both Eastern and Western Europe, including the U.S.S.R.). The third edition covers the rest of the world. It starts with Canada, moves to the Caribbean, Mexico, and Central and South America, and the last part of the edition covers Africa, Asia, Australia, and the Pacific. Each section of each edition starts with a listing of hotel representatives and hotel chains. There is an alphabetical listing by hotel representative/chain code (normally a three or a four letter code) identifying the hotel representative company that goes along with the code and referencing a page number for the hotel representation company. When one looks up the reference page for the hotel representation/chain company, one finds a listing that will include address, telephone number, telex number, fax number, and other related data. Often cross-reference data is also included. As noted, this is perhaps the most complete reference of hotel

Fig. 8-1. F.I.T. clients often insist on staying in the finest hotels. The Grand Hotel in Stockholm is one of the best. (Courtesy of The Leading Hotels of the World.)

representation companies in any major travel industry reference publication. Other advantages of reviewing hotels listed in the *O.H.R.G.* include: (1) often photos of the hotels are in the listing for the hotel; (2) hotel representation firms are presented next to the listing of each hotel so that one can rapidly identify what hotel representation company to contact in order to book a room for a client at that property; (3) the cost of all hotels is provided in local currency (and sometimes in American dollars); and, (4) perhaps most important, the *O.H.R.G.* guarantees commissions. This unique *O.H.R.G.* commission guarantee is especially welcome to many agency owners and executives. The process to follow if a hotel does not pay the travel agency is to send a card to the hotel advising that the *O.H.R.G.* will not list that hotel in the next year's edition of the *O.H.R.G.* unless the agency is paid. If the payment is still not forth coming, notification to the *O.H.R.G.* will bring a note from the *O.H.R.G.* representative to the senior hotel marketing executive for the property advising that the hotel will not be listed in the next edition unless the agency receives its commission. Finally, if the agency does not receive its commission within a reasonable period of time, the *O.H.R.G.* will follow through and not list the property in the next edition. As a result of this process, travel agency management and F.I.T. specialists can be confident that the vast majority of all reservations made for clients in properties listed in the *Official Hotel and Resort Guide* will result in the receipt of commissions knowing that the hotels listed have a history of paying commissions rather than risking not being listed in the guide the next year.

Other excellent sources for listings of hotel representative firms include *Travel 800* (813–980–6200; Cable Travel Publications, 1411 Cumpston St., North Hollywood, CA 91601) and the American Society of Travel Agents Membership Roster (703-739-ASTA, 1101 King Street, Alexandria, Virginia 22314). The *Travel 800* publication has the additional advantage of listing the "800" numbers, which are toll-free, for each of the hotel representation firms. The ASTA membership listing has the advantage of identifying hotel representation companies that support the American Society of Travel Agents with their membership and therefore tend to be stronger in their support of retail travel agents than some other hotel representation firms. This does not mean that if a hotel representation firm is not listed in the American Society of Travel Agents Roster that hotel representation firm is not good. It simply indicates that those that are members tend to support the travel agency association and the association encourages return support by travel agents.

Another excellent hotel guide, utilized by a large number of F.I.T. specialists is a guide that is designed primarily for selecting hotels for F.I.T. clients. This is the *Star Guide to Elegant Properties* (c/o ABC International, 131 Clarendon Street, Boston, MA 02116). The *Star Guide* does not take advertisements and it has a team of unbiased observers who stay in listed hotels and write their exact impressions. They provide both favorable and unfavorable comments about the hotels. Of special value to F.I.T. specialists, they often provide comments on individual rooms and hotel amenities. These comments can help the F.I.T. specialist to select not only a better hotel, but better rooms in hotels and a hotel with an amenity package matching the needs of the F.I.T. client.

Specialized guides are often available for the selection of special types of properties throughout the world. Many of these guides can be located by looking in the *Books In Print* publication available in large commercial book stores throughout the United States. These hotel guides vary from year to year, but often include some top quality hotel guides that specialize in regional properties or properties of one particular type (castle hotels, for example). For those who speak other languages, hotel guide publications in French, German, Spanish, and other languages are often available through national tourist bureau listings. These guides sometimes provide information on properties not published in any English language version. Simply write to the consulate or the tourist bureau of the destination country and ask for a listing of hotels and/or hotel representation firms.

In reading guide descriptions, some of the things that one should look for include: (1) the hotel's star ratings; (2) hotel restaurant star ratings; (3) staff-to-client ratios; (4) special services and/or amenities; and, (5) the few guide book client references that are sometimes made. Each of these factors are discussed in the following paragaraphs.

Hotel Star Ratings   Hotel star ratings are designed to give the client or agent who is reading a hotel brochure or a guide book some idea as to the quality of a hotel. Unfortunately, however, the star rating system can be confusing. Since there is no international agreement on how a star rating system will work, the criteria for awarding one or more stars to a hotel varies with the authors/editors of guide books, policies of countries—regions or cities, or with the concern of person(s) who have made the evaluation on which the star ratings are to be based. Adding to this confusion is the fact that the total number of stars that can be awarded will vary as well. Some are five-star systems. Others are four-star systems. A few others can range from a maximum of three stars on up to ten stars as a maximum. Therefore, when one learns that a certain property might be a four-star hotel, one must then determine whether this is based on a four-star system, a five-star system, or some other system.

The hotel star rating system does provide a guideline, however, to the quality and range of services and amenities of a hotel. All the major guides will have a section that deciphers their star system, indicating the number of maximum stars in the system and the major factors considered in awarding stars to a hotel. By reviewing this section of the guides, F.I.T. specialists will know whether a four-star hotel is one ranked at the top and is to be considered one of the very best hotels in the region or if a four-star hotel is somewhat below the best (five star being best).

Restaurant Star Ratings   The restaurants in many of the better hotels of the world are often rated by culinary associations, national tourist boards, restaurant associations, and restaurant guides. When a hotel has one or more restaurants that are considered among the best in the city, region, or country, one will often find that the hotel is of top quality as well. Occasionally a hotel's reputation is built around that of its restaurant. The Sacher Hotel in Vienna, for example, is known for its restaurant that is known for its internationally famous Sacher Torte. Though many an F.I.T. client plans to dine at the restaurant, finishing the meal with a Sacher Torte, the availability of some of the best hotels in the world being located in Vienna results in most F.I.T. clients selecting a hotel with a larger range of amenities. This is not to say that the Sacher Hotel is not a fine hotel, but rather that there are so many excellent hotels in Vienna to choose from. Nevertheless, it should be kept in mind that there is a strong correlation between top quality restaurants and top quality hotels.

Staff-to-Client Ratios   Staff to client ratios are often hard to find. Some tourists bureaus will provide staff/client ratio data for the better properties in their country, most hotels will provide the data if it is specifically requested, and the *Star Guide to Elegant Properties* provides staff/client data for some of the hotel properties it lists. Obviously the more even the staff-to-client ratio, the more personal service clients can expect. A hotel with one staff person for each thirty clients will provide much less service than a hotel with a staff person for every five clients. There are a few hotels in the world where the ratio is better than even, for example, there are more staff members than clients. Obviously, these hotels cater to F.I.T. clients and provide a very high level of personal service.

Special Services and/or Amenities   All but budget hotels try to stress the importance of their services and amenities. In reviewing these services and amenities in the hotel guide books and the hotel's own literature, it is important to identify which of the services and amenities are directed to F.I.T. clients and which ones are directed to other types of clients. Most F.I.T. clients prefer to stay in those properties that offer specific services and amenities for them although some do not mind staying in properties that cater to other clients as well. Determine whether or not the property is also directing its services and amenities toward attracting large groups. Many F.I.T. clients prefer not to be in hotels that work with very large groups because the F.I.T. client in such an environment can sometimes be treated in a less than desirable manner.

Guide Book Client References   Hotel guides and travel guide books usually do not specifically indicate that a hotel caters to F.I.T. clients (or to any other specific group of clients). However, sometimes references are made to the types of clients that are attracted to the hotel. One must be careful in evaluating these statements when they appear in hotel guides as the descriptive sections on hotels are frequently written by hotel marketing personnel themselves and can be quite biased. The *Star Guide,* unlike most, does not accept hotel advertisements and does provide considerable editorializing in its evaluations. The descriptions sometimes specifically indicate the type of clients, but more often, they suggest appropriate client types. Such words as "family hotel" or "few groups" can give the reader a good idea as to whether or not this is a hotel that should be considered.

Location

Another major factor to consider when selecting a hotel for an F.I.T. client is location. Transportation to and/or from a hotel is sometimes a concern if the client will not have a rental car. Some hotels and resorts, however, have airport or rail station pickup and delivery, making a rental car less necessary. Some F.I.T. clients prefer to stay in a hotel close to the places they will be visiting. A client going to Paris might ask for a hotel within walking distance of the Louvre museum, for example. Or a client destined for Rome might request the Hassler because of its convenience to chic shops and sightseeing. The F.I.T. specialist needs to determine how important convenience is to the client before suggesting a hotel that might be out of the way.

Cost

Although many F.I.T. clients might give the impression that cost is less important than quality, most clients will want to consider cost factors. As pointed out in the costing section of the book, it is usually better to discuss cost in terms of a total budget for the trip rather than individual hotel costs. If in the early stages of discussion an overall budget has been agreed upon and a level of hotel quality and hotel costs have been considered when working out the overall budget, hotel selection becomes a matter of finding the hotel that best suits the client's needs for the money budget. In following along with this process, it is usually best to break out a total accommodations cost from the total budget, divide by the number of hotel nights, and determine an average budgeted price per hotel night. This figure then becomes the guideline for making hotel selection cost decisions. If a hotel is slightly higher than the budgeted price per hotel night and other hotels on the itinerary will be slightly lower than the budgeted price per hotel night, the slightly higher hotel can be kept. Alternately, if all hotels selected exceed the budgeted price per hotel night, either the budget will need to be changed or the category/quality of hotel will need to be changed.

SUMMARY

Hotels for F.I.T. clients are selected on the basis of four major factors. Perhaps the most critical of these is the range of client preferences. A number of questions have been presented to elicit the preferences a client might have relating to hotels. A second factor is the hotel itself and how the hotel relates to F.I.T. clients. Most hotels cater to some type(s) of client(s) and many do not cater to F.I.T. clients. It is important to match the needs of clients with the amenities and services provided by hotels that cater to F.I.T. clients. A third important factor is location. Transportation considerations make hotel location important or unimportant, but so do the preferences of clients. The cost of a hotel is the final major consideration in the selection of a hotel. By breaking out the total accommodation budget into a daily average cost, the affordability of individually selected hotels can be rapidly judged. Although these four criteria for the selection of hotels for F.I.T. clients are the major criteria, they are not the only criteria. If several hotels seem to weigh equally or almost equally after analyzing them on the basis of these criteria, additional criteria should be considered in order to make a final decision.

■   ■   ■

❏ *REVIEW QUESTIONS*

1. What are the four major factors to consider when selecting a hotel for an F.I.T. client?
2. What are some of the questions a travel agency F.I.T. specialist might ask to determine the preferences a client might have regarding hotels and hotel room selections?
3. What are some of the ways in which the agency's F.I.T. specialist might find out if a hotel specializes in handling F.I.T. clients?
4. Is a four-star rating the best a hotel can possibly have?
5. What is meant by the term "Staff/Client Ratio"?
6. What are some examples of services and amenities a hotel might offer to attract F.I.T. clients?
7. What guide books might provide the best help in selecting a hotel for an F.I.T. client?
8. Why is location considered important in the process of selecting a hotel for an F.I.T. client?
9. How does the F.I.T. specialist determine the average daily hotel cost that is "affordable" for an F.I.T. client?

❏ *ROLE PLAY EXERCISE*

Two students may participate in this role play either out of class as a fun way to review the chapter or as an in-class exercise. One plays the role of the client and the other plays the role of the travel agency's F.I.T. specialist. Please read the script and then pick up the conversation in your own words.

F.I.T. SPECIALIST: I want to select the very best hotel and hotel room for you. We have some excellent reference material here at the agency and as a staff we have been in most of the best hotels in the world. However, my concern is to make sure that the hotels we select match your needs and wants.

F.I.T. CLIENT: That is very important to me, too. After all, my home away from home is the hotel that you tell me will be the best. How can I help in the selection process?

F.I.T. SPECIALIST: I will need to ask you a number of questions. It might take us some time and a few of the questions might seem elementary. Will it be okay?

F.I.T. CLIENT: No problem! Ask away!

Continue on your own.

HOTEL SELECTION FACTORS EXERCISE NUMBER ONE

ASSIGNMENT: You are the travel agency's F.I.T. specialist. Mrs. Johnson is at your desk discussing the upcoming trip of Mr. and Mrs. Johnson to Acapulco. You have asked Mrs. Johnson a number of questions regarding her preferences and have found out the information noted below. You have also reviewed several guide books to find out what they have to say about the Acapulco hotels and you have received hotel brochures from several of the better properties. You have narrowed the decision to two hotels. The Acapulco Princess and Las Brisas. Information on the two hotels from the guides and from their own brochures has been summarized on the following pages. Based on your discussion with Mrs. Johnson, make a recommendation of one of these two hotels and write out what you will say to Mrs. Johnson to back up your recommendation.

Mrs. Johnson prefers:

A large hotel with formal grounds, gardens, and a scenic view. She likes to have a large, well-appointed lobby. Mrs. Johnson prefers to have a choice of dining rooms and likes formal dining with soft musical entertainment. Although she wants to avoid excessive noise, a small amount of noise is tolerable in exchange for an excellent view. Service is very important to Mrs. Johnson. She prefers twenty-four-hour room service. Mrs. Johnson usually travels with expensive jewelry, but she plans to spend time at the beach on this trip and will be bringing only a few items of jewelry with her. A safe deposit box will be sufficient for her on this trip. Mrs. Johnson often books suites. If she is not in a suite, she expects to have a very large comfortable room with high-quality appointments. Bath appointments are not particularly important. Nothing exceptional is required. Older elegant hotels are preferred as compared with sleek hotels. Mrs. Johnson always expects to have a large staff at the hotel. Service is important and is expected.

At destinations that are new for Mrs. Johnson, she prefers to take a number of sightseeing trips and expects to have a sightseeing desk in the hotel and to have both sightseeing bus pickup and delivery at the hotel. For repeat destinations, Mrs. Johnson rents a car—usually at the airport. She prefers to use a car rental company with a rental desk at the hotel. She will sometimes change hotels to get one that has a car rental desk.

Some sporting facilities are important to Mrs. Johnson. She does not play many sports and she plays no physically active sports well. However, she does golf and plays a little tennis. At the beach she likes to work on her tan rather than swim and she insists upon being at a private—or at least an exclusive beach. She will not go to a crowded public beach.

Mrs. Johnson prefers to be right on the water. She likes to take the elevator to the beach and will not consider being across a busy street from the beach. She wants a room that looks out over the water with a full ocean view.

At destinations that are new for Mrs. Johnson, she asks many questions of the concierge and expects considerable help in finding out where to go and how to get there. When she has been to a destination several times, her reliance on a concierge is far less. She still expects the hotel to have a concierge, but she will only use him for a few times as compared to constantly.

When Mrs. Johnson entertains in her room or suite, she is very fussy about housekeeping. She often does entertain. At other times, Mrs. Johnson expects good, constant housekeeping service, but two or three daily checks are usually sufficient. Mrs. Johnson does take a nap many afternoons and expects to have her bed made up shortly after getting up.

Mrs. Johnson prefers valet parking in downtown hotels and she prefers parking the car herself when at a villa or a resort.

Mrs. Johnson always prefers to be on the executive suite floor when this is available. She expects to have a fully stocked bar in her room or suite and prefers to have an English-language newspaper (the Wall Street Journal or the New York Times, if possible) each morning. She prefers to have it brought with the room-service breakfast.

ACAPULCO PRINCESS HOTEL INFORMATION

The Princess is a relatively new hotel (latest addition in 1982) about halfway between downtown and the airport and right on Revolcadero Beach. It is a visually striking resort in a pyramid shape. The resort is one of the largest in Mexico, offering a wide range of water sports, golf, and tennis. Used by large conventions and incentive operators, the resort hotel has its own activities director and its own tour program. Known for its excellent beach and lush gardens, the Princess also offers a full range of dining and evening entertainment facilities. These include a disco and a nightclub, eight restaurants (Mexican, serve-yourself buffet, formal, western, and a number of others), and four bars. Several of the restaurants have live bands offering a wide range of dance music.

LAS BRISAS

Voted one of the ten best hotels in the world by several reviewers, Las Brisas is considered by many to be Westin Hotels and Resorts' premier property. Located on a sloping hillside, the resort is a series of luxury casitas (private bungalows) each one with either a private or a two-casita shared swimming pool. The Presidential Suite features an even more deluxe casita with a private indoor/outdoor swimming pool. Pink and white jeeps are provided with each casita, if desired. The casitas feature fully stocked bars, continental breakfasts served through trap doors (to retain privacy), full marble baths, verandas surrounding the pools, and sweeping views of the ocean. There is twenty-four-hour room service and both fresh fruit and fresh flowers are put in each casita every day. There is twice-daily maid service and turn-down service at night. Membership at the La Concha Beach Club is included for each guest. The club is one of the best (some say it is the best) in Mexico. It offers a gourmet luncheon buffet, rolling bars, and an oyster bar. Sporting facilities include snorkeling, scuba diving, parasailing, sailing, waterskiing, tennis (five lighted courts), and golf (nearby). There is a large saltwater swimming pool and a smaller children's pool. Three formal dining facilities are available at Las Brisas ranging from an ocean-front open-air restaurant with a live band and quiet dance music to a mountaintop restaurant with sweeping views of Acapulco. Las Brisas is located betwen the airport and the city almost an equal distance between the two.

Identify the hotel you selected and describe your selection reasons:

_____

_____

_____

_____

_____

Voucher No. 5737

To _____

Address _____

In accordance with our instructions, kindly provide

M _____

_____

with the following

Confirmed by _____
This voucher not valid
unless officially stamped

Coupon
Value $ _____

VALUE STATED INCLUDES RESERVATIONS ONLY AS SPECIFIED. OTHER
CHARGES INCURRED SHOULD BE PAID DIRECTLY TO HOTEL OR OPERATOR
SUPPLYING ADDITIONAL SERVICES.

Please honor accommodations
as shown above.

Date issued _____

Confirmed by Ltr.   Phone   Telegram   Date _____   By _____
This party will arrive at _____ Via _____
On _____ 19____ At _____ M   From_____

Rate _____ $ _____   Paid-in-full commission of $ _____
Comm _____   _____   Full amt. to be collected:
Net _____   _____   commission due
Serv. Chg. _____   _____   Deposit check enclosed $ _____
Tax _____   _____   Commission due
Total _____   _____   Deposit net of Commission
                                             Enclosed $ _____

The Patron holds the original voucher and should surrender it in exchange for services. The
amount shown represents our collection for services specified. If additional charges are
incurred, you should collect the difference from the Patron. Kindly extend your usual
courtesies to this party and confirm these arrangements by air mail to us.

By _____
Authorized Signature

(Courtesy of Willow Press. Reprinted with permission.)

BOROBUDUR INTERCONTINENTAL

BOROBUDUR INTERCONTINENTAL	702R	Rene Proot, General Manager
ADDRESS Jalan Lapangan Baneterey Station	PHONE L1 21370108	CABLE Borobudur
CLASS TYPE Moderate Deluxe Hotel	TELEX BDQ JKT 4, 156	Extra charges SC 10% Tax 5%
AFFILIATIONS Intercontinental Hotels	RESERVATIONS IHC UIL or any Pan Am Office	COM R-10

DESCRIPTION/LOCATION Modern 18-story hotel (1974) on a 23-acre site in central Djakarata, on the south side of Memorial Square. Within easy reach of shops, government offices and tourist attractions—5 minute drive from city center and 20-minute drive from Halim Perdankusmah Airport.

ACCOMMODATIONS Well-decorated guest rooms including 8 cabanas, 46 suites and 18 business professional's suites with extra large sitting/conference rooms—most rooms are split-level, all have private bath, radio, individual climate control, and spectacular view—24-hour room service.

DINING/ENTERTAINMENT Kejo Japanese restaurant—Nelayan Seafood restaurant—Toba rotisserie featuring grilled specialities—Bogor brasserie for informal meals and snacks—Pendopo bar and Pendopo lounge, both with entertainment nightly—Poolside snack bar.

CONVENTION/BANQUET FACILITIES Eight meeting rooms accommodating up to 1400 persons for banquets or conferences and 2500 for receptions. All rooms with microphones, telephone and electrical outlets, and individual controls for heat, air-conditioning, and sound—Separate outside entrance—Separate banquet kitchen—Registration area.

OTHER FACILITIES/SERVICES Olympic size pool with lounge area—Children's pool—Health club with sauna, steam room and massage—Squash and tennis courts—Jogging track—Bowling—Secretarial and translation services—Offices and business professional's lounge—Newstand—Hair salon—Art gallery—Shops—Travel agent—Car rental, tour and airline desks—Heliport—Parking.

RATES: EUROPEAN PLAN

Single with Bath   (100)
Double with Bath   (110)
Triple   (120)
Suite   (290)

Credit cards honored: AE CB DC VISA

HOTEL SELECTION EXERCISE NUMBER TWO

Mr. and Mrs. Johnson wish to stay at a Western Hotel near the National Museum in Djakarta, Indonesia, and will be arriving on Flight 002 at 6:10 A.M. on June 7. They will be leaving on JAL flight number 256 at 7:00 P.M. on the 23rd of June. You have selected the Borobudur Intercontinental Hotel for them and at their request, you have selected a business professional's suite with an extra large sitting-conference room.

Complete the reservation form, on page 103, and emphasize that they will need to have both early check-in privileges and late check-out privileges, if at all possible. Any additional recommendations you can make should be noted.

SCANDINAVIAN ITINERARY DEVELOPMENT EXERCISE NUMBER TWO

This is a continuation from Scandinavian Itinerary Development Exercise Number One. Please refer back to it.

SITUATION: You have scheduled Mrs. Johnson and Mrs. Taymore for the following flights for the Scandinavian trip.

TUE	30	JUN	MEMSTL	TW 580	8:49 A.M.	9:53 A.M.
TUE	30	JUN	STLJFK	TW 298	10:52 A.M.	3:07 P.M.
TUE	30	JUN	JFKCPH	TW 816	6:30 P.M.	10:20 A.M.
+1 (WED	01	JUL)				
SUN	12	JUL	CPHTRD	SK 842	10:10 P.M.	11:50 P.M.
MON	13	JUL	TRDFBU	BU 151	3:25 P.M.	4:15 P.M.
WED	15	JUL	FBUARN	SK 490	11:05 A.M.	12:00 Noon
SUN	19	JUL	ARNJFK	TW 817	9:05 A.M.	2:15 P.M.
			JFKSTL	TW 573	3:56 P.M.	6:18 P.M.
			STLMEM	TW 602	7:11 P.M.	8:26 P.M.

Transfer the flights to the draft itinerary forms on pages 106 to 115, leaving enough room to include hotel information in each city. When using the hotel descriptions for each of the above cities, keep in mind that the total budget for the trip is $3,500 per person, the cost of the air tickets (above) is $1,420 per person, and the cost of the sightseeing that will be done. Place hotel information on the draft itinerary.

ITINERARY DRAFT WORKSHEET FOR:

-1- Tue 30 Jun

_____

_____

_____

_____

_____

_____

_____

_____

_____

_____

-2- Wed 01 Jul

_____

_____

_____

_____

_____

_____

_____

_____

ITINERARY DRAFT WORKSHEET FOR:

-3- Thurs 02 Jul

-4- Fri 03 Jul

ITINERARY DRAFT WORKSHEET FOR:

-5-   Sat   04   Jul
_____

_____

_____

_____

_____

_____

_____

_____

_____

_____

_____

_____

-6-   Sun   05   Jul
_____

_____

_____

_____

_____

_____

_____

_____

_____

_____

ITINERARY DRAFT WORKSHEET FOR:

-7- Mon 06 Jul

_____

_____

_____

_____

_____

_____

_____

_____

_____

_____

_____

-8- Tue 07 Jul

_____

_____

_____

_____

_____

_____

_____

_____

ITINERARY DRAFT WORKSHEET FOR:

-9- Wed 08 Jul

_____

_____

_____

_____

_____

_____

_____

_____

_____

_____

-10- Thurs 09 Jul

_____

_____

_____

_____

_____

_____

_____

_____

ITINERARY DRAFT WORKSHEET FOR:

-11- Fri 10 Jul

_____

_____

_____

_____

_____

_____

_____

_____

_____

_____

_____

-12- Sat 11 Jul

_____

_____

_____

_____

_____

_____

_____

_____

_____

ITINERARY DRAFT WORKSHEET FOR:

-13- Sun 12 Jul

_____

_____

_____

_____

_____

_____

_____

_____

_____

_____

_____

-14- Mon 13 Jul

_____

_____

_____

_____

_____

_____

_____

_____

_____

ITINERARY DRAFT WORKSHEET FOR:

-15- Tue 14 Jul

-16- Wed 15 Jul

ITINERARY DRAFT WORKSHEET FOR:

-17-   Thur   16   Jul

_____

_____

_____

_____

_____

_____

_____

_____

_____

_____

-18-   Fri   17   Jul

_____

_____

_____

_____

_____

_____

_____

ITINERARY DRAFT WORKSHEET FOR:

-19- Sat 18 Jul
_____

_____

_____

_____

_____

_____

_____

_____

_____

_____

_____

-20- Sun 19 Jul
_____

_____

_____

_____

_____

_____

_____

_____

_____

SELECTING
GROUND OPERATORS

One of the most difficult aspects of F.I.T. development is finding quality vendors. The F.I.T. specialist might do an excellent job of developing an itinerary tailored to the exact specifications of the F.I.T. client. The client might be elated when leaving the agency with final documentation, expecting to experience the trip of a lifetime. But if even one vendor fails to provide a product and the degree of service expected by the client, the trip could be spoiled in the mind of the client. If there are several vendor failures or the quality of service is poor on two or three occasions, the agency might lose a client. Another agency will be selected for the next trip, or the client might simply decide foreign travel is no longer desirable and choose to spend money on other options than travel. And if the trip is really bad, the agent and the agency could be sued.

AGENT/VENDOR CONTROL

In spite of the extreme dependence the F.I.T. specialist has on vendors who provide products and service to other countries, the travel agent has no control whatsoever over the type of service or the quality of service rendered to F.I.T. clients when they arrive at each point on their overseas journey. Of course, the agent has some degree of recourse after the fact if clients are grossly mistreated. But, at the crucial time during which service is to be given to F.I.T. clients by overseas vendors, the F.I.T. specialist has absolutely no control. In essence, therefore, it is the threat of reprisals from an agency (as light as this threat might often be) and the reputation of the vendor that travel agents must rely on for the expectation of service and product excellence.

IMPORTANCE OF VENDOR SELECTION

Because of the total dependence agents have on F.I.T. ground operators and because after the client leaves the United States these vendors control the degree of client satisfaction with the F.I.T., ground operator vendor selection is crucial to the development and offering of an F.I.T. by a travel agency. In view of this importance, on what basis are ground operators selected? What criteria do F.I.T. specialists use in the selection of a vendor? And where do F.I.T. specialists turn to find quality vendors?

THE CHOICES

When an F.I.T. specialist needs to select a ground operator, the justifiable concern regarding the quality of the service that will be delivered usually results in the selection of a top quality operator that has been used before. However, there are times when the client will be traveling to a destination new to the F.I.T. specialist, for example, an area where a ground operator has not been used in the past. Under such circumstances, several sources are often turned to in finding a quality ground operator. The four major sources are WATA (World Association of Travel Agencies) ground operator members, American company organizations, national or regional tourist boards/bureaus, and the recommendations of other travel agents. In addition, there are several back-up sources available to the F.I.T. specialist. Each source has its advantages and disadvantages. But before looking at the pros and cons of each source, there is a problem of semantics that needs to be addressed.

The Many Names for Ground Operators

In the United States agents tend to lump all those vendors who provide meet and assist, sightseeing, and transfer services into the umbrella term of "ground operator." However, the types of firms offering these services are different in nature and structure and therefore, those outside the United States, many umbrella organizations, and the vendors themselves use a variety of terms as names for the companies that we refer to as ground operators. Although most tourist boards, especially those with offices in the United States, understand the term, ground operator, some look at ground operators as only those companies that provide ground transfers and/or car or limousine rentals. Therefore, in communicating to tourist boards outside the United States, it is better to clarify exactly what services are being sought so that vendors offering a full range of services will be referred to you.

American company organizations, on the other hand, are usually considered sightseeing companies first and ground operators second, even though they almost always offer a full line of ground operator services. Again, most American company organizations will understand the term, ground operator, but will use the term franchisee, or the term sightseeing company, in their literature and correspondence.

W.A.T.A. headquarters staff members in Geneva, Switzerland, understand ground operator, but its literature refers to member "agencies." These agencies are often travel agency retailers as we in the United States know travel agencies to be, but they also are wholesalers that put together tours (in many cases) and ground operators that provide inbound services for both F.I.T.s and tour groups. Some W.A.T.A. members offer sightseeing trips, while other do not. W.A.T.A. members can range from being small firms that provide few or no ground services to large organizations that provide a full range of ground services. W.A.T.A provides American travel agency F.I.T. specialists with a "tariff" or what they refer to as a "master key" to their member agencies services and these "master keys" identify the ground operator services provided by each agency listed. All services for which a price is provided are offered by the member agency. Some will be able to provide services not listed, but this will need to be clarified with the member agency itself. Therefore, the terminology an F.I.T. specialist might encounter for what we in the United States think of in terms of a ground operator, might be "franchisee," "sightseeing company," or "agency." If one enters into the selection process with this realization, it will help to keep from eliminating a potential vendor because the term used might otherwise have led the F.I.T. specialist to believe it was not a ground operator.

"Proven" Ground Operators

In surveying F.I.T. specialists, the most often selected technique of choosing a ground operator is reported to be the selection of one that has proven itself over and over again in the past. Typically, the staff of the vendor and the F.I.T. specialist know one another (by phone, at least) and over a period of time the vendor's staff members understand the exact specifications expected by the agency's F.I.T. specialist. A "favored vendor" status might have been established either formally or informally and a substantial amount of business might have been placed with the vendor by the agency over the years. This means that when something special is needed for an F.I.T. client, the proven ground operator will often go out of its way to provide the special service—sometimes at no additional charge. If the past agency volume of business with the vendor has been sufficiently substantial, the agency can expect the favored vendor to assign its best staff members to the agency's F.I.T. clients and to make continuing extra special efforts to be sure that a high degree of quality service is rendered.

American Company Organizations

Often F.I.T. specialists will have a client who will be traveling to areas where the specialist has not had an opportunity to build up a relationship with ground operators and/or where previous vendors that have been used provided an inferior quality of service. The F.I.T. specialist will not consider using these ground operators again. In such cases, it is necessary to select a vendor whose reputation for quality might be unknown. Although this can always mean taking a risk, there are ways to mitigate the risk. One of these ways is to select the franchisee of an American company. Many of the services provided to F.I.T. clients are provided by sightseeing companies. These services include meet and assist, airport transfers, and local sightseeing.

Some American companies have members and representatives in many cities of the world, as do Gray Line and American Sightseeing International. Both Gray Line and American Sightseeing produce annual publications detailing the services provided, sightseeing trips offered, and the costs in American dollars of all standard services. These books list destinations in alphabetical order by country and then by city. Typically, the listing will indicate contact information, booking process instructions, and service options. Daily sightseeing tours are usually listed first. The sightseeing listings will indicate the frequency of the trip (daily, every Monday and Wednesday, etc.), the times of the trips (departure times and sometimes return times), how long the trip is, pick-up point(s) (it is often helpful if a hotel is selected for the F.I.T. client that is a sightseeing trip pick-up and drop-off point, since such hotels can be especially convenient for F.I.T. clients), and a brief description of the sightseeing trip itinerary together with the points of interest that will be seen. The cost of the sightseeing trip will normally be listed after the description of the trip. It should be noted that this is sometimes a retail cost (the agency commission can then be deducted from the cost) and sometimes it is a net or wholesale cost (any commission the agency wants to have should be added onto the wholesaler's listed price when billing the client). Meet and assist and transfer services are also detailed and the cost for these are provided (again, the cost may be a retail cost or a net cost).

The publications provided to travel agencies by these operators allow the F.I.T. specialist and subsequently the client to select sightseeing and services from a wide range of options in each destination where one or more companies have member locations around the world. F.I.T. specialists find that working with U.S.-based organizations is especially convenient, since they can provide English-language guides and prices are usually held for the duration of the annual services publication. Equally important, each organization has established minimum service quality standards and makes an effort to ensure that its operators maintain the highest level of service. Although there might be no guarantees, the maintenance of these standards means the F.I.T. specialist can expect her client to receive a "reasonable" standard of service quality when dealing with a U.S.-based organization. In addition, each of the organizations has a U.S.-based toll-free phone number to call in order to book sightseeing, meet and assist, transfers (or other services), or to request additional information.

The major disadvantage to working with U.S. company organizations is that sometimes no representative is available in a destination country or a destination tourist area. A second, though much smaller, disadvantage is that the organizations are sometimes more expensive than competitors. The cost difference is seldom much and most of the time both the client and the F.I.T. specialist will prefer to pay the difference and use the U.S.-based organization.

W.A.T.A. Agencies

The most comprehensive listing of ground operators and the one that includes vendors in the largest number of cities and countries is the World Association of Travel Agency's list. As noted earlier, these are agencies that provide a wide variety of services. Although the F.I.T. specialist can find a listing in almost every major city of the world, it is necessary to read through the listing carefully to compare the services and the costs of vendors in any particular tourist destination. After identifying one or two vendors that might do the job based on the listings, it is wise to check out the vendor by asking tour operators, other travel agency F.I.T. specialists who might have used the vendor(s), and/or by calling the tourist board of the destination country.

W.A.T.A. has a list of vendors based on price structure. The master key is a list of vendors who quote a net or wholesale cost. In other words, no commission can be deducted from these prices. The entire amount of the price quoted is required by the vendor. If the F.I.T. specialist's travel agency wants a commission (and all expect to earn a commission), the dollar amount of the commission needs to be added to the prices quoted in W.A.T.A.'s master key for the price to be charged to the travel agency's F.I.T. client.

W.A.T.A. prefers that payment be made to W.A.T.A. agencies in advance of the client's arrival and that clients be provided fully paid-for service vouchers to present at the time of requesting local service. Because prepayment is often a requirement, one of the disadvantages of working with W.A.T.A. agencies is the time required to communicate back and forth and the time required to get the vendor full payment for the services to be rendered. It should be noted, however, that if an F.I.T. specialist sends a number of clients to a destination utilizing the same ground operator to a substantial degree, a billing system can sometimes be worked out. In addition, when a rush situation arises, a vendor that has been used a number of times in the past will sometimes provide service before payment on an exception basis only.

W.A.T.A. provides a set of guidelines for booking every service its agencies offer. It is wise for the F.I.T. specialist to read these guidelines and abide by them when booking services. Most are standard guidelines that are appropriate when booking arrangements with any ground operator. Others are more unique to W.A.T.A. agencies. For example, W.A.T.A. prefers that airport transfer bookings not be placed with ground operators prior to one month before the scheduled transfer. To obtain W.A.T.A.'s master keys and other data, write or phone them at the following address/phone: World Association of Travel Agencies, 1211 Geneva 1 (Switzerland) - 37, quai Wilson - P.O.B. 852, Phone: (022) 731.47.60. The cable address is WATRAV-EL and the telex address is: 22447 WATA CH.

Tourist Boards

Perhaps the best source to use in finding a quality ground operator is the tourist board or the tourist bureau (both terms are used). It is in the interest of the tourist board staff to know good ground operators in each area served by the board. The sole purpose of tourist boards is to promote inbound tourism. Therefore, putting the American travel agent in touch with a quality ground operator is an important part of the job of a tourist bureau and receiving the cooperation of tourist bureau staff can be expected.

When an F.I.T. specialist needs to find a vendor, a call to the CEO (Chief Executive Officer) of the tourist bureau serving the country, city, or area where the service is to be rendered will usually result in receiving several quality recommendations. The F.I.T. specialist benefits from the tourist bureau executive's first-hand knowledge of the area to be visited and of the local vendors who provide services for F.I.T. clients. Through discussion with tourist bureau executives the F.I.T. specialist can usually determine the pros and cons of several ground operators who provide the type of service being sought. One vendor may have a more up-to-date fleet of vehicles, for example, while another might employ a more experienced staff. Most tourist bureau executives will not hesitate to tell the F.I.T. specialist exactly what their opinions are about each of several possible vendors. Since the tourist board executive wants the F.I.T. specialist to send more people to his country, it is definitely in his interest to provide the best possible match between vendor and F.I.T. specialist. This source of recommendation is especially appealing to many F.I.T. specialists, since tourist bureaus do not charge agencies for their advice and many tourist bureaus have toll-free phone numbers. In addition, the tourist bureau will usually be up to date on all aspects of major vendor services for their geographical areas.

In working with a tourist bureau, however, there are some techniques to use in selecting a source that is more knowledgeable than other sources might be. Some tourist bureaus have offices in many of the larger cities of the United States, making it easy for local travel agencies to call a local number and reach the boards. However, these "branches" of tourist boards are often staffed with non-natives of the destination country. Many times they are staffed with Americans who have more than a casual knowledge of the country, but who sometimes do not have the detailed knowledge being sought by the travel agency F.I.T. specialist. It is often better to contact the main tourist board office (usually in New York City or Washington, D.C.) to get a good recommendation.

Although most tourist boards represent countries, some boards represent groups of countries, and a few represent areas of countries or individual cities. If the F.I.T. specialist contacts the tourist board representing the smallest appropriate geographic area where the F.I.T. client will need assistance, the information is likely to be more detailed and more up to date. For example, for information relating to ground operator services in Luasanne, Switzerland, it is better to contact the Luasanne Tourist Board in Atlanta rather than the Swiss Tourist Board in Washington, D.C.

Some tourist boards and their accompanying government controlled/directed travel affiliates might be the only source for F.I.T. ground operators. In many of the Communist countries, for example, all inbound travel is handled by the state or government travel organization. The tourist board is sometimes an extension or a branch of the same government organization. Therefore, all arrangements for ground operator services are arranged through the state/government tourist company. Typically, these state or government travel companies publish brochures for American travel agencies listing the ground services available in destination areas of their countries and a tariff or price list for each service. These are made available to travel agencies and F.I.T. specialists at little or no cost by requesting them from the appropriate country's tourist board in Washington, D.C.

A cost-saving hint to keep in mind when contacting tourist boards is to use their toll-free numbers. Although not all tourist boards have toll-free numbers, many do and the use of these numbers can save both the client and the travel agency in long-distance phone charges.

Also keep in mind that tourist boards (with the exception of some of those representing Eastern European countries) frequently do not maintain a supply of price lists or company brochures for ground operators. They can provide contact addresses and phone numbers (usually in the destination country), but usually the F.I.T. specialist will have to contact the ground operator directly and request service and price information. Some tourist boards will utilize their embassy mail services in getting information to the United States in an expedient manner when the F.I.T. specialist is in a hurry, but this additional and special service is rare.

It should be remembered that some government tourist bureaus are restricted in the recommendations that they are allowed to make in that being public servants they are not supposed to show a preference for one home country vendor over another or to show favoritism in any way. In such cases, the usual practice is to provide the F.I.T. specialist with the names and addresses of three ground operators from a list of those that have been asked to be represented by the government tourist board. There will be little or no quality differentiation made in the selection of companies on these lists and the F.I.T. specialist will need to make any quality judgments on her own through additional research.

Other Agency F.I.T. Specialist Suggestion

Although the competition in some communities is so considerable and so bitter, some agency F.I.T. specialists would never think of discussing a client's special needs with a person working for another agency. Fortunately, in most communities throughout the country, agents have developed a good rapport with one another and have learned that helping one another can be mutually beneficial even when a strong competitive environment exists. By identifying those at other agencies who specialize in F.I.T.s, an informal resource base can be established. With such a resource base, the F.I.T. specialist can usually find a good quality vendor in a very short time simply by calling a few friends in other agencies. If the F.I.T. specialists from other agencies all give the same recommendations and they all believe the vendor to be good, one can be fairly confident in the quality of service that will be provided to one's client.

OTHER APPROACHES

Although the previously mentioned four ways of selecting a ground operator are the techniques used most often, there are some other, less often used approaches as well. These include previous client suggestions and tour operator suggestions. Both approaches have their drawbacks, but they can supplement the vendor selection range and one's vendor data file listings.

Previous Client Suggestions

F.I.T.clients who travel often encounter a wide range of ground operators. Not only those vendors contracted to provide services to them, but many other vendors are met as well. When leaving the baggage control area and looking for the meet and assist representative, F.I.T. clients will often see other meet and assist representatives and say to themselves, "I wish I were being met by that person. He/she seems to be doing a better job than my meet and assist representative."

This type of comparison goes on all the time and F.I.T. clients returning from a trip will usually not be shy to tell the F.I.T. specialist that another vendor should have been used if the client feels strongly that another vendor was doing a better job.

There are several problems with depending on these clients recommendations, however. Clients seldom obtain the needed "contact" data. They might remember the color of the jacket the meet and assist representative was wearing, but they seldom get the name of the company the meet and assist representative was working for or a telephone contact number for the company. Client quality judgments can also be erroneous, since a more expensive service might have been requested by the other F.I.T. passenger being met or substitutes might be working the meet and assist duties for the client's company the day the client arrived. Many factors might color the individual F.I.T. client's experience.

However, client recommendations should be considered and followed up on—especially if the agency sends many F.I.T. clients to the destination area.

Tour Operator Suggestions

Tour operators deal extensively with ground service operators. They send large numbers of tourists to destinations and therefore are even more dependent upon local vendors than are F.I.T. specialists who have only one or two clients going to the area at a time. Therefore, quality tour operators check out vendors quite thoroughly. As with client recommendations, however, there can be problems in asking tour operators for their vendor suggestions. Willingness and ability to provide information constitutes the major constraint one can expect to encounter. Agents interact with tour operator reservationists, while vendor selection is usually made by those working in the operations division of a tour company. Therefore, it can be expected that the reservationist will not always know the vendors that are serving a specific tour.

Operations staff might be unwilling to discuss recommendations with agents, since their time is valuable and they might not want to divulge the names of vendors fearing that competitors might take advantage of such knowledge. Even when tour operators do provide the names and contact information for their preferred vendors, the F.I.T. specialist might find that the ground operator who was recommended only deals with groups and does not provide services for individual F.I.T. clients. Also they might find that a vendor who might provide excellent group service does not offer the same quality of service to individual F.I.T. clients.

In spite of the difficulty in getting tour operator vendor suggestions and in spite of a potential difference in the quality of service provided by tour company vendors, any suggestions generated from this source should be compared with suggestions received from other sources. If one finds that several sources are recommending the same vendor, the chances are good that the service will be of an acceptable degree of quality.

SERVICE SELECTION

Although the way in which data is provided by those ground operators suggested by national tourist boards, by W.A.T.A. agencies, and by others

PARIS, FRANCE

SIGHTSEEING PARIS AND SURROUNDINGS

INFORMATION: Tours depart from/return° to our Paris headquarters, 4 place des Pyramides (near the Louvre Museum). Metro stop: ("Palais Royal"). Tours include air-conditioned motorcoach transportation, services of a licensed multilingual guide (except tours C and VO) and entrance fees to places visited during the tours. (Lunch not included).

All tours are automatically confirmed as long as NET payment (After deducting your commission) is RECEIVED in our office at least two weeks prior to tour departure.
Children: Under 4: free. Age 4 to 10: 50% reduction.
°Optional drop off at the Opera.

PLEASE NOTE:
.Y: Year Round
.S: Summer schedule — from March 31 to November 1, 1988
.W: Winter schedule — from November 2, 1988 to March 31, 1989

All prices valid until March 31st 1989.

HALF DAY PARIS

C/CITYRAMA TOUR   2 hrs
FARE: FF100. / $18. – commission: 15%
.S: Daily at 9.30–10–10.30–11 AM and 1–1.30–2–2.30–3.30 PM
    Additional departures from May 12 to September 25 at 9–12.30 AM and 3–4 PM
.W: Daily at 9.30–10.30 AM and 1.30–2.30 PM
The most comprehensive orientation tour of Paris. Double decker motor-coach with recorded commentary. All major sights but no inside visits.

P/PARIS ARTISTIQUE   3½ hrs
FARE: FF195. / $35. – commission: 10%
.Y: Daily at 9.15 AM
The heart of Paris including a visit to Notre Dame and an orientation tour of the Louvre Museum (or Orsay Museum on Tuesday).

PP/PARIS PANORAMIQUE   3½ hrs
FARE: FF195. / $35. – commission: 10%
.S: Daily at 2 PM
.W: Daily at 1.30 PM
The Western districts of Paris with a cruise on the Seine river and a visit to the 1st floor of the Eiffel Tower..

I/ILLUMINATIONS   2 hrs
FARE: FF120. / $22. – commission: 15%
.S: Daily at 10 PM
.W: Daily at 8.30 PM
Guided tour or recorded commentary of the illuminated sights and floodlit monuments of Paris.

COMBINE TWO ½ DAY TOURS AND SAVE:
The two tours may be taken on the same day or separately. Any unused portions are non-refundable.

PJ/PARIS FULL DAY: Paris Artistique and Panoramique
FARE: FF350. / $63. – commission: 10%
.Y: Daily at 9.15 AM

CVA/CITYRAMA and VERSAILLES APARTMENTS
FARE: FF240. / $43. – commission: 10%
.S: Daily at 9.30-10 AM, Except on Monday and Sunday afternoon.
.W: Daily at 9.30 AM, Except on Monday and Sunday afternoon.

HALF DAY OUTSKIRTS OF PARIS

VO/VERSAILLES ORIENTATION   3¼ hrs
FARE: FF120. / $22. – commission: 10%
.S: Daily except on Monday at 9–10 AM and 1–2.30 PM
En route, tape recorded presentation of the palace, then, on your own, visit to the State Apartments and the wonderful gardens.

VA/VERSAILLES APARTMENTS   3½ hrs
FARE: FF170. / $31. – commission: 10%
.S: Daily except on Monday & Sunday afternoon at 9.30 AM & 2 PM
.W: Daily except on Monday at 9.30 AM and 1.30 PM.
With our guide, walk in the gardens then visit to the State Apartments and the new Restored Apartments.

VS/SPECIAL VERSAILLES WITH FOUNTAIN DISPLAY   4½ hrs
FARE: FF190. / $34. – commission: 10%
. At 2 PM, three Sundays a month from May to October Versailles plus a display of all the Versailles fountains in operation.

T/THE TRIANONS   3½ hrs
FARE: FF160. / $29. – commission: 10%
.S: Tuesday and Thursday at 1.30 PM
.W: Thursday at 1.30 PM
Guided tour to the Trianons and the Marie Antoinette's hamlet, located in the wonderful park of Versailles.

MA/MALMAISON   3½ hrs
FARE: FF170. / $31. – commission: 10%
.S: Wednesday and Friday at 9.30 AM
The castle of the happy days of Bonaparte and Josephine.

F/FONTAINEBLEAU and BARBIZON   5 hrs
FARE: FF225. / $41. – commission: 10%
.S: Monday, Wednesday, Friday, Saturday at 1.30 PM.
.W: Wednesday, Friday, Sunday at 1.30 PM.
The favorite hunting residence of the Kings of France.

CH/CHARTRES   5½ hrs
FARE: FF205. / $37. – commission: 10%
.S: Tuesday, Thursday and Saturday at 1.30 PM
.W: Tuesday and Saturday at 1 PM
Elegant medieval cathedral, world famous for its stained glass windows.

CY/CHANTILLY   5 hrs
FARE: FF240. / $43. – commission: 10%
.S: Sunday at 1.30 PM
The important museum and lovely castle of Chantilly.

G/GIVERNY — MONET'S HOME   5 hrs
FARE: FF250. / $45. – commission: 10%
Thursday from April 7 to October 27 at 2 PM
Tuesday from April 19 to October 25 at 2 PM
The flower garden and famous Japanese bridge. Visit to the painter's home.

FULL DAY OUTSKIRTS OF PARIS

VT/VERSAILLES and THE TRIANONS   7 hrs
FARE: FF280. / $50. – commission: 10%
.S: Tuesday and Thursday at 9.30 AM
.W: Thursday at 9.30 AM

COMBINE TWO ½ DAY TOURS and SAVE:
Any unused portions are non-refundable.

VF/VERSAILLES, FONTAINEBLEAU and BARBIZON
FARE: FF330. / $59. – commission: 10%
.S: Wednesday, Friday, Saturday at 9.30 AM
.W: Wednesday, Friday, Sunday at 9.30 AM

VC/VERSAILLES and CHARTRES
FARE: FF300. / $54. – commission: 10%
.S: Tuesday, Thursday and Saturdayat 9.30 AM
.W: Tuesday, Saturday at 9.30 AM

MV/MALMAISON and VERSAILLES
FARE: FF290. / $52. – commission: 10%
.S: Wednesday, Friday at 9.30 AM

MF/MALMAISON — FONTAINEBLEAU — BARBIZON
FARE: FF330. / $59. – commission: 10%
.S: Wednesday, Friday at 9.30 AM

Fig. 9-1. Gray Line's meet and assist and transfer services in Paris. (Courtesy of Gray Line Sight-Seeing Association, Inc.)

PRIVATE CAR SERVICES

For the discriminating traveller who would rather tour or sightsee in the comfort of a late model sedan with an English speaking driver, a chauffered car offers a leisurely and friendly way to travel.
PRICES INCLUDE: Driver's maintenance, expenses for the car (gas and maintenance), tolls for suggested tours (F.G.H.I.), insurance for passengers, mileage as quoted, duration of services as indicated.
NOT INCLUDED: Clients' lodging and meals, extra mileage or hours, entrance fees, items of a personal nature.
Note: Our English speaking drivers have some general knowledge but may not conduct inside visits of public monuments, castles or museums.
Services of multilingual licensed guides available: rates on request.

TRANSFERS

All transfers indicated are for Paris. They included assistance and porterage of one suitcase per person at rail station or aiport. Il you have additional luggage, you may have to arrange for a larger car or a minibus (Cat. 2). If any extra luggage cannot be accommodated in the car, it will have to be carried in a taxi hired at your own expense. For arrival transfers by private cars, it is the responsability of the clients to advise the operator of any changes or delays, as cars will wait only ninety minutes past the agreed time or will require local cash payment for extra waiting time. It is also necessary to advise the operator, at least 24 hours in advance, of any changes in your departure transfer schedule.
Night surcharge: from 8 PM to 8 AM.

A. From a Paris train station to a centrally located hotel or vice-versa.
B. From Orly Airport to Paris hotel or vice-versa.
C. From Charles-de-Gaulle Airport (Roissy) to Paris hotel or vice-versa.

AT DISPOSAL AND FOR SIGHTSEEING:

D. Half day at disposal within Paris. 35 km maximum within 3 1/2 hours.
E. Full day at disposal within Paris. 70 km maximum within 9 hours.
F. Half day to Versailles. 70 km maximum within 3 1/2 hours.
G. Full day to Giverny. Monet's home. 200 km maximum within 8 hours.
H. Full day to the landing beaches of Normandy or Mt-St-Michel full day. 700 km maximum within 14 hours.
I. Full day to the Châteaux Country. 550 km maximum within 14 hours.
J. Full day at disposal. 200 km maximum within 8 hours.

Catégorie 1:
MERCEDES LIMOUSINE 250 Longue (5/7 pax).
1 suitcase per person.

Catégorie 2:
MINIBUS LUXE (8 pax).
1 suitcase per person.

Catégorie 2:
MERCEDES BERLINE 230 E (3/4 pax)
CITROËN PRESTIGE (3/4 pax).
1 suitcase per person.

Catégorie 3:
CITROËN CX (3/4 pax) - RENAULT 25 GTX (3/4 pax) - RENAULT ESPACE (5 pax).
1 suitcase per person.

PRIVATE CAR SERVICES (RESA) See page 3

All rates are per car.
PRICES INCLUDE: Driver's maintenance, expenses for the car (gas and maintenance), tolls for suggested tours (F.G.H.I.), insurance for passengers, mileage as quoted, duration of services as indicated.
NOT INCLUDED: Clients' lodging and meals, extra mileage or hours, entrance fees, items of a personal nature.
Note: Our English speaking drivers have some general knowledge but may not conduct inside visits of public monuments, castles or museums.
Services of multilingual licensed guides available: rates or request.

TRANSFERS

All transfers indicated are for Paris. They include assistance and porterage of one suitcase per person at rail station or airport. If you have additional luggage, you may have to arrange for a larger car or a minibus (Cat. 2). If any extra luggage cannot be accommodated in the car, it will have to be carried in a taxi hired at your own expense. For arrival transfers by private cars, it is the responsability of the clients to advise the operator of any changes or delays as cars will wait only ninety minutes past the agreed time or will require local cash payment for extra waiting time. It is also necessary to advise the operator, at least 24 hours in advance, of any changes in your departure transfer schedule.

Night surcharge from 8 PM to 8 AM: $ 17 per car.

TRANSFERS: rates per car.

SERVICES	CATEGORY 3	CATEGORY 2	CATEGORY 1
A	$ 66	$ 81	$ 101
B	$ 102	$ 132	$ 162
C	$ 103	$ 134	$ 164
AT DISPOSAL and FOR SIGHTSEEING: rates per car.			
D	$ 133	$ 166	$ 202
E	$ 285	$ 343	$ 419
F	$ 179	$ 221	$ 273
G	$ 409	$ 502	$ 620
H	$ 940	$ 1173	$ 1469
I	$ 806	$ 996	$ 1246
J	$ 401	$ 495	$ 611

Fig. 9-1. Continued

PARIS, FRANCE

MULTIPLE DAY TOURS

CL2/CHATEAUX COUNTRY 2 Days
FARE: FF1,595. / $285. – commission: 10%
Single supplement: FF165. / $30.
.Sunday from April 3 to October 30 at 7.15 AM.
.Thursday from May 12 to October 13 at 7.15 AM.
Overnight in TOURS (Hotel Univers or Bordeaux). – Visit to: AMBOISE – LANGEAIS – AZAY LE RIDEAU – VILLANDRY GARDENS – CLOS LUCE (home of Leonardo da Vinci) – CHENONCEAU and CHAMBORD. Local wine tasting. Return to Paris around 7.00 PM.

ML2/MONT SAINT MICHEL and CHATEAUX COUNTRY 2 Days
FARE: FF1,690. / $302. – commission: 10%
Single supplement: FF165. / $30.
.Saturday: year round at 7.15 AM.
.Wednesday from May 11 to October 12 at 7.15 AM.
Overnight in ANGERS (Hotel Mercure). – The Mont Saint Michel "Marvel of the West" is one of the highlights of this tour. In the Chateaux Country, you will visit: ANGERS – CHINON – CHENONCEAU and CHAMBORD. Return to Paris around 8.00 PM.

PM2/NORMANDY, MONT SAINT MICHEL and SAINT MALO 2 Days
FARE: FF1,750. / $313. – commission: 10%
Single supplement: FF165. / $30.
.Friday from April 1 to October 28 at 7.15 AM.
.Tuesday from May 10 to October 11 at 7.15 AM.
Overnight in CAEN (Hotel Novotel) – HONFLEUR – DEAUVILLE – CABOURG – ARROMANCHES (Landing Beaches Museum) – CAEN – MONT SAINT MICHEL (Visit of the abbey) and SAINT MALO-CAEN (snack). Return to Paris around 10.30 PM.

ML3/MONT SAINT MICHEL and CHATEAUX COUNTRY 3 Days
FARE: FF2,380. / $425. – commission: 10%
Single supplement: FF330. / $60.
.Saturday from April 2 to October 29 at 7.15 AM.
.Wednesday from May 11 to October 12 at 7.15 AM.
Overnights in ANGERS (Hotel Mercure) and TOURS (Hotel Univers or Bordeaux). MONT SAINT MICHEL –ANGERS – CHINON – AZAY LE RIDEAU – VILLANDRY GARDENS – AMBOISE – CHENONCEAU – CHEVERNY – CHAMBORD. Return to Paris around 7.00 PM.

NBC3/NORMANDY, MONT ST MICHEL and CHATEAUX COUNTRY 3 Days
FARE: FF2,500. / $447. – commission: 10%
Single supplement: FF330. / $60.
.Friday from April 1 to October 28 at 7.15 AM.
.Tuesday from May 10 to October 11 at 7.15 AM.
Overnights in CAEN (Hotel Novotel) and ANGERS (Hotel Mercure). HONFLEUR – DEAUVILLE – LANDING BEACHES – BAYEUX – MONT SAINT MICHEL – SAINT MALO – ANGERS – CHINON – TOURS – CHENONCEAU – CHAMBORD. Return to Paris around 8.00 PM.

NBC4/NORMANDY, MONT ST MICHEL and CHATEAUX COUNTRY 4 Days
FARE: FF3,450. / $616. – commission: 10%
Single supplement: FF495. / $90.
.Friday from April 1 to October 28 at 7.15 AM.
.Tuesday from May 10 to October 11 at 7.15 AM.
Overnights in CAEN (Hotel Novotel), ANGERS (Hotel Mercure) and TOURS (Hotel Univers or Bordeaux). ROUEN – HONFLEUR – DEAUVILLE – LANDING BEACHES – BAYEUX – CAEN – MONT SAINT MICHEL – SAINT MALO – ANGERS – LANGEAIS – CHINON – AZAY LE RIDEAU – VILLANDRY GARDENS – TOURS – AMBOISE – CLOS LUCE – CHENONCEAU – CHAMBORD. Return to Paris around 7.00 PM.

BPR3/PARIS TO NICE: BURGUNDY – PROVENCE – RIVIERA 3 Days
FARE: FF3,550. / $634. – commission: 10%
Single supplement: FF330. / $60.
.Monday at 7.15 AM: May 16–June 6–June 20–July 4–July 18–August 8 –August 8–August 22–September 5–September 19– October 3.
ITINERARY: Day 1. 7.15 AM departure from Paris, the burgundy vineyards (visit to a cellar and wine tasting), the "wine road", lunch in Beaune east of the "Hospices", overnight in Lyon (Hotel Metropole) and gourmet dinner at the world famous Paul Bocuse restaurant. • Day 2. Depart Lyon to Orange and visit to the Roman Theater and Arch of Triumph, the Pont du Gard, free time in Avignon for lunch on your own, afternoon visit of Les Baux before driving on to Nimes for dinner and overnight (Hotel Imperator). • Day 3. Morning visit of Nimes including the Maison Carree, Diana's Temple and the Arena. Drive on to Arles where Gauguin and Van Gogh lived and painted, then continue on to Aix en Provence for lunch. After a short visit, drive on to Saint Raphael on the Mediterranean and follow the Esterel Corniche road to Cannes and on to Nice.

GENERAL INFORMATION

TOUR DEPARTURES: Tours depart from/return to our main office, 4 Place des Pyramides. phone: 42.60.30.14 (metro: Palais Royal). Arrangements can be made to pick up groups of 10 persons or more at centrally located hotels. Clients should arrive 15 minutes before scheduled departure time to exchange all prepaid orders and vouchers for final tickets.

BOOKINGS: Except for hotel packages, all tours are automatically confirmed as long as net payment (after deducting your commission) is received in our office at least two weeks prior to departure. No tour will be confirmed without a deposit of $100.00 or full payment. For late bookings, a cable charge might be added. With each booking, please indicate clients' names, date and means of arrival and contact (hotel) in Paris.

RESERVATIONS/CONFIRMATIONS: Necesary only for hotel packages. All tours need only to be prepaid two weeks in advance to our New York Office for U.S. clients.

REISSUE OF DOCUMENTS: In case of change of plans or loss, $20.00 charge will be levied if vouchers have to be reissued.

CHILDREN: Under 4 = free (any hotel and restaurant expenses to be paid directly). 4 to 10 = 50% on half and full day tours, 20% on multiday tours, no discounts on tours with night clubs. 10 and over = full price.

REFUNDS: The operator must be notified in writing of any cancellation 72 hours before the tour. A cancellation fee of $20.00 per person will be deducted from all refunds. For hotels, one night will be charged for reservations cancelled less than 7 days prior to arrival for individuals.
Cancellations received in Paris less then 48 hours before departure = 20% of price, less then 24 hours = 40% of price. No refunds for NO SHOW, unused components of a tour or any uncompleted tour.
No claim or refund will be considered unless it is submitted with proper documentation to Cityrama or its local office, in writing, no later than thirty days following completion of the tour or services.
RATES: All rates are based on current tariffs and are subject to modifications in case of currency fluctuation. In the event of an increase due in Paris over prepayment, adjustments will be made directly with the clients.
RESPONSIBILITY: Cityrama and its foreign ticket agents act only as agent for the passenger(s) and the various companies and assumes no liability for injury, damage, loss, accident or delay which may be occasioned through the act or default of any company engaged or in carrying out the tour arrangements. Cityrama reserves the right, at its sole discretion, to withdraw, modify or cancel any or all tours if it is necessary for the comfort or safety of the passengers.

FOR FURTHER INFORMATION REFER TO CONSUMER'S BROCHURE

GRAY LINE OF PARIS *Operated by Cityrama*
FOR INFORMATION AND RESERVATIONS, CONTACT: *New York Office:* CITYRAMA–CITYPLUS
347 Fifth Avenue, Suite 709, New York, NY 10016 – 5098
Telephone: (212) 683-8120 • Telex: 668 576 HEXA

Cityrama 4 Place des Pyramides, 75001 PARIS • Open 7 days a week – 7:00 AM / 10:00 PM
Mr. Noel CHARPENTIER, Vice President
Telephone: (1) 42-60-30-14 • Telex: 670532 CITYRAP • Telex: 240679 TOURAMA

Fig. 9-1. Continued

FRANCE   PARIS   FRANCE

AMERICAN SIGHTSEEING PARIS

Direct prepaid vouchers and checks to:*

For USA: **FRANCE TOURISME, INC.**
309 Fifth Avenue, Room 502
New York, New York 10016
Groups: (800) 882-2344; (212) 889-2344
FAX: (212) 889-9688

*For Sightseeing Tours for Individuals,** direct prepaid vouchers and checks
payable to:

AMERICAN SIGHTSEEING INTERNATIONAL
309 Fifth Avenue, Room 500
New York, New York 10016
(800) 225-4432; (212) 689-7744

Operated by: FRANCE TOURISME – PARIS VISION

5 Rue D'Alger

75001 Paris, France

General Manager: Georges Toromanof

Telephone: 42.61.85.50

Telex: 670024

FAX: 42.60.00.86

Member: ASTA, IATA, ATAF, SNAV, PATA, UFTAA, JATA, COTAL

GENERAL INFORMATION

Rates: The rates given in this tariff are in U.S. Dollars for your convenience. Prices are subject to change with or without notice due to fluctuation of currency. (US$1.00 = FF6.00)

Confirmation: Sightseeing tours, half day or full day excursions, should be considered as automatically confirmed, unless informed otherwise. Acknowledgement of orders should only be expected for groups, transfers and tours lasting at least two days.

WE ARE SPECIALISTS IN INCENTIVES, CONVENTIONS, LARGE GROUPS – SPECIAL RATES AS WELL AS HOSTESSES FOR HOSPITALITY DESKS, INTERPRETERS, MOTORCOACH HIRE ON REQUEST.

Cancellation: On Hotel Reservations: Hotels are legally entitled to charge a cancellation fee, for groups cancelling less than 30 days prior to arrival, for individuals cancelling less than 7 days prior to arrival, or, obviously, for any no-show; the cancellation fees are bond on a one night accommodation according to services requested: Bed and Breakfast, Half Pension or Full Pension.

In case of cancellation: France Tourisme will charge an additional standard amount of $17.00 per individual reservation and $38.00 per group, covering service charges.

On tours of 2 days or more: For cancellations made:

24 hours before departure, 50% of the total price.
48 hours before departure, transferring tour to a later date, $10.00 per person will be deducted as a service charge.
48 hours before departure, 25% of the total price.

Departure Point: From Paris Vision Terminal 214, Rue De Rivoli – No Hotel pick ups. Contact Paris Vision office at least 15 minutes before scheduled departure time. All prepaid orders and vouchers should be exchanged for final tickets.

Remittance: Payment must accompany all coupons or tour orders. Tours will not be provided unless full pre-payment is received.

Hotel Rates: On request.

Official Guides: Not available without sightseeing, excursions, tours, etc. Hostesses for hospitality desk (congresses and incentives) and guides for technical visits, prices on request.

IMPORTANT NOTICE FOR GROUPS AND INDIVIDUALS:

Pointed heel shoes are forbidden in National Museums.

When making your quotation, also remember that National Historical Museums (Louvre, Malmaison, Fontainebleau, Chambord, Chantilly, etc.) are closed on Tuesdays.

Versailles Museum and Palace are closed on Mondays.

Usually all Museums are also closed on legal holidays.

For Groups, do not forget that the number of persons is limited for admission with an official licensed guide for the visits in National or Historical Museums and Monuments:
 – 30 persons in Fontainebleau, Malmaison, the Trianons, the Louvre, and Chateaux Country castles, Versailles.

After this number of persons, a second guide is compulsory.

Entrance Fees to Museums:
Musee d'Orsay, Trianons, Pompidou Center $4.00
Louvre, Versailles, Fontainebleau, Ste. Chapelle, Invalides 5.00
Private Galleries, Chantilly, Villandry, Mont St. Michel 4.00/7.00

Reductions for Children: Not commissionable
Under 4 years:
 – on local excursions (½ day or full day): free
 – on 1, 2, 3, and 4 day tours with meals or hotels: For direct account of parents, where required.

From 4 to 10 years:
 – on local excursions: 50%
 – on 1, 2, 3, and 4 day tours with meals or hotels: 20% discount

Official Holidays: New Year: Jan. 1; Easter: April 3 and 4; Labour Day: May 1; Victory Day: May 8; Ascension Day: May 12; Witsun: May 22 and 23; Bastille Day: July 14; Assumption Day: Aug. 15; All Saints' Day: Nov. 1; Armistice Day: Nov. 11; Christmas Day: Dec. 25.

INDIVIDUAL TRANSFERS BY PRIVATE CHAUFFEUR DRIVEN CARS – NET

By private car with assistance of a multi-lingual chauffeur, porterage of 2 pieces of luggage, tips to driver (porterage at hotel not included).

NET RATES PER CAR

	1-2 Pax Berline Luxe	1-3 Pax Berline Grand Luxe	5-7 Pax Limousine Luxe or Mini-bus	5-7 Pax Limousine Grand Luxe
Paris Station/Hotel (one way)	$ 64.00	$ 75.00	$ 85.00	$110.00
Orly Airport/Paris (one way)	89.00	105.00	122.00	155.00
Charles de Gaulle Airport/Paris (one way)	103.00	124.00	145.00	192.00
Orly Airport/Charles de Gaulle Airport (one way)	146.00	178.00	209.00	265.00

SUPPLEMENTS FOR INDIVIDUALS – NET:

Waiting Time: 1st hour free of charge
between 7:00 a.m. and 8:00 p.m. $30.00
between 8:00 p.m. and 12:00 p.m.: 34.00
between 12:00 p.m. and 7:00 a.m.: 41.00

Overtime: between 8:00 p.m. and 8:00 a.m. $31.00

More than 3 hotels per transfer: 30.00

Fig. 9-2. ASI's meet and assist and transfer services in Paris. (Courtesy of American Sightseeing International.)

FRANCE   PARIS   FRANCE

INDIVIDUAL TOURS WITH PRIVATE CHAUFFEUR-DRIVEN CARS

Including insurance, gasoline, maintenance of the cars, gratuity, services, chauffeur's salary and meal, transportation of luggage (2 pieces per person), kilometrage as indicated, taxes, and driver's meals on full day tours.

TOURS	Duration	Distances	3rd category Citroen CX Peugeot 505 Renault 20 1-2 persons	2nd category Mercedes 230 Peugeot 604 Mini-bus 8 Pax 1-3 persons	1st category Mercedes Limo Citroen Prestige Peugeot Heuliez 1-7 persons	Grand Luxe Mercedes Limo 250 Mercedes Berline Cadillac Limo 1-7 persons
Paris ½ day	2 ½ hrs.	35 kms	$117.00	$139.00	$162.00	$211.00
Orientation tour	3 ½ hrs.	50 kms	141.00	166.00	194.00	253.00
Versailles ½ day	3 ½ hrs.	65 kms	157.00	186.00	218.00	283.00
Paris full day Versailles-Malmaison full day	7 hrs.	70 kms	249.00	293.00	340.00	438.00
Fontainebleau-Barbizon ½ day	5 hrs.	150 kms	221.00	267.00	310.00	402.00
Chartres or Giverny ½ day	5 hrs.	200 kms	267.00	321.00	379.00	482.00
Versailles + Fontainebleau full day	7 hrs.	175 kms	335.00	398.00	466.00	663.00
Versailles + Chartres + Fontainebleau full day	8 hrs.	300 kms	442.00	528.00	620.00	787.00
Rheims + Champagne full day Rouen + Giverny full day	9 hrs.	350 kms	514.00	587.00	700.00	878.00
Lisieux + Honfleur + Deauville full day	14 hrs.	400 kms	674.00	801.00	941.00	1194.00
Chateaux Country (Loire Valley) 1 day	14 hrs.	550 kms	682.00	862.00	1006.00	1293.00
Mont Saint-Michel 1 day	16 hrs.	800 kms	804.00	1041.00	1218.00	1533.00

PARIS SIGHTSEEING – Half Day – 15% Commission

TOUR AS/PC – PARIS VISION DISCOVERY TOUR

RATE: $18.00/person

DEPARTS: Summer: 9:00 a.m., 9:30 a.m., 10:00 a.m., 1:30 p.m., 2:00 p.m., 2:30 p.m., Daily + 10:30 a.m. & 3:00 p.m. May 12- Sept. 25.
Winter: 9:30 a.m., 11:00 a.m., 1:30 p.m., 2:00 p.m., 2:30 p.m., Daily + 10:00 a.m. Saturday & Sunday.

This tour aboard our famous double decker bus, lasts approx. two hours. It is a complete overview of the city accompanied by a multi-lingual taped commentary with background music. It includes the city's most interesting districts and every major landmark: Vendôme Square, Concorde Square, Louvre, Pont Neuf, Ile de la Cité, Notre Dame Cathedral, Hotel de Ville, Place des Vosges, Bastille Square, Ile St Louis, Sorbonne, Latin Quarter, Panthéon, Luxembourg Gardens, St Germain des Prés, Invalides, Eiffel Tower, Triumph Arch, Elysées, Madeleine Church, Opéra Square, Rivoli Street.

GROUP RATES NET PER PERSON

10-15	16-20	21-25	26-30	31-35	36-40
$23.00	$16.00	$14.00	$11.00	$10.00	$9.00

Fig. 9-2. Continued

might differ slightly from the way it is provided by American company organizations, the information presented tends to be quite similar. Therefore, to show how the F.I.T. specialist approaches the selection of services, a comparison of ground service presentations for Paris is provided together with an explanation of standard criteria and the processes used in making a selection of the ground operator that will "fit" the F.I.T. client best. The examples are taken from the Gray Line/Cityrama *"France"* brochure and the American Sightseeing International *Worldwide Tour Planning Manual.*

The American Sightseeing International listing for Paris, which is Paris Vision, starts by providing contact information in New York City (for pre-paid vouchers and checks) and for Paris (including Paris phone number, telex number, and address). The "General Information" section follows with an explanation that rates are quoted in U.S. dollars (they are based on French Francs and might change unless an expiration validity date is shown, rates quoted in U.S. dollars should always be verified), confirmation and cancellation policies, departure points (Note: there are no hotel pickup points.), remittance policies regarding pre-payment or payment accompanying tour orders, notes regarding closure days/dates for popular sightseeing points and pointing out that pointed heel shoes are forbidden in national museums, rate reductions for children, and museum entry fees. The next section provides policies and rates for net individual transfers by private chauffeur-driven cars. The net rates are provided on a per person basis and they go down depending upon how many people are being provided the service at the same time. Net group transfer rates are provided next, followed by supplements (for after-hour transfers, flight or train delays, no shows, and limousine transfers). Finally, net porterage charges are provided. See the sample page for details.

The Gray Line/Cityrama data is presented quite differently. Here the concentration is definitely on groups and sightseeing. The F.I.T. specialist will need to seek out individual F.I.T. transfer services, but the sightseeing information is easy to obtain by calling Gray Line at their posted New York City phone number (212-683-8120). A phone call results in finding out that the agent's commission is 10%. This means that the rates quoted are gross (the commission can be deducted). Transfer rates are per car. A night surcharge (from 8 P.M. to 10 A.M.) of 10% is charged. The client can select from three numeric categories of cars and three alpha categories of service.

If our clients wanted to arrange transfer services from the Charles-de-Gaulle Airport to the Intercontinental Hotel at Rue de Rivoli and if they are arriving on a morning flight scheduled to set down at the airport at 9:30 A.M., a cost comparison between the two companies would rapidly allow the F.I.T. specialist to determine that the net rate applicable from A.S.I./Paris Vision will be at least $103.00. Transfers will be made by private car with the assistance of a multi-lingual chauffeur. The rate includes four pieces of luggage (two per person) and the tip to the driver, but it does not include the porterage charges at the hotel. An off-hour supplement will not be required, since these are in effect only between 8 P.M. and 8 A.M.

On the other hand, if our clients made the transfer by using the services of Gray Line, the cost will be $103 gross if they arrive at the same time and utilize a Citroen or a Renault. This rate, however, includes only one suitcase per person. Again, an off-hour (night) surcharge is not levied since the surcharge is in effect only between 8 P.M. and 8 A.M.

It would appear that the A.S.I. rate is much better. However, remember that it is a net rate (no commission can be deducted by the travel agency), while the Gray Line is a gross rate (10% commission should be deducted). If the agent adds 10% for her commission to the A.S.I./Paris Vision rate, the charge will be $103.00 plus $10.30 or a total of $113.30. This is almost the same as the Gray Line rate. Before finally selecting the vendor, however, it might be important to find out what type of car will be used for the transfer and what the exchange rate will be which will be utilized in calculating the dollar cost of the service.

SELECTION FACTORS

In the above review, it was possible to identify several factors to consider when making the selection of a ground operator for any particular service. While the cost is an important consideration, even the cost may vary depending upon other variables. The number of persons in the traveling party can be most important. Had our clients brought their three children with them on their trip, for example, the A.S.I./Paris Vision rate would have been $145. This is a net rate, so 10% would have to be added to get a figure that would compare to the Gray Line/Cityrama rate and to include a commission for the travel agency. Adding the 10% will give us a rate of $145 + $14.50, or $159.50. Since no reduction for children is offered by the ground operator when the children are over ten (no reduction at all is offered for children when the service that is purchased is transfers), this can be considered a firm figure for A.S.I./Paris Vision. The Gray Line/Cityrama figure is based on a rate per car (with up to five persons per car), their rate will not change from the $103 gross rate calculated earlier. Therefore, if their children accompanied our clients on the trip, Gray Line/Cityrama would probably be selected to provide transfers if the decision is based on price.

Other selection factors are also important. The "off-hour" or "night" surcharge differs between A.S.I./Paris Vision and GrayLine/Cityrama in both the dollar amount and in the times that the surcharge is effective. The number of pieces of free luggage included in the cost of the transfer service can differ with ground operators and the difference may result in a considerable additional cost for clients. Sometimes if the client has additional luggage, he may have to arrange for a larger car or a minibus (at an additional charge). Alternately, if any luggage cannot be accommodated in the car, it may have to be carried in a taxi hired at additional expense. If there are flight delays, cancellations, or changes in the itinerary, they might add to the cost of service and sometimes will add substantially to the cost. The type of car utilized can result in a considerable difference in cost (as much as $61.00 in many cases). Having tips included or not included can make a difference as well. And, if the hotel is located some distance away from the city, an additional cost will often be levied. Porterage is usually included from the airport to the car (or vice versa), but sometimes it is not. Seldom is porterage included from the hotel to the car of vice versa. It is important to find out whether or not it is included and, if not, what the cost will be for porterage at either or both points.

SIGHTSEEING

In selecting sightseeing trips one will find that F.I.T. clients will differ considerably regarding what they want to book in advance. Many sightseeing excursions are easy to book on the spot and one of the advantages of an F.I.T. is the freedom to make a last-minute sightseeing decision. Therefore, some F.I.T. clients will not make any sightseeing arrangements until they have arrived in a destination city. Others, however, will want every detail planned prior to leaving home, and the ability to do so is an advantage of an F.I.T. as well. A large number of F.I.T. clients will want something between having all sightseeing planned in advance and having no pre-arranged sightseeing. Most clients visiting a new city will at least want to pre-arrange either a half day or a full day city "overview" sightseeing trip. In this way they can get a feel for the city and go back on their own for longer visits to the places of special interest.

In booking sightseeing trips several factors are important. Those aspects of greatest importance are:

1. Cost
2. Convenience of pick-up and drop-off points
3. Comfortable touring buses or limousines
4. English speaking guides
5. The quality of the sightseeing trip

The F.I.T. specialist cannot always determine all of the factors from ground operator literature. As with transfers and meet and assist services, the three U.S. organizations are usually sought out first since the guides speak English and quality levels are maintained. Costs can be compared in all ground operators' literature and most publish the pick-up/drop-off points. Only experience, however, will provide sightseeing comfort comparisons.

A special note should be made as to pick-up and drop-off convenience. When sightseeing buses/limousines pick up and drop off at only a few hotels, every reasonable effort should be made to place the F.I.T. clients in the same hotels. These are usually large, top-quality hotels that most F.I.T. clients find to be at least satisfactory. A second choice is a nearby quality hotel, close enough for the client to walk to the sightseeing bus pick-up/drop-off point. An excellent example is the Hassler Hotel in Rome. This is just a block from the top of the "Spanish Steps." On the other hand, the American Express sightseeing headquarters in Rome is around the corner from the bottom of the "Spanish Steps." All the American Express sightseeing buses start and stop from this convenient location. The F.I.T. client has about a block and a half to walk.

SUMMARY

The selection of ground operators that will do a good job and provide a high level of quality service is an imporant key to the happiness of F.I.T. clients. Vendor selection is especially important since the control the travel agency and the travel agency's F.I.T. specialist have over the amount of service provided or the quality of service rendered once the client leaves the United States is minimal. They must depend on the vendor's desire to maintain and retain a good reputation and must trust the vendor to provide the specific service and the quality of services purchased.

Because of this dependence and the desire to have happy customers who will return to the agency for future trips, F.I.T. specialists are justifiably concerned about the selection of ground operators. They rely heavily on those vendors that they have used in the past that have provided the kind and amount of service their F.I.T. clients want and expect. They especially depend upon those purveyors with which they have a "favored vendor" relationship. These are the vendors F.I.T. specialists give a lot of business to and these are the vendors F.I.T. specialists expect to have go out of their way to provide extra-special touches that will make their clients' trips happily memorable.

But when there are no "favored vendors" available and service for the F.I.T. client is needed, the F.I.T. specialist must find a way to locate a ground operator that can be trusted to provide good, quality service anyway. Several approaches are often used. There are four major sources for assistance. These include contacting U.S. sightseeing members and representatives, asking for recommendations from an executive working with the destination country's tourist bureau, working through the World Association of Travel Agencies, and requesting a suggestion from an F.I.T. specialist working in another agency. Less often utilized approaches include reviewing previous-client suggestions and/or tour operator suggestions.

Each approach has its drawbacks and its beneficial points. Many F.I.T. specialists will adopt two or three approaches in their search for a top quality ground operator. They will look for a company whose name comes up more than once in the search for a vendor—in the often-correct belief that several recommendations of the same firm is a quality indicator in and of itself.

In working with these sources, it is important to remember that the terminology can differ for the names used to identify a ground operator or a vendor providing ground services in its menu of services. Some of the terms one might encounter include: franchise, sightseeing company or agency(ies). In working with potential vendors or vendor referral sources it is best to clarify exactly what services are being sought so that only vendors providing that service or those services will be referred.

Tourist boards can provide excellent referrals of ground services vendors in their home countries or areas. Some boards, especially those of Eastern European countries, are extensions of government tourist organizations that provide all ground services themselves. Most tourist boards can only make referrals, however. While some might refer three of the many ground operators providing information to their home office and will provide no quality differentiation, most tourist boards will make a sincere effort to give the F.I.T. specialist the best possible quality recommendation. In working with tourist boards, it is generally better to contact those representing the smallest geographical area to which the client is traveling and to work with the main office of the tourist board in the United States.

U.S. company organizations are often preferred as ground service vendors by F.I.T. specialists. The members and representatives provide quality levels that are known in advance and they have U.S. offices through which the F.I.T. specialist can place reservations. Simply ask for their brochures, read them carefully, and make comparisons. Many have toll-free phone numbers to call for either making reservations or for requesting explanations regarding service and/or price comparisons.

W.A.T.A. agencies are members of a worldwide network of travel retailers. Some provide wholesale operations as well. Most offer a full range of ground services. W.A.T.A.s master key lists members who quote net or wholesale rates. Any commission must be added to these rates. The F.I.T. specialist should be very careful to follow the W.A.T.A. guidelines and procedures when booking ground arrangements with W.A.T.A. agencies.

Ground operators provide similar data in their literature. However, it is sometimes necessary to search the data to find all the information needed to make a good comparison between vendors. When a vendor specializes in providing services to groups or in providing sightseeing services rather than transfers, it is sometimes difficult to find the F.I.T. meet and assist and/or transfer services that might or might not be offered. In addition, when comparing prices and services, one should remember that some prices are quoted on a net basis, while others quote gross rates. Other variables that might make a difference include:

1. The number of travelers in the F.I.T. party
2. Possible off-hour or night surcharges
3. Any additional luggage charges
4. The "wait" charges for flight delays
5. Possible cancellation and/or itinerary change charges
6. The type of car being used for the transfer
7. Whether or not tips have been included in the rate that has been quoted (if so, what tips)
8. The location of the hotel vis a vis the airport (there might be a mileage surcharge if the hotel is located away from the middle of town)
9. Possible porterage charges (determining what porterage charges are included and what ones are not included in the quoted rate is important)

The sightseeing preferences of clients might vary from the F.I.T. client who wants to make all sightseeing arrangements in the destination country/city to the client who wants all sightseeing arranged in advance. Most prefer to have at least a city "overview" sightseeing trip set up prior to hometown departure. At least the following five factors should be kept in mind when selecting a sightseeing vendor:

1. Cost
2. Convenience of pick-up and drop-off points
3. Comfortable transportation
4. English speaking guides
5. Trip quality

Using U.S. company organizations will provide assurance that most of these factors are taken care of. Comparing costs and pick-up/drop-off points will provide the other factors.

■   ■   ■

❏ *REVIEW QUESTIONS*

1. Why is the selection of a ground operator for F.I.T. services important?
2. What is meant by the term "favored vendor" status?
3. What are the four major ground operator selection options?
4. What are the three U.S. companies that have sightseeing firms around the world?
5. What are the three sources that are often turned to in order to find a quality ground operator?
6. What are some of the other terms used for ground operator by vendors and others outside the United States?
7. Why is a tourist board often the best source for finding a quality ground operator?
8. If one has a choice between a city, a regional, or a national tourist board, which is most likely to provide detailed, up-to-date, and specific information for a client visiting the city that is in the region of the nation represented by the three tourist boards?
9. Can the tourist boards of Communist countries provide tariffs or price lists for ground operator services? Why?
10. Can the tourist boards of non-Communist countries provide tariffs or price lists for ground operator services? Why?
11. Why are the tourist boards of some countries limited in suggesting only three ground operator vendors and unable to provide vendor quality evaluations to F.I.T. specialists? What types of countries work under these restrictions?
12. Which two of the three major U.S. company organizations produce annual books that list member ground operators and their services by destination country or destination area?

13. What is the difference between a ground operator's "retail" or "gross" cost and the ground operator's "wholesale" or "net" cost? How do these costs affect a travel agency's commission?

14. What three factors can an F.I.T. specialist usually take for granted when working with a U.S. company organization?

15. Where will F.I.T. specialists find the most comprehensive listing of ground operators?

16. What are the pros and cons involved in utilizing one of the less-often-used approaches to finding an F.I.T. ground operator?

17. What is the title of the W.A.T.A. list of ground operators?

18. How can the F.I.T. specialist be sure that a commission is earned by working with vendors from each of the W.A.T.A. lists?

19. Will W.A.T.A. agencies provide services without being paid for the services in advance? If so, under what conditions?

20. What is the W.A.T.A policy regarding the placement of airport transfer bookings?

21. When vendor brochures or booklets quote rates in U.S. dollars, can these rates be considered as firm quotes?

22. How might the number of people in the F.I.T. client party affect the selection of a ground operator vendor based on cost? Can you give an example from the text material you have read?

23. Do all vendors agree on the times when off-hour or night surcharges are in effect?

24. What factors other than the number in the F.I.T. client party and off-hour or night surcharges might add to take away from the cost of airport to hotel transfer services for F.I.T. clients?

25. Is porterage usually included in transfer service quotes?

26. Do F.I.T. clients normally want all sightseeing arranged in advance? Explain.

27. What five factors are of greatest importance in booking sightseeing trips?

28. How might a U.S. company organization insure that some of the five factors are taken care of?

❏ *ROLE PLAY EXERCISE*

Two students may participate in this role play either out of class as a fun way to review ground operator vendor selection recommendation requests directed to a destination area tourist board executive or as an in-class exercise. One student plays the role of the travel agency's F.I.T. specialist and the other plays the role of the tourist board executive. Please read the script and then pick up the conversation in your own words.

TRAVEL AGENT: I am trying to find a top quality meet and assist vendor who I can count on to meet my clients, Mr. and Mrs. Johnson, when they arrive in your capital city during their trip in June. The Johnsons are very shy. They will not want to approach someone unless they are absolutely sure it is the person from the meet and assist company. Obviously, I must find them a vendor I can rely on.

TOURIST BOARD EXECUTIVE: We have several companies that provide meet and assist services, but there are two that are most reliable. The cost difference between them is substantial. Meet and Assist, Inc., is less expensive. They use younger, less experienced staff members, and their uniforms look similar to a standard blue suit. Your clients should be able to recognize them, but there is a possibility they might not. Grand Assist Associates cost a lot more, but their staff is excellent; they wear bright yellow jackets with pink handkerchiefs in the pockets. Which company would the Johnsons prefer?

Continue on your own.

❏ *ROLE PLAY EXERCISE*

Two students may participate in this role play either out of class as a fun way to review the chapter or as an in-class exercise. One plays the role of the ground operator vendor while the other plays the role of the F.I.T. specialist. Please read the script and then pick up the conversation in your own words.

F.I.T. SPECIALIST: My clients, John and Martha Johnson, will be arriving next month on the fourteenth and want to be met at the airport and transferred by private car to the downtown InterContinental Hotel. What will be the cost and what commission do you pay?

GROUND OPERATOR: We can quote net or gross and the rate will depend upon a number of variables.

F.I.T. SPECIALIST: Can I come out better with the net rate or the gross rate? And what are the variables?

GROUND OPERATOR: Well, let's talk about rates first and then the variables. The net rate is . . .

Continue on your own.

❏ *GROUND OPERATOR SELECTION EXERCISE*

Our clients, Mr. and Mrs. Johnson, expect to arrive in Israel on Saturday evening, the twenty-third of next month at 9:30 P.M. local time. They will be arriving via flight LY 296 from Rome and it is expected that customs clearance will take about an hour. It usually does for arrivals at this time on a Saturday evening. The Johnsons have never been to Israel before. They will be staying only a short period of time and are concerned about possible language differences. They have asked you to arrange for them to be met just as soon as they clear customs. They want to be transferred from the Ben Gurion, sometimes known as the Lod, airport to their hotel, the Ramada Renaissance Jerusalem Hotel. Review the information, relating to transfers described on the next page (the Gray Line brochure) and on the following page (the American Sightseeing International brochure), select the service you wish to book, and answer the following questions.

1. Which of the two services did you select? Why?

2. What is the total cost of the service you selected? How was this cost calculated?

3. Were there any add-ons to the base cost? If so, what were they and how much were they?

4. What is the dollar amount of the commission you will earn?

5. What would your commission be if you had selected the other vendor to provide meet and assist and transfer services?

ISRAEL

CIRCULAR TOUR
7 nights with 5 days of sightseeing

A meaningful journey to ancient and modern Israel. Arrive any day. Assistance at the airport and transfer to and from the hotel.

START OF TOUR:

Monday: Panoramic tour of Jerusalem, New City.

Tuesday: Old City of Jerusalem, Bethlehem (overnight in Jerusalem).

Wednesday: Massada, Dead Sea, Jericho.

Thursday: Nazareth, Sea of Galilee, Tiberias, Mt. of Beatitudes. Overnight in Kibbutz (except Jewish Holidays).

Friday: Safed, Acre, Haifa (overnight Tel Aviv).

Saturday: Leisure in Tel Aviv. Optional tour to the Golan Heights (overnight in Tel Aviv).

Sunday: Transfer to the Airport.

Departure: Any day. (Additional nights available.)

HOTELS			
1988/89	Deluxe	Superior First Class	First Class
	$685.00	$500.00	$360.00
Jerusalem	SHERATON PLAZA	RAMADA RENAISSANCE HYATT REGENCY	KNESER TOWER EILON TOWER
Kibbutz	KIBBUTZ	KIBBUTZ	KIBBUTZ
Tel Aviv	SHERATON	RAMADA CONTINENTAL MORIAH PLAZA	CONCORDE BASEL
ALL PRICES ARE NET			
Seasonal Supplement (April/May — Oct. - Nov. 15)	$ 90.00	$ 75.00	$ 45.00
Dinner Supplement	—	130.00	75.00
Single Supplement	390.00	180.00	120.00

◼ TOURS FROM JERUSALEM and TEL AVIV ◼

TOUR NO. 14A/39A: NAZARETH, TIBERIAS
Full day   Year round
Approx. 300 miles from Jerusalem   Approx. 200 miles from Tel Aviv
Departure from Jerusalem
7:30 a.m. Mondays, Thursdays, Fridays and Saturdays
Departure from Tel Aviv: 8:00 a.m. Mondays, Tuesday, Fridays and Saturdays
Travel along the coastal plain to Nazareth. Visit the Church of the Annunciation and St. Joseph's Workshop. Tour the ancient synagogue and St. Peter's house at Capernaum. Drive to the summit of the Mt. of Beatitudes. Then back to the Sea of Galilee for a swim. Optional cruise on the Sea of Galilee if weather and time allow. Return via "Yardenit" on the Jordan River.

Fare: $34.00   Commission: $4.00   Remit: $30.00

TOUR 14C/39C: ARMAGEDDON, SACHNE, BETH ALFA, MT. TABOR
Full day on Mondays
Departure from Tel Aviv: 8:00 a.m., from Jerusalem: 7:30 a.m.
A new tour from Tel Aviv and Jerusalem. Drive to Armageddon (Meggido) where more than 20 layers of civilization have been excavated. Drive to Beth Shearim, the Sanhedrin home of the second century. Continue on through the lush Jezreel Valley to Sachne with its natural swimming pool. Next, to Beth Alfa to visit the ruins of the ancient synagogue. End the tour with a visit to the top of Mt. Tabor with its view of the valley and surrounding area.
NOTE: Modest clothing is required.
Fare: $36.00   Commission: $4.30   Remit: $31.70

TOUR NO. 12/37A MASSADA, DEAD SEA, BEDOUIN MARKET
Full day   Year round
Approx. 220 miles from Jerusalem   Approx. 280 miles from Tel Aviv
Departure from Jerusalem and Tel Aviv: 8:00 a.m. Thursdays
Travel south to Beer-Sheva (the "capital" of the Negev). Walk through the colorful Bedouin market. Continue east through the Negev to the Dead Sea (the lowest point on earth). Then on to the Fortress Rock of Massada (ascent and descent by cable car). Conclude the tour with a swim in the Dead Sea.

Fare from Jerusalem: $40.00   Commission: $4.80   Remit: $35.20
Fare from Tel Aviv: 42.00   Commission: 5.00   Remit: 37.00

TOUR NO. 20/37 & 13/37B MASSADA, DEAD SEA
Full day   Year round
Approx. 200 miles from Jerusalem   Approx. 300 miles from Tel Aviv
Departure from Jerusalem: 9:00 a.m. Daily except Thursdays and Fridays
Departure from Tel Aviv: 8:00 a.m. Daily except Thursdays and Fridays
Travel via the Judean Desert to Massada (ascent and descent by cable car). Continue along the Dead Sea for a swim. Travel to the desert oasis of Jericho (the oldest city in the world).

Fare from Jerusalem: $40.00   Commission: $4.80   Remit: $35.20
Fare from Tel Aviv: 42.00   Commission: 5.00   Remit: 37.00

TOUR NO. 23A/38A: HAIFA, ACRE, CAESAREA
Full day   Year round
Approx. 300 miles from Jerusalem   Approx. 200 miles from Tel Aviv
Departure from Jerusalem: 7:30 a.m. Mondays, Saturdays
Departure from Tel Aviv: 8:00 a.m. Mondays, Saturdays
Travel along the coastal plain via Mt. Carmel to Haifa for a panoramic view of the city. Continue north to the ancient city of Acre to visit the Crusader Knights' Hall and the Old Port. Return south and tour Caesarea.

Fare from Jerusalem: $38.00   Commission: $4.55   Remit: $33.45
Fare from Tel Aviv: 33.00   Commission: 3.95   Remit: 29.05

TOUR NO. 23B/40B: HAIFA, SAFED, ACRE
Full day   Year round
Approx. 360 miles from Jerusalem   Approx. 280 miles from Tel Aviv
Departure from Jerusalem: 7:00 a.m. Wednesdays
Departure from Tel Aviv: 7:30 a.m. Fridays
Drive to Safed, visit the ancient synagogue and artists' quarter. Drive to Meron to visit the Holy Tomb of Rabbi Simon Bar-Yochai. On to Acre to visit the Crusader Knights' Hall and the Old Port. Ascend Mt. Carmel for a panoramic view of the harbour and the golden-domed Bahai Shrine.

Fare from Jerusalem: $38.00   Commission: $4.55   Remit: $33.45
Fare from Tel Aviv: 33.00   Commission: 3.95   Remit: 29.05

TOUR NO. 9B/35A: CAVES AND KIBBUTZ
Full Day on Wednesdays
Transfer from Tel Aviv to Jerusalem
Visit Absalom's cave, rich in multi coloured stalactites and stalagmites. Continue to Amazia cave, area of underground hiding places from the second temple period and the time of the Bar Kochba rebellion. Lunch in Kibbutz with kibbutz members (not included in the price. Visit in the kibbutz.
Fare: $35.00   Commission: $4.20   Remit: $30.80

Fig. 9-3. Gray Line's tours and transfer services in Israel. (Courtesy of Gray Line Sight-Seeing Association, Inc.)

ISRAEL

TOUR NO. 22/50: EILAT

3 days   *Year round*

Departure from Jerusalem and Tel Aviv Monday and Friday

Route identical to Tour No. 19A/48A. Second day at leisure in Eilat. It is possible to return from Eilat by flight to Tel Aviv after two days or to Tel Aviv and Jerusalem after three days. (Air fare **$62.00** subject to changes.)

Fare: In 4 Star Hotel H/B: **$200.00**   Single Supplement: **$32.00** (net)
Commission: 12%

TOUR NO. 15A/55A: GALILEE, GOLAN

2 days   *Year round*

Departure from Jerusalem: 7:30 a.m. Mondays and Fridays
Departure from Tel Aviv; 8:00 a.m. Mondays, Fridays.

1st day: Nazareth, °See Tour # 14A/39A for further itinerary.
2nd day: Golan. See Tour # 18A/43A for further itinerary.

Fare: In 4 Star Hotel H/B: **$125.00**   Single Supplement: **$16.00** (net)
In 5 Star Hotel H/B: 160.00   Single Supplement: 22.00 (net)
Commission: 12%

TOUR NO. 17A/56A
GALILEE, GOLAN, SAFED, ACRE, HAIFA

3 days   *Year round*

Departure from Jerusalem: 7:30 a.m. Mondays
Departure from Tel Aviv: 8:00 a.m. Mondays

1st day: Follow itinerary for Tour # 14A/39A.
2nd day: Follow itinerary for Tour # 18/43A.
3rd day: Follow itinerary for Tour # 23B/40B.

Fare: In 4 Star Hotel H/B: **$175.00**   Single Supplement: **$32.00** (net)
In 5 Star Hotel H/B: 219.00   Single Supplement: 44.00 (net)
Commission: 12%

COMPACT PACKAGE OF ISRAEL

4 days   *Year round*

Departure from Jerusalem: Daily except Fridays and Saturdays
Departure from Tel Aviv: Daily except Thursdays and Saturdays

DAY TOUR: Jerusalem — Old City, Bethlehem
DAY TOUR: Massada, Dead Sea, Jericho or Ein Gedi
DAY TOUR: Haifa, Safed, Acre
DAY TOUR: Nazareth, Tiberias, Sea of Galilee

Fare: In 4 Star Hotel H/B: **$240.00**   Single Supplement: **$48.00** (net)
In 5 Star Hotel H/B: 368.00   Single Supplement: 78.00 (net)
Commission: 12%

The package includes the four most popular tours in Israel. The tour price includes accommodations with 2 nights in Tel Aviv and 1 night in Jerusalem. The exact sequence of tours will be given to tourist upon arrival. Rates for additional nights prior to or after tours available upon request.

■ TOURS FROM JERUSALEM

TOUR NO. 1A: PANORAMIC JERUSALEM

2 hours

Departure: 9:00 a.m. Mondays, Wednesdays

A new relaxing way to see Jerusalem — especially designed for tour-sits who would rather ride than walk! Drive around the walls of the Old City to Mt. Scopus. View the Judean Desert and the New and Old City of Jerusalem from the Mt. of Olives. Pass by the Garden of Gethsamane, the Kidron Valley and the City of David on the way to Mt. Zion. Next, pass the Valley of Hinnom and the Road of the Patriarchs, to visit some of the architectural highlights of New Jerusalem — including the Jerusalem Theatre, the President's Residence, and the Knesset.

Fare: **$9.00**   Commission: **$0.90**   Remit: **$8.10**

TOUR NO. 1: OLD CITY OF JERUSALEM

3½ hours   *Year round*   *Approx. 2 miles*

Departure: 9:00 a.m. Sundays, Wednesdays; 1:45 p.m. Fridays

Three hour walking tour of the Old City. Visit the Western Wall (15 minute visit) and the Temple Mount (no visit to mosques). Continue along the Stations of the Cross (via Dolorosa) to the Church of the Holy Sepulchre.

Fare: **$13.00**   Commission: **$1.55**   Remit: **$11.45**

TOUR NO. 2A
GARDEN TOMB, MT. OF OLIVES, BETHANY

4 hours   *Year round*   *Approx. 20 miles*

Departure: 8:00 a.m. Wednesdays, 1:45 p.m. Fridays

Travel to Mt. Scopus and Mt. of Olives for a magnificent panoramic view of Old and New Jerusalem. Visit the Garden of Gethsemane, the Church of All Nations, and Mary's Tomb. Visit the Tombs of the Kings. Continue to the Garden Tomb and then to Bethany, home of Mary, Martha and Lazarus.

Fare: **$14.00**   Commission: **$1.65**   Remit: **$12.35**

TOUR NO. 3: KENNEDY MEMORIAL,
HADASSAH, YAD VASHEM

4 hours   *Year round*   *Approx. 30 miles*

Departures: 8:00 a.m., or 9:00 a.m. Sundays, Fridays; 1:45 p.m. Wednesday

Travel to the Kennedy Memorial. Then on to the nearby Hadassah Medical Center, to view Chagall's famous stained-glass windows. Continue to Yad Vashem, memorial to the six million Jews who perished in the Holocaust. Conclude the tour at Mt. Herzl.

Fare: **$12.00**   Commission: **$1.44**   Remit: **$10.56**

TOUR NO. 4: BETHLEHEM and HEBRON

4 hours   *Year round*   *Approx. 60 miles*

Departure: 1:45 p.m. Daily except Mondays and Fridays

Visit Rachel's Tomb on the outskirts of Bethlehem. In Hebron, tour the Cave of Machpelah (Tombs of the Patriarchs and Matriarchs). On the return trip make a short visit to the historic Etzion Bloc and drive past Solomon's Pools, then on to Bethlehem to visit the Church of the Nativity. On Moslem festivals Kiryat Arba will be visited instead of Hebron. On Saturday Rachel's Tomb is closed.

Fare: **$14.00**   Commission: **$1.65**   Remit: **$12.35**

TOUR NO. 5A: NEW JERUSALEM

4 hours   *Year round*

Departure: 9:00 a.m. Fridays, 1:45 p.m. Mondays, Wednesdays

Drive through the new city to the model of Jerusalem, a replica of ancient Jerusalem as it appeared 2000 years ago. Then on to the nearby Hadassah Medical Centre, to view Chagall's famous stained glass windows. Continue to Yad Vashem, memorial to the six million Jews who perished in the Holocaust.

Fare: **$15.00**   Commission: **$1.80**   Remit: **$13.20**

TOUR NO. 7: JERICHO & KIBBUTZ

4 hours   *Year round*   *Approx. 70 miles*

Drive to the green desert oasis of Jericho to visit the archaeological remains of the world's oldest city. Visit the 8th century Palace built by Arab Caliph Hisham. Travel along the western shore of the Dead Sea to Qumran to tour the site where the famous Dead Sea Scrolls were written and-discovered. Continue to Kibbutz Almog, pioneers in the desert to view the hand-written Qumran Scrolls (replicas) and audiovisual presentation.

Fare: **$19.00**   Commission: **$2.30**   Remit: **$16.70**

Fig. 9-3. Continued

ISRAEL

TOURS FROM TEL AVIV

TOUR NO. 18: GOLAN HEIGHTS
Full day   Year round
Approx. 440 miles from Jerusalem
Departure from Jerusalem: 7:00 a.m. Tuesdays, Saturdays

Drive across the Jordan River to Mizpeh Gadot for a panoramic view of the Hulah Valley. Continue to Qatzrin. Visit the natural blue pool of Birkat Ram. Visit the springs of the Banias.
Fare: **$38.00**   Commission: **$4.50**   Remit: **$33.50**
FROM JERUSALEM

TOUR NO. 44A: JERUSALEM OLD and NEW
Full day   Year round   Approx. 120 miles
Départure: 8:00 a.m. Mondays, Wednesdays, Fridays

Depart from Tel Aviv to Jerusalem. Drive through the new city to the model of Jerusalem, a replica of ancient Jerusalem as it appeared 2000 years ago. Then onto nearby Haddassah Medical Centre to view Chagall's famous stained glass windows. Continue to Yad Vashem, memorial to the six million Jews who perished in the Holocaust.
Fare: **$36.00**   Commission: **$6.00**   Remit: **$30.00**

TOUR NO. 44B
OLD JERUSALEM, BETHLEHEM, HEBRON
Full day   Year round   Approx. 160 miles
Departure: 8:00 a.m. daily except Mondays and Fridays

Depart from Tel Aviv to Jerusalem. Drive to the Jaffa Gate, for a 3 hour walking tour of the Old City. Visit the Western Wall (15 minute visit) by way of the Armenian and Jewish Quarters. Continue along the Stations of the Cross (via Dolorosa) to the Church of the Holy Sepulchre. Visit Rachel's Tomb. In Hebron tour the Cave of Machpelah. Then on to Bethlehem to visit the Church of the Nativity. Please note that there is no entrance to Rachel's Tomb on Saturday and Jewish Holidays. On Moslem festivals, Kiryat Arba will be visited instead of Hebron.
Fare: **$34.00**   Commission: **$4.00**   Remit: **$30.00**

TRANSFER SERVICE

One way to/from hotel (net rates 1-4 passengers). Each additional person **$6.00** up to 7 passengers. Airport-Jerusalem — **$60.00**. Airport-Tel Aviv — **$30.00**. Jerusalem-Tel Aviv — **$65.00**. Services include: Meeting and assistance at the airport, transportation in private car. Transfers operated at night (21:00 until 05:30) and on weekends (Friday from 16:00 until Sunday morning at 05:30) and holidays, **SURCHARGE OF 20% WILL BE ASSESSED.** All prices are subject to change. Please check with Gray Line office to confirm.

TRANSFERS TO EGYPT

Departure daily from Tel Aviv and Jerusalem (except Saturdays from Jerusalem). Fare one way: **$25.00**. Commission: **$2.50**. Remit: **$22.50**. Fare round trip: **$40.00**. Commission: **$4.80**. Remit: **$35.20**. Reduction for students below 26: **$10.00** for two-way transfers. **$5.00** for one-way transfer.

NOTE: Passenger must have entry visa to Egypt and must inform us of his passport number and nationality in advance.

GENERAL INFORMATION

TOUR DEPARTURES: Tours depart from our offices in Jerusalem, Centrel (near Central Station) and Tel Aviv, 142 Hayarkon St. Free transportation to and from the hotels in these cities (also from hotels in Netanya for full day tours from Tel Aviv). Client should be ready half an hour prior to departure time near the reception desk in his hotel.
BOOKING. All tours are automatically confirmed as long as payment is received in our office at least two weeks prior to departure. No tour will be confirmed without a deposit of **$100.00** or full payment with each booking. Please indicate clients' name, date and contact in Jerusalem or Tel Aviv. Children under 12 receive 20% discount on half day or one day tours and 10% discount on tours with overnight accommodations.
CHARTER SERVICE: Our fleet of luxury Mercedes or M.A.N. buses and mini buses (19-44-53-55 seats) or private limousines (5 or 7 seats) are available for hire. We can arrange transfers, excursions, etc. for your group. Our incoming department can handle your special group tours. We will be pleased to quote upon receipt of your inquiry.

GUIDES: Tours are conducted in English. Bi-lingual guides are provided in French, Spanish, German and other languages upon request.

RATES: All rates are shown in U.S. $.

REFUNDS: The operator must be notified in writing of any cancellation 72 hours before the tour. A cancellation fee of **$25.00** per reservation will be deducted from all refunds. For hotels, one night will be charged for reservations cancelled less than 7 days prior to arrival for individuals and less than 30 days prior to arrival by groups. No refund for NO SHOW, unused components of a tour or any uncompleted tour.

RESPONSIBILITY: Changes in routes or departure times may occur for reasons beyond the company's control. No tours are operated on Yom Kippur and Rosh Hashana. The company reserves the right to cancel tours due to force majeure. It is the responsibility of the tourist to stay with the guide at all times. Modest clothing is required at holy sites.

FOR FURTHER INFORMATION REFER TO CONSUMER'S OR AGENT BROCHURE.

GRAY LINE OF JERUSALEM AND TEL AVIV, ISRAEL
Operated by Galilee Tours Ltd.   •   Reuben Ben Dori, President
FOR INFORMATION AND RESERVATIONS, CONTACT: *Moshe Hananel, Director*
3, Ben Sira St., 94181, Jerusalem, Israel • Phone: (02) 231223, 247155, 246858
Telex: 26597 GALIL IL, 26116 GALIL IL • FAX (02) 231341

Avi Kenet, Director
New York Office: 2112 Broadway, Suite 500, New York, NY 10023
Phone: (212) 874-4000, Toll free 800-874-4445 • Telex: 8100070344 Sodaud
FAX (212) 769-8832

Fig. 9-3. Continued

ISRAEL   ISREAL

Direct prepaid vouchers and checks to:

AMERICAN SIGHTSEEING ISRAEL

Saladin Street – P.O. Box 19138
Jerusalem, Israel

Operated by: Dakkak Tourist Agency
Managers: Hilmi Dakkak; Sylvia Dakkak
Telephones: 282525, 282526
Telex: 26330 HILMI IL
Cable: DAKKAKTOUR
Member: ASTA

GENERAL INFORMATION

Reservations: Are required in advance for tours and hotels.

Equipment: Mostly Mercedes vehicles. Luxury limousines, 4- and 7- passengers; minibuses to 19 Pax, A/C; deluxe coaches, A/C, to 53 Pax.

Guides: Highly qualified; mostly English-speaking, but other major languages available on request. Guide rates included in tour costs.

Admissions/Entrance Fees: Included in rates.

Children: 50% reduction on daily tours when with an adult. Inquire about reductions on package tours.

Complimentary Seats: to agents or representatives accompanying group.

Holidays: Apr. 20, 26; May 10; June 9; Sept. 30; Oct. 1, 9, 14, 21.

Rates: To the best of our knowledge, rates will be effective to Feb. 28, 1990, but are subject to change if necessary.
Special prices will be given on package tours from Jan. 6 – Feb. 15; July 1 – Sept. 1; and Nov. 1 – Dec. 15.

INDIVIDUAL TRANSFERS – 10% COMMISSION

International arrivals are to Ben-Gurion (Lod) Airport, which is located approx. 11 miles from Tel Aviv, 35 miles from Jerusalem. Rates quoted are for one-way trip and include meeting by top driver and porterage of 2 cases per person. Driver meets clients immediately outside exit from customs area and will be carrying a sign with their name on it. 24-hour airport service.

Transfer from Jerusalem to Allenby Bridge or v.v $85.00

Bridge is open 8-2 Sun. – Thurs.; 8-12 Fri. & hol. eves; closed Sat. & all holidays listed above.

BY PRIVATE CAR, PER CAR, 1 to 4 persons*

Ben-Gurion Airport to Jerusalem or v.v	$ 55.00
Ben-Gurion Airport to Tel Aviv or v.v	45.00
Ben-Gurion Airport to Haifa (or Tiberias) or v.v	125.00
Jerusalem to Tel Aviv or v.v	60.00
Haifa Harbor to Jerusalem or v.v	150.00

Night charge (between 10 p.m. and 6 a.m.) 30% additional.

*For 5 to 7 persons, add $10 per car to any of our quoted rates.
Group transfers gladly quoted on request.

INDIVIDUAL SIGHTSEEING – JERUSALEM & VICINITY – 10% COMMISSION

Includes guide, entrance fees, insured cars. Meals not included.
Passengers picked up & returned to all hotels, Jerusalem.

	RATES PER PERSON BY PRIVATE CAR Group Rates on Request			
	1 Pax	2 Pax	3 Pax	4 Up Pax
TOUR AS/1 – BETHLEHEM, MOUNT OF OLIVES, GETHSEMANE, MOUNT ZION (Room of the Last Supper). **Duration:** 3 hours. **Departs:** 9 a.m. or 2:30 p.m., Daily.	$120.00	$ 65.00	$ 45.00	$35.00
TOUR AS/2 – JERICHO, DEAD SEA (lowest point on earth, 1300 feet below sea level), **BETHANY Duration:** 4 hours. **Departs:** 9 a.m. or 2 p.m., Daily. .... Available extension to QUMRAN, to see ruins of Essene community & caves where Dead Sea Scrolls were found, add $10/Pax.	130.00	70.00	50.00	40.00
TOUR AS/3 – JERUSALEM, OLD CITY: Way of the Cross, Church of the Holy Sepluchre. Also native bazaars. **Duration:** 3 ½ hours. **Departs:** 9 a.m. or 2:30 p.m., Daily.	80.00	45.00	30.00	25.00
TOUR AS/4 – JERUSALEM, OLD CITY: Temple Area, Dome of the Rock, Western (Wailing) Wall. Also Garden Tomb. **Duration:** 3 hours. **Departs:** 9 a.m., Daily ex. Fri.	85.00	50.00	35.00	30.00
TOUR AS/5 – WEST JERUSALEM: Israel Museum (Dead Sea Scrolls), Yad Vashem, Chagall Windows, Model/Jerusalem at time of 2nd Temple. **Duration:** 3 ½ hours. **Departs:** 9 a.m. , Daily ex. Sat.; 2:30 p.m., Daily ex. Fri. & Sat.	135.00	75.00	55.00	45.00
TOUR AS/6 – TIBERIAS & NAZARETH: Via Jordan Valley to visit Sea of Galilee area (boat ride, Capernaum, Mount of Beatitudes, headwaters Jordan River) and Nazareth (Church of Annunciation, Mary's Well, synagogue), return Jerusalem. **Duration:** About 10 hours. **Departs:** 8 a.m., Daily.	325.00	170.00	115.00	90.00
TOUR AS/7 – CAESAREA, HAIFA, ACRE: Roman ruins, Mount Carmel, panoramic view Haifa, St. John's Crypt, Jezzar Pasha Mosque. **Duration:** About 10 hours. **Departs:** 8 a.m., Daily.............	325.00	170.00	115.00	90.00
TOUR AS/8 – MASADA: Half day: Ascent & descent by cable car; ruins of fortress, Herodian palace, Roman camps. **Duration:** 5 hours. **Departs:** 8 a.m., Daily.	175.00	110.00	85.00	70.00
Full day: As above plus visit QUMRAN, stop to wade or swim in Dead Sea, return via Arad, Beersheba, Hebron. **Duration:** About 10 hours. **Departs:** 8 a.m., Daily.	335.00	180.00	125.00	100.00

OUR SPECIALTIES – **Package tours:** We specialize in **pilgrimage tours** for all faiths, and tours to visit places of special historical interest. For Catholics, we are ready to arrange Masses every day. For other denominations, we are glad to offer all their preferences. We gladly prepare and cost **special programs** of any length that may be desired; just tell us how long a time and a general idea of what you would like included. TWO (OR THREE) COUNTRY TOURS: We can also arrange to add a visit to **Jordan**, especially for the opportunity to visit **Petra**, the Rose Red City of the Nabateans, & **Jerash**; and /or add a visit to **Egypt**, to visit **Cairo**, the **Pyramids, Sphinx, Valley of the Kings,** etc. Full details gladly provided upon request.

Fig. 9-4. ASI's tours and transfer services in Israel. (Courtesy of American Sightseeing International.)

19

THE BOOKING/
CONFIRMATION PROCESS

THE THREE STEP BOOKING/CONFIRMATION PROCESS

The booking and confirmation process is essentially a three-step process. It starts with a recognition of the importance of accurate and timely bookings and confirmations. The second step is gathering the data needed by the F.I.T. specialist in making a booking and the data needed by the vendor in being able to confirm a booking. The final step is communicating booking and confirmation data back and forth between the travel agency and the vendors.

TIMELY BOOKINGS

The importance of timely booking of F.I.T. arrangements appears to be self-explanatory. Obviously, if the vendor receives a booking too close to the date when service is to be rendered, it might be impossible to provide the service desired by both the client and the agency F.I.T. specialist. Many agencies that concentrate on the sale of F.I.T.s have adopted the policy of sending out booking requests within 24 hours of determining the vendor and the specific service to be used. But even in those agencies where this is not a specific policy, experienced F.I.T. specialists rapidly learn the importance of giving the vendor sufficient time to receive and process a booking. Some vendors establish their own minimum and maximum advanced booking requirements.

However, when a client comes to the agency at an especially busy time or with only a few days before the date of departure, even the most experienced F.I.T. specialist can sometimes negate the importance of timely bookings and try to squeeze out a booking with far too little advance notice for the vendor. Sometimes satisfying the desire to make a client happy or to make a large commission can get in the way of judging the needed timeliness of bookings. Those few F.I.T. specialists who refuse to take chances or to be pushed and who tell a client that the client has started too late or that the client is attempting to make a reservation with too little notice are due the respect of all in the industry.

What is timely for one vendor, however, is not necessarily the same for other vendors. The following guidelines provide the F.I.T. specialist with a rough gauge of what usually can be considered the minimum number of advance booking days prior to the departure of the client. These guidelines should be used as an average only. There are exceptional F.I.T.s that will require much more advance booking time than the number of days listed below. An example is when booking a special event, like the Olympics, it is often necessary to book the hotel of choice as much as a year in advance. For the average F.I.T. the following guidelines can be used:

Hotel reservations	10–14 days
Sightseeing	21 days
Meet and assist	30 days
Transfers	30 days
Rail reservations	45 days
Rental cars	21 days
Chauffeur-driven cars	35 days
Cruise reservations	90 days
Restaurant meal reservations	30 days
Special food and beverage functions	60 days
Special events (happening once a month or more often	60 days
Special events (happening once a quarter)	120 days
Special events (happening once every six months)	220 days
Special events (happening once a year or less often)	18 months or more

Add at least fifteen days to the above advance booking times if communication of the booking and/or confirmation is to be handled by mail rather than telex or telephone. Some special events cannot be booked on an F.I.T. basis unless space held by a tour operator in a tour operator's prepaid block is booked from the operator. Other events hold open a limited number of places for F.I.T. clients and these are traditionally made available on a first-come, first-serve basis. In either case, bookings sometimes must be made more than a year in advance. Examples of such events are the Oberummagau Passion Play (held every ten years), and both the Winter and Summer Olympics.

ACCURATE BOOKINGS

The accuracy of bookings is also important. In a recent survey of bookings transmitted to vendors by fourteen travel agents (none were F.I.T. specialists), five had at least one error in a written booking transmittal and three had two or more errors. Although most of these errors were minor and made no difference in regard to obtaining the desired services or the quality of the services that were delivered, at least two of the errors were so major that had the booking been transmitted without correction, the client might not have received any services (the date of arrival of the client was wrong) or may well have received services other than those expected (the type of service booked was in error). At the high point of the season when there are many pressures on the F.I.T. specialist, work is often undertaken when the F.I.T. specialist is tired, pushed, or under extreme pressure. Errors can result. Some travel agencies have adopted a quality control process whereby all F.I.T. booking transmittals are submitted to crosschecks to make certain that they are accurate prior to leaving the agency. Simple checklists (similar to the listings provided later in this chapter) provide a rapid way of making sure all necessary data is included in the booking communication. However, only a person with a knowledge of the entire trip arrangements and client preferences can undertake a quality check that confirms such data as room type preferences, car rental preferences, etc. Some agencies are addressing a part of these areas of quality control by having multi-page detailed client preference inventories stored in the agency reservation computers and having a quality control staff member audit booking requests against preference inventories each evening before bookings are actually sent out of the agency. Although expensive, this quality control process can go a long way toward insuring that what the client gets is what the client wants. The result is a happier client, one who will no doubt return to book future trips rather than a disgruntled client who might never again book through the agency.

CONFIRMATIONS

Confirmations are often taken for granted in a travel agency. However, they can also be a source of major problems if they are either not received at all or if they are received after the client has left on the trip. To insure that confirmations are received early enough to take appropriate action if the booking cannot be confirmed (usually an alternative booking is requested), each booking should carry with it a confirmation deadline. It is suggested that this confirmation deadline be transmitted to the vendor in a polite manner so that the vendor understands the limitations within which the agency F.I.T. specialist is working. Although this should be a polite indication of a deadline, it must also be a firm deadline. Deadline dates will depend upon the form of booking communication. For example, if the reservation is made by phone, the vendor can often provide a confirmation number while on the phone with the F.I.T. specialist. This can be followed up with a letter or a telex confirming all details. The confirmation number allows the F.I.T. specialist to proceed with making other arrangements that might be contingent upon having a confirmation for the service being booked. On the other hand, if the booking request is sent to the vendor via international air mail and a response by air mail is expected, the confirmation deadline might have to be stretched three or four weeks. A telex booking request can often be confirmed within 24 hours.

However, if there is a local holiday or weekend at the vendor's location, a telex confirmation might not be received for as much as 72 or 96 hours. Whatever the deadline, the F.I.T. specialist should be prepared to follow up with another (follow-up) booking request to the same vendor or a new booking request placed through another vendor if the confirmation deadline date/time passes. A tickler system should be set up by the F.I.T. specialist to remind the specialist of all confirmation deadlines so that a timely follow-up is undertaken if deadlines are missed. It must be remembered that the client depends upon the travel agency to make sure all arrangements are made and confirmed prior to leaving on the trip. It is the F.I.T. specialist's responsiblity to always stay on top of confirmation deadlines.

Confirmations can sometimes present problems even when they are received by the established deadlines. The confirmation might be incomplete or it might confirm arrangements different than those requested. Confirmations should always be checked against the booking request to make certain that they confirm the exact arrangements requested. If there is a difference, an immediate clarification needs to be obtained. Usually time is short at this point. Therefore telephone or telex clarification messages should be transmitted. If the difference is resolved, a new "hard copy" confirmation should be requested (by telex, if possible) from the vendor confirming the arrangements now agreed upon. If the difference is not possible to resolve, the specialist either needs to seek another vendor or find out if the alternative (and confirmed) arrangements are satisfactory with the F.I.T. clients. In no case should a confirmation message be put in a client's file without checking that the confirmation is for the arrangements requested. To do so is to invite problems that might not be possible to resolve when the error is discovered (if it is discovered) when preparing the final documents just prior to the client's departure for the F.I.T. trip.

BOOKING REQUEST DATA

Booking request data requirements vary depending upon the service being requested and the vendor's information requirements. The following can be considered checklists for data requirements for each of the major F.I.T. services that F.I.T. specialists most frequently book. Individual vendors might require less data or other data, but they will advise accordingly in their brochures or confirmation messages. F.I.T. specialists might wish to copy these lists on check data pads or they might want to use these lists to develop form letters, form telex messages, and/or form data for telephone bookings.

Hotel Bookings

1. Client name (Mr., Ms., or Mrs. followed by first name, followed by last name)
2. Number of persons in party
3. Type of accommodation SWB (single with bath,) DWB (double with bath), Suite, etc.
4. Type of plan (if appropriate): AP (American plan), MAP (modified American plan), etc.
5. Arrival date/time
6. How arriving (airline flight number, car rental, private car, chauffeur-driven car, train, tour bus, etc.)
7. Client origin city
8. Rate at which the client is booked (per night)
9. Deposit or full payment amount enclosed with booking request
10. Amount of commission deducted from deposit or full payment, if appropriate
11. Service charges collected in advance, if any
12. Taxes collected in advance, if any
13. Any special requests from the clients (balcony, ocean side room, first or lower floor room only, especially quiet room, etc.)
14. After 6 P.M. arrival guarantee, if appropriate

Sightseeing Bookings

1. Client name (Mr., Ms., or Mrs. followed by first name, followed by last name)
2. Sightseeing tour number and name of sightseeing tour being booked
3. Date the sightseeing tour is being requested
4. Time of day of the sightseeing tour (absolutely required when there are two, three, or more of the same sightseeing tours going out the same day)
5. Name of client hotel
6. City where the sightseeing tour will be operated
7. Number of persons in the sightseeing tour party
8. Rate per person
9. If a gross rate is quoted by the vendor, commission taken
10. Total to be paid to the sightseeing tour operator
11. Deposit or full payment amount enclosed with booking request

Meet and Assist Bookings

1. Airline and flight number for passenger(s) arrival
2. Airport of passenger arrival
3. Time of passenger arrival

4. Client name (Mr., Ms., or Mrs. followed by first name, followed by last name)
5. Date the meet and assist is being requested
6. Time of day the meet and assist is being requested
7. City where the meet and assist service is being requested
8. Number of persons in the party to be met
9. Rate for the meet and assist service or rate per person
10. If a gross rate is quoted by the vendor, commission taken
11. Total to be paid to the ground operator
12. Deposit or full payment amount enclosed with booking request

Transfer Bookings

The data requirements for booking transfers is the same as that required for meet and assist services, except that some vendors provide a choice of type of transfer (private car or bus, for example). In such cases the type of transfer preferred by the client should be indicated. In addition, of course, the hotel (or other lodging) destination must be advised.

Rail Bookings

1. Client name (Mr., Ms., or Mrs. followed by first name, followed by last name)
2. Number of persons in the party
3. Class of rail service preferred (first or second class)
4. City pair (the city where the client will board the train and the city of destination of the train for the client)
5. Type of train accommodation (day car, suite, sleeper, couchette) (if a bedroom, whether for one, two, three, or four persons)
6. First or second seating in the dining room (if dining car reservations are possible and desired)
7. Cost of all services requested
8. Commission in dollar amount deducted
9. Net amount of deposit and/or full payment accompanying the reservation booking request

Rental Car Bookings

1. Client name (Mr., Ms., or Mrs. followed by first name, followed by last name)
2. Airport or in-town pick-up point
3. The type of car desired
4. Airline and flight number of arrival (if airport car pickup)
5. Time of scheduled flight arrival (if airport car pickup)

6. Client's international driving license number
7. Expected number of days' usage
8. Car return location (if different than pick-up point)
9. Client credit card number expiration date, and name of client as it appears on the credit card (this is the card against which payment will be made for the car rental)
10. Type of rate being used (daily, weekly, corporate, etc.)
11. Rate amount and calculated total charge
12. Deposit, if any, accompanying reservation
13. Any additional services needed (if known)
14. Advise if collision damage waiver is needed

Chauffeur-Driven Car Bookings

The data requirements for booking chauffeur-driven cars is the same as that required for rental car bookings, except that the client's international driving license is not required. Some vendors will provide the option of either a driver only or a driver/guide combination. In such cases, the driver/guide will be more expensive than if a driver only is requested. When such options are available, the reservation booking request should indicate "driver only" or "driver guide" preferred.

Cruise Bookings

1. Client name (Mr., Ms., or Mrs. followed by first name, followed by last name) (Note: This should include the names of each party)
2. Number of persons in the party
3. Cabin number or type of cabin desired (normally this will be a letter or name category corresponding to a price and cabin size level)
4. Sailing date
5. Name of ship being booked
6. Meal sitting (early or late)
7. Dining room table size (normally 2, 4, 6, or 8)
8. Dining room smoking or non-smoking section
9. Passport number (Note: The name on the passport should correspond with the client name indicated in number 1 above)
10. Payment amount accompanying the cruise booking (normally a deposit)
11. Cruise amount per person times the number of persons and total cruise cost
12. Port charges per person times number of persons and total port charge cost
13. Total cost (amount of total cruise cost and total port taxes combined)
14. Any additional costs such as, for example, add-on air fare

15. Special occasions to be celebrated by the client (normally birthday, anniversary, or honeymoon)
16. Client preference of either inside or outside cabin
17. If a preference is available, an indication of single or double bed
18. If a choice is available, an indication of either shower or tub, or shower and tub
19. Client arrival information (either airline flight number and time of arrival or hotel in which the client will be staying prior to the cruise)
20. Client contact information (client home address and phone number)

Restaurant Meal Reservations

1. Client name (Mr., Ms., or Mrs. followed by first name, followed by last name) (Note: This should include the names of each party)
2. Number of persons in the party
3. Table size (or number of people who will be at the table—usually the same as number of persons in the party)
4. Whether for lunch or dinner
5. Date reservation is requested
6. Time of day reservation is requested (in 24-hour clock)
7. Smoking or non-smoking preferred (optional, most restaurants outside the United States do not have smoking and non-smoking sections, but a few do)
8. Payment data (seldom required but usually preferred)

Special Food and Beverage Functions

The data needed for special food and beverage functions is essentially the same as that needed for restaurant meal bookings. However, since these functions might be in facilities that have limited space and/or are in high demand such as the medieval feast in castles or dinner shows at night clubs, advance payments and/or deposits are usually required. In some cases the vendor will require full payment in advance or a set and specified fee. In other cases, a deposit will be required. Literature from the vendor will normally specify the amount required, but if this is not known, a telephone call or letter will usually provide the information needed. It should be noted, that unless payment of the deposit or full payment is received by the vendor with or after the reservation booking request, the booking will probably either not be confirmed or it will be confirmed contingent upon receiving payment by a specified date.

Special Events

The data needed to book special events can vary with the event. However, the following data is the minimum amount of information needed to make a booking:

1. Client name (Mr., Ms., or Mrs. followed by first name, followed by last name)
2. Number of persons in party
3. Arrival date/time
4. The type of facility desired (if appropriate)
5. Payment information (usually a deposit or full payment will be required with the booking request)
6. Any special requests from the client(s)

COMMUNICATING WITH VENDORS

There are three customary forms of communicating with vendors. These are telex, mail, and telephone. Each form has both advantages and disadvantages, which are reviewed here. Whatever form of communication, getting in touch with vendors, booking with vendors, and keeping in touch with vendors is essential if a quality F.I.T. is to be expected for the client. Vendor booking communications start almost as soon as the client leaves the agency after the first agency visit (even sooner if the client has phoned and advised some basic details regarding the trip) and communication continues throughout the pre-departure planning process. It often continues even after the client has left on the first leg of the F.I.T. trip. If at any point messages are not clear or are misunderstood, there is a danger that the client will not receive some component of the trip that might be vital to the success of the F.I.T. It is, therefore, essential that communications be timely, clear, precise, and documented.

TELEX COMMUNICATIONS

One of the most popular forms of communication is telex. Although most U.S.-based travel agencies have never had a telex machine in their offices, a growing number of travel agencies that specialize in F.I.T.s have either had one installed or have made arrangements to use a commercial telex machine. Internationally, the reverse is true—almost all travel agencies and almost all vendors have telex machines and use them as a major form of communication. With the advent of telex capability being built into most of the major travel agency automated reservations systems, more and more American travel agencies are actively utilizing the telex communications capability.

Telex Advantages

There are three major advantages of communicating booking requests to a supplier via telex: (1) it is electronic; (2) it is almost instantaneous; and, (3) it provides a written "hard copy" of the communication. Looking at these advantages more closely, having electronic communication means that the chance of error during transmission is very low and the cost is economical (compared to telephone, overnight letter, and other rapid forms of communication). Speed is very important. Often the F.I.T. specialist expects and needs to obtain confirmation rapidly. The telex is probably the most rapid form of communication short of the telephone plus it is often not only more reliable than phone communication, but it is clearer, for example, one can go back and review the written word more rapidly than by phone. Having a written form of communication is especially advantageous. A copy of the telex communication from the vendor, run off on the agency's computer using plain "hard copy" paper can be placed in the client's file, kept for the agency's records, and/or given to the client to prove all confirmation details upon arrival. In addition, telex confirmation messages sent to American travel agencies are usually sent in English, whereas telephone conversations might or might not find an English-speaking person on the other end of the phone line.

Telex Disadvantages

Cost, especially start-up costs, constitute the major disadvantage of using the telex to communicate with suppliers. Getting a telex number and training staff to use the telex facility properly represent a significant start-up cost. In addition, the cost per message, although significantly less expensive than long-distance phone calls, is more than an international letter. Finally, there is a labor cost involved in changing computer paper to hard copy paper each time the incoming telex messages are to be transferred from the agency's computer to print (unless the agency has or purchases a hard copy printer).

Timing is another factor that can be a disadvantage. Although the message response will show whether or not the F.I.T. specialist's message is being received by the vendor at the time it is transmitted, the vendor might not see the message and/or might not reply to it for several hours or for several days. Timing is sometimes crucial and when it is, the only method fast enough might be an international phone call. Sometimes only the phones can provide the immediate two-way communication needed.

Telex Process

The procedures to follow in using the telex to book a hotel, car, ground operator service, etc., is discussed later in this chapter. However, an overview of the telex process is presented below for those who might never have used an agency computer-generated telex facility. There are three basic steps.

Step One: Find the Vendor Telex Number   Almost all standard hotel guides (the *Official Hotel and Resort Guide,* the *STAR,* and the *Hotel Index*), ground operator guides; sightseeing companies, such as Gray Line and American Sightseeing, car rental guides; and other vendor guides show the telex number of each company listed. After selecting the vendor of choice, make a written note of its telex number.

Step Two: Find the City/Country Telex Code   International Telephone and Telegraph (ITT) publishes a two-sided sheet that lists a telex code for every country of the world. It also provides a city code for each of the major cities of the world. These codes are like telephone number area codes. By looking up the country and then the city to which the telex is to be sent, one can rapidly determine the city/country telex code. Just as with the vendor telex number, the city/country telex number should be written down for further reference.

Step Three: Access the Telex Menu in the Reservation Computer   For most reservation computer systems in order to access the telex menu, it is necessary to enter a billing code. If you do not know what billing code to enter, check with the help desk of the reservation system vendor. The menu will provide choices for the agent to select from in sending a telex. The menu normally consists of at least the following three options: (1) the agent might send a telex with no response requested or expected; (2) the agent might send a telex with a response requested to the same reservation system computer as that from which the telex was sent (it will be stored in the reservation queues for access at a convenient time); or, (3) the agent might send a telex with a response requested to an alernate address (the client's telex, for example). Additional, less often used, options are also available on the menus of some computer reservation systems.

After accessing the menu, follow the step-by-step procedures outlined in the telex/response alternative selected until the message is ended and communication is closed. This usually consists of entering the two codes (the city/country code and the vendor code). Wait for a reponse. If a response is forthcoming, it means that the city/country and vendor codes entered are numbers that the telex system has accepted and the message can be transmitted. It is pointed out that this is no guarantee that the right vendor has been accessed, only that the system has accepted the codes.

Cost and Time

When checking the ITT country/city code list, it is suggested that a note be made of the cost per minute of telex time. This cost is listed across from the country/city code and varies from city to city around the world. Most telexes are transmitted at a rate of about ten lines per minute and most reservation requests are about fifteen lines in length. This means that the average reservation request telex takes about one and one-half minutes to send. Therefore, multiply the cost per minute times the total minutes of sending time to determine the telex transmission charge.

MAIL COMMUNICATIONS

If there is enough time, communication by mail is one of the best ways to book travel arrangements for F.I.T. clients. The mail has the advantage of allowing one to be very specific about what is communicated, while at the same time allowing one to keep accurate records of communications. Not only can the agency keep records, but copies of communications can be provided to the client, thereby giving the client that much more security that arrangements have been finalized in accordance with his needs. He can leave the country receiving no shocks or surprises when arriving at his destination. The completion of standard booking forms often supplied by vendors and mailed to vendors is frequently the vendor-preferred way of booking F.I.T. arrangements.

The major disadvantage of mail is that it can be very slow. In addition, there are few countries where guaranteed mail service is available. When a telex message is delivered, the travel agency is notified of its delivery right away (if the agency requests such notification). With mail, there is no way to know in most countries whether or not the message got delivered. One simply must wait and hope a reply is forthcoming. Few letters are lost anywhere in the world, but there is a greater incidence of loss in many other countries than in the United States.

Language Problem

Although a difference in language between those sending a message and those receiving it can be a problem with all forms of communication, it is sometimes more of a problem in communicating by mail. If on the phone there is a misunderstanding, it is often understood that a misunderstanding has taken place and continued discussion can often work out the misunderstanding. In mail communication, there is sometimes no way to understand that a misunderstanding has taken place until the misunderstanding has resulted in negative repercussions. The best way to communicate by mail, therefore, is often in the language of the person who will be receiving the message. Unfortunately, most Americans do not speak or write other languages fluently. A technique sometimes used is to have form letters made up in several languages. Having a key word translation guide for the same languages, it is fairly simple to fill in the blanks and send out letters in the language of the reader.

Hotel and Restaurant Mail Reservations

For both hotels and restaurants, reservations by mail can assure that the client receives what she expects to receive. Even if the client does not speak the language of the country, a copy of the reservation request, if it is in the language of the country of destination will tell the reader what has been requested, expediting the chances of the client getting what has been requested. If a confirmation back from the hotel or restaurant has been received in writing and a copy of the confirmation is attached to the reservation request, this provides even greater insurance that the client will receive what was asked for.

The ASTA standard hotel vendor voucher is suggested for hotel reservations throughout the world. Although it is written in English, it is designed so that the other language equivalent to our words for dates, types of accommodations, etc., can be filled in with the appropriate words in the other language and understood by most people working in the hotel industry. The use of this voucher is suggested whenever sufficient time allows.

Other language letters requesting restaurant reservations are similar in concept. Figure 10-1 shows an example of an English language letter re-

La Tour d'Argent
15 Quai Tournable
7005 Paris,
France

Dear Sir:

I would like to reserve a table for a party of _____
people, (client names), at dinner (lunch) on _____
199____ at _____ P.M. Would you kindly confirm this
reservation as soon as possible? Thanking you in advance, please accept
my very best wishes.

Signature
Name
Title

Fig. 10-1. English language version of a letter requesting a restaurant reservation. (Courtesy of Julie Westhoff, Awanderlust Travel, Denver, Colorado.)

La Tour d'Argent
15 Quai Tournelle
75005 Paris,
France

Monsieur:

Je voudrais réserver une table pour (number) personnes, (client name),
pour le dîner (déjeuner) le (day and month) 199___ (year) à (time
using the 24 hour clock) heures.

Auriez-vous la gentillesse de bien vouloir me confirmer cette reservation dès
que possible?

Avec mes remerciements, veuillez agréer, Monsieur, l'expression
de mes salutations distinguées.

Signature
(Your name and address)

Fig. 10-2. French language version of a letter requesting a restaurant reservation. (Courtesy
of Julie Westhoff, Awanderlust Travel, Denver, Colorado.)

questing a restaurant reservation. Figure 10–2 shows the same letter translated into French. It can easily be translated into other languages as well.
This provides an example of how fill-in-the-blank letters can get the kind of
reservation a client might prefer without having to be an expert in the
language of the country.

Sightseeing, Transfers, and Other Ground Transportation

In communicating by mail with ground operators who provide sightseeing,
transfers, and other ground arrangements, it is normally acceptable to
communicate by mail in English. Almost all ground operators that a U.S.
agent would use speak fluent English and it is the custom to communicate in
English. This is even true when they communicate between themselves in
many cases. Frequently standard or vendor-supplied fill-in-the-blank-type
vouchers are used to book travel arrangements with these vendors and in a

few cases vouchers constitute the only form of booking communication accepted by a ground operator.

PHONE COMMUNICATIONS

The third form of communication is by telephone. This has the advantage of being immediate and it lends itself to being able to straighten out misunderstandings immediately. A disadvantage is the cost. It is more expensive than either mail or telex compared to mail; many times more expensive. In addition, while there might be an understood agreement on the phone, there is no written record of the phone conversation. There is also the potential problem of not reaching the person(s) who can commit the vendor to a service, price, etc., and finally, one can only hope that the person picking up the phone in the other country will speak the same language that the F.I.T. specialist speaks.

Phone conversations should be undertaken if there is a time problem, for example, if the client is leaving in a day or two and if there are options that need to be clarified or from which a selection should be made prior to arrival. If time permits, it is essential that phone conversations be followed up with letters detailing what the F.I.T. specialist understands to be the agreement reached in the conversation.

THE SEVEN-STEP CAR RENTAL OR CHAUFFEUR-DRIVEN BOOKING PROCESS

Step One   Discuss the pros and cons of self-drive and chauffeured-driven car rentals versus other options with the client(s).

Step Two   From the client determine:

1. Type of car desired
2. Rough itinerary to be driven including:
   a. Number of days
   b. Any special features needed for the terrain to be covered on the itinerary
3. For self-drive, if the client has a valid international driving license
4. Client's car rental budget
5. Point of preferred pickup (airport or city)
6. Point of preferred car turn-in (return) (airport or city)

From the car rental company determine:

1. The availability of the type of car desired or, if not available, the availability of the next best car type choice
2. The cost and/or any special rate plans for which the client might be eligible

"J" Car	Manual Transmissions				Automatic Transmissions		
	Economy	Small	Medium	Large	Small	Medium	Deluxe
Austria (Shilling/U.S. $)							
—	2,350/ $200	2,849/ $240	3,395/ $290	4,494/ $380	4,396/ $375	—	9,394/ $795
Belgium (Belgian Franc/U.S. $)							
4,250/ $120	4,725/ $135	7,770/ $220	9,310/ $265	16,100/ $460	11,501 $330	13,440/ $385	22,050/ $630
Denmark (Danish Krone/U.S. $)							
1,000/ $150	1,120/ $175	1,295/ $200	1,435/ $225	1,995/ $310	—	3,717/ $580	3,850/ $600
Finland (Markkas/U.S. $)							
—	1,390/ $340	1,485/ $360	1,595/ $390	1,990/ $490	—	2,900/ $700	—
France (French Franc/U.S. $)							
1,100/ $190	1,225/ $215	1,400/ $250	1,645/ $290	2,401/ $425	2,065/ $365	—	3,780/ $670
Germany (Deutsche Mark/U.S. $)							
270/ $160	300/ $180	357/ $200	420/ $250	462/ $275	490/ $295	637/ $380	847/ $500
Greece (U.S. $)							
—	$200	$225	$260	—	$325	—	—
Ireland (Punt/U.S. $)							
—	112/ $175	119/ $190	147/ $230	189/ $300	182/ $290	315/ $500	476/ $750
Israel (U.S. $)							
—	$220	$275	$345	$415	$345	$515	$740
Italy (Lira/U.S. $)							
245,700/ $200	273,000/ $225	318,500/ $260	336,000/ $275	346,500/ $280	—	745,500/ $600	994,000/ $800

Fig. 10-3. A sample of weekly car rental rates in Europe during 1988 through 1989.

"J" Car	Manual Transmissions				Automatic Transmissions		
	Economy	Small	Medium	Large	Small	Medium	Deluxe
Luxembourg (Lux. Franc/U.S. $)							
3,822/ $100	4,249/ $120	5,628/ $160	7,966/ $225	13,300/ $380	9,835/ $280	11,494/ $325	20,300/ $575
Netherlands (Guilder/U.S. $)							
308/ $165	343/ $180	371/ $195	399/ $215	546/ $290	476/ $250	749/ $400	1,554/ $825
Norway (Nor Krone/U.S. $)							
—	1,400/ $215	1,715/ $265	2,065/ $325	2,450/ $380	—	2,450/ $380	—
Portugal (Escudo/U.S. $)							
—	16,100/ $115	20,300/ $145	21,700/ $155	26,460/ $190	—	48,300/ $350	—
Spain (Peseta/U.S. $)							
15,246/ $135	16,940/ $150	18,760/ $165	20,650/ $180	24,640/ $215	43,100/ $380	—	65,653/ $575
Sweden (Swedish Krone/U.S. $)							
—	1,495/ $250	1,695/ $280	2,150/ $355	2,350/ $390	—	2,895/ $480	3,795/ $625
Switzerland (Swiss Franc/U.S. $)							
210/ $150	238/ $175	280/ $200	329/ $250	399/ $290	469/ $340	504/ $370	686/ $500
United Kingdom (Pounds/U.S. $)							
98/ $175	105/ $190	133/ $235	140/ $250	154/ $275	175/ $310	273/ $485	350/ $625
Yugoslavia (U.S. $)							
—	$150	$245	$275	$390	$420	$575	$690

Fig. 10-3. Continued

3. Restrictions that might apply
4. If any required special features are available
5. Pick-up point (location and procedure)
6. Car return point (location and procedure)
7. The client documents that will be needed at the car pick-up point (passport, driving license, etc.)
8. VAT and/or other taxes that might apply

For chauffeur-driven car rentals, determine:

1. Cost options (driver only or driver/guide)
2. Driver or driver/guide minimum qualifications
3. Tip expectations

Step Three　Discuss the options with the F.I.T. client.

Step Four　Make a phone booking, getting:

1. Reservation confirmation number
2. Reservation agent's name
3. Agreement on the form of payment and applicable exchange rate

Step Five　Complete the car rental voucher.

Step Six　Send the prepayment (an agency check) and the voucher copy to the car rental company.

Step Seven　Collect payment from the client and give the client his/her car rental confirmation and/or voucher copy.

THE ELEVEN-STEP RAIL BOOKING PROCESS

Step One　Discuss the advantages and disadvantages of rail travel versus other options with the client(s).

Step Two   From the client determine:

1. Whether or not a day train (scenery) or a night train (transportation convenience) is preferred
2. Whether first or second class is preferred
   a. First is almost always needed if the trip is more than 4 hours
   b. Very short trips on Northern European or Canadian trains can be booked second class (If a Trans European Express—TEE—train is to be taken, it is all first class and no choice is available.)
3. The itinerary for each train segment (city pairs)
4. Whether or not sleeping accommodations are desired and if so (if traveling in Europe) the client(s) prefer a sleeper or a couchettte.

Travel Voucher	TRAVEL AGENCY COPY **1** ORIGINAL (NOT NEGOTIABLE)	**695409**	
CUSTOMER NAME	DATE OF ISSUE	AGENCY FILE NO.	
RENTAL STATION ADDRESS STREET [DOWN TOWN] [AIR-PORT]	DATE OF RENTAL DAY MONTH YEAR	TO BE COMPLETED ONLY IF PART OF TOUR PACKAGE TOUR NAME	
CITY	LENGTH OF RENTAL (24 HR DAYS)	TOUR NO. RATE CODE	
TELEPHONE NO. CITY OF RETURN	CAR GROUP OR CLASS	VOUCHER VALUE INCLUDES [CDW] [TAX] [UNL. MIL.]	
RATE NAME	RESERVATION NO.	ARC OR IATA NO.	AGENCY VALIDATION STAMP
REMARKS		ACCOUNT NO.	
VOUCHER VALUE (AMOUNT IN WORDS) IF NET RATE INCLUDE RATE CODE	AMOUNT	TRAVEL AGENCY NAME & ADDRESS	
— MAXIMUM VALUE $1000 (OR EQUIVALENT LOCAL CURRENCY). RENTAL NOT TO EXCEED 30 DAYS. — EXCHANGE RATES AT COMMENCEMENT OF RENTAL APPLY. — ANY EXCESS CHARGES OVER VOUCHER VALUE MUST BE PAID BY RENTER DIRECT TO COMPANY.	OFFICE USE ONLY RATE OF EXCHANGE APPLIED RENTAL AGREEMENT NO.		

Fig. 10-4. A sample of car rental reservation voucher.

Travel Voucher	TRAVEL AGENCY COPY **1** ORIGINAL (NOT NEGOTIABLE)	**695409**	
CUSTOMER NAME	DATE OF ISSUE	AGENCY FILE NO.	
RENTAL STATION ADDRESS STREET [DOWN TOWN] [AIR-PORT]	DATE OF RENTAL DAY MONTH YEAR	TO BE COMPLETED ONLY IF PART OF TOUR PACKAGE TOUR NAME	
CITY	LENGTH OF RENTAL (24 HR DAYS)	TOUR NO. RATE CODE [ ][ ][ ]	
TELEPHONE NO. CITY OF RETURN	CAR GROUP OR CLASS	VOUCHER VALUE INCLUDES [CDW] [TAX] [UNL. MIL.]	
RATE NAME	RESERVATION NO.	ARC OR IATA NO.	AGENCY VALIDATION STAMP
REMARKS		ACCOUNT NO.	
VOUCHER VALUE (AMOUNT IN WORDS) IF NET RATE INCLUDE RATE CODE	AMOUNT	TRAVEL AGENCY NAME & ADDRESS	
— MAXIMUM VALUE $1000 (OR EQUIVALENT LOCAL CURRENCY). RENTAL NOT TO EXCEED 30 DAYS. — EXCHANGE RATES AT COMMENCEMENT OF RENTAL APPLY. — ANY EXCESS CHARGES OVER VOUCHER VALUE MUST BE PAID BY RENTER DIRECT TO COMPANY.	OFFICE USE ONLY		
	RATE OF EXCHANGE APPLIED		
	RENTAL AGREEMENT NO.		

Travel Voucher	TRAVEL AGENCY COPY **2** ORIGINAL (NOT NEGOTIABLE)	**695409**	
CUSTOMER NAME	DATE OF ISSUE	AGENCY FILE NO.	
RENTAL STATION ADDRESS STREET [DOWN TOWN] [AIR-PORT]	DATE OF RENTAL DAY MONTH YEAR	TO BE COMPLETED ONLY IF PART OF TOUR PACKAGE TOUR NAME	
CITY	LENGTH OF RENTAL (24 HR DAYS)	TOUR NO. RATE CODE [ ][ ][ ]	
TELEPHONE NO. CITY OF RETURN	CAR GROUP OR CLASS	VOUCHER VALUE INCLUDES [CDW] [TAX] [UNL. MIL.]	
RATE NAME	RESERVATION NO.	ARC OR IATA NO.	AGENCY VALIDATION STAMP
REMARKS		ACCOUNT NO.	
VOUCHER VALUE (AMOUNT IN WORDS) IF NET RATE INCLUDE RATE CODE	AMOUNT	TRAVEL AGENCY NAME & ADDRESS	
— MAXIMUM VALUE $1000 (OR EQUIVALENT LOCAL CURRENCY). RENTAL NOT TO EXCEED 30 DAYS. — EXCHANGE RATES AT COMMENCEMENT OF RENTAL APPLY. — ANY EXCESS CHARGES OVER VOUCHER VALUE MUST BE PAID BY RENTER DIRECT TO COMPANY.	OFFICE USE ONLY		
	RATE OF EXCHANGE APPLIED		
	RENTAL AGREEMENT NO.		

Fig. 10-4. Continued

Travel Voucher

TRAVEL AGENCY COPY **3** ORIGINAL (NOT NEGOTIABLE)

695409

CUSTOMER NAME	DATE OF ISSUE	AGENCY FILE NO.
RENTAL STATION ADDRESS STREET [DOWN TOWN] [AIR-PORT]	DATE OF RENTAL DAY MONTH YEAR	TO BE COMPLETED ONLY IF PART OF TOUR PACKAGE TOUR NAME
CITY	LENGTH OF RENTAL (24 HR DAYS)	TOUR NO. RATE CODE
TELEPHONE NO. CITY OF RETURN	CAR GROUP OR CLASS	VOUCHER VALUE INCLUDES CDW TAX UNL. MIL.
RATE NAME	RESERVATION NO.	ARC OR IATA NO.
REMARKS		ACCOUNT NO. AGENCY VALIDATION STAMP

VOUCHER VALUE (AMOUNT IN WORDS) IF NET RATE INCLUDE RATE CODE	AMOUNT	TRAVEL AGENCY NAME & ADDRESS
— MAXIMUM VALUE $1000 (OR EQUIVALENT LOCAL CURRENCY). RENTAL NOT TO EXCEED 30 DAYS. — EXCHANGE RATES AT COMMENCEMENT OF RENTAL APPLY. — ANY EXCESS CHARGES OVER VOUCHER VALUE MUST BE PAID BY RENTER DIRECT TO COMPANY.	OFFICE USE ONLY RATE OF EXCHANGE APPLIED RENTAL AGREEMENT NO.	

Travel Voucher

TRAVEL AGENCY COPY **4** ORIGINAL (NOT NEGOTIABLE)

695409

CUSTOMER NAME	DATE OF ISSUE	AGENCY FILE NO.
RENTAL STATION ADDRESS STREET [DOWN TOWN] [AIR-PORT]	DATE OF RENTAL DAY MONTH YEAR	TO BE COMPLETED ONLY IF PART OF TOUR PACKAGE TOUR NAME
CITY	LENGTH OF RENTAL (24 HR DAYS)	TOUR NO. RATE CODE
TELEPHONE NO. CITY OF RETURN	CAR GROUP OR CLASS	VOUCHER VALUE INCLUDES CDW TAX UNL. MIL.
RATE NAME	RESERVATION NO.	ARC OR IATA NO.
REMARKS		ACCOUNT NO. AGENCY VALIDATION STAMP

VOUCHER VALUE (AMOUNT IN WORDS) IF NET RATE INCLUDE RATE CODE	AMOUNT	TRAVEL AGENCY NAME & ADDRESS
— MAXIMUM VALUE $1000 (OR EQUIVALENT LOCAL CURRENCY). RENTAL NOT TO EXCEED 30 DAYS. — EXCHANGE RATES AT COMMENCEMENT OF RENTAL APPLY. — ANY EXCESS CHARGES OVER VOUCHER VALUE MUST BE PAID BY RENTER DIRECT TO COMPANY.	OFFICE USE ONLY RATE OF EXCHANGE APPLIED RENTAL AGREEMENT NO.	

Fig. 10-4. Continued

Travel Voucher	TRAVEL AGENCY COPY **5** ORIGINAL (NOT NEGOTIABLE)	**695409**	
CUSTOMER NAME	DATE OF ISSUE	AGENCY FILE NO.	
RENTAL STATION ADDRESS STREET [DOWN TOWN] [AIR-PORT]	DATE OF RENTAL DAY MONTH YEAR	TO BE COMPLETED ONLY IF PART OF TOUR PACKAGE TOUR NAME	
CITY	LENGTH OF RENTAL (24 HR DAYS)	TOUR NO. RATE CODE [ ][ ][ ]	
TELEPHONE NO. CITY OF RETURN	CAR GROUP OR CLASS	VOUCHER VALUE INCLUDES [CDW] [TAX] [UNL. MIL.]	
RATE NAME	RESERVATION NO.	ARC OR IATA NO.	AGENCY VALIDATION STAMP
REMARKS		ACCOUNT NO.	
VOUCHER VALUE (AMOUNT IN WORDS) IF NET RATE INCLUDE RATE CODE	AMOUNT	TRAVEL AGENCY NAME & ADDRESS	
— **MAXIMUM VALUE $1000** (OR EQUIVALENT LOCAL CURRENCY). RENTAL NOT TO EXCEED 30 DAYS. — **EXCHANGE RATES** AT COMMENCEMENT OF RENTAL APPLY. — **ANY EXCESS CHARGES** OVER VOUCHER VALUE MUST BE PAID BY RENTER DIRECT TO COMPANY.	OFFICE USE ONLY RATE OF EXCHANGE APPLIED RENTAL AGREEMENT NO.		

Fig. 10-4. Continued

a. If a sleeper, which of the following is preferred:
   — a first class bedroom for one person
   — a first class bedroom for two people
   — a second class bedroom for two people
   — a second class bedroom for three people
b. If a couchette, which of the following is preferred:
   — a first class couchette (four couchettes per compartment)
   — a second class couchette (six couchettes per compartment)

Note: If train travel is outside of Europe, other sleeping arrangements might be offered. Discuss the following four potential options with the client at this stage, determining if the client(s) prefer(s) to:

a. Share a rail compartment—some are for four people with upper and lower beds at each wall
b. Take a pullman sleeping compartment (a train car made up of all beds usually two or three high at each wall)
c. Have a private couchette (a very small room with private chair and lavatory—the chair makes into a bed at night)
d. Reserve a private sleeping compartment (usually a day bed that converts to a night bed, a writing table that folds into the wall at night, and a lavatory/toilet)
5. If the trip is long enough that food service will be needed, find out if the client(s) prefer(s):
   a. A train with a dining car (most TEE trains and many others)
   b. A train with meals served at one's seat (all TGV high-speed trains from Paris to French Mediterranean, Alps, or Switzerland)

    c. If first or second sitting is preferred in the dining car

6. If the client(s) prefer(s) to make advance reservations for all train segments (Reservations are suggested on all segments and required for Italian Rapidos, Spanish Express Trains, French TGV Trains, sleepers and couchettes.)
7. Client's rail budget

Step Three From the *Thomas Cook Rail Guide* determine:

1. What trains (by number and/or name) traverse the city pairs the client wishes to travel at approximately the times the client prefers to travel
2. Whether or not sleeping cars are on evening or night trains, and if so, what type(s) of sleeping accommodations are standard
3. Exact arrival and departure times (especially important if the client has close air or sightseeing trip connections)
4. Dining and other facilities provided on the trains selected as options
5. Whether or not the train options are non-stop, or if they have stops, the frequency, duration and location of major city stops

Step Four Discuss the *Thomas Cook Rail Guide* options with the client(s) and determine a first and second choice of trains to be booked and first and second choices of sleeping accommodations, if appropriate.

Step Five Call the appropriate rail company and from the rail company determine:

1. If the type of train preferred is available on the dates needed between the city pairs being traveled

Fig. 10-5. The Venice Simplon Orient Express restores elegance to rail travel. (Courtesy of the Venice Simplon-Orient-Express-Library.)

2. If the class of service preferred is available
3. If the type of sleeping accommodation preferred is available
4. If the preferred sitting in the dining room is available
5. If window or aisle (whichever the client prefers) in a smoking or non-smoking compartment (whichever the client prefers is available)
6. The exact price of each client-preferred option

Step Six   If the first preference of train type, class of service, type of sleeping accommodations, preferred dining car sitting, window or aisle preference, or smoking or non-smoking car preference is *not* available

1. Put the rail reservationist on hold, if you perceive the client will take an option right away with little or no discussion. Discuss the option with the client and then confirm to the rail reservationst that the client will take the option, or
2. Hang up from the rail booking call, discuss the options with the client, determine option preferences, and call the rail company reservationist again. Advise the reservationist of the option preferences.

Step Seven   Make a booking getting:

1. The name of the agent making the reservation
2. Agreement on form of payment and U.S. dollar cost
3. Lag time in getting tickets and written reservation confirmations

Note: On most European trains reservations cannot be made more than two weeks in advance. The hotel concierge can reconfirm reservations for dates when the client leaves for Europe more than two weeks out.

4. Reservation confirmation data for each city pair being traveled as follows:
   a. Train name and/or number
   b. Train, seat, compartment, and car numbers (berth number, if appropriate)
   c. Couchette or sleeper assignment, compartment, and car number (if different than day car number)
   d. Preferred class of service confirmed
   e. Preferred dining car sitting confirmed
5. Appropriate confirmation numbers
6. The exact price and payment confirmation data including:
   a. The exact amount and date by which payment of the deposit needs to be made (including form of payment accepted and address to which it is to be sent)
   b. The exact amount and date by which payment of the final payment needs to be made (including form of payment accepted and address to which it is to be sent)
7. Reservation agent's name

Step Eight   Confirm all details arranged with the client(s) making sure all details arranged are agreeable to them.

Step Nine   Collect a deposit and/or full payment from the client(s), depending upon the amount of time and whether or not there is enough time to collect two payments. (Always collecting full payment and cancellation insurance payment is suggested.)

Step Ten   Send the prepayment (deduct agency commissions and send an agency check) and a letter detailing all reservation data that was confirmed in step seven to the U.S. office of the rail company; request (in the letter) documents and written reservation confirmations.

Step Eleven   Verify the accuracy and completeness of documents upon receipt and turn them over to the client, collecting full payment from the client (if not already paid in full).

RAIL CONTACT INFORMATION

RAILROADS

AMTRAK
National Railroad Passenger Corporation
400 N. Capital St. N.W.
Washington, D.C. 20001
(202) 383-3000
Telex 892624

Pres.   Alan S. Boyd
V. P. Marketing   William Norman
                                (202)383-2002
V. P. Pass. Sve.   John Lombardi
                                (202) 383 3914
Dir. Adv./Mktg. Sve.   Joe Falsetti
                                (202) 383-2030
Dir. Sales Prgrms.   K. Hartz
                                (202) 383-2051
Mng. Dir.   Brian Duff
                                (202) 383-3857
Tvl. Ed.   John F. McLeod
                                (202) 383-3850

Chicago, Ill. 60606:
309 W. Jackson Blvd.
Alfred J. Kaletta, Reg. Sales Dir.

New York, N.Y. 10001:
One Penn Plaza (212) 233-6457
Info. Res. (212) 736-4545
W. S. Smith, Reg. Sales Dir.

San Francisco, CA. 94105
100 Mission Street (415) 944-1896
Reg. Bell, Reg. Sales Dir.

RAILWAYS OF AUSTRALIA
N. A. Sales Office: Australian Travel Service/Tour Pacific
1101 E. Broadway
Glendale, CA 91205
Tel (800) 423-2880

Melbourne, Victoria, Australia 3000
85 Queen Street, Tel (03) 608-0811

AUSTRIAN FEDERAL RAILWAYS
545 5th Avenue
New York, N.Y. 10017
Info: (212) 697-0651
Tickets at French, German, Swiss rail offices

AUTO-TRAIN CORP.
1801 K. St. N.W.
Washington, D.C. 20006
Exec: (202) 785-4020
Res/Info E.U.S. 800-424-1111
Res/Info Can: Collect
Res/Info. Wash. D.C. (202) 785-4000

Pres.	Eugene K. Garfield
Sr. V.P./C.O.O.	Richard A. Goldstein
Mgr. Trv. Agcy. Sales	Lee Reidel
Dir. P.R.	Patricia A. Mason

BELGIAN NATIONAL RAILROADS
745 5th Ave.
New York, N.Y. 10151
(212) 758-8130
Tickets at French, German, Swiss rail offices

Dir.	Mrs. Frederique Raeymaekers
Mgr. Trvl. Trade Rel.	Beatrice Genart
Mgr. P.R.	Ann Neville

BRITRAIL TRAVEL INTERNATIONAL
630 3rd Ave.
New York, N.Y. 10017
Exec.: (212) 682-5150
Res.: (212) 599-5400

Pres.   Colin M. Hall

Los Angeles, Calif. 90017
800 South Hope St. (213) 624-8787
M. Fox, Marketing Manager, Western USA

New York, N.Y. 10017
630 3rd Ave. (212) 599-1467
D. Ralphs, Marketing Manager, Eastern USA

Toronto, Ont. M5R 1A3
94 Cumberland St. (416) 929-3334
V. Leddie, Sales Manager, Eastern Canada

Vancouver, B.C. V6C 1T2:
408 Granville St. (604) 683-6896
K. Bishop, Sales Manager, Western Canada

Dallas 75201
Suite 210, Cedar Maple Plaza
2305 Cedar Springs (214) 748-0860
J. Scott, Marketing Manager, Central USA

CIE TOURS, INTERNATIONAL
590 5th Ave.
New York, N.Y. 10036
(212) 944-8828
Res/Info Exc NYS: 800-223-8944
NYS: 800-522-5258

Exec. V.P.   Eamonn McKeon
V.P. Sls.   Ralph Mangini
V.P. Admin.   Patrick O'Connell
Sls. Mgr.   Vincent Callahan
Mgr. E. Coast   Ena Langan

Chicago, Ill.
1651 Clavey Road,
Highland Park 60035
(312) 831-2612

Joe Collins, Mgr. Midwest

Los Angeles, Calif.:
2322 E. Larch St. Simi Valley, 93065 (213) 888-7388
Evelyn Myers, Mngr. West Coast

**CONFERENCE OF EUROPEAN
RAILROAD REPRESENTATIVES**
c/o Britrail Travel International
630 5th Ave.
New York, N.Y. 10017
(212) 599-5400

Chmn.   John A. M. Watson

DANISH STATE RAILWAYS
(See listings for French, German, Italian, Swiss rail offices)

EURAILPASS EXECUTIVE COMMITTEE
610 5th Ave.
New York, N.Y. 10020
(212) 586-0091

Chmn.   Joseph Blumstein

EXPRESS INTERNATIONAL TICKET CORP.
P. O. Box A Main St.
Saltillo, PA. 17253
(814) 448-3941

Pres.   Linda Swinnerton
Mktg. Mngr.   Mike Swinnerton

FINNISH STATE RAILROADS
Rep: German Federal Railroad
630 5th Ave.
New York, N.Y. 10017
(212) 977-9300
800-223-6036

FRENCH NATIONAL RAILROADS
610 5th Ave.
New York, N.Y. 10020
(212) 582-2816

Gen. Mngr. N.A./Carib.   Joseph C. Blumstein
Depty. Mnge. N.A.   Michael J. Ponssot
Asst. Genl. Mngr.   Dagobert M. Scher

Beverly Hills, Calif. 90210:
9465 Wilshire Blvd.
Robert Berthe S.W. RM
(213) 274-6934

Chicago, Ill. 60603:
11 E. Adams St.
Horst Steinfer Midwest R.M.
(312) 427-8691

Coral Gables, Fla. 33134:
2121 Ponce de Leon Blvd.
Gisele Pauin, SE RM
(305) 445-8648

Montreal, Que H3A 183:
1500 Stanley St.
Jecques Meinner, Mgr. Can.
(514) 288-8255

San Francisco, Calif. 94108:
360 Post St.
Paul Avril, N.W. RM
(415) 982-1993

Vancouver, B.C. V6C 1T2:
409 Granville St.
(604) 688-6707

GERMAN FEDERAL RAILROAD
630 5th Ave.
New York, N.Y. 10111
(212) 977-9300
800-223-6036

Gen. Mngr.	Hermann Krueger
Asst. Gen. Mngr.	Juergen Arnold
Sls. Mngr.	Hartmut Lemke

Boston, Mass. 02116:
625 Statler Office Bldg.
Cindy Mac-Isaac. Off. Mngr.
(617) 542-0577

Chicago, Ill. 60603;
c/o German National Tourist Office
104 S. Michigan Ave.
Veronica Lupori, Sls.
(312) 263-2958

Houston, Texas 77002:
c/o DER Travel Service
1121 Walker Street
Peter Schaefer, RM
(713) 274-8781

Los Angeles, Calif. 90067:
c/o DER Travel Service
101000 Santa Monica Blvd.
(213) 553-7063

Jack Woldt, Sls.
c/o German National Tourist Office
700 Flower Street
Helmut Helas, Sls.
(213) 688-7332

Toronto, Ont:
c/o DER Travel Services
45 Richmond St. W.
Christina Holloway, RM
(416) 364-2214

ITALIAN STATE RAILWAYS
Pass. Ticket Agent: CIT Tours Corporation
666 5th Ave.
New York, N.Y. 10103
(212) 397-2667

Gen. Mgr.   Alan Pini

Bensonville, Ill. 60106:
CIT Tours Corporation
765 Route 83
(312) 860-1090

Los Angeles, Calif. 90036:
CIT Tours Corporation
5670 Wilshire Blvd.
(213) 938-2921

Montreal, Que.
2055 Peel St.
(514) 845-9101

New York, N.Y. 10019:
666 5th Ave.
(212) 397-2667

Toronto, Ont.:
111 Richmond St.
(416) 384-4724

JAPANESE NATIONAL RAILWAYS
45 Rockefeller Plaza
New York, N.Y. 10111
Info only: (212) 757-9070

Dir.   Takeshi Tamura

LAHAINA-KAANAPALI & PACIFIC RAILROAD
P. O. Box 816
Lahaina, Maui, Hawaii 96761
Honolulu: (808) 533-6980
Hawaii: (808) 667-6851

Pres.   Willis B. Kyle

MALAYAN RAILWAY
Discount passes good year-round available in
Singapore and 9 other train stations in Malaysia.
600 Montgomery Street
San Francisco, Calif. 94111
(415) 788-3344

MEXICAN GOVERNMENT RAILWAY SYSTEM
489 5th Ave.
New York, N.Y. 10017
(212) 682-1494

Gen. Agt.   Emita Rodriquez

NETHERLANDS RAILWAYS
576 5th Ave.
New York, N.Y. 10036
(212) 245-5320
Tickets at French, German, Italian, Swiss rail
offices: local tickets at stations in Holland

Gen Rep. U.S. Can.   John Bertram

NEW ZEALAND RAILWAYS
c/o New Zealand Govt. Tourist Board
630 5th Ave.
New York, N.Y. 10020
(212) 586-0060

Tvl. Commissioner   Bert Queenin

NORWEGIAN STATE RAILWAYS
(See listings for French, German, Italian, Swiss
rail offices)

SAR TRAVEL
610 5th Ave.
New York, N.Y. 10020
(212) 826-1245
NYS: 800-223-9870
Nationwide: 800-442-5985

SKAGWAY AND WHITEHORSE ROUTE
P. O. Box 2147
Seattle, Wash. 98111
(206) 623-2510

Mngr. Pass. Sls.   W. E. Feero

SOUTH AFRICAN RAILWAYS
(Publ. and Travel Dept.)
P. O. Box 1111
Johannesburg, South Africa
Telex: 8-0876 S.A.

Mngr.   J. Havenga

SPANISH NATIONAL RAILWAYS
(French National Railroads; Agents
for tickets, info only)

SWEDISH STATE RAILWAYS
(See listings for French, Italian, Swiss rail
offices)

SWISS FEDERAL RAILWAYS
The Swiss Center
608 5th Ave.
New York, N.Y. 10020
(212) 757-5944

Dir.   Helmut Klee
Mktg. Mngr.   Eric Buhlmann
Railway Dept. Mngr.   Robert Hager
Sls. Prod. Mngr.   Rene Steim

TRANSALPINO
Reduced rate-rail passes
c/o Express Int'l Main Street
Saltillo, PA. 17253
(814) 448-3941

VIA RAIL CANADA
P. O. Box 8116
1801 McGill College
Montreal, Que. H3A 2N4
(514) 286-2311

Chmn. of Bd./Pres.

V. P. Pass. Mktg.

Sys. Mngr. Sls. Pro.

Sys. Mngr. Mkt. Dev.

J. F. Roberts

G. C. Campbell

J. F. A. LeVasseur

G. Roberge

Banff, Alta, T0L 0C0:
Elk/Lynx
1-800-665-8630

Boston, Mass.
Tie line to Montreal
(617) 426-7974

Buffalo, N.Y. 14207
1765 Niagara St.
(716) 854-2842

Calgary, Alta 72G 0P6:
9th Ave/Centre
1-800-665-8630

Chicago, Ill. 60603:
105 E. Adams St.
(312) 263-3080

Detroit, Mich.
298 Walker
Windsor, Ont.
(313) 963-6037

Halifax. N.S. B3H 2P6:
1161 Hollis
(902) 429-8421

Jasper, Alta T0E 1E0:
400 Comnaught Dr.
1-800-665-8630

Moncton, N.B. E1C 1H7:
1234 Main
(506) 642-2916

Montreal, Que. H3B 4G1:
Gare Centrale, Central Station
J. Potvin, Super.
(514) 871-1331

New York, N.Y. 10036
630 5th Ave.
(212) 586-6066

Niagara Falls, Ont. L2E 2R6:
4267 Bridge
1-800-268-9511

Ottawa, Ont. K1G 3H5:
200 Tremblar
(613) 238-8289

Quebec, Que. G1W 1S1:
Gare Ste-Foy; Ste-Foy Station
1-800-361-5390

Prince George, B.C. V2L 2Y3:
1300 First Ave.
112-800-665-8630

Saint John, N.B. E2J 2B8:
Station
(506) 642-2916

San Francisco, Calif. 94103:
Hearst Bldg. 3rd & Market
(415) 543-4737

Saskatoon, Sask S7K 1J6
Chappel Dr.
1-800-665-8630

Saint John's Nflnd. A1C 5K1:
Water St. Call nearest Transport Ltd.
Office

Toronto, Ont. M5J 1E7:
Union Station-Gare Union
(416) 366-8411

Vancouver, B.C. V6A 2X7:
1150 Station
112-800-665-8630

Victoria, B.C. V8W 2M3:
325 Esquimait
112-800-665-8630

Winnipeg, Man. R3C 2P8:
123 Main
(204) 949-1830

VOYAGER SIGHTSEEING TRAIN
600 S. Seabreeze Ave.
Fort Lauderdale, Fla. 33316
(305) 463-0401
(306) 463-0401

Gen. Mngr.   Mrs. Gertrude Koch
Mngr. Trvl. Agy. Sls.   Z. Friedberg

SUMMARY

The three step booking and confirmation process consists of:

1. Recognizing the importance of booking and getting confirmations in an accurate and timely manner
2. Getting the needed data
3. Communicating the data to and from the appropriate vendors

Because of the potential for error in not booking in a timely manner, agencies have set up tickler systems to provide cross checks. Since vendors need varying amounts of lead time, a listing of minimum time guidelines has been provided by vendor type, ranging from ten days to over eighteen months.

Accurate bookings are important, too. Booking accuracy is harder to control, but some efforts at quality control have been made. It is important that systems be developed and followed to insure booking accuracy.

The other half of making a booking is receiving a confirmation. Rather than taking confirmations for granted, a tickler file needs to be established and response deadlines need to be set. If the vendor does not respond on time, either a follow-up booking request needs to be sent or a new booking with another vendor needs to be made. All confirmations need to be checked to make sure there is no deviation from confirming what had been requested. Any differences should be resolved right away.

Booking request data varies with the vendor. Standard data checklists have been provided for booking hotels, sightseeing, meet and assist services, transfers, rail, rental and chauffeur-driven cars, cruises, restaurants, special food and beverage functions, and special events.

Communication is the third part of the three-step booking and confirmation process. While there are other ways of communicating with vendors outside the United States, there are three ways that are common in working on F.I.T. client arrangements. These are telex, mail, and telephone. Each form of communications has its advantages and disadvantages. Telex is easy if the travel agency's reservations computer has been brought on-line and assigned a telex number. Telex is fast and it provides a hard copy. Messages can be transmitted between the vendor and the travel agency back and forth throughout a day working constantly to obtain exactly what a client wants and the total cost will normally be less than a single phone conversation would be. However, telex is more expensive than mail and the agency must pay an initial cost to be brought on-line.

Mail provides the opportunity to be most expressive and to provide the greatest amount of communication. It also provides a hard copy. However, mail is slow and mail messages can be misunderstood. Using form letters in the language of the recipient to request hotel and restaurant reservations is efficient and often results in getting the client exactly what the client requests. Vendors provide the exact data they need and often are the vendor preferred form of communication. A final advantage is that mail is the least expensive major form of communication.

Using the telephone is fast, but expensive. In addition to cost is the drawback of langauge. Unless both parties speak the same language, misunderstanding can occur. In addition, to get a hard copy of the telephone-generated confirmation, the vendor must follow up with a letter or a telex. Whatever the form of communication, it is important to keep good, accurate records and to make sure the client has copies of appropriate written documents to carry with him on the trip.

■   ■   ■

❑ REVIEW QUESTIONS

1. What are the three steps of the booking confirmation process?
2. Within how many hours of agreement on vendors and services needed do many agency policies call for sending out booking requests?
3. Do all vendors agree on their definitions of timely?
4. How long in advance should a special food and beverage function be booked?
5. How many days should be added to average F.I.T. booking guidelines if the booking is made by mail?
6. What quality control efforts are some agencies adopting to make sure booking transmittals are accurate?
7. Why should each booking request carry with it a confirmation deadline?
8. What kind of system might be set up to remind an F.I.T. specialist of confirmation deadlines?
9. Why should confirmations be checked against booking requests?
10. Why are hard copies of confirmations important?
11. What are some of the standard data transmitted to vendors in booking requests?
12. In what way might the data requirements differ when booking a "transfer" as compared to booking a "meet and assist" service?
13. What two driver-type options are often made available to F.I.T. clients when chauffeur-driven arrangements are booked?
14. What dining room table size options are usually made available to F.I.T. clients when they take a cruise?
15. What are the three standard forms of vendor communication?
16. Why is it essential that communications be timely, precise, clear, and documented?

17. Do most travel agencies in the United States and outside the U.S. have telex machines? Explain your answer.
18. Why is telex one of the most popular forms of communication?
19. What must a travel agency do to access computer reservation systems telex capability?
20. What are the disadvantages of using telex as a means of communication for F.I.T. specialists?
21. How does the F.I.T. specialist find a vendor telex number when a telex message is ready to be sent?
22. Where does the F.I.T. specialist find the appropriate country/city telex code when getting ready to send a telex message to a vendor located outside the United States?
23. Where can the F.I.T. specialist find the travel agency's billing code if the manager/owner of the agency is not present?
24. How long does the average reservation request telex take to send? How is this figure calculated?
25. What are the advantages of mail communications as compared to using telex or the phone for communicating?
26. In what way can form letters help to overcome the language problem in communicating by mail?
27. What type of voucher is suggested for hotel reservations throughout the world?
28. Why is communicating to ground operators in English normally acceptable?
29. What are the advantages and the disadvantages of using the phone to communicate with international vendors?
30. When booking a car rental, why might it be important to find out what restrictions might apply?
31. On what European trains are reservations required?
32. On most European trains reservations cannot be made more than how many weeks in advance?

❏ *ROLE PLAY EXERCISE*

Two students may participate in this role play either out of class as a way to review the chapter or as an in-class exercise. One plays the role of the F.I.T. specialist and the other plays the role of the ground service operator in London, England. Please read the script and then pick up the conversation in your own words.

F.I.T. SPECIALIST This is _____ with _____ Travel Agency in the United States. I would like to make ground arrangements for a party of two, Johnson, arriving on the 23 September via BA 548. Hotel arrangements have been made at the Bristol. Do you have sighteseeing pick up at the Bristol?

GROUND OPERATOR: It isn't one of our standard pickups, but we can arrange side lobby pickup and drop off at no additional cost with full advance payment less your commission and with five business days advance notice for full day and multi-day sightseeing only. Do you have one of our rate sheets?

F.I.T. SPECIALIST: Yes, and I would like to book the full day Oxford and Shakespeare Theater tour on the 25 September and the Thames River and and Castle cruise on the 28 and 29 September.

GROUND OPERATOR: Right. Give me the client booking data, contact information for you and your agency, and form of advanced payment and I'll process a confirmation number for you while you are still on the phone. Remember, it's self-canceling if we don't receive payment at least fifteen days in advance. Since we quote in pounds, please make sure you remit in pounds.

F.I.T. SPECIALIST: Fine, before giving you the client data and our agency information, I understand you book plays as well. Our clients want to stay in the Picadilly Circus area for evening plays. What's available for the evening of the 24 September?

GROUND OPERATOR: There are three theaters within four blocks of the Picadilly Circus underground. Only The Mad Englishman is sold out on the 24 September, but . . .

Continue on your own.

RAIL BOOKING PROCESS EXERCISE

SITUATION: Mr. and Mrs. Johnson wish to board trans European express train number 863 from Paris to Nice, departing at 9:30 P.M. January 10. They wish to reserve a first class compartment and Mrs. Johnson wishes to have a beauty parlor appointment made for her shortly after the evening meal. They would like reservations in the dining car at about 11:00 P.M..

ASSIGNMENT: Describe on a step-by-step basis how you will make the reservations, submit documentation and request tickets, vouchers, etc.

Please place your name and social security number on the right-hand corner of the page before you turn it in.

RAIL BOOKING PRACTICE EXERCISE

SITUATION: Mr. and Mrs. Jones want to take the Paris to Marseille TGV train leaving at 9:03 P.M. and arriving at 8:11 A.M. the next morning (train number 521). They want a two person first class sleeper. They wish to leave

Paris the evening of May 21 and will continue on to Rome the evening of May 26. For the Marseille-Rome trip they want the train leaving at 5:23 P.M. and arriving at 7:00 A.M. (train number 408). On that train they want second sitting in the dining car for dinner and a first class sleeper. On May 28 the Johnsons want to take the 12:50 Noon Rapido to Bari (train number 614) to connect with the ferry to Greece. It arrives in Bari at 7:25 P.M. They want first sitting in the dining room for dinner and a first class non-smoking compartment with both window seats for the Rapido.

ASSIGNMENT: You have discussed the above with reservationist (Ms. Mimi Dubonne) and she has confirmed everything for you. Since the Johnsons will not be leaving the United States until May 19, all reservations can be finalized before they depart. Write a letter to Mimi at: French National Railroads, 11 East Adams Street, Chicago, Illinois 60603 confirming the arrangements. Review the eleven steps of the "Rail Booking Process" to make sure you have covered everything in your letter.

CAR RENTAL BOOKING PRACTICE EXERCISE

Mrs. and Mrs. Johnson have asked to rent a car while they are in Paris. They will arrive in Paris on Saturday, June 10 at 11:00 A.M. via AF 269 and will be leaving on Thursday, June 15 at 1:30 P.M. via BA 551 for their stay in London. They will be using an airport transfer to their hotel in downtown Paris and do not want to pick up their car until Monday morning at about 10:00 A.M. They will pick it up at an in-town car rental office located at 23 Rue de Salle.

Travel Voucher	TRAVEL AGENCY COPY **1** ORIGINAL (NOT NEGOTIABLE)	**695409**	
CUSTOMER NAME	DATE OF ISSUE	AGENCY FILE NO.	
RENTAL STATION ADDRESS STREET · DOWN TOWN · AIR-PORT	DATE OF RENTAL · DAY · MONTH · YEAR	TO BE COMPLETED ONLY IF PART OF TOUR PACKAGE · TOUR NAME	
CITY	LENGTH OF RENTAL (24 HR DAYS)	TOUR NO. · RATE CODE	
TELEPHONE NO. · CITY OF RETURN	CAR GROUP OR CLASS	VOUCHER VALUE INCLUDES · CDW · TAX · UNL. MIL.	
RATE NAME	RESERVATION NO.	ARC OR IATA NO.	AGENCY VALIDATION STAMP
REMARKS		ACCOUNT NO.	
VOUCHER VALUE (AMOUNT IN WORDS) IF NET RATE INCLUDE RATE CODE	AMOUNT	TRAVEL AGENCY NAME & ADDRESS	
— MAXIMUM VALUE $1000 (OR EQUIVALENT LOCAL CURRENCY). RENTAL NOT TO EXCEED 30 DAYS. — EXCHANGE RATES AT COMMENCEMENT OF RENTAL APPLY. — ANY EXCESS CHARGES OVER VOUCHER VALUE MUST BE PAID BY RENTER DIRECT TO COMPANY.	OFFICE USE ONLY · RATE OF EXCHANGE APPLIED · RENTAL AGREEMENT NO.		

Fig. 10-6. Johnson car rental voucher.

However, they wish to turn the car in at the airport right before their BA flight.

You determine that the daily/hourly rate will be less expensive for Mr. and Mrs. Johnson, since they do not qualify for any of this company's specials. This rate is equal to USD 23 per day and USD 3.10 per hour including unlimited mileage and the collision damage waiver. VAT is extra at 15%. Mrs. Johnson wishes to pay you in advance in full and you need to present her with both your bill and a rental voucher showing full payment less your commission.

After calling the rental company to make a reservation, you confirm a "C" class Renault, standard drive with air conditioning, four-wheel drive, and four door. The confirmation number is AZ297448 and the reservation was confirmed by Bill Winchester in the U.S. headquarters office.

Prepare a completed car rental voucher for Mr. and Mrs. Johnson. Also prepare a written letter detailing all charges. Prepare the section of their itinerary that will give them the needed information they would need and/or prefer to have prior to their departure and while en route.

SCANDINAVIAN ITINERARY DEVELOPMENT
EXERCISE NUMBER THREE

SITUATION: You have confirmed arrangments for Mrs. Johnson and Mrs. Taymore to share a room (double occupancy) at the following hotels on the dates indicated:

IN: Wednesday, 03 July (morning arrival—about 11:30 A.M.)
OUT: Saturday, 04 July (late departure requested—about 4:00 P.M.)
HOTEL SCANDINAVIA
Amager Boulevard 70, Copenhagen
Confirmation No. BGK 57348288

IN: Sunday, 12 July (guaranteed arrival and will arrive after 6:00 P.M.)
OUT: Monday, 13 July (late departure requested—about 2:30 P.M.)
BRITTANIA HOTEL
Dronningensgt 5, Trondheim
Confirmation No. TD7730108559

IN: Monday, 13 July (guaranteed arrival but will arrive about 6:00 P.M.)
OUT: Wednesday, 15 July
GRAND HOTEL
Karl Johansgt 31, Oslo
Confirmation No. KKK66620041

IN: Wednesday, 15 July (early arrival—about 1:30 P.M.)
OUT: Sunday, 19 July
GRAND HOTEL
S. Blaseholmshammen 8, Stockholm
Confirmation No. STH74299368

Transfer the flights from "Scandinavian Development Exercise Number Two" and the above hotel information to the attached draft itinerary forms, leaving enough room to include sightseeing information in each city. Keep in mind the cost of the air, the total budget, and the cost of each of the hotels per night per person double occupancy, select sightseeing programs for each city (some should be scheduled sightseeing and some should be "on your own"). Since our "normal source" sightseeing firms do not offer sightseeing in Scandinavia, you will need to glean information from escorted tours to these cities, national tourist boards, and other industry sources. Although a firm cost on each of the sightseeing trips might not be possible at this time, provide a budgeted figure for each sightseeing trip for which an exact cost cannot be determined. Place the sightseeing information on the draft itinerary.

HOTEL COSTS PER NIGHT (DOUBLE OCCUPANCY)

Copenhagen	HOTEL SCANDINAVIA	$148 × 3 nights =	$ 444
Trondheim	BRITTANIA HOTEL	$165 × 1 night =	$ 165
Oslo	GRAND HOTEL	$150 × 2 nights =	$ 300
Stockholm	GRAND HOTEL	$180 × 4 nights =	$ 720
Total on a double occupancy basis			$1,629
Total for each person on a double occupancy basis			$ 814.50

ITINERARY DRAFT WORKSHEET FOR:

-1- Tue 30 Jun

_____

_____

_____

_____

_____

_____

_____

_____

_____

-2- Wed 01 Jul

_____

_____

_____

_____

_____

_____

_____

_____

ITINERARY DRAFT WORKSHEET FOR:

_____

-3- Thurs   02   Jul _____

_____

_____

_____

_____

_____

_____

_____

_____

_____

_____

_____

_____

-4- Fri   03   Jul _____

_____

_____

_____

_____

_____

_____

_____

_____

_____

_____

_____

ITINERARY DRAFT WORKSHEET FOR:

-5- Sat 04 Jul

_____

_____

_____

_____

_____

_____

_____

_____

_____

_____

_____

-6- Sun 05 Jul

_____

_____

_____

_____

_____

_____

_____

_____

ITINERARY DRAFT WORKSHEET FOR:

-7- Mon 06 Jul

_____

_____

_____

_____

_____

_____

_____

_____

_____

_____

_____

-8- Tue 07 Jul

_____

_____

_____

_____

_____

_____

_____

_____

_____

_____

ITINERARY DRAFT WORKSHEET FOR:

-9-   Wed   08   Jul

-10-   Thurs   09   Jul

ITINERARY DRAFT WORKSHEET FOR:

-11- Fri 10 Jul

_____

_____

_____

_____

_____

_____

_____

_____

_____

_____

_____

-12- Sat 11 Jul

_____

_____

_____

_____

_____

_____

_____

_____

_____

ITINERARY DRAFT WORKSHEET FOR:

_____

-13- Sun 12 Jul

_____

_____

_____

_____

_____

_____

_____

_____

_____

_____

_____

-14- Mon 13 Jul

_____

_____

_____

_____

_____

_____

_____

_____

ITINERARY DRAFT WORKSHEET FOR:

-15- Tue 14 Jul

_____

_____

_____

_____

_____

_____

_____

_____

_____

_____

_____

-16- Wed 15 Jul

_____

_____

_____

_____

_____

_____

_____

_____

_____

ITINERARY DRAFT WORKSHEET FOR:

-17- Thur 16 Jul

-18- Fri 17 Jul

ITINERARY DRAFT WORKSHEET FOR:

-19- Sat 18 Jul

_____

-20- Sun 19 Jul

PRICING

F.I.T. PRICING VERSUS TOUR PRICING

"In establishing the tour price, the agency manager feeds all the data into a computer or cost sheet . . . computing . . . expenses . . . taking all legitimate mark-ups, calculating commissions, and adding on a factor for other expenses and profit. The goal would be to realize a profit of ten to fifteen percent," according to Robert Reilly in his *Handbook of Professional Tour Management.* Pricing an F.I.T. is similar in concept, but different in the mechanics.

A COMMON PRICING APPROACH

Many who plan F.I.T.s work strictly on a product commission basis. They price the F.I.T. by adding the total of the commissionable components and the total of the non-commissionable components and charging the client the resulting figure. The advantage, they say, is that they can go over each and every item in the F.I.T. with the client, showing an exact breakdown of each element. In this way the F.I.T. client can add to or drop parts of the F.I.T. based on the cost of each part. In addition, the client will know that the F.I.T. specialist is not padding the total tour cost or building in excessive profits.

A MORE PROFITABLE APPROACH

Those who have specialized in F.I.T.s the longest tend to agree that the best approach and the most profitable approach is to start with a total budgeted figure that the client is willing to pay and expects to pay for the trip. Working within that figure, roughly calculate at the initial meeting whether or not the F.I.T. can realistically be undertaken within the budget figure framework. If it cannot, advise the client accordingly and either modify the F.I.T. to the budget that is available or do not do the F.I.T. If the specialist believes the F.I.T. can be done within the client's budget, but that it will be close, advise the client accordingly (the client should know it if the cost will run a few hundred dollars over budget or if something might have to be cut).

In such a case, determine up front how firm the budget is. If the F.I.T. can comfortably fit within the budget, advise the client accordingly and set about developing it after obtaining an up-front F.I.T. deposit.

With this approach, additions and subtractions (within a reasonable range) can be dealt with based upon the perceived satisfaction level of the client, not strictly from a cost standpoint. The client is given a total cost figure at the end of the planning stage when final payments are needed. A detailed cost-breakdown is never given and should never be promised. Most important, with this approach the F.I.T. specialist can charge for her time and expenses and the agency can realize a profit as well.

THE COMMISSION-ONLY APPROACH VERSUS THE TIME/EXPENSE/PROFIT APPROACH

Although the commission-only approach has some merits, it usually does not work well. F.I.T. clients go to a travel agency F.I.T. specialist who they can trust to know what is most enjoyable and what is available within their price range. They can expect a quality job. While it would be a mistake to believe that most F.I.T. clients think cost is no object, at the same time F.I.T. clients will value satisfaction above a few dollars of additional cost. If the F.I.T. specialist is spending less time on the F.I.T. than it needs, trying to cut corners on expenses, or including F.I.T. elements because they pay commission (as opposed to those that might be more satisfactory to the client, but that do not pay a commission), the specialist is doing the client a disfavor. Yet, if all travel agency remuneration is to come from commissions only, the F.I.T. specialist might have to spend less time, cut corners, and include only commissionable items. The F.I.T. specialist might well find himself in a position of not making the client happy and at the same time, not making money for the travel agency. It can easily be a double-bind.

On the other hand, if the F.I.T. specialist has been honest about estimating the real costs (including his time and expenses) when first talking with the client and if the F.I.T. still falls comfortably within the client's budget, the agency can make a profit and have a satisfied client. The time/expense/profit approach can take time to develop and document, but it can also earn a reasonable profit for the agency. The time/expense/profit approach requires the F.I.T. specialist to keep a record of the time spent on each F.I.T. much like lawyers do to bill for their time. It also requires the specialist to keep good records of the expenses and the commissions on all F.I.T. costs. This record keeping allows a total time and expense record to be calculated. When this cost figure is compared to the total commissions earned figure, the difference can be added to the client's total bill. By taking this approach, the travel agency is insured of a profit on the transaction, the client gets all the time needed from the F.I.T. specialist, and only items that are most enjoyable are included on the itinerary. Both the client and the travel agency win. Because of the advantages of using the time/expense/profit approach to F.I.T. pricing, the rest of this chapter and the balance of the book will be based on this approach.

RECORD KEEPING

If the travel agency expects to make a profit on F.I.T. sales, keeping good records is essential. Since a profit can only be made if all commissions are received, it is necessary to keep a record of what has been ordered from vendors, the cost of each service to be provided by vendors, the services for which commissions have been deducted prior to payment and of greatest importance, the commissions that are owed to the travel agency by vendors. Consultants who audit travel agencies often express surprise at the amount of uncollected commissions. Profits are reduced and in many cases they are eliminated when commissions due to the agency are unpaid. Good record keeping, re-billing vendors for unpaid commissions, and eliminating vendors from further bookings when they do not promptly pay commission are some of the best ways to make sure that profits are not lost because vendors do not pay commissions.

A second justification for keeping good records is the potential loss from expenses paid by the agency, but not reimbursed from any payment source. Communication charges are a good example. Telex and long-distance telephone charges might seem very small on each F.I.T., but for many agencies they constitute as much as 7% of all agency expenses. It should be possible to totally recover these expenses by including them in the time/expense/profit calculations.

Costing Worksheets

Most travel agencies keep track of expenses using worksheets. When an F.I.T. is started for a client, blank costing worksheet forms are inserted into the client F.I.T. file. As costs are determined, the published prices, commissions to be paid, and net prices are entered into appropriate blanks on the forms. Costing worksheets are provided for transportation (air, rail, bus, ship, etc.), accommodations (hotel, villa rental, kibbutz, pension, etc.), ground transfers (meet and assist, airport/hotel transfers, hotel/airport transfers, sightseeing, etc.), prepaid meals on the F.I.T. (not including those included on a sightseeing trip), car or limousine rentals, prepaid entertainment, and so forth. Each time an itinerary item is added to the itinerary for which a pre-payment is needed or on which a commission would be paid, an entry to this effect is made on the appropriate blank costing worksheet form. By entering the costs in pencil, calculating the totals for each costing page weekly, and totaling each page weekly, the F.I.T. specialist can determine the F.I.T.'s weekly status.

Air Fare Costing Worksheet

The air fare costing worksheet is designed to track all costs involved with air transportation in conjunction with the F.I.T. Often this is just an international air fare. However, even when only an international air fare is involved, the F.I.T. specialist must add the $3.00 departure tax to determine the total amount to be paid by the client. In calculating the commission, the F.I.T. specialist must determine what the percentage of commission is and any overrides for which the agency is eligible should be collected.

COSTING WORKSHEET NUMBER _____

AIR FARE COSTS	Quoted or Published Price	Commission	Net
Total ticket price (gross)			
Base			
Tax (U.S. domestic—outbound)			
Tax (U.S. domestic—return)			
Tax (U.S. domestic outbound and return)			
Tax (international departure tax)			
Tax (other—designate)			
Tax (other—designate)			
Domestic add-on fare			
Other			
Other			
Other Air Costs			
V.I.P. room admission charge			
Airline V.I.P. handling charge			
Overweight baggage charge			
Headphone charge			
Drink chits			
Other			
Other			
Total This Page			

Fig. 11-1. Sample air fare costing worksheet.

COSTING WORKSHEET NUMBER _____

RAIL COSTS	Quoted or Published Price	Commission	Net

Railpass (type: _____)
Circle appropriate:
  1st cl   2nd cl
Circle appropriate:
  15 day   21 day   1 mo.
  2 mo.   3 mo.
Cost			

Point-to-Point Rail Day _____ Date_____ City pair _____ Ticket cost 1st cl 2nd cl Reservation cost(s) Sleeper or couchette cost BBR or exchange rate costs Other Other			
Day _____ Date_____ City pair _____ Ticket cost 1st cl 2nd cl Reservation cost(s) Sleeper or couchette cost BBR or exchange rate costs Other Other			
Day _____ Date_____ City pair _____ Ticket cost 1st cl 2nd cl Reservation cost(s) Sleeper or couchette cost BBR or exchange rate costs Other Other			
Total This Page			

Fig. 11-2. Sample rail costing worksheet.

If domestic flights are involved (and they usually are), the taxes must be deducted from the air fare before calculating the commission; there might be more than one tax involved. Canadian tax, landing fee surcharges, overweight charges, and departure taxes are all costs that might be involved in determining the totals to be paid for airline tickets. While some air costs are commissionable, taxes are not. Therefore, special attention must be paid to calculating the correct U.S. dollar commission amount. A sample of the air fare costing worksheet appears in figure 11–1 and air fare costing worksheets are included in the destination exercises.

Rail Costing Worksheet

The rail costing worksheet is designed to track all rail costs involved with the F.I.T. Some F.I.T. specialists will use a separate rail costing worksheet for each rail ticket purchased since tickets might come with varying additional charges (reservation charge, sleeper or couchette charge, first-class surcharge, and so forth). Other F.I.T. specialists add up all rail ticket charges and each additional charge by type of charge, calculating all rail costs on one rail costing worksheet. It is easier to use separate rail costing worksheets for each rail ticket if there are many additional varying costs and this is especially so since most, but not all, additional varying costs are not commissionable. In addition, the commission rate and/or amount might vary from one rail service to another and from one rail product to another. If, however, there are very few or no additional rail services, only two or three rail tickets involved, and especially if the rail bookings are all with one rail company in one country, a single rail costing worksheet will suffice quite well. A sample of a rail costing worksheet appears in figure 11–2 and rail costing worksheets are included in the destination exercises.

Bus Costing Worksheet

Few F.I.T.s involve bus travel and bus costs are normally straightforward. Some bus travel is commissionable, but most is not. There are no standard additional bus charges as there are with train travel, for example. Although the bus costing worksheet is self-explanatory and is seldom used, a copy of the bus costing worksheet appears in figure 11–3.

Ship Costing Worksheet

Most ship bookings in conjunction with F.I.T.s are for cruises, but there is also ferry service and, increasingly, barge travel that is sold to those taking an F.I.T. As with other transportation, the cruise, ferry, and/or barge trip ticket is usually commissionable (some ferrys and barge trips are not), but other connected expenses either are never commissionable (port charges, for example) or are sometimes commissionable (shore excursions purchased prior to departure, for example). As with rail travel, some F.I.T. specialists use a separate form for each cruise, ferry trip, or barge trip booked while other specialists will combine all F.I.T. ship costs into one costing form. A sample of the ship costing worksheet appears in figure 11-4.

Other Transportation

Other transportation is rarely arranged in advance. Hot air balloons and helicopter transfers are exceptions. They are usually included in the price,

COSTING WORKSHEET NUMBER _____

BUS COSTS	Quoted or Published Price	Commission	Net
Day _____ Date _____ City Pair _____			
Day _____ Date _____ City Pair _____			
Day _____ Date _____ City Pair _____			
Day _____ Date _____ City Pair _____			
Day _____ Date _____ City Pair _____			
Day _____ Date _____ City Pair _____			
Day _____ Date _____ City Pair _____			
Day _____ Date _____ City Pair _____			
Day _____ Date _____ City Pair _____			
Day _____ Date _____ City Pair _____			
Day _____ Date _____ City Pair _____			
Day _____ Date _____ City Pair _____			
Day _____ Date _____ City Pair _____			
Day _____ Date _____ City Pair _____			
Day _____ Date _____ City Pair _____			
Day _____ Date _____ City Pair _____			
Day _____ Date _____ City Pair _____			
Day _____ Date _____ City Pair _____			
Day _____ Date _____ City Pair _____			
Day _____ Date _____ City Pair _____			
Day _____ Date _____ City Pair _____			
Day _____ Date _____ City Pair _____			
Day _____ Date _____ City Pair _____			
Day _____ Date _____ City Pair _____			
Day _____ Date _____ City Pair _____			
Day _____ Date _____ City Pair _____			
Day _____ Date _____ City Pair _____			
Total This Page			

Fig. 11-3. Sample bus costing worksheet.

COSTING WORKSHEET NUMBER _____

SHIP COSTS	Quoted or Published Price	Commission	Net
Basic fare (berth or cabin) cost			
Reservation fee			
Port charges			
Deck chair charges			
Air supplement (for air/sea programs)			
Cruise provided transfer costs			
Taxes			
Other			
Other			
Other			
Basic fare (berth or cabin) cost			
Reservation fee			
Port charges			
Deck chair charges			
Air supplement (for air/sea programs)			
Cruise provided transfer costs			
Taxes			
Other			
Other			
Other			
Total This Page			

Fig. 11-4. Sample ship costing worksheet.

paid for in advance and especially if such other transportation is commissionable, it should be described and the costs for it should be itemized under the "Other Costs" category in the "Other Costs Costing Worksheet." A sample of the other costs costing worksheet appears in figure 11–5.

Meet and Assist Costing Worksheet

Meet and assist charges will vary depending on which ground operator is used. Most quote flat standard fees for meet and assist services, but some will have special or V.I.P. handling services (and appropriate charges for same) as well. Most ground operators pay a flat fee or a straight percentage for meet and assist services. Commissions on special handling or V.I.P. services vary from no commission paid to fairly substantial flat fees and as high as twenty percent commission have been paid. Each of these costing/ commission arrangements can be documented on the meet and assist costing worksheet. Where no special services or V.I.P. services are involved on an F.I.T., a single meet and assist costing worksheet can be utilized to detail all meet and assist services arranged for during the F.I.T. When special or V.I.P. services are involved, it is suggested that separate meet and assist costing worksheets be prepared for each meet and assist. A sample of a meet and assist costing worksheet appears in figure 11-6.

Ground Transfer Costing Worksheet

Ground transfers are normally from the airport or rail station of arrival in a destination city to a hotel and back. They are often sold in conjunction with

COSTING WORKSHEET NUMBER _____

OTHER TRANSPORTATION COSTS	Quoted or Published Price	Commission	Net
Total This Page			

Fig. 11-5. Sample costing worksheet for other transportation.

COSTING WORKSHEET NUMBER _____

MEET AND ASSIST COSTS	Quoted or Published Price	Commission	Net
Airport/rail station meet and assist			
Special or V.I.P. handling			
Airport/rail station meet and assist			
Special or V.I.P. handling			
Airport/rail station meet and assist			
Special or V.I.P. handling			
Airport/rail station meet and assist			
Special or V.I.P. handling			
Airport/rail station meet and assist			
Special or V.I.P. handling			
Airport/rail station meet and assist			
Special or V.I.P. handling			
Airport/rail station meet and assist			
Special or V.I.P. handling			
Airport/rail station meet and assist			
Special or V.I.P. handling			
Airport/rail station meet and assist			
Special or V.I.P. handling			
Airport/rail station meet and assist			
Special or V.I.P. handling			
Airport/rail station meet and assist			
Special or V.I.P. handling			
Airport/rail station meet and assist			
Special or V.I.P. handling			
Total This Page			

Fig. 11-6. Sample meet and assist costing worksheet.

meet and assist services; usually, separate charges are quoted. It is for this reason that they are costed separately by most F.I.T. specialists. Usually a flat fee commission is paid, but some ground operators pay a percentage-based commission. A sample of a ground transfer costing worksheet appears in figure 11-7.

Sightseeing Costing Worksheet

Sightseeing trips pay a flat fee or a percentage-based commission for each sightseeing trip or tour booked. Most F.I.T. specialists will complete a sightseeing tour costing worksheet for each sightseeing company used even if only one or a few sightseeing trips are booked per company (vendor). In this way, not only will all sightseeing cost information be readily available, but total amounts to be sent and commissions to be deducted or collected from each sightseeing vendor can be rapidly computed. A sample of a sightseeing costing worksheet appears in figure 11-8.

Accommodation Costing Worksheet

There are many variables to be considered in costing accommodations. Most hotels, resorts, and other lodging facilities providing overnight ac-

COSTING WORKSHEET NUMBER _____

GROUND TRANSFER COSTS	Quoted or Published Price	Commission	Net
Airport to hotel			
Hotel to airport			
Service charges and gratuities			
Taxes			
Other			
Other			
Airport to hotel			
Hotel to airport			
Service charges and gratuities			
Taxes			
Other			
Other			
Airport to hotel			
Hotel to airport			
Service charges and gratuities			
Taxes			
Other			
Other			
Airport to hotel			
Hotel to airport			
Service charges and gratuities			
Taxes			
Other			
Other			
Total This Page			

Fig. 11-7. Sample ground transfer costing worksheet.

COSTING WORKSHEET NUMBER _____

SIGHTSEEING TOURS	Quoted or Published Price	Commission	Net
Date _____ Tour title _____			
Date _____ Tour title _____			
Date _____ Tour title _____			
Date _____ Tour title _____			
Date _____ Tour title _____			
Date _____ Tour title _____			
Date _____ Tour title _____			
Date _____ Tour title _____			
Date _____ Tour title _____			
Date _____ Tour title _____			
Date _____ Tour title _____			
Date _____ Tour title _____			
Date _____ Tour title _____			
Date _____ Tour title _____			
Date _____ Tour title _____			
Date _____ Tour title _____			
Date _____ Tour title _____			
Date _____ Tour title _____			
Date _____ Tour title _____			
Date _____ Tour title _____			
Date _____ Tour title _____			
Date _____ Tour title _____			
Date _____ Tour title _____			
Date _____ Tour title _____			
Date _____ Tour title _____			
Date _____ Tour title _____			
Total This Page			

Fig. 11-8. Sample sightseeing costing worksheet.

commodations quote a rate per night, but day rates are available when a room is occupied only during day hours (often the case with international airport properties) and there are sometimes the add-on prepaid costs of porterage (baggage handling) in and out of the hotel, tips, taxes, service charges, gratuities, and other fees or charges to be considered. Although these add-ons need to be calculated to make certain the correct payment for the client is made to the vendor property, the add-ons seldom, if ever, are commissionable. In addition, add-ons both required and optional vary radically from property to property. A sample of the accommodation costing worksheet appears in figure 11-9.

Car/Limo Costing Worksheet

The base rate on car and limousine rentals is normally all that is commissionable. However, for a chauffeur-driven car, the base rate usually includes the cost of both the car or limousine and the chauffeur with the total base rate being commissionable. When both the chauffeur and the car or limou-

COSTING WORKSHEET NUMBER _____

ACCOMMODATION COSTS	Quoted or Published Price	Commission	Net
Day _____ Date in _____ Date out _____ Hotel, inn, etc., name			
Per night $ _____ × _____ nights =			
Porterage in			
Porterage out			
Tips			
Housekeeping			
Other			
Taxes			
Service charges and gratuities			
Other			
Day _____ Date in _____ Date out _____ Hotel, inn, etc., name			
Per night $ _____ × _____ nights =			
Porterage in			
Porterage out			
Tips			
Housekeeping			
Other			
Taxes			
Service charges and gratuities			
Other			
Total This Page			

Fig. 11-9. Sample accommodation costing worksheet.

sine are combined in a base rate, this rate is normally quoted on a daily, weekly, or monthly basis and the separate cost line for chauffeur should be marked, "Cost included in base rate." The balance of the line should be left blank. Other normal car/limousine rental costs, such as the collision dam-

COSTING WORKSHEET NUMBER _____

CAR OR LIMO RENTAL	Quoted or Published Price	Commission	Net
Day ____ Date of pickup ____			
Date of return ____			
Rate per ____:			
$ ____ × ____ days/weeks =			
Chauffeur cost			
C.D. waiver			
Insurance			
Taxes			
Other			
Day ____ Date of pickup ____			
Date of return ____			
Rate per ____:			
$ ____ × ____ days/weeks =			
Chauffeur cost			
C.D. waiver			
Insurance			
Taxes			
Other			
Day ____ Date of pickup ____			
Date of return ____			
Rate per ____:			
$ ____ × ____ days/weeks =			
Chauffeur cost			
C.D. waiver			
Insurance			
Taxes			
Other			
Total This Page			

Fig. 11-10. Sample car or limousine rental costing worksheet.

COSTING WORKSHEET NUMBER _____

MEALS	Quoted or Published Price	Commission	Net
Day _____ Date _____ Meal _____			
Day _____ Date _____ Meal _____			
Day _____ Date _____ Meal _____			
Day _____ Date _____ Meal _____			
Day _____ Date _____ Meal _____			
Day _____ Date _____ Meal _____			
Day _____ Date _____ Meal _____			
Day _____ Date _____ Meal _____			
Day _____ Date _____ Meal _____			
Day _____ Date _____ Meal _____			
Day _____ Date _____ Meal _____			
Day _____ Date _____ Meal _____			
Day _____ Date _____ Meal _____			
Day _____ Date _____ Meal _____			
Day _____ Date _____ Meal _____			
Day _____ Date _____ Meal _____			
Day _____ Date _____ Meal _____			
Day _____ Date _____ Meal _____			
Day _____ Date _____ Meal _____			
Day _____ Date _____ Meal _____			
Day _____ Date _____ Meal _____			
Day _____ Date _____ Meal _____			
Total This Page			

Fig. 11-11. Sample included meal costing worksheet.

age waiver (CDW), insurance, and taxes are not commissionable unless it is clearly stated that they are included in the base rate. A sample of a car/limousine costing worksheet appears in figure 11–10.

Meal Costing Worksheet

There are two types of meal costing worksheets used in the industry. One shows the day of the tour for each meal listed, making its tie-in with the itinerary especially easy. The other carries a "Restaurant" line, providing a place to identify the name of the restaurant where the meal will be served

COSTING WORKSHEET NUMBER _____

MEALS (Sold as meals—not included on a tour)	Quoted or Published Price	Commission	Net
Date _____ Meal _____ Restaurant _____			
Date _____ Meal _____ Restaurant _____			
Date _____ Meal _____ Restaurant _____			
Date _____ Meal _____ Restaurant _____			
Date _____ Meal _____ Restaurant _____			
Date _____ Meal _____ Restaurant _____			
Date _____ Meal _____ Restaurant _____			
Date _____ Meal _____ Restaurant _____			
Date _____ Meal _____ Restaurant _____			
Date _____ Meal _____ Restaurant _____			
Date _____ Meal _____ Restaurant _____			
Date _____ Meal _____ Restaurant _____			
Date _____ Meal _____ Restaurant _____			
Date _____ Meal _____ Restaurant _____			
Date _____ Meal _____ Restaurant _____			
Date _____ Meal _____ Restaurant _____			
Date _____ Meal _____ Restaurant _____			
Total This Page			

Fig. 11-12. Sample optional meal costing worksheet.

making vendor identification tie-in especially easy. Some F.I.T. specialists prefer one type of form, while others prefer the other type. Whichever form is used, only meals that are not included on tours or sightseeing trips should be shown on the pricing worksheet since those that are included as part of sightseeing or tour packages are already paid for in the sightseeing or tour price. Prepaid meals almost always include the tips and gratuities. If clients wish to provide an additional tip "on site," they are usually allowed to do so (some vendors prohibit additional tipping to make certain that service staff members do not encourage it). When tips and gratuities are included in the meal cost, it is normal to pay commission for the total meal cost including tips and gratuities. If tips and/or gratuities are not included, they will normally be charged to the client at the end of the meal and are not prepayable or commissionable. The client(s) should be advised accordingly in order to avoid any unexpected surprises. Samples of both meal costing worksheets appear in figures 11-11 and 11-12.

Entertainment Costing Worksheet

Entertainment costing worksheets should be completed only for those entertainment functions that are not sold as tours, sightseeing trips, or as a part of tours or sightseeing trips. Entertainment costs normally include only the cost of the ticket to enter the entertainment function. Food and/or beverages consumed during the entertainment function, the cost of which is not included in the cost of the function, normally are paid for at the time of consumption. Tips to get good or better seats than those reserved in advance are provided by the client at the time of entering the entertainment facility. Entertainment ticket costs usually do include any applicable taxes. Commission policies vary widely, but sometimes do include the total price of the ticket (including tax) as being commissionable. The F.I.T. specialist should check when making the reservation for entertainment to determine what the commission amount or percentage is and whether or not it is based on a percentage of taxes and ticket or just the ticket price. A sample of an entertainment costing worksheet appears in figure 11-13.

Administrative Costing Worksheet

The administrative worksheet provides a vehicle for recording administrative costs, staff time charges, other costs that do not fit anywhere else, and a vehicle for carrying over the total costs of other worksheets in order to come up with a total price for the client. Often memos or receipts reflecting the various administrative costs are stapled to the administrative costing worksheet as they are incurred or paid. Since entries on the administrative costing worksheet are made in pencil, new figures can be entered each time they are developed. Mail costs are usually reflected by post office receipts.

COSTING WORKSHEET NUMBER _____

ENTERTAINMENT COSTS (Including taxes and service charges)	Quoted or Published Price	Commission	Net
Day _____ Date _____ Show/Event _____			
Day _____ Date _____ Show/Event _____			
Day _____ Date _____ Show/Event _____			
Day _____ Date _____ Show/Event _____			
Day _____ Date _____ Show/Event _____			
Day _____ Date _____ Show/Event _____			
Day _____ Date _____ Show/Event _____			
Day _____ Date _____ Show/Event _____			
Day _____ Date _____ Show/Event _____			
Day _____ Date _____ Show/Event _____			
Day _____ Date _____ Show/Event _____			
Day _____ Date _____ Show/Event _____			
Day _____ Date _____ Show/Event _____			
Day _____ Date _____ Show/Event _____			
Day _____ Date _____ Show/Event _____			
Day _____ Date _____ Show/Event _____			
Day _____ Date _____ Show/Event _____			
Total This Page			

Fig. 11-13. Sample entertainment costing worksheet.

COSTING WORKSHEET NUMBER _____

ADMINISTRATIVE COSTS	Cost	Markup	Total
Communication			
Mail charges			
Phone charges			
Telex charges			
Other communication charges			
Delivery charges			
Duplication charges			
Give Aways			
Flight bag			
Flowers			
Liquor			
Toiletry kit			
Other (specify):			
Other (specify):			
Time Charges			
Name: _____ @ $ ____ per hour =			
Name: _____ @ $ ____ per hour =			
Name: _____ @ $ ____ per hour =			
Other costs (itemize):			
Other costs (itemize):			
Other costs (itemize):			
Total Costs			
Page 1			
Page 2			
Page 3			
Page 4			
Page 5			
Page 6			
Grand Total			
Markups			
Total per Person Price to the Clients			

Fig. 11-14. Sample administrative costing worksheet.

Telephone and telex charges are normally identified when reviewing the end-of-month bills from the telex and telephone vendors. Delivery charges are billed on a monthly basis when the service is contracted to the travel agency. If the agency employs a delivery person, delivery records can be reviewed to determine a pro-rated delivery charge for each F.I.T. client. Duplication charges can be computed and recorded by assigning each client a client number and recording either that number or the client name on a running list kept near the copy machine. Give-aways such as flight bags and toiletry kits are normally charged as promotional items and charged to clients' accounts at cost.

F.I.T. specialist time costs are often the most difficult to keep up with. Few F.I.T. specialists keep good time records, but an increasing number of them are copying the techniques used in the legal profession. This means that a time log is kept on all phone calls, all appointments, and all other working time. Each F.I.T. client's appropriate charges are extracted (usually weekly) from the time log with the hours and minutes multiplied times the predetermined cost per hour of the F.I.T. specialist and any other agency employees who may have worked on the F.I.T. The weekly figures are added together to determine the total time or labor charges to be applied to the F.I.T.

The "Other Costs" section of the administrative costing worksheet provides a place to itemize any costs that do not fit any of the above categories. Some of these costs will be commissionable, but most are not. As with the administrative costs (which are not commissionable), a mark-up is possible and a section is provided for mark-up (either flat charge or percentage) on each administrative and other cost item. A sample of an administrative costing worksheet appears in figure 11–14.

Total Cost Review

The last section of the administrative costing worksheet is a page by page review of costs taken from each of the other costing worksheets. By transferring all costing worksheet totals to this page and adding the columns, the F.I.T. specialist can rapidly determine

1. Total costs of the F.I.T. at any point in time
2. If budget constraints have been complied with
3. What type of costing problems might be developing

By providing an additional line for any additional mark-ups; and adding these additional mark-ups to the grand total figures determined by adding each of the individual costing worksheet totals, the F.I.T. specialist can calculate a final per person client price for the F.I.T.

Cost Summary Sheet

Many F.I.T. specialists, however, will not want such a detailed accounting for F.I.T. costs as the worksheet system provides. They prefer to keep track of costs by keeping notes and receipts in the client files and summarizing costs on a single cost summary sheet. A copy of a sample cost summary sheet appears in figure 11–15. The costs are calculated in a manner similar to the cost calculations described above.

Costs Versus Pricing

In determining the price that the client will pay for the F.I.T., the F.I.T. specialist starts with the total cost figures as determined on the cost summary sheet or the totals section of the administrative costing worksheet. Next, the F.I.T. specialist determines from these same forms what the total commission on the F.I.T. will be. This includes both the commission deducted prior to making payments to vendors and the commissions that should be received from vendor payments. The F.I.T. specialist then subtracts commission totals from agency overhead costs (administrative costs, including personnel costs) and adds only these costs to the vendor costs to determine the price to be paid by the client. Although there are agencies that will charge administrative costs, mark-ups, and any additional fees possible in addition to keeping the vendor commissions, most agencies will make sure that their administrative costs are covered, but will use commission earnings to cover these as much as possible.

PROFIT

Travel agencies were not established to be non-profit ventures. They do not stay in business by breaking even or by losing money. By following the costing and pricing approach discussed, the agency should break even, but it might not make a profit. Agencies should decide what a reasonable per F.I.T. profit should be based upon a percentage factor. Most commercial businesses expect to turn a profit between 15% and 40%, but most travel agencies make far less in annual profits (when they are profitable). Therefore, it is suggested that a figure of between 5% and 15% of costs should be added to the F.I.T. and taken as an agency profit. After the profit is added to the total costs, the resulting figure will be the F.I.T. price.

SUMMARY

In determining pricing one must start with deciding to follow a commission only or a time/expense/profit approach. The time/expense/profit approach or some variation of it is used by most experienced professional F.I.T. specialists. In utilizing this approach, accurate record keeping is essential. Two types of records are available. The more detailed, but for many, the

COST SUMMARY SHEET

	Quoted or Published Price	Commission	Net
Transportation			
Air			
Rail			
Bus			
Ship			
Other			
Ground Transfers			
Meet and assist			
Transfers			
Other			
Accommodations			
Other			
Car/limo rentals			
Other			
Tour costs			
Other			
Meal costs			
Other			
Entertainment costs			
Other			
Administrative costs			
Other			
Total			
Markup			
Total price			

Fig. 11-15. Sample cost summary worksheet.

more handy approach is to use a series of costing worksheets. These worksheets identify gross costs, commissions, and net costs by the following cost categories: air fare, rail, bus, ship, other transportation, meet and assist services, ground transfers, sightseeing, accommodations, cars or limousines, meals, entertainment and administrative costs. An alternative approach is a cost summary sheet. Whichever approach is utilized, administrative costs should be covered. Some administrative costs can be paid for out of earned commissions. Adding a reasonable profit to the cost total provides the travel agency with an opportunity to

1. Make money on the F.I.T.
2. Provide good service to the F.I.T. client
3. Not price the F.I.T. too high to be competitive

■   ■   ■

❏ *REVIEW QUESTIONS*

1. There is a common pricing approach and a more profitable pricing approach. What are the differences between the two approaches?
2. In what way(s) can the time/expense/profit approach to pricing benefit the client more than the commission-only approach?
3. Why is good record keeping considered essential to making a profit on F.I.T. sales?
4. Working with costing worksheets, what must the F.I.T. specialist do to determine the financial status of an F.I.T. each week?
5. What data needs to be considered in determining a total figure on the air fare costing worksheet?
6. Under what circumstances might it be easier to use separate rail costing worksheets for each rail ticket as compared to a single rail ticket costing worksheet for all rail tickets?
7. Are port charges commissionable?
8. Under what circumstances might shore excursions taken by an F.I.T. client in conjunction with a cruise be commissionable?
9. Do most ground operators quote standard flat fees for meet and assist services?
10. Why do most F.I.T. specialists cost out ground transfers separately from meet and assist services?
11. Do most F.I.T. specialists prepare a cost worksheet for each sightseeing trip or do they prepare one cost worksheet for all sightseeing trips booked by a sightseeing company in a destination city/area for the F.I.T. client? Why?
12. Under what circumstances are day rates quoted by hotels for F.I.T. clients?
13. When quoting a cost for a chauffeur-driven car, is it customary for the vendor to quote a single rate for car and driver or to quote two different rates, for example, one rate for the driver and another rate for the car?
14. What are the two types of meal costing worksheets and what are the easy "tie-ins" associated with each?

15. Under what circumstances are meal tips and gratuities commissionable?

16. What commission questions should be asked by the F.I.T. specialist when booking entertainment reservations?

17. On what costing worksheet are staff time charges recorded?

18. What system is sometimes used to compute duplication (copying) charges incurred for F.I.T. clients?

19. Where are costs recorded that do not fit any identified or specified category?

20. Under what circumstances might an F.I.T. specialist elect to work with a cost summary sheet instead of costing worksheets?

21. What steps does the F.I.T. specialist follow in determining the price that the client will pay for an F.I.T.?

22. How do F.I.T. suggested profits compare to the profits most commercial businesses expect to earn?

❏ *Role Play Exercise*

Two students may participate in this exercise either out of class as a fun way to review pricing discussions with F.I.T. clients or as an in-class exercise. One student plays the role of the travel agency's F.I.T. client and the other plays the role of the travel agent F.I.T. specialist. Please read the script and then pick up the conversation in your own words.

TRAVEL AGENT: It's good to see you again, Mrs. Johnson. On the phone you said you want to take a long weekend trip to Mexico. What specifically do you have in mind?

F.I.T. CLIENT: Mr. Johnson wants to do some fishing in Acapulco and I want to shop in Mexico City. We want to stay at Las Brisas and relax mostly. Mr. Johnson only wants a half day of fishing.

TRAVEL AGENT: Las Brisas has the pink and white jeeps you enjoyed on your last trip. Would you like for me to reserve one after arranging for a transfer from the hotel? You can turn it in at the airport if you like.

F.I.T. CLIENT: That's fine. But do set up a transfer to Las Brisas on Friday night. We won't want to get the jeep until Saturday morning. And my husband will want the fishing excursion on Saturday afternoon.

TRAVEL AGENT: I will arrange it exactly that way. You do want a private pool instead of a shared one, don't you?

F.I.T. CLIENT: Yes, and we want a casita as high up the mountainside as possible. The views are so much better, you know. Now in Mexico City I want a chauffeur and driver. I want to go to the better shops in the Pink Zone, but I also know some little out-of-the-way places in other parts of the city I want to get to. And we want to fly back and get home Sunday night. Can we get it all in on a budget of about $1,300—plus our expenses there, of course?

TRAVEL AGENT: It will be close. Let me start working it out. Will you be in this area the day after tomorrow or shall I phone you?

F.I.T. CLIENT: I'll be here in the afternoon. Do you have a one or two o'clock time open?

TRAVEL AGENT: One thirty is open. I think we will only need about half an hour. Is that okay?

F.I.T. CLIENT: Fine. What additional information do you need before you can start?

Continue on your own.

F.I.T. PRICING EXERCISE

SITUATION: Mr. and Mrs. Johnson have decided to take a short trip to Acapulco with a six-hour stopover in Mexico City on the way back home for shopping. Review the prices on page 214, complete the cost summary sheet on page 215, and determine a total F.I.T. price. After completing this exercise, proceed to the next pricing role play which follows. It is based on this exercise.

❏ *Role Play Exercise*

Two students may participate in this exercise either out of class as a fun way to review pricing discussions with F.I.T. clients or an in-class exercise. One student plays the role of the travel agency's F.I.T. client and the other plays the role of the travel agent F.I.T. specialist. This role play is based on the "Pricing Role Play Exercise Number One" on the preceding page and on the F.I.T. pricing exercise (above). Please read the script and pick up the conversation in your own words.

TRAVEL AGENT: Mrs. Johnson, everything you asked for has been worked out. The casita we requested is as high up as they go and I understand the view is magnificent. To do it the way you want, however, will be right at $1,400—maybe a little under. I know you said you wanted to keep it around $1,300. May I suggest one or two alternatives that will let us get down to $1,300 or will the $1,400 range be okay?

Continue on your own.

NUMBER	ITEM/ACTIVITY	GROSS COST	COMMISSION	NET COST
One	Round trip air tickets—base fare of each	$298.00	$23.84	$274.16
Two	Round trip air tickets—departure tax of each	3.00	-0-	3.00
One	Private car, transfer airport to hotel	31.00	3.10	28.90
Two	Hotel nights @ 141.00 each	282.00	28.20	253.80
One	Half day fishing boat excursion (Mr. Johnson)	147.00	14.70	132.30
One	One day jeep rental—payment to be made in Acapulco Pick up at hotel— turn in at airport, two day rate including drop off charge	76.00	7.60	Client will pay $76.00 car rental. Rental company to pay agency its commission.
One	Meet and assist and six-hour chauffeur-driven car hired in Mexico City—pre-payment required, commission deducted before payment	188.00	18.80	169.20

COST SUMMARY SHEET FOR _____
                                              Name(s) of Client(s)

TRIP DESTINATION: _____

	Quoted or Published Price	Commission	Net
Transportation			
Air			
Rail			
Bus			
Ship			
Other			
Ground Transfers			
Meet and assist			
Transfers			
Other			
Accommodations			
Other			
Car/limo rentals			
Other			
Tour costs			
Other			
Meal costs			
Other			
Entertainment costs			
Other			
Administrative costs			
Other			
Total			
Markup			
Total price			

SCANDINAVIAN ITINERARY DEVELOPMENT EXERCISE NUMBER FOUR

SITUATION: You have confirmed the following sightseeing arrangements for Mrs. Johnson and Mrs. Taymore and have suggested the following "On Your Own" arrangements for them on the dates indicated:

WEDNESDAY, JULY 01, AFTERNOON

City sightseeing tour departing at 2:00 P.M. with pickup at your hotel and return to your hotel at 5:30 P.M. You will see the highlights of the city, many of which you may want to return to on your own. Present your Copenhagen City Tour voucher to the guide when boarding the tour bus. Note: Meet at the hotel tour desk.

WEDNESDAY, JULY 01, EVENING

This evening is on your own. You may want to relax with a delightful dinner at the Scandinavian Room in your hotel. This is a quiet dining room with piano music. The lengthy menu is in both English and Danish.

THURSDAY, JULY 02, MORNING AND AFTERNOON

A full-day sightseeing tour is scheduled for the Tivoli Gardens. Your guide will pick you up at the hotel at 10:15 A.M. and you will return to your hotel at 4:05 P.M. A picnic basket has been prepared for you to enjoy at the gardens, famous throughout the world for their unique statuary and gentle paths with overwhelming views of the bay. Several picnic areas are designated by signs that are pictures of picnics.

THURSDAY, JULY 02, EVENING

Copenhagen is the home of the smorgasbord and tonight you will feast at the Smorgasbord Copenhagen. Over one hundred hot and cold dishes will amaze you and provide a feast for your eyes as well as your stomach. Variety entertainment is included in this all-evening affair. Your bus will pick you up at the door of the hotel at 5:45 P.M. and after a short drive you will arrive at the Smorgasbord Copenhagen. Dinner and festive activities last until at least 10 P.M. Enjoy a brief walk through the gardens of the restaurant before returning to your tour bus. It leaves promptly at 10:30 P.M. and will get you back to your hotel in time for a pleasant night's sleep before a relaxing day tomorrow.

FRIDAY, JULY 03, MORNING

This is a morning of leisure. We suggest a light breakfast in your room on the balcony overlooking the harbor. Try the Danish hot chocolate. It is world famous and justifiably so.

FRIDAY, JULY 03, AFTERNOON

The brief tour of the Christianborg (Royal) Palace and the Rosenborg Castle takes you back in history and architecture. Your guide will pick you up at the main entrance to your hotel at 1:15 P.M. and will bring you back to the hotel at 3:30 P.M. You will have an opportunity to pick up some beautiful paintings at the castle annex. This small gallery offers some of the best original paintings available in Scandinavia. They wrap them for air shipment back home to the United States.

FRIDAY, JULY 03, EVENING

Nothing is scheduled for this evening as we know you want to pack and prepare to depart tommorrow for the long-awaited visit with your Scandinavian relatives.

SATURDAY, JULY 04, MORNING

After meeting with your relatives, check out of your hotel before 12:00 Noon and travel by car with your relatives to their home in the country where you will spend the next eight days. Enjoy this long-awaited family reunion. We understand it is the capstone of your trip around which the entire itinerary has been organized.

SATURDAY, JULY 04, AFTERNOON THROUGH
SUNDAY, JULY 12, EVENING

Visit with your relatives. They will drive you to the airport the afternoon and evening of July 12 to take your flight to Trondheim.

SUNDAY, JULY 12, AFTERNOON

You will be met at the airport upon arrival by SWS Transfer Service. Their representative wears a blue blazer with the initials "SWS" on the jacket pocket. She will meet you at the baggage claim area and and will drive you to the Brittania Hotel. Remember, this is a city far in the north. We suggest warm sweaters or jackets while outside even at this time of year.

You may want a late night meal. If so the delightful Johansen's Restaurant is right across the street from the Brittania Hotel. This is the "in" dining spot in Trondheim. Try their Arctic Reindeer Steak. It is a delicacy difficult to find in the rest of the world.

MONDAY, JULY 13, MORNING

This morning is free for you to discover the wonders of this Scandinavia gem of a city on your own. We suggest you get an English-language copy of the Trondheim Walking Tour from the concierge at the Brittania and take a leisurely walk before having a light lunch at Johansen's Restaurant. Remember to bring a sweater or jacket to ward off the chill in the air.

MONDAY, JULY 13, AFTERNOON

Your SWS Transfer Service representative will meet you at the check-out desk at the Brittania at 1:00 P.M. She will drive you to the airport and will make sure both you and your baggage are properly checked in for your flight at 3:25 P.M. to Oslo. On arrival in Oslo a representative in the distinctive blue SWS blazer will meet you at the baggage claim area and will drive you to the Grand Hotel. One of the largest hotels in Scandinavia, if any hotel deserves the title grand, this one does.

MONDAY, JULY 13, EVENING

Dining this evening is an event you will remember. We have made dinner reservations for you for 8:00 P.M. at the Valdres, about a four-minute taxi ride from the Grand Hotel. The doorman will flag a taxi for you. The Valdres, named after the famous Valdres mountains of Norway, is famous for its seafood specialties. These delightful specialties are innovatively prepared and the menu changes each evening. Ask you waiter and he will guide you to a feast you will not forget.

TUESDAY, JULY 14, MORNING

This morning is free, giving you an opportunity to sleep late or to buy gifts from the nearby elegant shops. Handmade ski sweaters, crystal, and Scandinavian furs are all good buys here in Oslo.

TUESDAY, JULY 14, AFTERNOON

The city sightseeing tour leaves your hotel at 12:00 Noon. Guests meet at the concierge desk and are escorted to a waiting bus. You will visit Frogner Park with Vigeland's unique and controversial sculptures. After a Scandinavian shortbread and wine snack at a typical pub-like worker's cafe, the tour visits the Bygdoy Peninsula where the Kon Tiki Raft and Viking ships are on display. A late-afternoon return gets you back to the Grand Hotel between 5:15 P.M. and 5:30 P.M.—still enough time to dress for dinner.

TUESDAY, JULY 14, EVENING

This evening is "on your own." A dinner cruise can be arranged by your concierge at the Grand Hotel. Or, perhaps you will want to try one of the several specialty restaurants for which the Grand Hotel is justly famous. If fine dining close to the hotel is what you feel like, may we suggest The Midnight Sun. All meals are at least six courses and the wine cellar is outstanding.

WEDNESDAY, JULY 15, MORNING

The efficient SWS Transfer Service representative will meet you at the check-out desk at the Grand Hotel at 9:30 A.M. She will drive you to the airport, check you and your luggage in, and be sure you make the 11:05 A.M. flight to Stockholm without difficulty. When you arrive in Stockholm at 12:00 Noon, the SWS Transfer Service representative will meet you at the baggage claim area. She will be wearing the distinctive SWS blazer. After driving you to the Grand Hotel, Stockholm, she will make sure you are properly checked in.

WEDNESDAY, JULY 15, AFTERNOON

This afternoon and evening are at leisure to relax after your flight. From your hotel room balcony you will have a panoramic view of the Saltsjon Canal, Stockholm's largest. This is the main part of the city with both the best shopping and Stockholm's famous National Museum within a five-minute walking distance. Enjoy discovering Stockholm by strolling at your own pace this afternoon and evening. Stockholm is far enough south that the average evening temperature in July is a comfortable 55 degrees.

WEDNESDAY, JULY 15, EVENING

The evening is on your own. There are excellent well-known restaurants in the vicinity of the hotel, but there are also a good number of small out-of-the-way places as well. For your first night in Sweden, we suggest The Viking. Decorated like a viking ship with many authentic relics, The Viking presents food in a unique and memorable manner. Although their wine cellar is excellent, we suggest the stout Viking beer.

THURSDAY, JULY 16, MORNING AND AFTERNOON

Meet this morning at 10:30 A.M. at the tour desk in the hotel for a complete city sightseeing trip. Stockholm's "Old Town" (Gamia Stan) is first on the itinerary. Medieval buildings, cobblestone streets, and Stockholm's Town Hall share an ambiance that seem made for each other. Weaving in and out are the Stockholm canal's reminiscent of those for which Venice is famous. The bus returns to the Grand Hotel about 3:30 P.M., leaving enough time to take a cat-nap before the evening's festivities.

THURSDAY, JULY 16, EVENING

Stockholm is famous for its nightlife and dancing. This evening is free to explore the many nightclubs, a large number of them within walking distance of your hotel. Ask the concierge if there is a particular type of nightclub you prefer. Stockholm has them all.

FRIDAY, JULY 17, MORNING AND AFTERNOON

Get an early start this morning for a visit through the Swedish countryside and the lake district. The highlight is a visit to Jonkoping at the head of Lake Vattern. Lunch is a typical Swedish buffet at a country restaurant. After lunch the tour bus heads back to Stockholm getting to the hotel at about 4:30 P.M.

FRIDAY, JULY 17, EVENING

Tonight enjoy the special experience of dinner in a castle. Two of our tour members will be crowned. One will be king for the night and the other will be tonight's queen. Court maidens will serve a meal that seems to go on and on. This is the Scandinavian Medieval feast, a repast with international fame. You will be entertained by the court jester, a dance troupe appointed by this evening's king, and a ballad master who strolls throughout the vaulted dining rooms all evening long. Swedish ale is the drink of the evening and a powerful drink it is. The bus does not get back until 1:30 tomorrow morning, so plan to make a night of it.

SATURDAY, JULY 18, MORNING, AFTERNOON, AND EVENING

This last day in Scandinavia is free to visit the many places that have become special in Stockholm once again. Shop for those last minute gifts or just relax in this land of the midnight sun.

SUNDAY, JULY 19, MORNING, AFTERNOON, AND EVENING

The SWS Transfer Service representative will be waiting at the hotel check-out counter at 7:00 A.M. to escort you to the airport for your journey back to America. He will make sure you get checked in and cleared through customs before bidding a final adieu from SWS. Your flight leaves from Stockholm at 9:05 this morning and lands at JFK Airport in New York City at 2:15 P.M.. Reclaim your baggage for customs clearance, proceed through customs, and then check your baggage back in with TWA. Although you will change planes in St. Louis, your baggage will be waiting for you when you arrive in Memphis. Your flight to St. Louis leaves at 3:56 P.M. After a brief plane change, you will depart from St. Louis at 7:11 P.M. and arrive back in Memphis at 8:26 P.M. Welcome back!

SCANDINAVIAN ITINERARY DEVELOPMENT EXERCISE NUMBER FOUR

Transfer the flights from "Scandinavian Itinerary Development Exercise Number Two," the hotel information from "Scandinavian Itinerary Development Exercise Number Three," and the above sightseeing booking information to the following draft itinerary form. Keep in mind the cost of the air, the hotels, and the total budget. Prepare a cost budget, estimate commissions and markup, and make certain the total cost is within the specified client budget. Use the tour cost information below. Add any mark-ups and/or other costs and prepare a total cost to client figure using the costing worksheets on pages 232 through 248.

TOUR COST INFORMATION

01 July	Copenhagen city tour	$25 per person
02 July	Tivoli Gardens tour	$22 per person
02 July	Smorgasbord Copenhagen dinner	$31 per person
03 July	Palace and Rosenborg Castle tour	$08 per person
12 July	SWS Transfer Trondheim Airport to Brittania Hotel	$15 per person
13 July	SWS Transfer Brittania Hotel to Trondheim Airport and from Oslo Airport to Grand Hotel	$18 per person
14 July	Oslo City Sightseeing tour	$27 per person
15 July	SWS Transfer Grand Hotel to Oslo Airport	$18 per person
15 July	SWS Transfer Stockholm Airport to Grand Hotel, Stockholm	$17 per person
16 July	Stockholm city tour	$29 per person
17 July	Swedish countryside tour with lunch	$38 per person
17 July	Castle medieval banquet	$64 per person
19 July	SWS Transfer Grand Hotel Stockholm to Stockholm Airport	$17 per person

Total Tour Cost per Person $329 per person

ITINERARY DRAFT WORKSHEET FOR:

-1- Tue 30 Jun
_____

_____

_____

_____

_____

_____

_____

_____

_____

_____

_____

-2- Wed 01 Jul
_____

_____

_____

_____

_____

_____

_____

_____

_____

ITINERARY DRAFT WORKSHEET FOR:

-3- Thurs 02 Jul

-4- Fri 03 Jul

ITINERARY DRAFT WORKSHEET FOR:

-5- Sat 04 Jul

_____

_____

_____

_____

_____

_____

_____

_____

_____

_____

-6- Sun 05 Jul

_____

_____

_____

_____

_____

_____

_____

_____

_____

ITINERARY DRAFT WORKSHEET FOR:

-7- Mon 06 Jul

_____

_____

_____

_____

_____

_____

_____

_____

_____

_____

_____

-8- Tue 07 Jul

_____

_____

_____

_____

_____

_____

_____

_____

ITINERARY DRAFT WORKSHEET FOR:

-9-   Wed   08   Jul

-10-   Thurs   09   Jul

ITINERARY DRAFT WORKSHEET FOR:

. -11- Fri 10 Jul
_____

_____

_____

_____

_____

_____

_____

_____

_____

_____

_____

_____

-12- Sat 11 Jul
_____

_____

_____

_____

_____

_____

_____

_____

_____

ITINERARY DRAFT WORKSHEET FOR:

-13- Sun 12 Jul

_____

_____

_____

_____

_____

_____

_____

_____

_____

_____

_____

-14- Mon 13 Jul

_____

_____

_____

_____

_____

_____

_____

_____

ITINERARY DRAFT WORKSHEET FOR:

-15- Tue 14 Jul

-16- Wed 15 Jul

ITINERARY DRAFT WORKSHEET FOR:

-17- Thur 16 Jul

-18- Fri 17 Jul

ITINERARY DRAFT WORKSHEET FOR:

-19- Sat 18 Jul

_____

_____

_____

_____

_____

_____

_____

_____

_____

_____

-20- Sun 19 Jul

_____

_____

_____

_____

_____

_____

_____

_____

COSTING WORKSHEET NUMBER _____

AIR FARE COSTS	Quoted or Published Price	Commission	Net
Total ticket price (gross)			
Base			
Tax (U.S. domestic—outbound)			
Tax (U.S. domestic—return)			
Tax (U.S. domestic outbound and return)			
Tax (international departure tax)			
Tax (other—designate)			
Tax (other—designate)			
Domestic add-on fare			
Other			
Other			
Other Air Costs			
V.I.P. room admission charge			
Airline V.I.P. handling charge			
Overweight baggage charge			
Headphone charge			
Drink chits			
Other			
Other			
Total This Page			

COSTING WORKSHEET NUMBER _____

RAIL COSTS	Quoted or Published Price	Commission	Net
Railpass (type: _____) Circle appropriate: 1st cl 2nd cl Circle appropriate: 15 day 21 day 1 mo. 2 mo. 3 mo. Cost			
Point-to-Point Rail Day _____ Date_____ City pair _____			
Ticket cost 1st cl 2nd cl			
Reservation cost(s)			
Sleeper or couchette cost			
BBR or exchange rate costs			
Other			
Other			
Day _____ Date_____ City pair _____			
Ticket cost 1st cl 2nd cl			
Reservation cost(s)			
Sleeper or couchette cost			
BBR or exchange rate costs			
Other			
Other			
Day _____ Date_____ City pair _____			
Ticket cost 1st cl 2nd cl			
Reservation cost(s)			
Sleeper or couchette cost			
BBR or exchange rate costs			
Other			
Other			
Total This Page			

COSTING WORKSHEET NUMBER _____

BUS COSTS	Quoted or Published Price	Commission	Net
Day _____ Date _____ City Pair _____			
Day _____ Date _____ City Pair _____			
Day _____ Date _____ City Pair _____			
Day _____ Date _____ City Pair _____			
Day _____ Date _____ City Pair _____			
Day _____ Date _____ City Pair _____			
Day _____ Date _____ City Pair _____			
Day _____ Date _____ City Pair _____			
Day _____ Date _____ City Pair _____			
Day _____ Date _____ City Pair _____			
Day _____ Date _____ City Pair _____			
Day _____ Date _____ City Pair _____			
Day _____ Date _____ City Pair _____			
Day _____ Date _____ City Pair _____			
Day _____ Date _____ City Pair _____			
Day _____ Date _____ City Pair _____			
Day _____ Date _____ City Pair _____			
Day _____ Date _____ City Pair _____			
Day _____ Date _____ City Pair _____			
Day _____ Date _____ City Pair _____			
Day _____ Date _____ City Pair _____			
Day _____ Date _____ City Pair _____			
Day _____ Date _____ City Pair _____			
Day _____ Date _____ City Pair _____			
Day _____ Date _____ City Pair _____			
Day _____ Date _____ City Pair _____			
Day _____ Date _____ City Pair _____			
Total This Page			

COSTING WORKSHEET NUMBER _____

HIP COSTS	Quoted or Published Price	Commission	Net
asic fare (berth or cabin) cost			
eservation fee			
ort charges			
eck chair charges			
ir supplement (for air/sea programs)			
ruise provided transfer costs			
axes			
ther			
ther			
ther			
asic fare (berth or cabin) cost			
eservation fee			
ort charges			
eck chair charges			
ir supplement (for air/sea programs)			
ruise provided transfer costs			
axes			
ther			
ther			
ther			
otal This Page			

COSTING WORKSHEET NUMBER _____

OTHER TRANSPORTATION COSTS	Quoted or Published Price	Commission	Net
Total This Page			

COSTING WORKSHEET NUMBER _____

MEET AND ASSIST COSTS	Quoted or Published Price	Commission	Net
Airport/rail station meet and assist			
Special or V.I.P. handling			
Airport/rail station meet and assist			
Special or V.I.P. handling			
Airport/rail station meet and assist			
Special or V.I.P. handling			
Airport/rail station meet and assist			
Special or V.I.P. handling			
Airport/rail station meet and assist			
Special or V.I.P. handling			
Airport/rail station meet and assist			
Special or V.I.P. handling			
Airport/rail station meet and assist			
Special or V.I.P. handling			
Airport/rail station meet and assist			
Special or V.I.P. handling			
Airport/rail station meet and assist			
Special or V.I.P. handling			
Airport/rail station meet and assist			
Special or V.I.P. handling			
Airport/rail station meet and assist			
Special or V.I.P. handling			
Airport/rail station meet and assist			
Special or V.I.P. handling			
Total This Page			

COSTING WORKSHEET NUMBER _____

GROUND TRANSFER COSTS	Quoted or Published Price	Commission	Net
Airport to hotel			
Hotel to airport			
Service charges and gratuities			
Taxes			
Other			
Other			
Airport to hotel			
Hotel to airport			
Service charges and gratuities			
Taxes			
Other			
Other			
Airport to hotel			
Hotel to airport			
Service charges and gratuities			
Taxes			
Other			
Other			
Airport to hotel			
Hotel to airport			
Service charges and gratuities			
Taxes			
Other			
Other			
Total This Page			

COSTING WORKSHEET NUMBER _____

SIGHTSEEING TOURS	Quoted or Published Price	Commission	Net
Date _____ Tour title _____			
Date _____ Tour title _____			
Date _____ Tour title _____			
Date _____ Tour title _____			
Date _____ Tour title _____			
Date _____ Tour title _____			
Date _____ Tour title _____			
Date _____ Tour title _____			
Date _____ Tour title _____			
Date _____ Tour title _____			
Date _____ Tour title _____			
Date _____ Tour title _____			
Date _____ Tour title _____			
Date _____ Tour title _____			
Date _____ Tour title _____			
Date _____ Tour title _____			
Date _____ Tour title _____			
Date _____ Tour title _____			
Date _____ Tour title _____			
Date _____ Tour title _____			
Date _____ Tour title _____			
Date _____ Tour title _____			
Date _____ Tour title _____			
Date _____ Tour title _____			
Date _____ Tour title _____			
Date _____ Tour title _____			
Total This Page			

COSTING WORKSHEET NUMBER _____

ACCOMMODATION COSTS	Quoted or Published Price	Commission	Net
Day _____ Date in _____ Date out _____ Hotel, inn, etc., name			
Per night $ _____ × _____ nights =			
Porterage in			
Porterage out			
Tips			
Housekeeping			
Other			
Taxes			
Service charges and gratuities			
Other			
Day _____ Date in _____ Date out _____ Hotel, inn, etc., name			
Per night $ _____ × _____ nights =			
Porterage in			
Porterage out			
Tips			
Housekeeping			
Other			
Taxes			
Service charges and gratuities			
Other			
Total This Page			

COSTING WORKSHEET NUMBER _____

CAR OR LIMO RENTAL	Quoted or Published Price	Commission	Net
Day _____ Date of pickup _____			
Date of return _____			
Rate per _____ :			
$ _____ × _____ days/weeks =			
Chauffeur cost			
C.D. waiver			
Insurance			
Taxes			
Other			
Day _____ Date of pickup _____			
Date of return _____			
Rate per _____ :			
$ _____ × _____ days/weeks =			
Chauffeur cost			
C.D. waiver			
Insurance			
Taxes			
Other			
Day _____ Date of pickup _____			
Date of return _____			
Rate per _____ :			
$ _____ × _____ days/weeks =			
Chauffeur cost			
C.D. waiver			
Insurance			
Taxes			
Other			
Total This Page			

COSTING WORKSHEET NUMBER _____

MEALS (Sold as meals—not included on a tour)	Quoted or Published Price	Commission	Net
Date _____ Meal _____ Restaurant _____			
Date _____ Meal _____ Restaurant _____			
Date _____ Meal _____ Restaurant _____			
Date _____ Meal _____ Restaurant _____			
Date _____ Meal _____ Restaurant _____			
Date _____ Meal _____ Restaurant _____			
Date _____ Meal _____ Restaurant _____			
Date _____ Meal _____ Restaurant _____			
Date _____ Meal _____ Restaurant _____			
Date _____ Meal _____ Restaurant _____			
Date _____ Meal _____ Restaurant _____			
Date _____ Meal _____ Restaurant _____			
Date _____ Meal _____ Restaurant _____			
Date _____ Meal _____ Restaurant _____			
Date _____ Meal _____ Restaurant _____			
Date _____ Meal _____ Restaurant _____			
Total This Page			

COSTING WORKSHEET NUMBER _____

MEALS	Quoted or Published Price	Commission	Net
Day _____ Date _____ Meal _____			
Day _____ Date _____ Meal _____			
Day _____ Date _____ Meal _____			
Day _____ Date _____ Meal _____			
Day _____ Date _____ Meal _____			
Day _____ Date _____ Meal _____			
Day _____ Date _____ Meal _____			
Day _____ Date _____ Meal _____			
Day _____ Date _____ Meal _____			
Day _____ Date _____ Meal _____			
Day _____ Date _____ Meal _____			
Day _____ Date _____ Meal _____			
Day _____ Date _____ Meal _____			
Day _____ Date _____ Meal _____			
Day _____ Date _____ Meal _____			
Day _____ Date _____ Meal _____			
Day _____ Date _____ Meal _____			
Day _____ Date _____ Meal _____			
Day _____ Date _____ Meal _____			
Day _____ Date _____ Meal _____			
Day _____ Date _____ Meal _____			
Day _____ Date _____ Meal _____			
Day _____ Date _____ Meal _____			
Total This Page			

COSTING WORKSHEET NUMBER _____

ENTERTAINMENT COSTS (Including taxes and service charges)	Quoted or Published Price	Commission	Net
Day _____ Date _____ Show/Event _____			
Day _____ Date _____ Show/Event _____			
Day _____ Date _____ Show/Event _____			
Day _____ Date _____ Show/Event _____			
Day _____ Date _____ Show/Event _____			
Day _____ Date _____ Show/Event _____			
Day _____ Date _____ Show/Event _____			
Day _____ Date _____ Show/Event _____			
Day _____ Date _____ Show/Event _____			
Day _____ Date _____ Show/Event _____			
Day _____ Date _____ Show/Event _____			
Day _____ Date _____ Show/Event _____			
Day _____ Date _____ Show/Event _____			
Day _____ Date _____ Show/Event _____			
Day _____ Date _____ Show/Event _____			
Day _____ Date _____ Show/Event _____			
Total This Page			

COSTING WORKSHEET NUMBER _____

ADMINISTRATIVE COSTS	Cost	Markup	Total
Communication			
Mail charges			
Phone charges			
Telex charges			
Other communication charges			
Delivery charges			
Duplication charges			
Give Aways			
Flight bag			
Flowers			
Liquor			
Toiletry kit			
Other (specify):			
Other (specify):			
Time Charges			
Name: _____ @ $ _____ per hour =			
Name: _____ @ $ _____ per hour =			
Name: _____ @ $ _____ per hour =			
Other costs (itemize):			
Other costs (itemize):			
Other costs (itemize):			
Total Costs			
Page 1			
Page 2			
Page 3			
Page 4			
Page 5			
Page 6			
Grand Total			
Markups			
Total per Person Price to the Clients			

COST SUMMARY SHEET

	Quoted or Published Price	Commission	Net
Transportation			
Air			
Rail			
Bus			
Ship			
Other			
Ground Transfers			
Meet and assist			
Transfers			
Other			
Accommodations			
Other			
Car/limo rentals			
Other			
Tour costs			
Other			
Meal costs			
Other			
Entertainment costs			
Other			
Administrative costs			
Other			
Total			
Markup			
Total price			

12

DOCUMENTS, RECORDS, INSURANCE, AND MONEY

THE IMPORTANCE OF DOCUMENTS, RECORDS, INSURANCE, AND MONEY

Perhaps because they seem more mundane than some of the more exciting aspects of F.I.T. development, document gathering, record keeping, determining the appropriate insurance and obtaining it, and helping the client with monetary transfers and safekeeping are all aspects of the F.I.T. that sometimes get overlooked or handled in a less than professional manner. Indeed, it is often these seemingly small points that can make the difference between completing a professional job that is appreciated and commented about by clients and completing a poorly finished job that might provide the client with a technically acceptable F.I.T., but sometimes leaves the client with the uneasy feeling that something might go wrong. These areas of work often provide the finishing touches that are the mark of having completed a professional job.

THE IMPORTANCE OF HAVING A DOCUMENTATION PROCESS

The documentation process and documentation checks constitute one of the weakest areas in the F.I.T. development process at many travel agencies. As worldy as many travel agents are, they seem to take it for granted that the clients know what documents are needed and where to get the documents. These agents send their clients on their trips presuming documentation is in order. More experienced F.I.T. specialists, however, will not take such risks. They set up a system early in the F.I.T. development process to ensure that appropriate documentation is identified, requested well in advance, and verified prior to departure of the F.I.T. client. They make this process work for every client, including the very experienced client.

255

Page One of _____

Client Name: _____

Trip Dates: _____

Documents	Needed	Ordered	Checked	Received
Passport				
Immunization records				
Document: _____				
Document: _____				
Document: _____				
Country: _____				
Visa				
Entry card				
Currency declaration				
Other: _____				
Other: _____				
Country: _____				
Visa				
Entry card				
Currency declaration				
Other: _____				
Other: _____				
Country: _____				
Visa				
Entry card				
Currency declaration				
Other: _____				
Other: _____				

Fig. 12-1. A simple documentation checklist form.

DOCUMENTATION CHECKS

Documentation processes involve two aspects: a checklist and a good visa service. Once the itinerary destinations are identified, a checklist is inserted into the client file. The checklist shown in figure 12-1 is one of the simplest types of documentation checklists used. It simply identifies all countries to be visited and has blocks to indicate the documents needed for each country. A column next to each document block is completed to show status. The first,

"Needed," column indicates whether or not the document is needed or not needed. The next column, "Ordered," indicates the date the document has been requested. "Check" columns are included to show when phone calls have been made to determine the status of documents in process. The final, "Received," column is filled in with the date the document is received. In addition to the country blocks is a section for the passport, for the immunization records, and for "Other" documents. F.I.T. specialists working several F.I.T.s at a time usually try to check the documentation checklist of each F.I.T. client on a weekly basis to identify any problem situations early enough to make sure no last minute documentation problems are encountered. Some agencies—usually those having a large F.I.T. clientele—have a secretary or a clerk who checks all current client documentation checklists weekly, bringing potential problem situations to the attention of the F.I.T. specialist handling the client involved. However, most F.I.T. specialists prefer to handle documentation checks themselves.

VISA SERVICE

The second part of the documentation process is the retention of a good visa service. These services obtain passports, visas, and many other travel documents for clients and they usually work closely with F.I.T. specialists. Although some travel agents will simply refer their clients to a visa service and forget about the documentation—leaving the rest to the client and the visa service to work out; F.I.T. specialists usually make the initial call to the visa service, set up an appointment for the F.I.T. client(s) with a visa service specialist, call back after the appointment to confirm that their checklist of documents needed matches the visa service specialist's evaluation of needed documents, and checks with the visa service weekly to determine the status of requested documents.

PASSPORT

The passport is the single most important document required of F.I.T. clients as they travel throughout the world. Many other documents may be required, but F.I.T. experts agree that the passport is the primary one needed. Although U.S. citizens are not required to have a passport for travel out of the United States and they do not need one for entry into several countries; re-entry into the United States always requires some form of proof of citizenship and most countries of the world require a valid passport as a basic document for entry into their country. Most F.I.T. clients will already have a passport, although it might have expired and no longer be valid, before they become F.I.T. clients. They will have obtained a passport for business travel, tours, cruises, or other travel prior to taking their first F.I.T. However, a few F.I.T. clients will not have a passport and a few of these clients might argue that they do not want to spend the money and time to get a passport. They have a choice in some countries. In Mexico, Canada, and some Caribbean countries, a United States passport is not required for entry into or exit from the country. However, upon re-entry into the United States, the traveler will need to prove that he is an American citizen. This may be done by showing a valid, up-to-date voter's registration or an "original" (it must be imprinted with a raised seal) birth certificate. In either of these cases, however, the proof of citizenship document might be challenged and it sometimes is. A passport is definitely recommended.

In addition to the importance of having a passport in order to re-enter the United States, it should be pointed out to F.I.T. clients that having a valid passport can give them better protection outside the United States than will a birth certificate or a voter's registration card. A Texas travel agent recently recounted an incident involving a wealthy, influential client of latin heritage who visited Mexico with only a birth certificate as proof of citizenship. He and his wife were in a street when an antigovernment demonstration broke out. They were arrested. It took several days before lawyers were able to get them released from jail. When they were released, the Mexican authorities told them that if they had been carrying valid United States passports, they would have been released immediately.

Getting a Passport Getting a passport for them is a service many clients expect from a travel agent. However, U.S. government legal restrictions prohibit a travel agent from obtaining a passport for her client(s). Passports must be requested by the applicants (client) only. This is because some application questions must be sworn to.

There are two ways in which a passport may be obtained. These are:

1. For the client to order the passport through the United States Post Office or at one of the United States Passport Offices (if outside the Unites States, it can be ordered through a U.S. consulate)
2. For the client to order the passport through a visa service

If the passport is ordered through a visa service, it can be done on an appointment basis and it can be obtained quickly (sometimes as rapidly as forty-eight hours). However, it will be expensive (sometimes as much as four times the cost of ordering it through the post office). If the passport is ordered through the post office or at one of the United States Passport Offices (located in Washington, D.C., New York City, Chicago, Seattle, and Los Angeles), there may be long lines; normal waiting periods can stretch to six weeks or longer (the usual processing time is three to four weeks during non-peak periods, but the cost is a lot less. Good visa services will maintain a file showing the passport number, date of issue, and expiration date of each client's passport. They will notify the traveler and the travel agency when the passport needs to be renewed. However, with the new ten-year validity of passports, this service is less important than it was before, when passports were renewed every three years. The most important aspect of this service's record-keeping is the protection it offers in case of passport theft or loss. To expedite obtaining a duplicate passport, it is beneficial to have the passport number and date of issue for the state department or the U.S. consulate. However, these records are often kept by the travel agency as well as a service to its clients. Therefore, the decision to order a passport through the Post Office or the United States Passport Office or to order it through a visa service is often a decision based totally on cost, convenience, and especially how fast the passport is needed.

Passport Application Forms There are two types of passport application forms. The long white form is used for those applicants who have never had a United States passport before. The shorter, pink form is used for those who have had a United States passport in the past and wish to obtain a new passport. New passport applicants are expected to furnish considerable information supporting their eligibility for a United States passport. They must have original birth certificates and these are checked for authenticity by having a raised seal embossed on them indicating the country in which they were issued. Normally the page and date of birth registration are noted on the birth certificate. Original birth certificates can be obtained from the county in which the applicant was born. Usually these records are kept by the county courthouse. There is normally a cost levied for the issuance and mailing of original birth certificates, so clients should be advised to phone ahead to determine:

1. If the county has the record of birth on file
2. What the cost will be to obtain an original birth certificate

Once this information is known, a letter and appropriate check can be sent requesting the birth certificate. If the applicant is a naturalized citizen, notorized copies of the naturalization papers (the citizenship certificate) must be sent with the passport application to authenticate citizenship.

For those who have had a passport in the past, the process is much easier. It is presumed that citizenship proof was presented when the original passport was issued. Therefore, the old passport is sent with the application for a new passport, thereby providing the needed documentation. Some clients might be concerned that the expiration of the old passport may render it invalid for documentation purposes, but the United States Passport Office does not differentiate between a currently-valid-but-soon-to-expire passport, a recently expired passport, or a passport that expired many years ago. All are accepted as new passport documentation proof. Therefore, advise clients that they should not throw their expired passports away just because they have expired. This will save them considerable time, effort, paperwork, and money if and when they wish to get a new passport.

The passport application forms call for specific information designed to determine passport eligibility. The names and addresses of relatives, the birth dates and the birth places of parents, siblings, and spouses are requested. Previous addresses of the applicant are called for. The client is urged to complete all data to the best of his knowledge. Many elderly passport applicants do not remember and, in some cases, do not know the information asked. Nevertheless, they should be advised to provide as complete information as possible and to send a cover letter with the application if there is some reason why they do not know some of the information asked for. The United States Passport Office has the right to refuse to issue a passport, they have acted on this right a number of times in the past. The requirement to provide proof of eligibility to obtain a passport lies with the applicant and if such proof is not provided, a passport will not be issued.

VISAS

Visas are stamps stamped on the blank pages of passports. Normally, they must be obtained before entering a country. They are issued by the country to be visited and reflect permission from the government of that country to enter that country. The issuance or non-issuance of a visa is totally up to the host country and some countries, Albania, for example, will not issue a visa to an American citizen. There are many types of visas, each carrying specific privileges and obligations. Diplomatic visas are issued to official representatives of one government traveling to other countries representing their government. Business visas are issued to those traveling to the host country for the purpose of conducting business. And tourist visas, the type obtained by most travelers, are issued to those visiting a country to see the sites and for other tourism reasons. There are countries that will not issue tourist visas (Saudi Arabia, for example) and there are countries that wish to limit the number of tourists and only issue up to a specified quota of tourist visas (until recently, China was such a country).

How does the F.I.T. expert determine whether or not a tourist visa is required by a host country? There are three standard ways.

1. To reference the *Pan American World Guide*
2. To reference the country documentation data in their reservations computer
3. To consult the visa service with which the travel agency works

The most up-to-date and accurate information comes from the visa service. A quality visa service updates its records daily. The computer reservation data will normally be up-to-date as well, although some systems update this data only once every two weeks or once a month. The *Pan American World Guide* is updated at each publication and, therefore, might be outdated when the F.I.T. specialist consults it. Although the *Pan Am World Guide* is convenient, data should be verified if the book being used for reference is more than a month old.

Visas are issued by the consular services of the host countries. Almost all of these are headquartered in Washington, D.C., but many have offices in

New York City, Chicago, San Francisco, and/or Los Angeles plus other major cities. Although a few countries will only issue visas out of their Washington, D.C., consulate headquarters, most countries will issue visas at any of their consular offices.

Since visas are stamped on pages in the traveler's passport, the client must first have a passport before getting a visa. And since it might take several days to process a visa request at a consulate, if the client is visiting several countries and must obtain visas from each country, the processing time to obtain a passport and all visas can extend for several months. This time concern might be crucial if the client starts the planning process only a short time before the intended trip and/or if the client wants to attend an event that only occurs at a specific time. Visa services can reduce the time considerably, however. Most good visa services will send the passport request via overnight mail to their Washington, D.C., or other office headquarters and can request rush service, often obtaining the visa in as little as twenty-four hours. The Washington, D.C., staff will hand-carry a passport needing multiple visas to each consulate for which a visa is needed and because they work closely with consulates, they can usually expedite the issuance of each visa along the way. Visa services, therefore, can often cut down a two- or three-month task of getting a new passport and the visas for each country to be visited to a one week time frame. Visa service charges, however, can be considerable—often running as high as $200 to $400.

If an F.I.T. client wishes to obtain visas personally, this can be done. The passport is mailed to each consulate with a completed visa application form, the appropriate visa fee, and a check covering return postage. Of course, getting the application form will take time, since most application forms must be requested by mail and many consulates will expect the client to pay the postage fee to send the application form. The passport should always be mailed via certified mail to avoid loss in the mailing process. Passport crime is still a major danger for those requesting visas themselves, however. But a greater potential problem is the possibility that a visa that was obtained early will expire before all other visas can be obtained. Many tourist visas are issued with a one month validity from the date of issue. If the client is still trying to get all the visas needed for the trip a month after getting the first visa and that visa will expire in thirty days, the client will go around in circles never getting all the visas needed. In such situations using a visa service is the only practical alternative.

Many clients, however, will not need any visas. Until 1986 no Western European country required a tourist visa from a United States citizen. Now, only France requires a tourist visa and these can usually be obtained quite rapidly (assuming a number of travel agencies keep French visa applications on file). Many other countries exempt United States citizens from having a tourist visa also. Therefore, trips to these countries can be made rapidly—sometimes on the spur of the moment—if one is holding a valid United States passport.

Other Documents

Several additional documents are needed by F.I.T. clients varying some-what with the destination country and the duration of their visit. These documents include health cards, entry cards, declaration forms, airline tickets, and miscellaneous other documents. Some are required by many countries, while others are required for only a few countries. In each case, the visa service should be able to advise the F.I.T. specialist of up-to-date documentation requirements.

Airline Tickets

Perhaps the least often required and most easily provided document that is sometimes needed for entry into a few countries of the world is an airline ticket. There are governments that are concerned about the tourist's ability to leave the country after the tourist has been admitted. In such circumstan-ces, the common document required to prove ability to depart from a host country is a valid, fully paid airline ticket out of the destination country. Some consulates will require proof of ability to depart from their country before a visa is issued. In such circumstances, a copy of the airline ticket showing departure flights is usually submitted with the visa application when requesting the visas. In other cases, the F.I.T. client will be required to show a valid airline ticket together with the appropriate visas upon arrival in the destination country before being allowed to clear customs and leave the arrival airport in the destination country. If this is the case, F.I.T. clients should be advised accordingly so that they will be prepared to show proof of departure ability upon arrival.

Immunization Records

Health cards, better known as immunization records, and the medical cov-erage against disease that they represent, are inspected as soon as the passengers arrive at the airport in many countries. There are even a few countries where health inspectors board the aircraft and inspect health certificates prior to allowing passengers to disembark from the plane. This is especially true when the plane is coming from a part of the world that is affected by an outbreak of a deadly disease. The United States is one of the most stringent countries to screen out those who are arriving without proper inoculations. If the F.I.T. client arrives in a country without the required shots, one of three courses of action is usually taken. The traveler may be given the appropriate shot and allowed to enter the country. The client might be sent back to the country of origin (the country from which he last departed or the country in which he last traveled.) Or, the client might be quarantined for a period of time to see whether or not an infection from the disease will develop. Because most countries require airlines to take passengers who do not have appropriate documents back to the country where they boarded the flight and because airlines want to avoid incurring this loss of revenue, many carriers adopt the policy of checking each document and each area of concern before allowing passengers to enter the aircraft before taking off on an international flight.

Although travel agents are advised not to act in the role of doctors and should avoid advising clients directly regarding shots (some clients might be allergic to or have had bad reactions to inoculations), they need to advise their clients that shots might be required before entering another country and they should advise their clients to see a physician to get the needed inoculations well in advance of starting the international trip.

F.I.T. specialists should advise clients that they might bring certain medications with them, but that other medications are not allowed. Generally, anything that can be construed to be a non-prescription or over-the-counter drug cannot legally be brought into most foreign countries, and there is often some diagreement between customs inspectors and travelers as to what is an allowable over-the-counter drug. Clients should be advised to consult with their personal physician to determine which countries allow medications to come in and which ones do not. Clients might want to obtain a letter from their physician on letterhead stating that the traveler is required to take this medication (when this is the case), and to obtain sufficient supplies of prescribed medications prior to the trip so that refills en route will not be needed.

For clients who are concerned about medical facilities in other countries, several referral services listing U.S.-trained doctors and hospitals that provide services for English-speaking clients operate throughout the world and are listed with major medical associations. Most of these services are located in European countries. Most physicians will be happy to research the services and provide a recommendation to their patients upon request. Some travel agents also provide recommendations to their clients, but because of the medical nature of the referrals, many F.I.T. specialists prefer to have the client consult his or her personal physician, since that physician will know the client's medical history.

Entry Cards

The entry cards required by many countries come in an assortment of sizes, shapes, and designs with varied questions. Not all countries require entry cards and those that do require them have no uniformity in their requirements. Either the F.I.T. specialist should provide copies of the blank entry cards obtained from each country that requires an entry card or the specialist should advise clients to pick up blank cards at the visa service (if the client is using a visa service). If the client has difficulty completing the entry cards, the F.I.T. specialist should help to interpret entry card regulations and procedures that must be completed before a traveler is allowed to enter the country. For most countries that require them, these forms are normally restricted to declaring the amount and types of currency or currency equivalents (checks, bank drafts, etc.) being brought into the country. Currency controls and the options travelers have in order to bring in or transfer money when traveling are discussed later in this chapter.

In completing the declaration form, it is essential that the client be advised to declare all currency and/or currency equivalents being brought into the country (seldom, but once in awhile travelers are searched), that a copy of the declaration (or at least the amount declared) be kept with the traveler, that all exchanges while in the country be made at an official bank, that receipts for all exchanges be requested and kept, and that an exact accounting of all monies spent and exchanged be balanced to the declaration completed when leaving the country so that the incoming amounts will balance to the monies and receipts for purchases taken out of the country.

Vouchers and Letter Copies

Other documents needed by F.I.T. clients include vouchers and letter copies. Vouchers will be needed to show that reservations have been made, deposits have been sent, and/or full payment has been provided to travel suppliers. The vouchers not only confirm the arrangements made with a supplier, but they often provide an exchange document that the traveler can give to the travel supplier in exchange for the service(s) provided. Vouchers are commonly used in conjunction with hotel arrangements, tours, sightseeing, meet and assist arrangements, and car or limousine rentals. In some cases, however, vouchers are not the commonly used means of confirming arrangements. Letters often constitute the means of confirmation. When a vendor responds via letter, a copy of the letter carried by the F.I.T. client will provide the vendor representative with the necessary on-site confirmation needed. Copies of telexes provide the same on-site confirmation.

Financial Documents

Still other documents the clients will carry are financial in nature. While clients on short F.I.T.s will carry the needed cash, traveler's checks, and credit cards with them, those taking lengthy F.I.T.s will need to arrange for money transfers. Often the travel agency F.I.T. specialist will assist clients in obtaining the needed traveler's checks, advising which will be best for each country, and keeping a record of the travel check numbers (sometimes even making a copy of the receipts in case the travel checks are lost). Advising clients on bank or other financial institution transfers of funds to similar institutions in countries to which the clients are traveling and assisting them in contacting those who can be of help in making such transfers is often of considerable importance.

Obtaining letters of credit and bank fund transfers, making certain that the documents are in order, and keeping the documents safe during travel are all concerns the F.I.T. specialists will need to address when working with F.I.T. clients who might be taking trips that are several months in length. They are also very sensitive areas of concern. On the one hand, the F.I.T. specialist does not want to seem to pry into the financial business of the client(s). On the other hand, the client(s) want to be certain that funds are available when they are needed and that they are secure up to the time they are to be needed. The key is to work with a safe financial institution that has experience in helping F.I.T. clients with the transfers of sometimes substantial funds.

Deak Perrera specializes in financial assistance to and for travelers and they are of special help for F.I.T. clients. Not only do they have their own offices in major tourist cities in Europe and other areas of the world, but they work closely with international banks in capital cities (and many other cities) in almost all countries of the world. If the travel agency is located in a city where Deak Perrera has an office, the F.I.T. specialist can set up an appointment for the client and know that all details will be taken care of in a professional manner. If Deak Perrera does not have an office in the city where the client lives, arrangements can often be worked out via long-distance phone calls and mail. Deak Perrera provides money packets for each country to which the client will be traveling, travel checks in the currencies of many destination countries, and money transfers to its own and other financial institutions. By combining all these services plus credit cards, F.I.T. clients can have not only financial flexibility, but financial security throughout the trip. Many Deak Perrera offices also sell money belts and leather financial document envelopes that can be strapped onto any part of the body and worn underneath the clothing for travel to provide the maximum degree of financial document safety. Some F.I.T. specialists buy the leather document envelopes and straps in bulk and provide one free to each F.I.T. client who is taking a trip for several months.

In some cases F.I.T. clients might be spending a considerable amount of time in one or a few neighboring countries. When this is the case, establishing a bank account prior to the trip (normally in the city where the client will be spending the greatest amount of time) and transferring funds prior to starting the trip will be of considerable benefit for the client. Either Deak Perrera or the international service office of the client's bank will be able to arrange for both the establishment of the bank account in the other country and the transfer of funds to the account. In almost all cases, a bank savings book, a checkbook, or some other document will be provided by the bank for the client. Some banks will mail these documents to the F.I.T. client in the United States. However, it is usually safer for the bank to arrange to hold the bank books for the client's arrival. In such circumstances the client's passport will be required to show proof of identity. In addition, a letter documenting the financial transfer or a receipt for the transfer will normally be needed before the bank books are turned over to the client. Of course, the F.I.T. specialist will want to make sure that such documents are included in the papers the client carries when departing the U.S. and that the documents are carried in a safe place (preferably in a strap-on leather envelope).

THE CLIENT FILE

To make sure that all F.I.T. arrangements are handled expeditiously and that all documents are in order prior to the client's planned departure date, most F.I.T. specialists work with a client file system. The system that works best for many F.I.T. specialists is a dedicated expandable cardboard file holder with an envelope-type tie-down flap and several inside pockets large enough to hold individual file folders. This system allows for considerable flexibility. When the folder is placed into a file cabinet, individual file folders can be placed into the holder and taken out of it with ease. The holder itself can be removed from the file cabinet with ease, the envelope cover closed and tied for ease of transfer, and all documents are readily retrievable when the holder is placed on a desk for either working the F.I.T. or going over details of the F.I.T. with the client(s).

If such a system is used, it is suggested that a document envelope (something which the client will carry during the trip) be placed in the file holder with the client's name typed on the outside of the document envelope. A checklist of all needed documents can be stapled to the outside of the document envelope and the inside flap document list can be filled in as each document is received and placed into the document envelope. In this way the F.I.T. specialist will be able to tell at a glance whether or not needed documents have been received. In addition, when the client is ready to start the trip, the F.I.T. specialist needs only to remove the document envelope from the file holder and give it to the client, knowing that all is in order.

Another section of the file holder should be devoted to vendor correspondence. Some F.I.T. specialists keep all vendor correspondence in the same file. However, if the F.I.T. is a lengthy one, separate correspondence files should be set up for each country or area to be visited. In some cases, F.I.T. specialists set up an individual file for the correspondence with each vendor. Having a file holder to work with makes any of these alternatives easy. Whichever system is used, it is suggested that a checklist be attached to the outside of each file so that the F.I.T. specialist will know at a glance what the status is with the arrangements being made with each vendor.

Still another section of the file relates to the F.I.T. costs and the financial records pertaining to the F.I.T. When starting the F.I.T. development, the F.I.T. specialist pulls cost sheets for every category of costs expected. These are placed into the financial records file. As costs are committed or incurred, the cost sheets are completed and receipts are attached. It is suggested that the cost sheets be kept in pencil since changes are frequent. When the F.I.T. has been put together, the cost sheets and receipts can be totaled and interim balances can be run up on an adding machine or calculator at any time during the F.I.T. development process (giving both the F.I.T. specialist and the client an up-to-the-minute financial status report with very little effort).

THE IMPORTANCE OF INSURANCE

In many ways for the F.I.T. client, insurance is even more important than it is for other travel agency clients. In terms of total dollars spent, the F.I.T. client is spending more than any other client on the basis of averages. And because the itinerary is tailored to the client, the potential for problems becomes even greater than with clients on package tours, cruises, or domestic trips. Therefore, the four key areas of personal insurance for travel agency individual client travelers should be presented to F.I.T. clients for their consideration. These four areas are:

1. Luggage
2. Accident/medical/sickness
3. Trip cancellation/interruption
4. Death, dismemberment, or sight loss

In some cases, other insurance should be considered also.

Baggage Insurance

International air carriers have sophisticated the baggage handling and baggage transfer process to a considerable extent over the last twenty years. Many have moved to the containerization of baggage. The end result is that there is less loss of baggage than there once was. Fortunately, most F.I.T. clients travel all over the world with no baggage mishaps whatsoever. But when a suitcase is lost, a client's trip can be seriously affected. Insurance will not find the missing suitcase, but insurance will help in making up for the monetary losses incurred in losing a suitcase.

Baggage Insurance Limitations Standard travel insurance policies have strict limitations on the maximum amounts that will be paid for baggage that is lost, stolen, or damaged. In some policies the limitations are variable and there is a sliding scale that equates with a sliding premium scale. In other words, the greater the coverage, the greater the cost for the coverage. The client selects a coverage amount and goes across the scale to determine how much that amount will cost. Even with the sliding scale, there is a limit to the amount of coverage that a client can purchase. Most sliding scale policies have a cap at between $7,000 and $10,000. If a client wants more coverage than the cap allows, but the additional coverage is not much more than the cap, a phone call to the insurance company giving the reason(s) why the additional coverage is desired and the amount of additional insurance needed will sometimes result in a waiver of the cap. Of course, the cost will be increased as well. If the waiver is not provided, the travel agency might look for another travel industry company in an attempt to find one that provides the amount of coverage the client desires. If the coverage desired is beyond what any of the standard travel insurance limitations will provide and no company will waive its limitations to cover the amount desired by the client, a special policy can sometimes be written for the client. This is expensive and it can be hard to find a company that will write such a policy. It is suggested that the travel agent contact Lloyds of London. Lloyds has a long history of writing special travel insurance policies and, while the premiums can be expensive, Lloyds has written such policies for years; more than any other insurance company and is famous for its history of making travel claim payments.

Although sliding scale baggage insurance policies are popular, specific limitation policies are often found as well. For many F.I.T. clients the specific limitation policy will provide more than enough coverage. This often tends to be the least expensive policy for the client. It is easier for most clients to understand, and it is usually easier to sell.

If the client is concerned about cost, however, and the policy amount desired is $2,500 or less, search out sliding scale policies because they might be slightly less expensive. A standard limitation policy has a cap of $3,000. This can apply to either an individual or a family. Consider writing policies on two or more travel insurance carriers if two or more family members are traveling together since most insurance carriers will interpret the limitation cap to apply to a total family when it is their option (and it usually is).

Collecting insurance on lost, stolen, or damaged baggage can be time consuming and does nothing for the immediate problem of having no packed clothing when arriving at the destination. There is an immediate problem for most clients. This is that they arrive at the international destination with the clothes they are wearing and often with nothing to change to. Most but not all policies, provide for an emergency purchase allowance (usually deducted from the maximum payment amount cap). The emergency purchase allowance does not normally go into effect immediately as the title of the allowance might suggest. Usually there is a waiting period of at least twenty-four hours after filing a lost baggage claim with the air carrier involved (and notifying the insurance carrier) before emergency purchases can be made. If the client makes clothing or other emergency purchases before the end of the twenty-four hour (or other, as specified) waiting period and the air carrier notifies the client that the baggage is found or returns the lost baggage to the client within the twenty-four hour waiting period, the client will normally not be reimbursed for the purchases. Therefore, this waiting period limitation should be explained to the F.I.T. client at the time the insurance is purchased. Clients should be advised that emergency purchase allowances are usually quite limited. The standard limit in the industry is $100. Check the limit on the policy being sold as the limitations might vary. Few, if any, however, exceed $100. Receipts detailing the purchases, time of purchase, what was purchased, and the cost of each item will normally be required before the insurance company will provide emergency purchase allowance reimbursement. Also clients should be advised that it might take several months after filing a claim before receiving their reimbursement.

Baggage Insurance Exceptions   One of the problems faced by F.I.T. clients who take out baggage insurance is the exceptions. There are two broad areas of exceptions that both the F.I.T. specialist and the client need to know. Exceptions are those conditions under which payment will not be made and those items that might be lost or stolen for which no or only limited coverage will be extended. Although policies vary regarding the conditions under which items in baggage or luggage as a whole will not be covered, there are three areas that are standard for most policies. These are:

1. Damage or loss from normal wear and tear
2. Damage or loss during a war or warlike situation
3. Damage or loss to property covered by other insurance

Of the three, the most commonly applied exception is the last one. F.I.T. clients often find that other insurance might be construed to be covering the items lost, damaged, or stolen. When this is claimed by the company providing the coverage, no payment is made. Therefore, clients should determine from their current insurers whether or not coverage to baggage or the items carried in their luggage is covered by their current insurers. Usually if they ask for a letter specifying the extent to which they are currently covered in advance, this will help them to decide whether or not they want to take out baggage insurance.

A second area of exceptions is those items specifically not covered or better put, not insurable under baggage and personal effects insurance. These normally fall into two categories: (1) those items totally excluded from coverage; and, (2) those items for which damage, theft, or loss liability is severely limited. The categories of items most commonly excluded altogether include household goods (furniture, rugs, etc.), items normally sent as freight, vehicles (cars, motorcycles, etc., but not bicycles when bikes are checked as baggage), money or money substitutes (credit cards, checks, etc.), pets, and body replacement parts (false teeth, artificial limbs, etc.). Items for which there are strict limitations on coverage (usually a maximum coverage of no more than $1000) normally include at least the following three categories: (1) jewelry (rings, watches, necklaces, etc.), (2) furs, and (3) cameras and camera equipment. Most clients who travel with these limited coverage items have insurance for these items covering them while they are at home. Sometimes a rider to their current policies will cover them fully while traveling will be less expensive and more inclusive than baggage insurance. The F.I.T. specialist should point out to clients that they might want to investigate obtaining such riders when they will be traveling with items of considerable value. This is especially true if the client will be traveling to one or more high risk destination(s).

Baggage Insurance Time Limitations   Most baggage insurance rates are time based and increase with the number of days of coverage. Many clients believe the insurance starts automatically on the first day of the trip and with some new policies this is the case. With other policies, however, the policy effectiveness hour and date must be specified before the policy will commence. In such cases, it is the client's responsibility to notify the insurance carrier the hour and date when the policy should start. This is normally done by making an appropriate notation on the policy application form. Most policies will not accept a start-up date that is significantly earlier than the first air trip of the journey.

Chart Baggage Insurance Selection Process   Review the following baggage insurance premium selection chart, figure 12-2. This is Mutual of Omaha's 1987 baggage insurance rate chart. Options for the number of days of coverage are provided vertically along the left margin of the chart. Options for the dollar amount of coverage are provided horizontally along the top of the chart. The cost of the insurance, depending upon which number of day option and which premium amount was selected by the client, is provided in the center of the chart.

Accident/Medical Sickness Insurance

In reviewing the types of people who take F.I.T.s, it is possible to immediately conclude that the two groups with the largest numbers of F.I.T. travelers are also high-risk groups when it comes to the potential for accidents and sickness. These two are the elderly and the adventuresome. While the adventuresome risk accidents, the elderly are more often sick. For both groups, therefore, accident/medical/sickness insurance should be considered. Obviously, there are many other F.I.T. clients who might want to consider this type of insurance coverage as well.

Accident/Medical/Sickness Insurance Limitations   Limitations vary depending upon three factors:

1. Cost scale
2. Term or number of days scale

Baggage Rates

NOTE: Baggage premiums cover either an individual or a family. All other premiums are individual rates.

For baggage coverage of $3,000, simply double the $1,000 rates. The maximum family limit for this coverage is $3,000.

Term of Coverage	Amount of Insurance				
	$500 Premium	$800 Premium	$1,000 Premium	$1,500 Premium	$2,000 Premium
1-3 days	$ 8.25	$ 11.50	$ 14.00	$ 17.50	$ 21.25
5 days	11.50	16.50	20.00	25.00	30.25
7 days	14.00	20.75	25.25	31.50	38.00
8 days	15.25	22.25	27.25	34.00	41.00
10 days	17.25	25.50	31.00	38.75	46.75
11 days	18.25	27.00	33.00	41.25	49.50
14 days	20.75	32.00	38.75	48.50	58.25
15 days	21.75	33.25	40.75	51.00	61.00
17 days	23.75	36.50	44.50	55.75	66.75
18 days	24.25	38.00	46.25	57.75	69.25
21 days	26.50	41.25	50.25	63.00	75.50
22 days	27.25	42.25	51.75	64.75	77.50
24 days	28.50	44.50	54.50	68.25	81.75
27 days	30.75	48.25	58.50	73.25	88.00
28 days	31.50	49.25	60.00	75.25	90.00
30 days	33.00	51.50	62.75	78.50	94.00
31 days	33.50	52.50	64.00	80.00	96.25
45 days	41.50	64.00	78.00	97.50	117.25
60 days	50.00	77.50	95.00	118.25	142.00
90 days	63.00	97.25	119.00	148.50	178.25
120 days	76.00	118.25	144.00	180.00	216.25
150 days	88.50	138.00	168.00	210.50	252.50
180 days	100.00	156.00	190.00	238.00	285.50

Fig. 12-2. Baggage rates. (Courtesy of Tele-Trip, Inc., an affiliate of the Mutual of Omaha Companies.)

3. Type of problem—for example, there is a different limitation maximum for loss of life (also loss of limb or loss of sight), accident medical expenses, and sickness payments

For most policies the maximum life insurance coverage is $100,000. The maximum for accident medical expenses is $10,000. And the average for sickness benefits is $50 per day.

Accident/Medical/Sickness Insurance Exceptions   Major exclusions are for suicide, participation in military activities, participation in some sports (check out your client's sport before finding out that the insurance she took out does not include her), illegal activities, or taking or being on drugs.

Accident/Medical/Sickness Insurance Time Limitations   As with baggage insurance, coverage is limited to the number of days selected in the premium program a client elects. The policy effectiveness must be specified by the client before the policy will commence. In addition, specific aspects of the coverage have their own time limitations. For example, accidental loss of life, limb, or sight is usually covered no more than six months after an accident even though the lingering effects of the accident might cause loss of life, limb, or sight more than six months after the accident. In addition,

**Accident — Medical —
Sickness Rates**

	Plan 1	Plan 2	Plan 3
Principal Sum	**$25,000**	**$50,000**	**$100,000**
Accident Medical Expense	**2,500**	**5,000**	**10,000**
Sickness Benefit	**$50/Day**	**$50/Day**	**$50/Day**
Term of Coverage	Premium		
1-3 days	$ 4.20	$ 7.25	$ 14.10
5 days	8.85	15.30	28.20
7 days	10.80	18.75	35.05
8 days	11.90	20.75	40.35
10 days	14.95	26.60	50.35
11 days	15.35	27.25	51.25
14 days	17.10	30.05	56.25
15 days	18.30	31.95	61.80
17 days	20.75	36.35	68.05
18 days	21.05	36.85	68.90
21 days	22.00	37.95	71.15
22 days	22.60	39.05	72.45
24 days	23.65	40.70	75.30
27 days	25.80	44.10	81.20
28 days	26.50	45.15	83.10
30 days	27.85	47.30	86.90
31 days	28.50	48.35	88.75
45 days	33.65	58.40	108.75
60 days	43.60	73.75	135.05
90 days	56.15	94.35	173.40
120 days	66.60	109.95	198.00
150 days	76.65	125.85	225.60
180 days	84.75	138.40	247.40

Fig. 12-3. Accidental—Medical—Sickness rates. (Courtesy of Tele-Trip, Inc., an affiliate of the Mutual of Omaha Companies.)

sickness benefits are normally not paid within the ninety days prior to the accident.

Chart Accident/Medical/Sickness Insurance Selection Process Review the following accident, medical, sickness insurance premium selection chart, figure 12-3. This is Mutual of Omaha's 1987 rate chart for accident, medical, and sickness insurance. Options for the number of days of coverage are provided vertically along the left margin of the chart. Three options for the dollar amount of coverage (premium) ranging from $25,000 to $100,000 for life, limb(s), or sight; from $2500 for accident/medical expenses; and a flat fee of $50 per day for sickness benefits are provided horizontally along the top of the chart. The cost of the insurance, depending upon which number of day option and which premium group was selected by the client, is provided in the center of the chart.

Trip Cancellation/Interruption Insurance

The most popular insurance with travelers, one of the easiest to sell, and one of the best policies for F.I.T. travelers is trip cancellation/interruption insurance. For many years this has been a popular insurance, but with the advent of non-refundable fares and fares with high cancellation penalties in the United States, the insurance has grown to be even more popular. Now that a growing number of international flights are also offering non-refundable and high cancellation fares, the policy is gaining still more popularity with F.I.T. clients. The policy pays non-refundable pre-paid fees for missed travel arrangements in the event of trip cancellation or interruption. For F.I.T. clients many more fees are non-refundable than for clients. Not only are many of the air fares for F.I.T. clients non-refundable, but also most ground arrangements are non-refundable. Of special interest to the F.I.T. specialist is that this insurance helps the travel agency almost as much as it does the client. Without the insurance when a client misses a part of an F.I.T., the client often expects the travel agency to contact all suppliers requesting a refund. This is both expensive and time consuming and the travel agency gets paid nothing for doing it. To the contrary, if a supplier fails to answer or does not provide the expected refund, the F.I.T. client might blame the F.I.T. specialist or the travel agency for not trying hard enough. It is for this reason that a growing number of travel agencies are requiring F.I.T. clients to take out trip cancellation/interruption insurance as a condition of arranging their F.I.T.s for them.

Trip Cancellation/Interruption Insurance Limitations and Conditions Although most in the industry feel that cancellation/interruption insurance is generous in what it covers and who it covers, clients need to be told that the policy does not cover the voluntary cancellation or interruption of a trip. In fact, the conditions under which trip cancellation or interruptions are covered are very specific. These are for six situations relating to the traveler or the traveler's traveling companion(s) and sickness, injury or death suffered by the traveler, the traveler's travel companion, and three other categories of people. These other categories are the:

1. Traveler's family members
2. Traveler's business partner
3. Traveler's traveling companion's family members

These terms, "family members," "traveling companions," and "business partner" are specifically defined. Family members are usually determined to be only spouse, child, son-in-law, daughter-in-law, parent, step-parent, parent-in-law, grandparent, grandparent-in-law, grandchild, aunt, uncle, nephew, niece, brother, sister, stepbrother, stepsister, brother-in-law, and sister-in-law. The term "traveling companion" is usually determined to be only a person or the persons with whom the traveler has coordinated travel arrangements and intends to travel during the trip. And the term "business partner" is usually determined to be only a person with whom the traveler co-owns a business.

The conditions under which payment will be made and that relate specifically to the traveler and the traveler's traveling companion are:

1. Must serve on a jury
2. Is quarantined
3. Is subpoenaed as a witness (unless the person subpoenaed is a law enforcement officer)
4. The home or main residence burns down or is rendered otherwise uninhabitable due to a fire or some other unforeseen circumstance
5. Miss their transportation connection because of a car or carrier accident while en route to depart on the trip or a section of the trip
6. Cannot take part or all of the trip because of a bankruptcy of an airline, tour operator, or cruise line

Sickness or injury must require medical treatment and such treatment must be documented if the policy is to pay the client. Normally payments will be limited to what is required (not exceeding economy air fare cost) for the client to continue the scheduled trip (if possible) or to return back to the point where the trip was started. Substitute travel arrangements usually must begin within ninety days of the accident or illness. If the trip is interrupted by weather, hijacking, or an unannounced strike, payment will usually be limited to three days and to not more than 10% of the amount of daily coverage.

Trip Cancellation/Interruption Insurance Exceptions and Time Coverage   War, military activities, suicide, sports activities, and aircraft damage or accident are the exceptions under which the trip cancellation/interruption insurance will not pay benefits. This policy goes into effect as soon as the policy is both applied for and paid for. However, travel arrangements must have been made before the policy becomes effective.

Flight Insurance

Flight insurance covers accidental death, dismemberment, or loss of sight sustained while traveling. Although many people have the impression that flight insurance only covers the traveler while the plane is in the air, most policies also cover the passenger while he is en route to the airport to start a trip, from the airport to local destination when the trip is over, and while the passenger is waiting in the airport. To be covered under this policy, a traveler must be a ticketed passenger on a scheduled air carrier, in the airport terminal or grounds immediately prior to or right after one's scheduled flight, or either en route to the airport to catch a flight or from the airport after having taken a flight. War, military activity, and suicide are the major exclusions relative to flight insurance. The insurance starts when the F.I.T. client starts to the airport for the flight(s) that are covered and the insurance continues until the passenger arrives at the first surface destination after air flight(s) arrive in the destination airport(s). Many policies have an additional restriction in that they cover only flights for which tickets were issued prior to the processing of flight insurance applications.

Chart Flight Insurance Selection Process   The selection process for flight insurance is straightforward. Standard premium rates are $5.00 for $150,000, $7.50 for $225,000, and $10.00 for $300,000. The F.I.T. client selects the amount of coverage ($150,000, $225,000, or $300,000) fills out an application form, pays the travel agency, and the policy is processed.

Chart Trip Cancellation/Interruption Selection Process   Trip cancellation/interruption rates tend to be right at $5.50 per $100 of coverage. The amount of coverage runs from a low of $100 to a high of $3,000 and most policies will allow the F.I.T. client to select any amount of coverage desired as long as it is in $100 increments. The following chart shows premium options and insurance amounts ranging from $100 of coverage to $3,000 of coverage.

**Trip Cancellation —
Interruption Rates**

Amount of Insurance	Premium
$ 100	$ 5.50
200	11.00
400	22.00
600	33.00
800	44.00
1,000	55.00
1,500	82.50
2,000	110.00
2,500	137.50
3,000	165.00

**Any amount of Coverage C
may be purchased at the rate
of $5.50 per $100 of coverage.**

Fig. 12-4. Trip cancellation—interruption rates. (Courtesy of Tele-Trip, Inc., an affiliate of the Mutual of Omaha companies.)

INSURANCE PROCESSING

For most trip insurance the completion of the application for insurance is self-explanatory since a large number of the applications are filled out by the client at home without the assistance of the travel agent. However, it is important to recognize there are two approaches to the completion and processing of insurance applications and there are pros and cons to both for the travel agency. One approach is for the F.I.T. specialist to complete the application for the client, obtain the client's check (made out to the travel agency), and send an agency check to the insurance company (after having deducted the agency commission) at the end of the month for all insurance policies written in the agency during the month. The second approach is to give the client the insurance application form. The client completes the form, mails it to the insurance company together with her check, and the insurance company sends a commission check to the travel agency.

The advantage of the first approach is that all handling is in-house within the travel agency. The F.I.T. specialist is certain that the insurance has been applied for and paid for and the agency is certain that commissions are received on all insurance sales. In addition, if it is agency policy not to handle an F.I.T. unless trip cancellation/interruption insurance is taken out, the agency can monitor each F.I.T. and be certain that the insurance has been applied for and paid for. This approach makes for far better tracking of insurance sales. The disadvantage to the first approach is that it leaves the agency exposed legally to a much larger degree. There have been cases where travel agency management has failed to pay for insurance written in their agency, simply banking the client checks and hoping no client claims would be filed. There have been other cases where an agent has misplaced or lost an insurance application form. Both of these situations leave the agency exposed to lawsuits if a claim against the insurance company is filed, the insurance company has not been paid for the insurance, and it is discovered that the travel agency has been paid, but has not paid the insurance company for the client's insurance. Even under normal circumstances when the agency processes the application forms and sends a check to the insurance company on a monthly basis, the agency can be caught in the middle. If the agency sends its check to the insurance company at the end of the month, the client purchases trip insurance at the beginning of the month, and a claim is filed in the middle of the month, the insurance company can rightly say that is has not received payment and that, therefore, the policy is not in effect. Again, the travel agency is exposed to a potential lawsuit. Finally, even when it can be proven that the insurance company has been paid on time and before a claim was filed, if the client sues the insurance company, the travel agency and the F.I.T. specialist can be named as parties to the suit. Although there is much less legal exposure than when payments were not received by the insurance company, there is still a very real legal exposure for both the travel agency and the F.I.T. specialist.

The second approach removes the degree of legal exposure found with the first approach. If the F.I.T. client has the responsibility of completing the insurance application form and sending it to the insurance company together with his check, the agency has been left out of the insurance application process and, therefore, the only potential legal exposure might be that the agency made a poor choice in recommending an insurance company (not a very serious legal exposure when the travel agency works with standard, reputable insurance companies). The disadvantage of the first approach, therefore, becomes the advantage of the second approach. However, the reverse is also true. The advantages of the first approach no longer apply when the client applies for insurance himself. There is no way for the travel agency to be certain that the client has actually completed the application form and sent his application and check to the insurance company. The travel agency has no way of knowing whether or not the checks it receives from the insurance company cover every client's insurance or if the insurance company mistakenly does not send a commission check, and the agency must wait until commission checks are written by the insurance company to receive the commissions it gets. There is no way, under this approach, to be certain that the agency policy of not handling an F.I.T. for clients who have not applied for insurance has been maintained. And such a policy cannot be enforced. Finally, the F.I.T. specialist cannot be certain that the client is protected by appropriate insurance if the processing is left up to the client.

There are some modifications to the second approach that can modify the disadvantage of not knowing what insurance has been applied for. Some F.I.T. specialists ask their clients to bring in the insurance application form prior to mailing it and allow them to review the application to discuss any coverage inadequacies the F.I.T. specialist might find and to photocopy the insurance application so that if the client has a concern that arises while she is outside the United States, the F.I.T. specialist can assist and so that in the case of death, a copy of the policy application is held by the agency for the survivors to process claims. Most F.I.T. clients will bring in their applications for insurance when the F.I.T. specialist explains the reasons along these lines. Some insurance companies help the travel agency to stay informed by including an agency notification copy in the insurance application form. This copy is either mailed to the agency by the client at the time of insurance application or, as is more often the case, it is sent to the agency by the insurance company—sometimes at the same time the commission check is mailed to the travel agency.

Both approaches, therefore, have major advantages and disadvantages. Each travel agency should review both the advantages and disadvantages to determine for itself what is most important before adopting a travel insurance company to work with and an insurance processing approach to follow within the agency.

DOCUMENT PACKAGING

When travel documents are turned over to F.I.T. clients, they should be packaged in a way that will be orderly, easy to retrieve, and easy to carry. In addition, the packaging should be good looking, if not impressive. F.I.T. specialists sometimes forget that the client is not buying a hard product that can be seen and touched when the F.I.T. purchase is made. The documents are the only tangibles the client has to show for what is often a very large expenditure of money. Therefore, packaging takes on significant importance. Willow Press (phone 516-231-1234) provides two types of document holders that allow an F.I.T. specialist to provide good looking, yet economical F.I.T. document packaging. The first of these is a voucher cover. Hotels and service companies to which vouchers have been issued usually received a copy of the voucher, but the original voucher can be stapled into a postcard-thick cardboard cover with the name, address, and logo of the travel agency on the front and a liability limitation statement on the back. The voucher looks professional and is packaged professionally.

The document envelope offered by Willow Press is a large imitation leather-grain, light-colored cardboard stock envelope in a pleasant pastel color. It is clearly marked, "TRAVEL PAPERS—Property of" and provides lines for the client's name, address, and city/state. It provides a bon voyage message from the travel agency and has the agency's name, address, phone number, and logo on the front cover. Below the envelope flap is a travel checklist with four categories of items that can be checked off as they are packed or included. The first checklist is for items that will go into the document envelope. This includes tickets, passports, vaccination certificates, traveler's checks, itinerary, reservations, phone numbers, and wallet. The F.I.T. specialist might want to add (and there are spaces for additions together with blocks to check off when the item is placed into the envelope) vouchers, entry cards, declaration forms, letter copies, and bank transfer documents, if appropriate. The second checklist category is a general list of items the F.I.T. client might want to pack. The final two checklist categories are a "his" and a "hers" list of frequently packed items. In both columns additional space has been left for the client to add what he/she may wish to pack. It is suggested that the F.I.T. specialist place documents into the document holder in the order that they should be reviewed and discussed in the final meeting with the F.I.T. client.

SUMMARY

Countries vary in what they require in the way of documentation for those who travel within their borders. Some countries allow American citizens to enter and leave freely, asking for no documentation at all. Others require only proof of citizenship. This can be a passport or birth certificate, a voter's registration card, and in a few cases, one of several other types of documents. More stringent countries require a valid United States passport, but no other documentation. Most of Western Europe requires nothing more from American citizens than a valid passport. Many other countries require a valid tourist visa stamped in a valid U.S. passport. A few countries will not issue visas to tourists, thereby not allowing tourists to enter their countries. A few others restrict tourists by issuing only a few tourist visas each year.

There are also countries that will require other documents from travelers entering their countries. The most common of these other documents are health records, which show that the traveler has had shots to insure that the traveler will not bring in a communicable disease, and airline tickets proving that the traveler has the ability to leave the country after completing his trip. Entry cards are required by many countries. Although some of these can be obtained and filled out on the airplane or at the border, other entry cards take longer to complete and should be requested in advance. Declaration forms are expected in some countries (including the United States). These declarations allow the country to control money flows into and out of the country and most countries that have declarations as a part of their travel system are very strict about good accounting for money brought into the country and about allowing their currency to leave the country.

Documentation checks require a good checklist reviewed by the F.I.T. specialist on a regular basis. If visas are obtained by a visa service, the visa service should assist the travel agency in making sure documentation is in order before the client departs on the trip.

Most clients apply for their own passport, but visa services can apply for it on behalf of their clients. An original birth certificate will be needed and the appropriate form (first-time or renewal) needs to be completed. If visas are required, the client might either apply for the visas herself or the visa service will do it for her. It is safer and faster to use a visa service, but the cost is greater. The client's medical doctor should advise on and should administer any needed shots and should complete the immunization record. Some countries check these carefully, denying entrance to the country if they are not completed accurately. Vouchers, commonly issued in conjunction with hotel arrangements, tours, meet and assist arrangements, and car or limousine rentals, and letter or telex correspondence with vendors might also constitute document copies that clients might wish to or need to take with them when embarking on an F.I.T.

Financial documents are also important. Traveler's check receipt copies and bank transfer documents will be needed during the trip if there is a loss of traveler's checks and when obtaining funds from banks outside the U.S. to which funds have been transfered. Working with Deak Perrera and/or the client's personal bank to make sure financial documents are in order is a part of the responsibility of the F.I.T. specialist if the client wishes to receive assistance along these lines. It should always be remembered that a client's financial matters are confidential until the client decides to disclose financial information. By advising clients of financial travel options, the F.I.T. specialist has opened the door to lending assistance if the client wishes to have assistance.

Having a good record keeping system is critical to keeping up to date on the status of a client's F.I.T. A client-dedicated expandable cardboard file holder kept in a client multi-drawer file cabinet is the foundation of the system recommended. One section of the file holder will contain a document envelope and all documents the client will need to carry on the trip will be placed in the document envelope in the file holder. Other sections of the file holder are dedicated to vendor correspondence. By attaching a checklist to the outside of each file, the F.I.T. specialist will be able to check the status of arrangements with vendors rapidly. A final section of the file holder relates to costs and the F.I.T. costing records. Cost sheets for all aspects of the F.I.T. are pulled when the file is opened and data is entered on the cost sheets each time some aspect of the trip is worked. This system allows the F.I.T. specialist to develop interim and final financial status reports both rapidly and accurately.

Because of the length of the trips, the often-frequent changes from one location to another during a trip, and the fact that the traveler is so much on his own while traveling, insurance is even more important for an F.I.T. traveler than for other travelers. There are baggage, accident/medical/sickness trip cancellation/interruption, and death/dismemberment/sight loss insurance policies. Baggage insurance limitations can be considerable. It is essential to advise clients that compensation is severely limited and that such items as jewelry and furs, if covered at all, will be covered at only a fraction of their value. In addition, baggage insurance exceptions exclude any compensation for losses under some circumstances and limit the compensation under other circumstances. Baggage insurance normally goes into effect the day and time of client notification and is limited to the number of days of elected term of coverage. In selecting a baggage insurance policy, client's need to study the time options, the premium options, and the compensation amounts before determining what the right combination is for them.

Both the older client and the adventuresome client should consider accident/medical/sickness insurance. This compensates for sickness and accidents anywhere in the world. Although there are limitations on the coverage, for many clients having the policy brings a peace of mind that is essential for an enjoyable trip.

With the increase of non-refundable fares and high cancellation penalties for air fares, trip cancellation/interruption insurance has grown in popularity. Since the policy pays the non-refundable pre-paid fees for missed travel arrangements when a trip must be cancelled or interrupted, the policy helps the F.I.T. specialist as well as the client by eliminating the need for letters and phone calls to explain why a refund should be made anyway. It is partly because of this feature that many travel agencies are requiring their F.I.T. clients to take out trip cancellation/interruption insurance as a prerequisite to their handling the F.I.T. However, clients need to be warned that, while policy payment interpretations tend to be generous (they will even pay when mother-in-law gets sick), compensation is dependent upon providing documented proof of sickness, injury, or death of the person or persons specified in the policy.

Flight insurance covers accidental death, dismemberment, or loss of sight. It is especially valued by those who fly frequently and those who are afraid of flying. Because the premiums and the policy payments are so high, many F.I.T. clients take it whenever they fly.

There are two approaches to insurance processing and both have advantages and disadvantages. The first approach is for the travel agency to do all the processing for the client. This gives the agency immediate commissions, good record keeping relating to insurance sales, and can help an agency maintain a policy of requiring trip cancellation/interruption insurance for every F.I.T. client. However, this approach carries with it potential legal exposure. The second approach is for the client to complete the insurance application and send it to the insurance agency together with her check for the coverage she wants. This carries little or no legal exposure for the travel agency, but does not give the agency immediate commission and leaves the agency with incomplete knowledge about the status of each client's insurance. It makes it very difficult for an agency to enforce a regulation of requiring trip cancellation/interruption insurance for all F.I.T. clients. Modifications of the second procedure include having the client bring in the policy for review and photocopying prior to sending the policy application to the insurance company and the insurance company sending a copy of the policy application to the travel agency. Both the pros and cons of each approach need to be studied by agency management before adopting a travel insurance vendor and an insurance application approach.

Keeping in mind that the client might spend a great deal of money for an F.I.T. and that what the client is purchasing is an intangible, the documents constitute the only tangible evidence of the expenditure prior to departure on the trip. Therefore, packaging of documents is very important.

Not only must the documents be packaged in a way that they are orderly, easy to carry, and easy to retrieve, but the packaging must be of top quality and appearance as well. Voucher covers keep vouchers in an easy-to-find manner and make a good impression on both the client and the vendor. A good quality document envelope can personalize the trip for the client and presents a way to keep documents organized in an envelope that fits carry-on baggage, a purse, or can be carried loosely. In addition, the document envelope has checklist reminders to make sure all appropriate documents are included inside.

❑ *Review Questions*

1. Why might a technically-acceptable F.I.T. still sometimes leave the client with the uneasy feeling that something might go wrong?
2. What are some of the reasons why the documentation process and documentation checks constitute one of the weakest areas in the F.I.T. development process at many travel agencies?
3. What are two aspects of the documentation process?
4. When is the "Received" column on a documentation checklist filled in and what information is filled in on the "Received" column?

5. What kind of services do F.I.T. specialists provide for clients in conjunction with working with a visa service?
6. What is the single most important document required of an F.I.T. client?
7. What are some countries for which a United States passport is not required for entry?
8. Can a travel agent apply for an F.I.T. client's passport? Why?
9. What is the shortest amount of time for a passport to be obtained through a visa service?
10. In what way(s) might a travel agent help an F.I.T. client if the client's passport is lost?
11. What are two types of passport application forms and under what circumstances can each type be used?
12. From what source can an original birth certificate be obtained?
13. Does the United States Passport Office have the right to refuse to issue a passport?
14. Name a country that will not issue a tourist visa to a citizen of the United States?
15. What are the three ways of determining whether or not a tourist visa is required by a host country?
16. What document must a client have before getting a visa? Why?
17. What are the dangers and/or potential problems involved in a client applying for visas himself?
18. What is the only Western European country to require a tourist visa for U.S. citizens traveling in the country?
19. Why do some countries require those applying for tourist visas to have an airline ticket?
20. What are three countries that require those applying for tourist visas to have an airline ticket?
21. Are all entry cards uniform in their requirements?
22. What should be in balance when leaving a country having currency declaration requirements?
23. Why might copies of letters and telexes be carried by an F.I.T. client?
24. What is the key to working with F.I.T. clients regarding the transfers of funds?
25. In what ways might Deak Perrera be of assistance to F.I.T. clients?
26. Under what circumstances might an F.I.T. client consider establishing a bank account in another country prior to leaving the United States?
27. What type of client file system works best for many F.I.T. specialists?
28. There are three sections to a file holder. What goes into each section?
29. What are the four kinds of personal insurance often sold to F.I.T. clients?
30. What is the cap for reimbursement of most baggage insurance when luggage is lost or stolen?
31. Which insurance company will write an insurance policy for any amount of baggage insurance?

32. What is the standard waiting period before a baggage loss emergency purchase allowance can be spent?
33. What is the standard industry limit on baggage emergency purchase allowances?
34. There are two broad luggage insurance exception areas. What are they?
35. What are the two high-risk groups of F.I.T. travelers when it comes to the potential for accidents and sickness?
36. Accident, medical, sickness insurance limitations vary depending upon what three factors?
37. Trip cancellation/interruption insurance is especially beneficial when the traveler is flying on what kinds of fares?
38. What people are considered to be included in the traveler's "family members" for the purposes of trip cancellation/interruption insurance?
39. Under what conditions will payment be made that relate specifically to the traveler and the traveler's traveling companion when covered by trip cancellation/interruption insurance?
40. If a traveler files a claim for reimbursement of sickness or injury costs when the traveler is covered by trip cancellation/interruption insurance, what will be required by the insurance company?
41. Does flight insurance cover death due to suicide?
42. If a passenger buys flight insurance but is allowed to fly on the air carrier free and without a ticket to compensate for poor service rendered by the carrier on a flight several months before will the policy cover the passenger? Why?
43. What are the two approaches used in processing F.I.T. client applications for insurance?
44. In what way should travel documents be packaged when they are turned over to F.I.T. clients? Why?
45. What two types of document holders does Willow Press offer?
46. When a client buys an F.I.T., what tangibles does the client leave the agency with after having paid for the F.I.T.?
47. In what way(s) is a document envelope "personalized" for an F.I.T. client?
48. What are the four categories of items found on the document envelope checklist?
49. In what order is it suggested that the F.I.T. specialist place documents into the document envelope?

❏ *Role Play Exercise*

Two students may participate in this role play exercise either out of class as a fun way to review the chapter or as an in-class exercise. One plays the role of the client and the other plays the role of the travel agency's F.I.T. specialist. Please read the script and then pick up the conversation in your own words.

F.I.T. SPECIALIST: You will need eight visas for this trip. They are for the countries noted on the itinerary I gave you. Each one has the word "visa" marked in red. You can either apply for them yourself by contacting the consulate of each country or you may want to have a visa service apply for them for you. Which approach do you think you would like to follow?

F.I.T. CLIENT: I don't know. What are the pros and cons of each approach? Which way do you suggest and why?

F.I.T. SPECIALIST: There certainly are pros and cons to each approach. Let's start with . . .

Continue on your own.

❑ *Role Play Exercise*

Two students may participate in this role play exercise either out of class as a fun way to review the chapter or as an in-class exercise. One plays the role of the client and the other plays the role of the travel agency's F.I.T. specialist. Please read the script and then pick up the conversation in your own words.

F.I.T. SPECIALIST: There are several types of insurance that you may want to consider in conjunction with your trip. These include baggage, accident/medical/sickness, trip cancellation/interruption, and flight insurance, which covers death, dismemberment, or loss of sight. Since your trip is a hazardous trek in Nepal, you are bringing a number of valuable items with you in your luggage, and since you are almost ninety-two-years old now, these policies really should be considered seriously.

F.I.T. CLIENT: I always take your suggestions seriously. I will take out all of the policies. Tell me what they cover and what they don't cover and tell me how much I should get. Also, how do I apply for these policies?

F.I.T. SPECIALIST: Thanks for agreeing. Let's start with . . .

Continue on your own.

INSURANCE APPLICATION EXERCISE

ASSIGNMENT: You are the travel agency's F.I.T. specialist. Mrs. Johnson is at your desk discussing her upcoming trip to Europe. The subject of insurance has come up and Mrs. Johnson has decided she wants to obtain several policies. Her trip will run twenty-nine days from the time she leaves home in the United States to the time she returns home. She wants to make sure she is covered wherever possible from the time she leaves home until she returns. Mrs. Johnson wants to have both herself and her husband covered. She wants the maximum amount of flight insurance, at least $4,000 of accident/medical expense coverage, at least $900 of baggage coverage, enough trip cancellation coverage to cover each of their round trip tickets ($628 apiece), and non-refundable car rental deposits of $1,229, at least $40 per day of sickness benefits, and she wants to know if the coverage will cover her fur coat valued at $18,000, if it is sent in the luggage. Mr. and Mrs. Johnson will be flying to Europe on the following itinerary:

CO	34C	03Sep	DENLGW	19:30	0730+1
CO	47C	02Oct	LGWDEN	11:45	18:20

As you know the Johnsons live at 1229 Century Way, Cherry Hills, Colorado 80111 and their phone number is 303-755-6361.

Complete the insurance application form on the next page for Mr. and Mrs. Johnson.

Coverage A — Accident — Medical — Sickness Rates

	Plan 1	Plan 2	Plan 3
Principal Sum Accident Medical Expense	$25,000	$50,000	$100,000
Sickness Benefit	2,500 $50/Day	5,000 $50/Day	10,000 $50/Day
Term of Coverage	Premium		
1-3 days	$ 4.20	$ 7.25	$ 14.10
5 days	8.85	15.30	28.20
7 days	10.80	18.75	35.05
8 days	11.90	20.75	40.35
10 days	14.95	26.60	50.35
11 days	15.35	27.25	51.25
14 days	17.10	30.05	56.25
15 days	18.30	31.95	61.80
17 days	20.75	36.35	68.05
18 days	21.05	36.85	68.90
21 days	22.00	37.95	71.15
22 days	22.60	39.05	72.45
24 days	23.65	40.70	75.30
27 days	25.80	44.10	81.20
28 days	26.50	45.15	83.10
30 days	27.85	47.30	86.90
31 days	28.50	48.35	88.75
45 days	33.65	58.40	108.75
60 days	43.60	73.75	135.05
90 days	56.15	94.35	173.40
120 days	66.60	109.95	198.00
150 days	76.65	125.85	225.60
180 days	84.75	138.40	247.40

Coverage B — Baggage Rates

NOTE: Baggage premiums cover either an individual or a family. All other premiums are individual rates.

For baggage coverage of $3,000, simply double the $1,000 rates. The maximum family limit for this coverage is $3,000.

	Amount of Insurance				
Term of Coverage	$500 Premium	$800 Premium	$1,000 Premium	$1,500 Premium	$2,000 Premium
1-3 days	$ 8.25	$ 11.50	$ 14.00	$ 17.50	$ 21.25
5 days	11.50	16.50	20.00	25.00	30.25
7 days	14.00	20.75	25.25	31.50	38.00
8 days	15.25	22.25	27.25	34.00	41.00
10 days	17.25	25.50	31.00	38.75	46.75
11 days	18.25	27.00	33.00	41.25	49.50
14 days	20.75	32.00	38.75	48.50	58.25
15 days	21.75	33.25	40.75	51.00	61.00
17 days	23.75	36.50	44.50	55.75	66.75
18 days	24.25	38.00	46.25	57.75	69.25
21 days	26.50	41.25	50.25	63.00	75.50
22 days	27.25	42.25	51.75	64.75	77.50
24 days	28.50	44.50	54.50	68.25	81.75
27 days	30.75	48.25	58.50	73.25	88.00
28 days	31.50	49.25	60.00	75.25	90.00
30 days	33.00	51.50	62.75	78.50	94.00
31 days	33.50	52.50	64.00	80.00	96.25
45 days	41.50	64.00	78.00	97.50	117.25
60 days	50.00	77.50	95.00	118.25	142.00
90 days	63.00	97.25	119.00	148.50	178.25
120 days	76.00	118.25	144.00	180.00	216.25
150 days	88.50	138.00	168.00	210.50	252.50
180 days	100.00	156.00	190.00	238.00	285.50

Coverage C — Trip Cancellation — Interruption Rates

Amount of Insurance	Premium
$ 100	$ 5.50
200	11.00
400	22.00
600	33.00
800	44.00
1,000	55.00
1,500	82.50
2,000	110.00
2,500	137.50
3,000	165.00

Any amount of Coverage C may be purchased at the rate of $5.50 per $100 of coverage.

Coverage D — Flight insurance Rates

Principal Sum	Premium
$300,000	$10.00
225,000	7.50
150,000	5.00

Insurance Schedule

Only Coverages for which premiums are paid will be in effect.

Family Members Covered

Insured: _____

Insured Spouse: _____

Insured Child: _____

Insured Child: _____

Effective Date for A & B Coverages
(Effective Date for Coverage C is Postmark Date.
Effective Date for Coverage D is Date of first Flight.)

Term of Coverage for A & B

Date: _____ Hour _____ ☐ a.m. ☐ p.m. _____ Days

PLEASE PRINT! BEAR DOWN

Name of Insured

Address

City _____ State _____ ZIP

X _____
Signature _____ Place _____ Date Signed

A. TRAVEL ACCIDENT

		Principal Sum	Premium
Enter one amount for each person.	Insured: $		$
Enter premium on line at far right.	Spouse: $		$
	Child: $		$
	Child: $		$

B. BAGGAGE

One amount covers Insured and family members traveling with the Insured.

	Amount of Insurance	Premium
	$	$

C. TRIP CANCELLATION

		Amount of Insurance	Premium
Enter one amount for each person.	Insured: $		$
Enter premium on line at far right.	Spouse: $		$
Departure Date: _____	Child: $		$
	Child: $		$

D. FLIGHT INSURANCE

		Principal Sum	Premium
Enter one amount for each person.			
Enter premium on line at far right	Insured: $		$
Departure City: _____	Spouse: $		$
Date: _____	Child: $		$
Destination: _____	Child: $		$

TOTAL PREMIUM $ _____

(Courtesy of Tele-Trip, Inc., an affiliate of the Mutual of Omaha Companies.)

13

CLIENT CONTACT

THE IMPORTANCE OF CLIENT CONTACT

Keeping in touch with clients is one mark of professionalism. Whether a client is spending a small amount of money on a short F.I.T. or a much larger amount on a long F.I.T., the planning of an F.I.T. is often even more important for the F.I.T. client than trip planning is for any other type of client. The very essence of having a tailored trip suggests how important the details can be for F.I.T. clients. They want to know what is happening and they expect the F.I.T. specialist to stay in touch.

Staying in touch, however, does not have to mean meeting after meeting. Too frequent meetings with clients means a waste of time and with F.I.T.s, the old adage "Time is money." definitely applies. Therefore, the F.I.T. specialist should plan a campaign whereby phone calls and letters are the vehicles that keep an F.I.T. client happy and knowledgeable, and allow the F.I.T. specialist the opportunity to constantly keep in touch.

THE STATE OF THE TOUR REPORT

David Lundquist, founder of Lundquist Travel in Denver and one of the country's top F.I.T. specialists, uses a "State of the Tour Report" as his vehicle to keep clients knowledgeable regarding the status of their F.I.T.s. This report is a simple one or two page letter that advises what confirmations have been received, those arrangements that still have pending confirmations, aspects of the F.I.T. that will need to be changed because they could not be worked out (and alternative options), and little points that David suggests which will make the F.I.T. special. David sends out two or three of these "State of the Tour Reports" on each F.I.T. that he plans, spacing them about an equal number of days apart. Over the years he has been able to calculate that F.I.T. clients need a written status report about every two weeks throughout the planning process. Of course, there are telephone calls every few days as well. The key here is to make sure the F.I.T.

specialist contacts the client advising the status of the tour before the client calls the F.I.T. specialist. By doing so, worries are addressed immediately and not allowed to build into major concerns. The client needs to feel confident at all times that her F.I.T. is important, is being worked on, and that problems are addressed immediately.

THE PRE-DEPARTURE MEETING

Perhaps the most crucial meeting between the F.I.T. specialist and the F.I.T. client is the pre-departure meeting. This is when all documents are turned over to the client, all last minute concerns are addressed, and any payments still due from the client are collected. For many F.I.T. clients, and especially for first-time F.I.T. clients, this can be a time of considerable concern and a time of mixed emotions. Most clients are excited about getting away on the adventure they have helped to plan, but many have strong concerns about all details working out. The experienced F.I.T. client will know that things can and do go wrong even with the best planned F.I.T. They will accept this with the knowledge that the occasional mishap is part of the excitement of travel. Typically, however, the less-experienced F.I.T. client will want to go over F.I.T. details several times—especially those they are less sure of or those involved in travel of a type or in an area where they feel somewhat uncomfortable. An example is the client who was scheduled for a two-hour camel ride in Egypt. Prior to departure he continually went back to questions about riding the camel. He wanted to undertake the ride; but was fearful of it at the same time. When he returned he reported that the camel ride was a highlight of the trip.

In preparing for the pre-departure meeting, the F.I.T. specialist should set aside a solid block of time, preferably with no interruptions from phone calls, other staff members, or walk-in clients. One F.I.T. specialist always blocks out one and a half hours for the pre-departure meeting. This is usually sufficient. Holding the meeting in a private office or a conference room is also important. This is a critical time for the client and it should be recognized as that by the F.I.T. specialist.

The purpose of the pre-departure meeting is three-fold:

1. To turn over the documents needed for the trip
2. To conduct a final briefing
3. To collect any payments still owed to the travel agency

These activities are usually undertaken simultaneously. As documents are reviewed, the F.I.T. specialist needs to go over the documents explaining the details of the documents and any special points relating to that aspect of the trip. For example, when reviewing the airport to hotel voucher, the F.I.T. specialist might want to say something like, "Remember, the transfer service representative will be holding a placard with your name on it and she will be wearing a blue blazer." In other words, the final briefing is usually conducted at the same time as the document review. This is especially true when reviewing the final itinerary. It is during the itinerary review that all aspects of the trip are discussed. Some F.I.T. specialists will start the pre-departure meeting with a review of the itinerary, tying in their briefing and a review of the other documents with a line-by-line discussion of each detail on the itinerary. By the time the itinerary is finished, all documents have been reviewed and all aspects of the trip have been discussed.

Many who are new to F.I.T.s look at the pre-departure meeting as a time for the F.I.T. specialist to constantly take the initiative and do almost all of the talking by "briefing" the client. More experienced F.I.T. specialists recognize that the clients will have concerns and might be too shy or too inhibited to share the concerns. These specialists will encourage the client to talk about the trip, sharing both his excitement and his concerns. They spend a lot of time listening. One goal is to make sure that when the client leaves the travel agency he is excited about the trip, confident that all will go well, and not worried that everything will go wrong. Listening carefully helps the F.I.T. specialist to pick up on concerns and talking to the client helps the client to vent any emotional concerns.

Some F.I.T. specialists find it hard to collect final payment from their clients. This need not be an uncomfortable experience. In reviewing the financial aspects of the trip, the F.I.T. specialist can be as up-front and as matter of fact about money matters as about any other aspect of the F.I.T. As with the itinerary review, the F.I.T. budget should be reviewed in detail discussing the total cost agreed on for the F.I.T., payments that have been made and the final payment that is due. As noted earlier, it is wise to avoid talking about specific costs of each element of the trip. The F.I.T. is costed out as a package and just like a packaged tour has a single total price, the F.I.T. should have a single total price. Just like a packaged tour often requires deposits (sometimes several deposits) and a final payment, so also the F.I.T. should require clients to make one or more deposits and to make a final payment.

Most F.I.T. specialists prefer to collect final payment early or in the middle of the pre-departure meeting and many avoid making final payment collection the last activity undertaken during the pre-departure meeting. They prefer that the client leave the office thinking positively about the F.I.T. and being excited about the trip rather than that they leave thinking about the check they just wrote out. While it is suggested that collecting final payment right at the beginning of the pre-departure meeting is inappropriate as most feel that the final itinerary review needs to be completed before final payment is collected, most also agree that final payment can be collected at any time after the final itinerary review.

Before the client leaves the office and usually after the itinerary review and the document review have been completed, the F.I.T. specialist should replace all documents into the document envelope in the proper order (usually in an order of time/date needed). After this has been done, the F.I.T. specialist hands over the documents in the document envelope to the client. The documents at this time become the responsibility of the client. Remind the client that pertinent document copies are being retained by the travel agency so that in case of loss, contact with the agency will bring rapid copies to the client wherever on the trip the client might be. With the new facsimile transfer equipment, copy transfers by phone can be accomplished almost anywhere in the world in just a few minutes. This knowledge gives the F.I.T. client a greater sense of security as she travels from one destination to another.

Finally, before the pre-departure meeting is over, assure the client that you will stay in touch with her during the F.I.T. She needs to be reassured that if any problem with a vendor occurs down-the-line (at a destination she will be getting to later in her trip), the F.I.T. specialist will stay on top of the problem and inform her as much in advance as possible if a change needs to be made.

IN TOUCH EN ROUTE

While many travel agents consider their work on an F.I.T. to be over when the client leaves the office after having received the final briefing of the F.I.T. documents, the F.I.T. specialist considers his job to be over only after the client has finished the trip and a follow-up call has been made to the client a few days after the trip is over.

Keeping in touch en route should be a planned activity, even if it only means writing a postcard saying you hope all is going well and the client is having fun. Some F.I.T. specialists write these cards in advance and mail them to a client even before the client leaves on the trip. If the envelope or card is addressed to the client in care of her hotel and is clearly marked to hold for her arrival and the date of arrival, quality hotels are very good at holding mail and giving it to a client at the time of check-in.

Keeping in touch while the client is on the F.I.T. is even more important if the trip has had little advance planning and some of the down-the-line details have not been confirmed prior to the client's departure. In such situations, it is essential that all details be confirmed as soon as possible and that the clients be contacted to advise them of the confirmations. Usually phone calls to the clients at their first stop hotels is the best way to handle after-departure confirmations. A facsimile transfer of the confirmation document(s) can usually be sent to the hotel where the client is currently staying or a telex confirmation can be sent in order to give the client a hard copy confirmation.

POST-TRIP FOLLOW UP

A large number of travel agents do not build post-trip follow ups into their F.I.T. systems. However, following up with an F.I.T. client after the trip is over provides a number of important benefits. Of perhaps greatest importance is the ability to initiate another F.I.T. sale. When the client returns from a trip that really was everything the client hoped it would be, there often is an immediate desire to start planning the next trip. If the F.I.T. specialist can capture this travel urge while the client is still excited about the trip just completed, the commitment to the next F.I.T. trip can often be forthcoming right away. This not only keeps the client in a constant circle of trip planning and trip taking (making more profits for the travel agency), but it also gives the F.I.T. specialist the maximum amount of time to work out trip details.

A second benefit to post-trip follow up is the ability to get up-to-date details on vendor services. If a vendor has rendered especially good service or if a vendor's service has fallen down in terms of quality, timeliness, etc., the F.I.T. client will usually volunteer the information right away. This provides the F.I.T. specialist with the ability to constantly judge whether or not to continue using a vendor. It also gives the specialist an understanding of what is new regarding services or programs offered by vendors and how well these new programs/services are working out.

Finally post-trip follow up gives the client a release of emotion, both positive and negative, related to the trip. This, in turn, creates a greater bonding between the F.I.T. specialist and the client. Each time there is a post-trip review, the F.I.T. specialist gains a better understanding of the nuances of the client's preferences. As a result, each new trip can be planned with a little better "feel" for what is right for this client.

Timing of the post-trip follow up is important. It needs to be soon after the client has returned, but not immediately after the return. Many feel that a phone call two or three days after the return is appropriate. If possible, schedule a visit in the agency office. Sometimes the client will have many personal affairs to attend to after having been gone on the trip and will want to just talk on the phone. If so, conduct the follow up discussion via phone.

Listening is important, but the F.I.T. specialist needs to provide involved and interactive listening. Take notes—especially when it comes to comments about vendors and about client preferences. Ask questions to show that you are following what the client is saying and that you want to understand completely. Reaffirm when a client preference seems to be coming clear. Statements like, "It sounds like you enjoyed the views from your hotel rooms in both Athens and Rome. Getting rooms with good views is a very important part of your vacation experience, isn't it"?

Perhaps most important to the post-trip follow up is the opportunity to sell the next F.I.T. This is usually the best time to get the client started on planning the next trip. Include a subtle, but definite sell in the post-trip follow up conversation. Ask questions like, "Where do you want to travel next"? Either/or questions can help a client in making the next trip decision. For example, "Both summer and winter are bad travel times there. The winter is very cold and the summer is both hot and humid. However, both the spring and the fall are delightful. Do you think you will be ready to go by the fall or would you prefer to start working on a spring trip"?

Finally, reconfirm the value to the client of the F.I.T. that has just been completed. Talk in terms of the memories that will last for a lifetime, the new friends that were made while on the trip, the beauty that was awesome, and perhaps the small points that made the trip so very worthwhile. It is usually wise to avoid talking about money and monetary value, but rather emphasize what a wonderful experience the F.I.T. has been for the client and how nothing else can really compare to the rewards and the sense of fulfillment that an excellent F.I.T. experience provides.

SUMMARY

Maintaining good client contact is both professional and important—especially for F.I.T. clients who often justifiably feel that a tailored vacation experience requires knowing exactly what they want and giving them all the options. However, time is money. Client contacts, therefore, need to be regular, concise, and to the point. Few in-office meetings are needed. Telephone calls and "State of the Tour Reports" can give the F.I.T. specialist the information needed to design an excellent F.I.T. experience and the client the feedback needed to feel comfortable.

The pre-departure meeting is perhaps the most crucial of all meetings. Clients are worried at this time and often fear something will go wrong. Although false promises should not be given, the clients should be reassured. By setting a time block and meeting in a quiet area without interruptions, the F.I.T. specialist can direct the meeting to an itinerary review that is also a final briefing. Collect final payments that might be due either before or during the briefing and turn over all trip documents at the end of the meeting.

Before the client leaves, assure her you will stay in touch while she is on the trip and plan to do so. Send cards, notes, and especially send facsimiles of confirmations that might arrive after the client has started the trip. Send these to the client's hotel so they arrive only a day or two before the client arrives.

Post-trip follow up is also important. Not only does it provide the client with an opportunity to release built up emotions, but the F.I.T. specialist has another opportunity to learn more about the preferences of the F.I.T. client. Perhaps even more important, both the client and the F.I.T. specialist have a perfect opportunity to start planning the client's next F.I.T.

■   ■   ■

❏ *Review Questions*

1. Why is keeping in touch with clients considered a mark of professionalism?
2. What information does a "State of the Tour Report" provide to F.I.T. clients?
3. How often throughout the planning process do F.I.T. clients need a written status report?
4. Why is the pre-departure meeting between the F.I.T. specialist and the F.I.T. client considered the most crucial meeting?
5. What three things are accomplished during the pre-departure meeting?
6. In what way is the itinerary review used as a guide in directing the final briefing and the document review?
7. Why is final payment collection undertaken early or in the middle of the pre-departure meeting?
8. When do documents become the responsibility of the client?
9. Why should keeping in touch en route be a planned activity?
10. What are some of the benefits post-trip follow ups provide?
11. How soon after an F.I.T. is over should the F.I.T. specialist initiate a post-trip follow-up phone call?
12. In what ways might an F.I.T. specialist reconfirm the value to the client of the F.I.T. just completed?

❏ *Role Play Exercise*

Two students may participate in this role play either out of class as a fun way to review the chapter or as an in-class exercise. One plays the role of the client and the other plays the role of the travel agency's F.I.T. specialist. Please read the script and then pick up the conversation in your own words.

F.I.T. SPECIALIST: Welcome back, Mrs. Jones. Thanks for the post-card you sent. It sounds like you had another wonderful trip.

F.I.T. CLIENT: Yes, we did. That little mountain hotel in Nepal and the houseboat you got for us in Kashmir were highlights. Both were so serene and they provided absolutely beautiful views.

F.I.T. SPECIALIST: You and your husband seem to appreciate quiet, comfortable stays, and beautiful scenery in off-the-beaten-track countries.

F.I.T. CLIENT: Yes, and native, well-prepared cuisine.

Continue on your own.

INDEX